destination BRIDE

A complete guide to planning your wedding anywhere in the world

lisa light

NORTH LIGHT BOOKS

Cincinnati, Ohio
www.artistsnetwork.com

10 09 08 07 06   5 4 3 2 1

Distributed in Canada by Fraser Direct
100 Armstrong Avenue
Georgetown, ON, Canada L7G 5S4
Tel: (905) 877-4411

Distributed in the U.K. and Europe by David & Charles
Brunel House, Newton Abbot, Devon, TQ12 4PU, England
Tel: (+44) 1626 323200, Fax: (+44) 1626 323319
e-mail: mail@davidandcharles.co.uk

Distributed in Australia by Capricorn Link
P.O. Box 704, S. Windsor, NSW 2756 Australia
Tel: (02) 4577-3555

Library of Congress Cataloging-in-Publication Data

Light, Lisa.
Destination bride : a complete guide to planning your wedding anywhere in the world / Lisa Light.
    p. cm.
Includes index.
ISBN 1-55870-703-4 (alk. paper)
1. Weddings--Planning. 2. Travel. I. Title.
  HQ745.L545 2006
  395.2'2--dc22

2005015490

F+W PUBLICATIONS, INC.

Editor: Jennifer Fellinger, Christine Doyle
Designer: Karla Baker
Illustrator: Rachell Sumpter
Layout Artist: Jennifer Fellinger
Production Coordinator: Robin Richie
Maps by Hartgen Archeological Associates, Inc.

THIS BOOK IS DEDICATED TO MY GRANDMOTHER, DOROTHY J. BAILEY, A CHILDREN'S LIBRARIAN, A WORLD TRAVELER, AND A WONDERFUL STORYTELLER, WHO SHOULD HAVE PUT PEN TO PAPER HERSELF. I ALSO WANT TO DEDICATE IT TO MY LITTLE WOMEN, OLIVIA, GRACE, AND MAISIE ALICE, WHOM I HOPE WILL ALL BE DESTINATION BRIDES SOME DAY.

——✠——

I would like to thank my mother, who has always encouraged me to write and taught me that you can do anything you set your mind to. I would also like to thank Jane Friedman for encouraging me to write the proposal for Destination Bride, and my editors at F+W Publications: Christine Doyle, for her patience and guidance, and Jennifer Fellinger.

Because this was my first book, I had no idea how much work goes into researching, writing, editing, designing, and publishing one. Many, many dedicated people made this project possible. It never would have gotten done without the help of Catherine J. Light, Cassandra Tinger, and Lisa Ross, who put in almost as many hours as I did researching and verifying information and photos. I also want to mention the contributions of Sumaya Conners, Leslie Craigmyle, Jennifer Light, Erin Delos, Patricia Decker, and Jarret Gregory.

I want to thank all the tourism bureaus, embassies, consulates, and venues that supplied information and answered numerous questions; all the photographers who graciously submitted photos; and Christine Smith of Hartgen and Associates for designing the maps. I am also tremendously grateful to my staff and my wonderful family who have lent support in so many ways.

Most importantly, I want to thank my groom, Glenn E. Rugen, with whom I planned a memorable wedding, and with whom I have shared all the ups and downs of raising children and growing businesses. From here on in, he will be referred to as "Saint Glenn" for his unfailing patience and support of my pursuits.

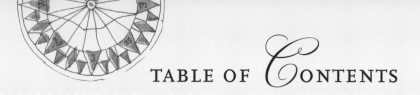

TABLE OF CONTENTS

PART ONE: THE DETAILS

CHAPTER ONE:

CHAPTER TWO:

CHAPTER THREE:

CHAPTER FOUR:

CHAPTER FIVE:

PART TWO: THE DESTINATIONS

THE DETAILS

What is a destination wedding? A destination wedding is a once-in-a-lifetime experience and a wonderful adventure, not just for the bride and groom, but for everyone involved. When you combine the allure of travel, a remarkable location, and an extraordinary cause for celebration, the mix is rich with meaning, memories, and opportunities for bonding. When most of us think of weddings, we probably imagine a church ceremony followed by a three-hour reception at a local hotel, or perhaps a backyard celebration with vows exchanged under a grape arbor. I have attended—and planned—many fabulous weddings like these. Destination weddings, however, have a few common characteristics that set them apart from other weddings: They take place away from home, they last more than one day, and they involve travel. Aside from those common elements, destination weddings are as varied as the couples who design them and the places they choose to go.

A destination wedding might be a Las Vegas elopement for two or a Riviera extravaganza for 1,000. It may be a simple country wedding for a couple living in New York City, an autumnal New England wedding for a Floridian bride and groom, or a warm Caribbean wedding in December for a couple from Maine. A destination wedding can be a simple, straightforward package offered by a resort, travel agent, or wedding planner, or it can be a detailed, custom-designed, and highly orchestrated event. Destination weddings take many forms, but they all center around travel. Perhaps it is a love of travel that draws you to the idea of a destination wedding in the first place. You might be intrigued by the unknown and the unexpected, or enamored with the romance of a foreign land, or fascinated by new sights, cultures, and traditions. But, romance and fascination aside, you probably know that travel invariably involves complications. Because destination weddings are far from home, they *can* be more challenging to plan. Often they necessitate the assistance of someone at the destination.

It's true that the element of travel makes a destination wedding a bit more complicated than a wedding at home. Yet, when I think of the destination weddings I have planned and all the wonderful possibilities I have discovered, I am struck more by their richness than their complexity. What I have found to be at the very heart of destination weddings—what distinguishes them most from other wedding celebrations—are the unique opportunities they present for the couple and the guests to get to know each other. Is it the travel? Is it being far from home, removed from "everyday life"? I think it is a magical mix of both, magnified in the context of a celebration, that makes people open up and connect with one another in extraordinary ways. Spirited and festive, destination weddings tie separate families and friends into one amiable group sharing a very special and very memorable experience.

A growing number of couples are discovering the appeal of destination weddings. According to a survey conducted by The Knot, forty percent of couples in the United States are planning destination weddings, and that number is sure to rise. Why the surge in popularity? One reason is the Internet, which has improved global communications, put international resources at our fingertips, and made other cultures more accessible. At the same time, the global economy is making the world an increasingly smaller place, allowing us to explore and exchange ideas well beyond our own backyard. Another reason is that today's brides and grooms are willing to push the boundaries of a traditional wedding in order to have a truly fun, unique, and memorable celebration. Raised by baby-boomer parents who nurtured a *carpe diem* spirit of adventure in their children, many couples are more well-traveled and more receptive to new experiences than previous generations. Modern couples also offer a changing perspective of the wedding day itself. Weddings used to be considered a party that parents hosted in honor of their children, but this notion is gradually being replaced by the idea that the wedding day belongs to the bride and groom. After all, it is not uncommon for couples to pay for at least a portion of their own weddings. It seems only fair that the bride and groom shape their celebration into an expression of their own individual personalities and their identity as a couple.

Whatever *your* reason for considering a destination wedding, this book is for you. It is designed to whet your appetite and fuel your dreams, but it is also designed to give you a very practical overview of the elements involved in planning a destination wedding, whether you intend to do so yourself or with the help of a wedding planner. My aim with this book is, first, to help you answer the question, *Is a destination wedding right for us?*, and second, if the answer is *Yes!*, to guide you through the planning stages. So, if you think you have what it takes to be a "Destination Bride," turn the page and get ready to explore the possibilities!

CONSIDERING A DESTINATION WEDDING:
Deciding, then Organizing

Destination weddings have captured the imagination of the modern American bride for a number of reasons. A destination bride may be geographically separated from her family, or she may be marrying someone from another region. She and her fiancé may be avid travelers, driven to broaden their horizons through journeys abroad. Or, with the attitude that the world is her oyster, she may desire a wedding that is the most amazing adventure of her lifetime. There are many reasons to choose a destination wedding and perhaps just as many reasons not to. The decision is not one to be made lightly, and it is important to go through the decision-making process before committing to a marriage celebration far from home. It is always unfortunate to watch a couple face disappointment, having plunged deep into their planning before honestly assessing what kind of celebration was truly appropriate for their circumstances. If your number-one priority on your wedding day is to be surrounded by everyone who has ever meant anything to you, a destination wedding may not be the best choice. If, however, you are set on having a once-in-a-lifetime romantic adventure surrounded by those dearest to you, then a destination wedding may be just the thing.

IS A DESTINATION WEDDING RIGHT FOR YOU?

Like any important decision, the choice can seem daunting, but it needn't be, once you weigh all the relevant pros and cons. By understanding what goes into a destination wedding, you can decide not only if it *appeals* to you but, more importantly, if it is *right* for you. I often consult with brides and couples who are considering various wedding options, including the possibility of a destination wedding. Within an hour, it is usually very clear to me whether a destination wedding makes sense for them. If you consider the questions in this book while keeping in mind your own objectives and priorities, I think you will arrive at an equally clear answer. First, ask yourself why you are considering a destination wedding. There are plenty of motivations, but some of the more common ones are:

- **Sheer logistics,** as when the destination is equidistant between his and her families. I have found this to be a common concern for couples who marry in the upper Hudson Valley, where I live. For guests coming from New York, Boston, and points west, a central location, such as the Hudson Valley and the Berkshires, is desirable. Some couples even plan progressive destination weddings. One couple I know hosted a wedding in California for their friends, another celebration in upstate New York for her parents and family, and a third in the Czech Republic for his parents and family. (I'd note that this is not a cheap option!)

- **The desire to travel and/or the romance and adventure of another country or culture.** This is a large category that includes many kinds of people with many different expectations. I worked with one couple—a pair of mountain climbers—who were bound and determined to marry on top of Mt. Kilimanjaro. Another couple e-mailed me during a trip around the world, requesting help for a wedding in Zanzibar because they knew they'd be there at Christmastime.

- **The wish to marry in a location of personal significance,** as when a couple journeys to a place of ancestral heritage or returns to the place where they first met. These weddings often become a meaningful celebration of ethnic roots and cultural traditions. I planned a destination wedding in the Czech Republic, the homeland from which the bride's father fled during World War II. Another couple decided to marry in a castle in southern England because they had met there during their college semester abroad.

- **A desire to save money.** Destination weddings can be expensive, but when planned with realistic wishes and well-defined priorities, they do not have to be. (Read more about this in *Setting Your Budget*, pages 27–33.)

- **The commitment to a nontraditional wedding.** Destination weddings often appeal to couples who are not particularly drawn to a conventional wedding. For some couples, especially those entering a second marriage, an important priority is to have a celebration that is decidedly "outside the box" of a typical ceremony and reception. These couples want to shed the confines and expectations that a traditional wedding holds. Other couples plan a destination wedding as a lively "encore" to a traditional wedding.

- **A need to escape.** This is a less-common scenario, but it does happen. I remember a bride who, after being engaged for only one month, found herself with a budget reaching six figures. Her future mother-in-law was insisting on inviting 175 personal friends, her own mother was already stressed out about the proper way to address invitations, and everyone from her next-door neighbor to her fourth cousin was offering unsolicited advice. The bride-to-be came to realize that she did not want a wedding dictated by the rules of etiquette and attended by 200 strangers. She wanted a wedding that she and her fiancé could truly enjoy.

If you can relate to any of these reasons or scenarios, a destination wedding is certainly worth considering. But one couple's ideal may be another couple's nightmare. How do you know if it is right for you? Below I've listed some basic characteristics of a destination wedding. Depending on your own situation, priorities, temperament, and style, you'll see these qualities as either advantages or disadvantages. By carefully and honestly considering the positive and negative aspects of each, you'll be making an informed decision.

Use this list as a springboard for your decision-making process, but be sure to consider and discuss the list *as a couple*. Perhaps you are a wanderlust-driven adventurer marrying a couch potato. While you may find wonderful ways to compromise with your partner during your marriage, your wedding may not be the best time to push the envelope! Ask yourselves: When you consider these aspects of a destination wedding, are your eyes lighting up with excitement and your imaginations sparked by possibilities, or are your palms sweating and your hearts pounding with anxiety? Your responses will depend on your wishes and your situation as a couple, so consider what is feasible for you both.

WHEN IT COMES TO A DESTINATION WEDDING, THE POSSIBILITIES ARE ENDLESS.
On one hand: With the world as your oyster, you'll never be at a loss for options.
On the other: With so many possibilities, the prospect of deciding and making plans can be overwhelming and perhaps too daunting.

A DESTINATION WEDDING OFFERS THE OPPORTUNITY TO MARRY AWAY FROM HOME, IN A LOCATION AS DISTANT, UNFAMILIAR, AND EXOTIC AS YOU CHOOSE.
On one hand: If you are passionate about traveling, exploring new places, and experiencing the unknown, a distant destination guarantees excitement!
On the other: Marrying in a foreign region and/or culture means dealing with uncharted territory, so it can be a great challenge, especially if you are not terribly comfortable traveling in unknown areas.

A DESTINATION WEDDING PROMISES A MEMORABLE EXPERIENCE.
On one hand: "Unforgettable" may be just the kind of wedding you are seeking, especially if you do not mind the possibility of facing the unexpected and being spontaneous when necessary.
On the other: The possibility of the unexpected could make the wedding "the wrong kind" of memorable. After all, it is harder to control every aspect of a wedding when planning it from afar.

A DESTINATION WEDDING ALLOWS YOUR GUESTS TO SPEND MORE TIME WITH YOU AND EACH OTHER.

On one hand: If you enjoy being with your family and friends, and they enjoy being with each other, this could be the trip of a lifetime. Everyone will get to know each other better and take pleasure in each other's company.

On the other: You love your friends and family individually, but perhaps together they are a combustible mix. If you cannot imagine the group dynamics working for longer than a few hours, this may create an uncomfortable situation.

A DESTINATION WEDDING IS A LONGER CELEBRATION, OFTEN SPREAD OUT OVER THE COURSE OF SEVERAL DAYS.

On one hand: A longer celebration means your wedding won't be over in a flash, like so many traditional one-day affairs. You and your guests can revel in the festivities for a few days.

On the other: One day may be all you need for your wedding, especially if you prefer an affair that is short and sweet!

BECAUSE OF THE TIME AND EXPENSE REQUIRED FOR TRAVELING, A DESTINATION WEDDING TYPICALLY INVOLVES FEWER GUESTS.

On one hand: With a guest list limited to your closest friends and family, you will be surrounded by those who mean the most to you.

On the other: The distance of a destination wedding may prevent some guests from attending your wedding, so "the whole gang" may not be able to make it.

YOUR PRIORITIES AND EXPECTATIONS WILL DETERMINE THE EXPENSE OF A DESTINATION WEDDING.

On one hand: If you invite fewer guests and/or choose a less expensive destination and reasonable sites, a destination wedding need not break the bank—in fact, it can be less expensive than the average wedding.

On the other: A destination wedding can be quite expensive. If you insist on a large guest list, foot the traveling bill for all your guests, or select an expensive destination such as Japan or Switzerland, or if you want a five-star quality wedding in any location, you will need a very large budget indeed.

THE DEGREE OF PLANNING REQUIRED FOR A DESTINATION WEDDING VARIES, DEPENDING ON YOUR EXPECTATIONS AND THE DESTINATION YOU SELECT.

On one hand: If you have a small group of guests, hire a wedding coordinator, and/or choose a site that offers wedding services, planning a destination wedding can be a straightforward process.

On the other: If you have a large group of guests, select a foreign destination, face a language barrier, and/or choose a site that offers no wedding services, you can expect to encounter problems during your planning process. This is especially true if you tend to agonize over every detail.

On one hand: If you are looking for ways to break the boundaries of a traditional wedding celebration, a different location and culture can give you the perfect opportunity to try new and unusual things.

On the other: It is difficult—sometimes even insensitive—to force your traditions and ideas in a foreign country. In some cultures, it can even be hard to *find* options for your traditions.

DESTINATION WEDDINGS TAKE YOU FAR FROM HOME.

On one hand: Sometimes there is nothing like escape… being absolutely removed from everyday stresses and entering fully into the fantasy and euphoria of realizing your dreams.

On the other: And sometimes the prospect of being away from home and disconnected (even temporarily) from all that is familiar holds no allure whatsoever.

While considering this list, think first and foremost about your own priorities as a couple. But also think about the people you love and ask yourselves if they would be able to attend a faraway wedding. Be sure to ask the really important people in your life—your "must-have" guests—if they are agreeable to the idea of a destination wedding. I have had more than one couple find out in the early stages of planning that a close relative was afraid to fly. That was enough to change the couples' minds about having a destination wedding. After discussing the pros and cons as a couple, ask yourselves these additional questions:

+ Is an interesting destination a priority?
+ Are you comfortable planning an out-of-town wedding?
+ Do you have time to plan a faraway wedding?
+ Do you want to hire somebody to coordinate the wedding? If so, can you afford to hire a professional planner?
+ Whom would you invite? And how many would you invite?
+ Would your closest family and friends be able to attend a destination wedding?
+ Are you ready to deal with potentially complicated planning logistics?
+ Can you afford to make a planning trip?

Phew! You have asked yourself some of the difficult questions and pondered the advantages and disadvantages of a destination wedding. It is only after you've wrapped your mind around some of these major issues that you can accept your heart's choice with confidence. By taking the time now to make an informed decision, you won't find yourself furiously backpedaling later on. If you do decide on a destination wedding for the right reasons, with all of the pros and cons on the table, it is sure to be a wonderful experience for you and all your guests.

FIVE PHASES TO MAKING IT A REALITY

In the coming chapters, I will take you step-by-step through the phases of making a destination wedding a reality. On pages 22–23, you will find a sample schedule, which is broken down into five phases. Because you may still be pondering several options, I have provided a brief overview of these phases below. This will give you a general sense of what is involved before you get into the "brass tacks" of the planning process.

PHASE *One*: READY, SET, GO!
Once you decide on a destination wedding, it is time to get organized, marshal your resources, and prepare yourself for one of the most meaningful projects you'll ever undertake. In this initial phase, you will gather and assess your collective thoughts, desires, priorities, finances, and human resources. Start designing your dreams by making some preliminary decisions about size, style, budget, and other basic elements of your wedding celebration.

PHASE *Two*: WHEN AND WHERE IN THE WORLD?
One of the most exciting decisions you'll make about your destination wedding is, of course, the destination. Whether or not you have a clear sense of your destination already, this part of the planning can be a wonderful process of discovery. You will want to collect as much information as possible to decide on a destination as well as specific sites for the ceremony and reception. If you are not short on time or money, you and your fiancé might even go on a tour to see all the destinations you are considering. I once sent a couple on a luxury tour of several Caribbean islands because they could not make a decision without visiting the possibilities first. Once you decide on a place, you'll experience a new level of exhilaration as you begin to see your dreams take shape.

PHASE *Three*: THE DREAM TEAM AND THE DETAILS
Next, you have to start the grunt work of determining what kind of details you want and who is going to provide them. This can be a tedious phase with lots of questions to answer and logistics to work out, but it can also be fun, especially if you like the idea of designing the wedding and you enjoy working with your service providers. Travel, accommodations, guest considerations, wardrobe, menus, décor—I'll show you how to pull it all together. Because this phase includes making plans with your service providers, it is advantageous to schedule a planning trip to your destination. That way, you'll not only be able to meet the service providers face-to-face, but you'll also have the opportunity to experience firsthand how everything will actually look, taste, sound, and feel.

PHASE *Four*: CONFIRMATION

With all the details in place, it is almost time to sit back and relax. First, though, you will have to confirm all the details. And reconfirm. When I plan a wedding, my motto is: *Confirmation is the key to a flawless event!*

PHASE *Five*: COORDINATION

As the big day approaches, someone other than yourself—a trusted family member, a friend, or a hired wedding planner—should coordinate all the elements you've designed. This will ensure that everything goes as planned, which will in turn allow you to complete your final and most important task—relaxing and thoroughly enjoying your wedding celebration.

GETTING THE TOOLS YOU NEED

You have imagined yourself being married far from home, you have weighed the pros and cons, and you have finally decided that it is right for you. Now that you are committed to having a destination wedding, what do you do? And how will you get it all done? Dreaming is easy. Making it happen, on the other hand, can seem overwhelming. But every journey, even the longest one, begins with a single step. Do not be scared, do not procrastinate—just get started. Start planning as soon as possible, especially if you are inviting guests. If you are anticipating a large group, I recommend starting at least one year in advance. The following chapters will help you from the first step of planning to your walk down the aisle, whether that aisle is on a sandy beach or in a ski lodge. To get started, equip yourself with a few essential tools. These tools, listed below, will facilitate your organization and make the planning process as smooth as possible.

BINDER...A BIG ONE!

Purchase a large binder to hold all your correspondence, contracts, and wedding-related documents. Divide the binder into categories, such as *Travel, Photography, Décor,* and *Music.* You will be organizing your papers as you go along, so do not worry about the fine details in the beginning. For now, it is important that you have one central place for all the important papers—from contracts to scribbled notes—that you generate during the months of planning. This binder will be your memory (when you've lost yours), your organizer (when you are not sure what day it is), and your lifesaver. One of my clients had a great idea for her binder: She glued a wonderful picture of her smiling fiancé onto the inside cover. At bumpy times along the wedding planning road, she could just look at the picture for a reminder of why the effort was well worth making.

SOFTWARE

Select wedding planner software to help you keep track of information, either online or in book or digital format. Planning software offers checklists and forms that will help you keep track of the details as you plan, enabling you to stay on schedule. You can purchase a quality software program such as Wedding Magic by FrogWare, or you can refer to various wedding Web sites, including *Destination Bride*'s site (www.destinationbride.com), where you will find online planning tips and tools. Make sure your software will allow you to open, view, and use graphics during the planning process.

INTERNET ACCESS

Internet access and an e-mail address are musts for group communication, especially when guests and service providers are scattered across a long distance and perhaps even different time zones. E-mail, which saves time and prevents miscommunication, is often the easiest way to keep everyone on the same page. With e-mail, you can simultaneously send notes to everyone and anyone who needs to stay informed. As a planner, I appreciate being able to communicate with both the bride and groom at the same time, regardless of where they may be. This eliminates comments such as, "You didn't tell me we were doing that!", which can add stress to the situation. Call it marriage mediation before the marriage!

You may want to set up a separate e-mail account designated for wedding planning only. An e-mail address devoted specifically to wedding matters is helpful, even if you already have a personal e-mail account at work or at home. With spam messages and personal correspondence pouring in every day, it is easy for wedding-related messages to slip through the cracks. Resist the temptation to get a free e-mail account because such accounts do not allow you to transfer large documents or send and receive graphics. It is always exciting to get your first photographs attached to an e-mail—"Oh! Pictures from the dress designer!"—but excitement quickly turns to frustration if you are unable to open them.

MOBILE PHONE

Whoever is planning the wedding should have a mobile phone with the proper national or international coverage to access your service providers. Compare rates to get the best plan available and, if you find you are using more minutes than your plan allows, upgrade. It is possible to get international service through various mobile phone companies; inquire about the different programs available to find the best option for you. If you are mid-contract with a company that does not cover your wedding destination, you might consider renting a phone when you need it most: during the planning trip (if you take one) and during the wedding trip. Mobile phones can be rented through companies such as Global Phoneworks (800-556-0530 / www.globalphoneworks.com). Don't forget to figure the mobile phone expense into your budget!

HARDWARE

The "wedding coordinator," whether that will be you, a friend, or a hired professional, should have a laptop computer and a portable printer so she can travel with all the wedding documents, send out e-mails when necessary, and create important notices as needed. I learned this the hard way when I was hired to coordinate a very complicated wedding in England; the wedding had already been planned, and my job was to orchestrate the events on-site. Once I arrived and was able to communicate face-to-face with the vendors, I discovered that many of the details differed from what I had been told by the client. Therefore it was necessary for me to rewrite and reprint several documents so the guests and the various service providers could be made aware of the changes. All was well until I faced the dilemma of not being able to print from the hotel's computers. I vowed then and there that I would never again be caught without a way of printing my documents. Nowadays, business centers are common in hotels, but I still keep to my vow. If you do not want to travel with a computer and printer, be sure your hotel has *exactly* what you need to edit and print documents from a disc, and verify that the hotel's computer center is available to guests 24 hours a day, seven days a week.

WEDDING INSURANCE

Wedding insurance is a tool intended to protect you throughout the planning process and the event itself. You will be investing a tremendous amount of money as you plan your wedding celebration, and you will be exposing yourself to liability as the host of the events. I consider insurance important—so important that I require all my clients to purchase both wedding and travel insurance. For companies that specialize in wedding insurance, I recommend Weddingsurance by R.V. Nuccio & Associates, Inc. (800-364-2433 / www.rvnuccio.com) or WedSafe (877-723-3933 / www.wedsafe.com).

You can get liability insurance closer to the wedding date (see chapter five, page 100), after you have confirmed the wedding location and caterer. However, I advise getting wedding insurance, which covers cancellation and/or postpone-ment, photographs, attire, gifts, rings, loss of deposits, and professional counsel-ing, right away to secure the coverage before you start spending money. The cost of this policy will depend on the amount of money you want to cover; ask yourself how much it would cost you if your wedding were cancelled. Make sure you can add additional people to the policy should you find out, for example, that your wed-ding planner or the property owner wants to be added to the list of insured. You can supply copies of your insurance to your planner and the wedding location if they request it.

DESIGNING YOUR PLANNING DOCUMENTS

Your planning documents—a planning schedule, guest list, service provider list and budget—will be constant companions through the months and weeks leading up to the wedding. Preserve your sanity by keeping the documents in one place (your binder) and keeping the information accurate and up-to-date.

THE PLANNING SCHEDULE

A planning schedule lays out the tasks to be completed, the dates by which they need to be completed, and the people responsible for completing them. It is wise to formulate this "master plan" early and revise it as you go along. As I mentioned before, wedding software programs offer ideas and forms for planning schedules. On pages 22–23, I have provided an example of one of my own planning sched-ules. There may be more details included in my sample than are relevant to your wedding, but you can easily adapt it to reflect your own plans and timeline.

Once you have organized your own planning schedule, you will no doubt refer to it often. It will give you a sense of where you are in the process, remind you of deadlines, and ease your mind when you feel overwhelmed. You cannot do every-thing at once, nor should you try; the planning schedule will remind you that everything can and should proceed step-by-step. With your schedule in hand, you can begin to divide up tasks between the bride and groom. Though you each may have your own tasks, you will probably have to pinch-hit for one another from time to time. In this case, the schedule will keep you both on track. If you are working with a professional planner, decide which decisions and choices you definitely want to make as a couple, and be clear in identifying which tasks and responsibil-ities you want to assign to the planner.

SAMPLE *P*LANNING SCHEDULE

*phase O*ne: READY, SET, GO!

12 MONTHS BEFORE: ORGANIZATION
- Organize wedding binder and digital files
- Prepare a planning schedule
- Purchase wedding insurance
- Compile a guest list
- Set a budget
- Prepare a service provider sheet
- Enlist a wedding planner and/or travel consultant

*phase T*wo: WHEN AND WHERE IN THE WORLD

11 MONTHS BEFORE: DESTINATION RESEARCH
- Profile destination
- Research wedding destinations and venues
- Verify legality for both religious (church) and civil (state) ceremonies
- Decide on a date
- Research travel and accommodation options and rates
- Check for travel advisories
- Get family approval
- Research and select honeymoon destination
- Assess need to take a planning trip

*phase T*hree: THE DREAM TEAM AND THE DETAILS

10 MONTHS BEFORE: THE PLANNING TRIP
- Reassess need for assistance
- Make travel arrangements for planning trip
- Determine your mission
- Research service providers
- Check service provider qualifications
- Set up meetings with service providers
- Confirm meetings with service providers and venues
- Pack for planning trip

ON PLANNING TRIP:
- Tour reception venues and meet with banquet managers
- Decide on reception venue
- Taste reception food and plan menu
- Interview local wedding coordinators
- Meet with and select religious and/or civil officiants
- Decide between civil and/or religious ceremony
- Decide on ceremony location
- Meet with officiant and work out ceremony details
- Determine who will assist with marriage license
- Determine where license must be filed
- Visit guest accommodation options: hotels, villas, resorts, etc.
- Interview and select a pastry chef to provide wedding cake
- Investigate and select music options
- Research florists and decorators
- Explore artisan shops and markets for design resources
- Interview photographers
- Interview videographers
- Investigate wedding transportation options
- Explore salon and/or stylist options by having a test-run

ON PLANNING TRIP (CONTINUED):
- Investigate rental companies
- Research favor and/or welcome gift ideas and resources
- Browse through jewelry stores for wedding rings
- Try different restaurants for rehearsal dinner and/or welcome party
- Research local activities for guests
- Decide on itinerary for you and guests
- Find a tour and/or transportation company for ground transport
- Inquire at local banks about opening a bank account
- Reassess and finalize honeymoon destination

9 MONTHS BEFORE: CONTRACTS
- Reasses (wo)man power
- Contract all service providers and send deposits
- Start getting your legal and religious documents in order
- Make all travel arrangements
- Book all accommodations
- Finalize the tour and activity itinerary
- Book ground transportation
- Purchase travel and (additional) wedding insurance
- Start writing a detailed order of events

8 MONTHS BEFORE: DESIGN AND GUEST COMMUNICATION
- Register for gifts
- Decide on wedding style, theme, and/or colors
- Set up wedding planning Web site or write first introduction letter
- Design, print, and send save-the-dates and preliminary wedding information
- Start designing or considering stationery: invitations, programs, seating cards, menus, and thank-yous
- Find and book a calligrapher

phase Three (CONTINUED):

7 MONTHS BEFORE: FASHION
- Select and order bride's gown
- Select and purchase bride's accessories: shoes, head piece/veil, jewelry, makeup, perfume
- Select and order bridesmaids' gowns
- Select and order groom's tuxedo or suit
- Select and order groomsmen's tuxedos or suits
- Purchase trousseau and honeymoon wardrobe
- Select and order wedding rings

6 MONTHS BEFORE: DESIGN DETAILS AND UPDATES
- Finalize menu(s)
- Finalize wedding cake
- Make final selections for flowers and décor
- Send idea pictures to florist/decorator
- Work on ceremony details and purchase ceremonial items
- Select music and entertainment
- Consider special effects for reception
- Hire wedding transportation

5 MONTHS BEFORE: GIFTS
- Purchase wedding gift for fiancé(e)
- Purchase gifts for bridal party, parents, and service providers
- Order welcome gifts
- Order favors

4 MONTHS BEFORE: INVITATIONS AND MORE
- Finish stationery design or order invitations
- Deliver stationery design to printer
- Send completed invitations to calligrapher
- Address and send invitations

3 MONTHS BEFORE: UPDATES AND WELCOME LETTERS
- Update budget, service provider list, and order of events
- Update Web site or send final update letter
- Review hotel contracts and release any unnecessary rooms
- Write welcome letter/itinerary for guests' arrival
- Order maps and brochures for welcome packages

2 MONTHS BEFORE: RESPONSES AND MARRIAGE LICENSE
- Start creating seating charts as people RSVP
- Call guests who have not responded by RSVP date
- Finalize marriage license

phase Four: CONFIRMATION

1 MONTH BEFORE: FINAL ORDERS
- Release final unnecessary rooms
- Conduct final meeting with coordinators and banquet manager in person or by phone
- Finalize all documents: budget, service provider list, and order of events
- Confirm travel reservations and seating

3 WEEKS BEFORE: CONFIRMATION E-MAILS AND FAXES
- Send confirmation e-mails or faxes, along with order of events and final numbers, to service providers
- Organize final payments and submit any payments due before the event
- Start packing

1 WEEK BEFORE: PACKING
- Finish packing

phase Five: COORDINATION

3–5 DAYS BEFORE: DEPARTURE AND VIS-À-VIS CONFIRMATONS
- Arrive at wedding destination
- Meet with banquet manager and wedding planner/coordinator
- Meet with all service providers
- Assemble and deliver welcome packages
- Get gown steamed
- Pick up tuxedo
- Have manicure, pedicure, massage, facial, etc.

1 DAY BEFORE: PRESERVING YOUR SANITY
- Totally relax!

THE GUEST LIST

Putting together a guest list is one of your first steps because this list will factor into almost every other planning decision. Because so much is dependent upon this list, it is important to establish one right from the beginning. It allows you to begin visualizing your wedding, its size, and the personalities involved. Knowing the "cast of characters" will also help you identify your resources and even help you determine what kind of a destination you should choose. Start your guest list by including everyone you think you might want to invite. Consider this a working list, as you may have to pare down the list once you know more about your budget and priorities.

© JOHN W. CORBETT PHOTOGRAPHY. WWW.CORBETTPHOTOGRAPHY.NET

Compile the guest list directly into a digital file, using Microsoft Word, Excel, Access, or a wedding planning software program, such as Wedding Magic by FrogWare. Enter the guests in alphabetical order by last name. You will be using this database in many ways, so it is important to organize it in a versatile format. If you seek another format to follow, refer to the sample guest list form on page 25. Add columns or lines for any additional information you might need to gather from the guests, such as events they will be attending, rooming information, arrival and departure dates, transportation needs, dietary needs, or child care. In a section for notes, you may want to keep track of a disability or preferences for smoking or nonsmoking rooms. In addition, include columns or lines for events at which you plan to have assigned seating. You will later be able to turn this database or form into a seating chart if necessary.

THE SERVICE PROVIDER LIST

Your team of service providers—the banquet manager, caterer, photographer, musicians, and so on—will be determined after you have selected your destination. Nevertheless, I suggest setting up a service provider list as soon as possible. To minimize documents, you can combine the service provider list with the budget form, as I have done with the sample form on pages 30–31. This is an easy way to consolidate important information.

TITLE   Mr. & Mrs.   LAST NAME   Rugen   FIRST NAMES   Glen and Lisa

ADDRESS   Post Office Box 142, Chatham, New York, 12037   PHONE   518-392-7766   E-MAIL ADDRESS LisaLight@destinationbride.com

RSVP   x Y   ○ N   ARRIVAL DATE   20 / June   DEPARTURE DATE   25 / June   HOTEL   Four Seasons

WELCOME PARTY   ○ Y   x N   REHEARSAL   x Y   ○ N   DINNER   x Y   ○ N

WEDDING TRANSPORT   no, will have car   TABLE NUMBER   11   BRUNCH   x Y   ○ N

TITLE   LAST NAME   FIRST NAMES

ADDRESS   PHONE   E-MAIL ADDRESS

RSVP   ○ Y   ○ N   ARRIVAL DATE   /   DEPARTURE DATE   /   HOTEL

WELCOME PARTY   ○ Y   ○ N   REHEARSAL   ○ Y   ○ N   DINNER   ○ Y   ○ N

WEDDING TRANSPORT   TABLE NUMBER   BRUNCH   ○ Y   ○ N

TITLE   LAST NAME   FIRST NAMES

ADDRESS   PHONE   E-MAIL ADDRESS

RSVP   ○ Y   ○ N   ARRIVAL DATE   /   DEPARTURE DATE   /   HOTEL

WELCOME PARTY   ○ Y   ○ N   REHEARSAL   ○ Y   ○ N   DINNER   ○ Y   ○ N

WEDDING TRANSPORT   TABLE NUMBER   BRUNCH   ○ Y   ○ N

TITLE   LAST NAME   FIRST NAMES

ADDRESS   PHONE   E-MAIL ADDRESS

RSVP   ○ Y   ○ N   ARRIVAL DATE   /   DEPARTURE DATE   /   HOTEL

WELCOME PARTY   ○ Y   ○ N   REHEARSAL   ○ Y   ○ N   DINNER   ○ Y   ○ N

WEDDING TRANSPORT   TABLE NUMBER   BRUNCH   ○ Y   ○ N

TITLE   LAST NAME   FIRST NAMES

ADDRESS   PHONE   E-MAIL ADDRESS

RSVP   ○ Y   ○ N   ARRIVAL DATE   /   DEPARTURE DATE   /   HOTEL

WELCOME PARTY   ○ Y   ○ N   REHEARSAL   ○ Y   ○ N   DINNER   ○ Y   ○ N

WEDDING TRANSPORT   TABLE NUMBER   BRUNCH   ○ Y   ○ N

TITLE   LAST NAME   FIRST NAMES

ADDRESS   PHONE   E-MAIL ADDRESS

RSVP   ○ Y   ○ N   ARRIVAL DATE   /   DEPARTURE DATE   /   HOTEL

WELCOME PARTY   ○ Y   ○ N   REHEARSAL   ○ Y   ○ N   DINNER   ○ Y   ○ N

WEDDING TRANSPORT   TABLE NUMBER   BRUNCH   ○ Y   ○ N

By organizing all your service provider contact information on one sheet, you create a quick reference that will make the tasks of coordinating and confirming much easier. As you identify and contract your service providers, enter all their

contact information directly into the document. Include the service being provided, the company, the contact person, contact numbers (phone, fax, and mobile) and addresses (postal, e-mail, and Web site). Turn the list into a checklist by adding columns alongside the contact. This checklist can be used to keep track of coordination and confirmation information. You can note, for example, when you sent, e-mailed, or faxed the order of events, when the receipt of the order of events was confirmed, when each service provider is scheduled to arrive at the wedding, and when the final payments are due. Once you have contracted all the service providers, it may prove helpful to send the service provider list to your officiant, banquet manager, and if appropriate, your photographer and emcee.

THE BUDGET

The budget is a crucial factor in planning a destination wedding, so I have dedicated an entire section (following on pages 27–33) to this topic. You can go ahead and set up the budget document even before you start working with the actual numbers. As I have already noted, my sample service provider list on pages 30–31 serves double duty as a budget form. To keep track of your budget, you can adopt this system or you can use a spreadsheet software program, such as Excel. You also have the option of utilizing an online program, such as those provided by the Wedding Channel (www.weddingchannel.com) or The Knot (www.theknot.com). Or you can visit the *Destination Bride* Web site (www.destinationbride.com), where you will find another sample budget that can be used as a model.

Be sure to include all the possible expenses you might incur, and delete items from the sample form that are not applicable. If, for example, your parents are paying for the catering and you are paying for the rest of the wedding, delete the "Caterer" section from your budget. Leave in any items you are getting free—perhaps your best friend is designing the invitations or your sister is baking the cake—so you have a record of the gift, but assign it a cost of zero dollars.

SETTING YOUR BUDGET

Here is the bottom line, the rule that will save you much trouble and heartache: *Set up a budget, and don't cheat.* The more comprehensive and accurate your budget, the easier time you will have throughout the planning process.

THE IMPORTANCE OF A BUDGET

One of the initial steps in planning any wedding is deciding on a realistic budget. Destination wedding budgets vary dramatically. According to the Association for Wedding Professionals International, the average wedding in the United States is attended by 178 guests and costs an average of $28,000. However, a wedding in a resort destination such as Newport, Rhode Island or a metropolitan area such as New York City will easily drive up that figure. If you are not prepared, the budget in *any* destination can exceed your expectations. Couples paying for their own wedding will, in all likelihood, find their nuptial celebration to be the third most

costly investment of their lives, topped only by raising children and buying a home. Unlike the experience of buying a house or a car, you do not have to prove to a wedding vendor that you can afford the purchase. And, unlike most large investments, most wedding expenses have to be paid within a year, sometimes less. So it is your responsibility to make sure your budget reflects what you can honestly afford.

For these reasons, I cannot overstress the importance of a budget. You and your fiancé must make yourselves sit down, with or without your parents, to establish your spending limits. This will empower you throughout the planning process, it will equip you to deal with vendors, and it will protect you from financial ruin. I was recently interviewed on *Inside Edition* along with a couple who went bankrupt, which led to their eventual divorce—all because they didn't have a wedding budget! Don't let it happen to you. If you are on a tight budget, you will have to find creative ways to save money without sacrificing what is most important to you. There are many ways to save money when planning a wedding, but my top five rules for cutting costs are listed on the following page.

RULE 1: DETERMINE YOUR PRIORITIES

Identify what is most important to you and your intended. The destination? The guests? The location? The planning trip? The flowers? The music? The food? The photographs? The ceremony? Your highest priorities, which could be anything from the invitations to the dress, are where you put the most money. Once you've established what is really important, cut corners everywhere else.

RULE 2: KEEP YOUR GUEST LIST TO A MINIMUM

Remember: Numbers mean money. For the average American wedding with 175 guests, the couple spends $160 per guest. Keep that in mind as you ponder inviting your tenth cousin or your elementary school bus driver! If you love gourmet food, haute couture, and white-glove service but your budget screams "firehouse hall," you may want to invite a very intimate group with whom you can enjoy those luxuries. On the other hand, if the company of friends and family is your highest priority, invite them all to a casual (but no less festive) celebration.

RULE 3: DECIDE ON AN APPROPRIATE STYLE

Choose a style for your wedding, then carry it through the entire event. Your wedding can be an elegant, traditional affair; a laid-back, informal gathering; or something in between. If you cannot afford a mansion, plan on a slightly more casual wedding at a country inn. The nice thing about destination weddings is that "anything goes." When you are all on vacation, nobody will give a second thought to attending a wedding on a Wednesday. This relaxed attitude gives couples the flexibility to do both what they want and what they need to save money.

RULE 4: IDENTIFY YOUR RESOURCES

Consider your resources. Is there family property that could be used for the ceremony or reception? Look at your guest list. Who on that list can sing or play an instrument for the ceremony? Whose artistic talent could help you create the invitations and stationery? Is anyone a photographer? Is anyone skilled at arranging flowers or sewing? Your friends and relatives may be able to fashion the most memorable wedding at little cost, if you let them. What better gift? Just remember: When calling on loved ones for help, be careful not to make any one guest work so much that they cannot enjoy the event.

RULE 5: BE INFORMED

Investigate the wedding destination to identify your resources and your options for the best and most affordable service providers. You can get this information by reading books and magazines, researching Web sites, contacting the local chamber of commerce or tourism bureau, and/or consulting with a wedding or travel professional who can advise you on service providers and venues within your budget. If you are reluctant to seek help from an expert, consider planning a one-time consultation to get yourselves started on the right foot; in such a consultation, an expert can offer basic information specific to your wedding and your chosen destination.

ESTABLISHING YOUR BUDGET

As a general rule, you can begin by assigning 50 percent of the budget to the reception location and dinner. Assess the remaining amount by deciding which items are highest priority to you, then assign each of them ten percent of the budget. This will vary from couple to couple; it could be anything from a wedding planner to the music. As you consider your priorities, decide where the lower priority miscellaneous items will fit into the budget. The basic idea is not to spend a lot on the less important items, making them all fit within 10 to 20 percent of your budget. If you identify three top priorities and assign them each ten percent of the budget, you will still have 20 percent left for the miscellaneous items. If your miscellaneous items are few, you may be able to have four top priorities. Your budget should reflect expenses in your chosen destination. You may not yet know where you will be getting married, but remember that costs are always changing and are different all over the world. In Italy, for example, photography is relatively inexpensive by American standards, while hair and makeup services are quite pricey.

KEEPING EXPENSES DOWN

Destination weddings have often been promoted as a money-saving alternative to the traditional wedding. They can be, but only if you are mindful of a few important ways to keep expenses down. Remember, five-star hotels cater to the wealthy and charge the same high rates all over the world, even if they are in "developing nations." You cannot expect to have a wedding for 100 for $15,000 in a five-star hotel unless you do not want music, flowers, or any of the other niceties associated with weddings. As you are developing your budget, remember that you can save money with a destination wedding if:

+ You invite a small group of people, or at least a significantly smaller group than you would invite at home.
+ You choose a destination that is not frequented by wealthy tourists.
+ You choose a three-star venue to host the reception.
+ You find a wedding location that is not in the business of offering weddings to wealthy foreigners. You might choose something else off the beaten track, such as a quaint, authentic restaurant or a privately-owned hacienda. (Just remember such places may not be in a position to provide any kind of wedding services.)
+ You invite your guests to an all-inclusive resort, where the resort covers the cost of the wedding as long as the wedding group occupies a certain number of rooms for a guaranteed number of nights.
+ You (or a close friend) plan the entire wedding.

SERVICE ROVIDER LIST / BUDGET

SERVICE	LAST UPDATE	COMPANY	CONTACT	ADDRESS
Wedding Insurance				
Financial Consultant				
Bank or Credit Card				
Wedding Planner				
Travel Consultant				
Wedding Web Site				
Gift Registry				
Stationery Designer				
Stationery Company				
Calligrapher				
Wedding Coordinator				
Airline				
Hotels				
Ground Transport				
Tour Company				
Tour Guide / Escort				
Bridal Gown / Accessories				
Rings				
Dry Cleaner				
Tuxedo Shop				
Welcome Packages				
Welcome Party				
Rehearsal Dinner				
Other Activities				
Hair / Makeup Stylist				
Wedding Party				
Wedding Transport				
Designer / Florist				
Rentals				
Table Settings				
Linens				
Lighting				
Audio				
Favors				
Photographer				
Videographer				
Ceremony Location				
Officiant(s)				
Ceremony Music				
Reception Location				
Caterer / Banquet Manager				
Pastry Chef / Wedding Cake				
Reception Music				
Special Effects				
Honeymoon Location				

WEB SITE	E-MAIL	PHONE / FAX	MOBILE	TOTAL DUE	DEPOSIT / 2ND PAYMENT	FINAL PAYMENT

Along with these tips, a spirit of resourcefulness can help cut costs for your destination wedding. A small budget does not make a wedding any less special or less meaningful. In fact, it can make a wedding more heartfelt and sentimental because it often prompts the couple to reach out to their close friends and relatives. If you haven't yet considered how friends and family members can lend a hand with their talents and efforts, do so now. In addition, ask yourself if there are ways to save money by making things, either by yourself or (preferably) with help from the wedding party. Or are there items you can borrow or services you can barter from friends, relatives, or community organizations you belong to.

MICRO-BUDGETS

As you develop your budget, it may help to include micro-budgets. A micro-budget is an itemized list of expenses under one single line item. I usually make a micro-budget that outlines the décor expenses because this tends to be the most complicated segment of the budget. The micro-budget accounts for the individual costs of flowers, lighting, linens, china, utensils, and props. I then add up all the individual costs and record the micro-budget total on the overall wedding budget.

WORKING WITH SERVICE PROVIDERS

Once you have a budget, you will be able to go to service providers knowing exactly what you have to spend on a particular product or service. Your planning should be driven by your budget; do not allow yourself to be steered otherwise. The service providers want you to be happy with their services, so they will try to interest you in what they think you'll like best. The natural instinct of a chef or designer will be to offer you his masterpiece, which will also be the most expensive option. But be careful, because what you love may not fit the budget. If you are worried about money, you must always communicate the importance of your budget and reiterate it to all of your service providers by saying, for example, "I love tulips but only if they are available within my budget." When I appeared on *Inside Edition* with the bankrupt couple, I was asked if their wedding vendors were to blame for budget-busting. My reply: If a couple does not go into a meeting with a service provider prepared with a budget, they are inviting problems.

With your budget in hand early on, you will have a guide for future decisions. It is your most important tool in being an informed consumer. If you were buying a house, you wouldn't go to a real estate agent and ask her to show you "everything," from modest homes to mansions. In planning your wedding, you will be making a variety of consumer decisions, and you will want to approach each one knowing the appropriate range. For example, when choosing a wedding reception site and caterer (if your caterer is independent of the site) with an overall wedding budget of $28,000, you know you cannot go over $14,000 for the entire reception location and banquet. Consider only reception facilities within the set range. During your search, you will be equipped with the right information and ready to ask the right questions. Ask the location manager or caterer what menus they can offer within your particular budget. Everything—food, beverage, service, rentals, tax, and gratuity—must be included in the projected cost to make your budget work. You do not want any surprises, so be clear that the *bottom-line* figure must be within your budget. To give you some wiggle room in your budget, you can also request a proposal that falls a little under the amount you plan to spend.

As you gather prices from vendors, you can make adjustments—as long as you remain within your budget framework. It is fine to deviate from your budget by spending less than you originally allotted for an item. It is also acceptable to use that savings in another area of your budget. For example, if you plan on spending $14,000 for the reception but manage to get it for $10,000, you can apply the remaining $4,000 to another expense. On the other hand, if you spend more than

you had planned on one item, you will have to adjust the budget somewhere else to accommodate the change. In the end, it all must be reconciled. By sticking to your overall budget and resisting the temptation to "cheat," you will make appropriate choices and avoid anxiety. And, as you select your service providers according to priority and budget, you will gain a clear sense of how feasible your guest list is.

Are you still not sure if you can afford the wedding you would like to have? Then enlist the help of a wedding consultant and/or financial planner who is familiar with the cost of wedding services. It is important to plan a wedding within your immediate means, but if you must, you can research other funding options. Talk to a professional about funding your wedding through a wedding loan, home equity loan, your 401(k), or your life insurance policy. The American Express Web site (www.americanexpress.com) offers a list of financial planners nationwide, as well as information on wedding financing and budgeting tips.

PLANNING THE WEDDING WITH PROFESSIONAL HELP

With your planning schedule in one hand and your budget in the other, you can decide if you need help pulling everything together. Your schedule will show how much work is involved, while your budget will show how much assistance you can afford for wedding planning and coordinating. Some couples, knowing their limits on time and patience, immediately recognize their need for someone else to oversee the details. Others know they cannot afford full service but still desire as much help as they can get. I suggest that couples enlist the help of a planner or consultant at least in the beginning of the process to start them on the right track. In order to determine how much and what kind of help you might need, consider the options for professional assistance. You may want to find a wedding professional in your immediate area, if only for a one-time consultation. Or, once you've determined your destination, you can check with the wedding venue to see if they offer planning assistance or are able to recommend reliable consultants.

© LONGUEVILLE HOUSE

WEDDING PLANNERS

When a 2003 *Wedding Bells* magazine survey asked brides what they would have done differently, many said they wished they had had more help and had hired a wedding planner. Few engaged couples know what lies ahead when they begin planning a wedding. Professional planners *do* know, and their job is to help you avoid the potential pitfalls and common mistakes. As you begin to see what kind of work is involved in the planning process, consider your own resources and schedule, then ask yourself, "Can I do this on my own, or am I already feeling overwhelmed?" If you are already feeling overwhelmed, it may be time to hire a professional wedding planner.

Many people still cringe when they hear the words "wedding planner" because they instantly imagine a strong personality who takes over the wedding. A quality wedding planner, however, focuses on making the wedding a reflection of *your* personality, not her personal showcase; the planner's objective is to make *your* dreams a reality. As with any successful professional relationship, you need to feel personally comfortable with your planner and confident of his or her working style. If you find a planner who seems too forceful, you can either be more forceful yourself or find another person to help you. A wedding planner should be able to offer you the necessary resources and referrals, provide guidance and direction, and coordinate your wedding events calmly and competently.

Professional planners can help with any and all aspects of your wedding, from assisting with the initial decision-making to coordinating the actual event. If you aim to plan your wedding yourself, a planner can be used strictly on a consultation basis at various points along the process. When clients hire me as a consultant only, I serve as their resource, supplying them with referrals and direction, and they do the legwork. I meet with them periodically to address their current issues—maybe invitations this month, musical options the next.

LOCATING A WEDDING PLANNER

It is possible to locate professional wedding planners through wedding associations, tourism bureaus, the Internet, and referrals from wedding venues. There are two primary wedding associations in the United States: the Association of Bridal Consultants (www.bridalassn.com) and the Association for Wedding Professionals International (www .afwpi.com). In Part II of this book, you can find contact information for wedding associations in various destinations throughout the world.

Wedding planners who specialize in destination weddings can be a valuable resource in planning travel, accommodations, and service providers in your chosen locale. Most have experience in assisting couples with the legal aspects of an international wedding, which can be quite tricky, considering the requirements and laws of different countries. Destination wedding planners are also accustomed to working with both clients and service providers all over the globe. In most cases, you can rely on these planners to handle travel services and guest coordination because either they are certified to provide travel services or they have partnered with a travel agency.

Wedding planners charge in a variety of ways, including a flat rate, an hourly rate, or a percentage/commission. Flat rates are estimated according to the job at hand. I used to charge flat rates, but I gave up because it is very difficult to anticipate the complexity of the job and estimate in advance the amount of time that will be required. When determining a flat rate, a planner will consider a combination of factors: how many months they have to plan, how easy the client is to work with, how many times they will have to travel to the destination, how many days they will be away coordinating the event, how many assistants will be needed at the event, how difficult the destination and service providers are to work with, how many service providers will be needed, and how many guests will have to be coordinated. Some wedding planners charge a flat fee that is simply based on a percentage (usually 10 to 15 percent) of your overall wedding budget. Wedding planners who charge a percentage usually provide you with an all-inclusive wedding package. The client pays the planner for everything, including the catering and the location, and the planner adds 10 to 15 percent to the bill to cover their fees. Finally, a planner may charge an hourly fee, which I feel is the most fair and flexible system because it correlates with the actual amount of time she spends working. This system also motivates the couple to do as much of the work themselves as possi-

© CHARITY DE MEER

ble. I charge an hourly rate, and I give my clients an estimate of the time I'll need for the job. I also encourage my clients to work with me to keep the costs down. Before hiring a wedding planner, make sure you understand what the rates are and how those rates are determined. Also keep in mind that a planner should be able to offer a plan of action so everybody is on the same page. You, your fiancé, and the planner should all be clear on each others' expectations and responsibilities throughout the process.

When meeting with a potential wedding planner, keep a few things in mind. First, ask yourself if this person is pleasant. Do you think you could relate to and work with him? Is he organized, accessible, and easy to communicate with? Also clarify that he will be the person with whom you will be working. If the company has several employees, your initial meeting may be with somebody other than the actual wedding planner; in this case, make sure you have the opportunity to meet the planner who would be assigned to your wedding. You will want to feel comfortable with your planner, and you will want the confidence of knowing he is experienced, qualified, and capable. For this reason, arm yourself with a list of questions to ask your candidates. The following questions are good ones to include:

- Are they members of a professional association?
- What kind of training have they had?
- How many years have they been planning destination weddings, or how many weddings have they actually planned?
- Can they provide a list of references for you to check?
- Are they legitimate businesses? Are they insured?
- What services do they offer? Consulting? Research? Planning? Design? Décor? Travel coordination? Guest escorting and guiding? Event coordination or orchestration? They may also sell wedding invitations and accessories, or offer dress and bouquet preservation, as my company does. If you are looking for full service from one service provider, be sure to make that clear.
- Do they have experience with the destination you have chosen? Do they have contacts there? If you have chosen a unique destination, you may have to hire a planner with little or no experience in that locale. However, if they are savvy destination wedding planners, that should not be a problem. Do they speak the destination language? If you have chosen to be married in Mexico because you and your fiancé speak Spanish, it will not help much if your planner doesn't. They will end up depending on you to translate!
- What and how do they charge? Do their fees include expenses or are they additional? What expenses need to be reimbursed? Mileage? Phone? Air? Rental car or ground transportation? Food? What do they charge for travel time? In other words, if they charge an hourly or daily rate, is it the same rate on travel days? Many companies charge less, even half rate, on travel days.
- What is the payment schedule? Many ask for a large nonrefundable deposit in the beginning, then schedule later payments to be made throughout the process. Final payments are usually due the week of the wedding, and if there are unexpected expenses when coordinating the events, you will be invoiced for those afterwards.

TRAVEL CONSULTANTS

Travel consultants specialize in helping their clients with all aspects of travel, including airfare and accommodation options, special fare packages, and services at their destination. Some destination clients work with a wedding planner who also provides travel services, some work just with a travel consultant/agent, and some with both. Note that travel agents no longer get paid commissions by the airlines. As a result, they often charge a booking fee to cover the time they spend researching and booking the reservation. This fee may not reflect a set percentage of the value of the booking. For example, they may charge $25 per booking, regardless of the cost of the ticket. If the travel agent is a destination wedding specialist, she will probably offer packages that are routinely sold to clients. The agent may be willing to custom design a destination wedding package for you, perhaps for an hourly fee, but most likely for a commission on the package.

It is often—but not always—the case that the cost of a travel consultant is less than that of a destination wedding planner. Travel consultants, however, do not necessarily offer the extent of services that planners do. Travel agents can coordinate all the travel for the guests. They can put together a package including air, ground transfers, hotel, meals, and a full itinerary of events if you wish. In this case, they add a 10 to 15 percent commission onto the package price, which is how they make their money. Consult the American Society of Travel Agents, www.astanet.com, to find an agent. When you hire a travel consultant, be sure to know exactly what you are paying for. Travel consultants may be able to provide you with possible locations and travel coordination for your wedding, but they may not have the resources to help you find service providers, coordinate the services, and address other planning issues.

WEDDING COORDINATORS

Wedding coordinators oversee all the details on the big day and make sure everything runs smoothly. However you plan your wedding and no matter what help you enlist along the way, you will want to have a wedding coordinator for the event—whether a hired professional or a trusted friend—so you can relax and enjoy your wedding. While you are busy with your own preparations, the coordinator will make sure the flowers arrive as planned (not just any flowers, but the ones you ordered!), the caterer is not substituting veal piccata for coq au vin, and the whole "hillside reception" is moved indoors if storm clouds threaten.

If you have hired a wedding planner, he may be a natural choice for the wedding coordinator. There are distinct advantages to having a coordinator who has been involved in the wedding throughout the planning process. Sometimes clients hire coordinators at their destination, perhaps suggested or even provided by the reception location. If you choose not to hire a coordinator, you may find that the maître d' or banquet manager at your location (armed with a detailed order of events) is capable of effectively overseeing the event. Or you may seek out an organized, detail-oriented, and reliable friend who is game to be your coordinator.

Now that you understand your options for assistance, you can begin to consider your own needs in the context of your budget. As you proceed through the planning, you will have the opportunity to reassess those needs and reconsider the question of assistance. Is it possible to plan your own destination wedding? Yes, provided you have a good deal of time, access to the Internet, some help from the wedding venue—and this book! If you want to tackle the planning on your own, I suggest you first contact the tourism bureaus near your home and at the destination to see what kind of resources they can provide. Ask the wedding venue to furnish a list of service providers. Find out if there is a wedding association you can contact. Subscribe to any local wedding publications and check out any wedding Web sites in the region. You might also obtain a telephone book from your destination area as a resource. If you have lots of time, patience, persistence, and resourcefulness, you can certainly do all the legwork on your own. However, I strongly advise against taking on the actual event orchestration yourself. If you want to keep your sanity and truly enjoy the most important trip and day of your life, enlist the help of a wedding coordinator. His assistance will make all the difference in allowing you to relax and have fun at your own wedding.

LOOKING AHEAD

At this point, I hope you are feeling less overwhelmed than when you first considered the prospect of having a destination wedding. Once you have gathered the tools you need, set up your planning documents, and determined how

© DAVID BECKSTEAD

much assistance you may require, you are well on your way to planning an unforgettable wedding. What's your next step? Choosing a destination! It is true that there will be many choices and details to consider, but you are now organized and ready to approach each one, step by step. It is said that nothing worth doing is ever easy. That maxim applies to marriage in general, and it certainly applies to planning a destination wedding!

{2} WHICH DESTINATION IS *Right for You?*

Where in the world *do* you want to be married? What kind of destination would best suit you as a couple? What destination holds meaning for you or reflects your personalities? Which destinations fit the dreams or fantasies you have about your wedding? Some couples just know, while others just know that they want to go *somewhere*. Even if you have not yet chosen your destination, you have probably dreamt about the ideal setting for your wedding. Your dreams provide a fine springboard for the tasks laid out in this chapter, beginning with profiling and researching your destination.

PROFILING AND RESEARCHING YOUR DESTINATION

If you are among those who have no particular destination in mind but are sure you want to combine your wedding with travel, begin to narrow down your options by asking yourselves these questions:

- If you could be married anywhere in the world, where would you go?
- What time of year would best suit your schedule?
- Do you have any ethnic ties to any particular part of the world?
- Do you have any history in any particular part of the world?
- Do you have friends or family in any fabulous destinations?
- What is your definition of romance: a beach, a mountain, a castle, a yacht?
- Do you see yourselves wearing a flowing gown and tuxedo or shirts and trousers? Cotton? Silk? Velvet? Furs?
- What type of flowers would you like to carry or wear? In what countries or regions would they be easy to find?
- What kind of cuisine makes your mouth water? French, Indian, Mediterranean?
- What else do you want to be able to do on your trip: play golf, swim, sail, hike, shop, visit museums, attend plays?

- What kind of music makes you want to dance? Calypso, big band, merengue, polka, rock, rhythm and blues, Celtic?
- What languages do you and your fiancé speak?
- Do you want a religious ceremony?
- Is it important to you to be legally married at the destination, or are you willing to go through the legal steps at home, either before or after the destination wedding celebration?
- How far are you willing to fly? How far are you willing to ask your guests to fly? Does it have to be a direct flight?
- How much do you want the flight and accommodations to cost you and your guests?

Once these questions are answered, you should have a workable profile of your preferred destination. You will have eliminated several options and perhaps identified a general area (a country, or at least a continent) or type of area (an island or a ski resort, for example) that appeals to you most. You are now ready to begin your research. At least 11 months before the wedding, you should start investigating potential destinations. Part II will allow you to zero in on your ideal destination and venue options. If you do not find what you are looking for in this book or if you want more information on a chosen destination, contact the tourism bureau either by phone or e-mail; they will have the most up-to-date resources.

Travel and bridal magazines, such as *Condé Nast Traveler*, *Modern Bride Connection* (a regional version of *Modern Bride*), and *National Geographic Traveler*, are excellent sources for information. Most wedding publications have a travel section detailing fabulous wedding and honeymoon destinations. You might also refer to the latest issue of any wedding periodicals published in your destination(s) of choice; I have listed some of these in Part II. If you enjoy the thrill of the hunt, the Internet is an easily accessible and often fruitful resource. The Appendix (pages 370–375) includes an extensive list of Web sites you may find helpful.

NARROWING THE LIST:
DOES IT PASS THE DESTINATION TEST?

After narrowing down your wedding destination possibilities, it is time to consider the practical aspects of each. Do as much research as possible to answer the four basic questions discussed on the following pages. Your destination may lose its appeal and its viability if it doesn't offer a few standard features: location, travel, and lodging options; safety; and a legal wedding ceremony.

DOES YOUR DESTINATION OFFER LOCATION OPTIONS?

Consider what location options your potential destination offers. Where will you actually hold the ceremony and reception? You do not have to choose the sites yet—whether a hotel, a redwood forest, or a chalet in the Italian Alps—but you do need to determine what options exist. I know of one couple who fell in love back-packing in a remote area of Idaho. On their wedding day, they wanted to share their favorite spot there—a mountain peak with an amazing view, a place they considered their own private piece of heaven—with their friends and family. However, the closest restaurant (a diner) was seven rigorous miles away. Your ideal destina-

© DAVID BECKSTEAD

tion, even if it is less remote than this couple's mountaintop, may have limited venue options for the ceremony and the reception, so be sure to investigate before you commit to a destination. In this early phase, you do not need to decide on a specific location. You do, however, need to narrow down your destination choices to those with interesting *and* feasible venues.

DOES YOUR DESTINATION OFFER TRAVEL AND LODGING OPTIONS?

How will people get to your destination, where will they stay, and what will it cost? As you research your destination choices, look into general travel and accommodation options for your guests. Will your guests have various travel options available to them, or is there only one way to reach your destination? Is that one way a reasonable flight or a 12-hour flight with three connections followed by a bus ride? Is the only option for accommodations an expensive hotel on a secluded island? While you do not have to limit yourself to only those options that would be easy and ideal for your guests, keep in mind that if you want to share your wedding with others, you should aim to strike a balance between your dreams and their comfort. If your destination holds appeal to both you and your guests, you will be happier planning the wedding and your guests will be happier attending it.

At this point you probably have a good idea of whether or not you are looking at a relatively safe destination. Just to cover all your bases, check the travel advisories. These advisories will alert you to any dangers or concerns, such as an outbreak of disease or a terrorist threat. You can obtain this information by contacting the United States Department of State (www.travel.state.gov).

CAN YOU BE LEGALLY MARRIED AT YOUR DESTINATION?

If it is important to you to have a legal marriage at your destination, be sure to choose a place that will allow foreigners to be married there. Most countries will allow foreigners or noncitizens to be legally married, but some countries make it challenging, and a few make it downright impossible. I've consulted with numerous couples who have had their hearts set on marrying in France, only to find out they cannot have a legal marriage there unless either the bride or the groom has lived in the country for 40 days before the wedding. The following pages offer a general overview of what may be involved in making your marriage legal abroad. In Part II, I have provided information on the level of difficulty, the residency requirements, the waiting period, if any, and who to contact for the further instructions you'll need for a legally binding ceremony in your chosen destination.

If having a religious ceremony is equally as important to you, check with the powers-that-be before you settle on a destination. Many churches and temples around the world will only marry members of their own congregations, so be aware of this pitfall before you get your hopes up. On the Italian island of Capri, for example, the Catholic Church will no longer marry foreign Catholics in their churches. If at all possible, determine who is going to perform the ceremony before committing to the destination. Talk to your local religious leader; perhaps he can connect you with religious leaders in your destination. The wedding venue may also be of help, as many resorts have a list of clergy with whom they work.

MAKING YOUR MARRIAGE LEGAL

Generally, if a marriage performed in a foreign country has met that country's legal requirements, the marriage will be legally valid in the United States. You can read more about this on the State Department's Web page for the Marriage of United States Citizens Abroad (www.travel.state.gov/family/issues_marriage. html). I recommend that couples first check the validity of a marriage abroad with the attorney general of the state in which they plan to reside.

Every country has its own set of rules and regulations for a legally binding marriage. Before finalizing your wedding destination, thoroughly acquaint yourself with the country's requirements and the process by which they must be met. Start by contacting the embassy and consulate of your chosen destination to obtain the requirement information. To find contact information for foreign embassies in the United States, visit the Electronic Embassy Web site (www.embassy.org). You may be directed to check on any local requirements by contacting the registry office in the specified city. The consulate should be able to tell you how to reach certain registry offices. You can also find contact information for some foreign registry offices on the Social Security Administration's Web page for Sources of Vital Statistics Records in Foreign Countries (http://policy.ssa.gov/poms.nsf/lnx/0200307990). In addition, it is advisable to touch base with the United States embassy in the host country; have them confirm what they know to be the letter of the law for foreign marriages. The State Department's Web page for United States Embassies and Consulates (http://usembassy.state.gov) lists contact information for American embassies all over the world. Laws do change, so do not make any travel arrangements or sign any contracts until you are certain you understand and are able to comply with your destination country's legal marriage requirements.

On the following pages I have provided an overview of the types of requirements you may be expected to meet, the documents you may have to supply, and the steps you may have to take to ensure that your marriage is legally recognized. This section provides more detail than you might expect for such an early phase of planning, but try not to be overwhelmed. You will see that it is necessary to start this process as soon as possible, and the details will prove helpful. Some countries have simple requirements and procedures. For those destinations with more complicated processes, you can seek professional assistance from a lawyer; to do so, visit the American embassy Web site of your chosen destination country, as several sites include a list of lawyers. Or you can request help from an on-staff wedding planner at your wedding location or an independent planner with experience in the area. Many of the locations featured in Part II will assist you in making your marriage legally binding. If you have your heart set on marrying in a country with stringent requirements, you can alway have a civil ceremony in your home country either before or after your destination wedding celebration.

DOCUMENTATION

Regardless of where you plan to be married, you can be sure that *some* documentation will be required. As you are researching the legal requirements, find out from your destination's embassy or consulate which documents you will need and whether these documents will need to undergo any of the following processes:

DUPLICATION

You may need more than one copy of certain documents, as different departments and offices may require the same paperwork. If necessary, find out if each copy has to be notarized and/or authenticated, or if you can get one document notarized and/or authenticated and then make copies.

NOTARIZATION

When a document is notarized, it is embossed and certified by a notary public as proof that the document is legal and authentic. Make sure you know the correct order of steps; check to see if the documents need to be notarized before and/or after they have been duplicated, translated, and authenticated. To have a document notarized, take it to a local notary public, located in any number of places including banks and municipal offices. This is not to be confused with the legal process of *authentication*, described in detail below.

TRANSLATION

If you are planning a wedding in a country where English is not the official language, you will most likely have to have some, if not all, of the required documents translated. Find out if your documents need to be translated and if so, by whom. You may have to complete a particular form and use an official embassy translator.

AUTHENTICATION

Authentication is a legal process to formally confirm that a signature, seal, or stamp appearing on a document is genuine. An authenticated document has an official signature of a notary public, judge, circuit clerk, or state registrar *and* an embossed seal of a currently commissioned state official. If a document needs to be "legalized" or it needs an *apostille*, this means it requires authentication. If duplicates of an authenticated document are necessary, find out if each copy has to be authenticated or if you can make copies from the original authenticated document. Authentication submittal forms are available in the Authentications Department of the Office of Secretary of State in every state, and they are also usually available through the state's Web site. Most states have a document authentication help line as well. For information, call 1-800-688-9889 or visit the Office of Authentications Web site (http://www.state.gov/m/a/auth/). Expect to pay a fee for the authentication of each separate document.

ENTRY REQUIREMENTS

If you plan on traveling abroad, you must first find out what documents are required to enter the country. This usually includes a form of photo identification, such as a passport. Sometimes, in addition to a passport, you need other documents, such as a birth certificate, baptismal record, naturalization record, census record, immigration record, or employment identification. You may also be required to get a visa, which is a permit to enter a country for a specific purpose, such as tourism, education, or business. Though few countries require visas, you should still make a point of checking. To find out if your destination requires a visa, you can visit or call that country's consulate or embassy in the United States. You can also get up-to-date visa information by referring to the Web sites for Travisa Visa Service, Inc. (www.travisa.com) and Travel Document Systems (www.traveldocs.com).

Always check to see if there are any health risks to consider when traveling to a destination. Note whether certain precautions should be taken, such as taking malaria medication or water purification tablets. Entry requirements may include a list of mandatory immunizations for hepatitis, yellow fever, or other diseases. Be sure you know what immunizations, if any, you need to get and what documentation you will need to present as proof of immunization.

For your destination country's entry requirements, contact the consulate or tourism department of the country's embassy in the United States. You can also write to the American government's Overseas Citizens Services Department (Room 4811, Deptartment of State, Washington, DC 20520) or visit the State Department Web site (www.travel.state.gov).

PASSPORTS

If you (and your guests) need a passport to enter your destination country, do not wait until the last minute to get one. It can take eight weeks or more to process a passport, and you won't need the added pressure of worrying whether your passport will arrive in time for your wedding trip! For information on getting a passport, call the United States State Department (202-647-4000) or visit their Web site (www.travel.state.gov) and click on "Passports." You can usually obtain passport application forms at your local post office or county clerk's office.

POSSIBLE LEGAL REQUIREMENTS FOR MARRIAGE

If you marry in another country, or even in another state, you may be asked to meet several marriage requirements. Because the process of meeting these conditions can be confusing, I have defined and described each possible requirement;

this will help you be prepared when you contact your destination's embassy, consulate, or state office. Don't let the number of requirements I've listed below intimidate you, as many destinations call for only a few to be met.

PROOF OF IDENTITY

Every destination in the world will require that you prove your identity before you can get married. This requirement is usually satisfied with a passport. In countries where a passport is not needed for entry, you may be able to use a birth certificate, a driver's license, or another official identification document. Confirm which form of identification is accepted in your destination country. Some forms of identification may need to be translated, as they are not written in an international format. Your destination country may also ask that you provide information about your parents, such as their names and/or addresses and, rarely, where they were born.

RESIDENCY

The residency requirement dictates how many days you have to be in the state, province, or country before you can legally be married there. This is often the "make or break" consideration when choosing a destination, as some couples may not be able to afford the luxury of being in a country for a month, for example, before their wedding. Some countries such as France simply state that one of you must reside in France for 40 consecutive days before you can apply to be married. If a country's residency requirement seems too difficult for you to fulfill, you may want to consider choosing a country that has a shorter (or no) residency requirement, such as Italy or many of the Caribbean islands.

If you opt for a destination that has a long residency requirement, you will have to plan and budget for this pre-wedding period. Pay specific attention to the legal process required. The registry office may need a copy of your passport page that shows your date of entry. Keep your plane ticket stub and any papers showing your itinerary as proof of your arrival date, just in case your passport was not stamped.

WAITING PERIOD

Some destinations have a waiting period, an amount of time required between the license application date and the date of the wedding. In the United States, there is no residency requirement, but many states have a waiting period ranging anywhere from 24 hours to three days.

Some countries have a residency requirement *and* a waiting period. To get married in England, you must arrive in the district where you plan to marry seven days before you apply for the license. An additional waiting period is also mandated in order for the couple to "give notice of their intent to marry." This is a remnant of an old practice first established by the Church of England, called "posting the banns." A couple's intent to marry was posted on the church door for a period of time, allowing anyone who did not agree with the marriage to formally object before the wedding day. Now notices of marriage are displayed on the notice board at the register office for a period of 15 days. So any couple wanting to be legally married in England would have to plan on being there for three weeks before the wedding to comply with British residency and waiting requirements.

PROOF OF AGE

Every state, province, and country has an age requirement for marriage. If you do not meet that requirement, you will have to submit a notarized letter of permission from your legal guardians.

PROOF OF SINGLE STATUS

Another universal requirement is proof of your eligibility for marriage. In other words, you must prove you are single and legally free to be married. In some countries, you will be asked to provide divorce decrees for past marriages or death certificates of past spouses. You may also be asked for an Affidavit of Eligibility to Marry, sometimes referred to as an Affidavit of Single Status, which is a legal statement certifying that no impediment to marriage exists and confirming that you are free to be married. While no such legal document exists in the United States, the destination country's consulate in the United States may be able to supply you with one if necessary. Or you may have to get it once you arrive at the destination, either at the civil registry office where you apply for your license or at the American embassy or consulate. Some countries also require witnesses to sign the affidavit as additional proof that you are free to be married. You will most likely need to bring along authenticated copies of any divorce decrees or death certificates to apply for the affidavit; sometimes these documents need to be notarized in that country as well as translated into the native language. If so, a list of official translators will be provided, either by the foreign consulate in the United States or by the American embassy in the host country.

MEDICAL DOCUMENTS

Some states and countries, such as Massachusetts and Puerto Rico, require couples to undergo a physical and/or blood test before marrying. Costa Rica and Puerto Rico, among others, require that the medical exam be done in the country. A few countries such as Costa Rica also require a pregnancy test.

CRIMINAL RECORDS

Some countries, such as Brazil, require that you submit an authenticated copy of your criminal record, which you can obtain at your county police department or by contacting the FBI. You may also be asked to verify that you have no criminal record in the destination country; this process can take five or more days.

WITNESSES

Most countries require that one to four people witness the wedding ceremony. This is usually not problematic for the couple, as a witness can simply be anyone who is willing to stand up with you and sign the license. However, some countries also require documented proof of age and identity from the witnesses. In Mexico, the witnesses must have their birth certificates notarized and translated at a Mexican consulate or embassy unless they are Mexican nationals, in which case they may have to present different documentation and identification.

Once you have gathered the necessary documentation and fulfilled all the requirements, you can go ahead and file for the marriage license. Before you do, however, find out how long the license will be valid. In other words, confirm how much time you have to get married using that license. Some licenses never expire, others do in six months, and others in one month. If, for whatever reason, you would have to postpone your wedding, you'll want to know how much time your license allows to reschedule your wedding.

If the license is valid for six months, you may be able to file for it if and when you take a planning trip (see chapter three), leaving one less thing to be done when you arrive for your wedding. By filing for the license during a planning trip, you may be able to get around long or difficult residency and waiting period requirements. For example, in Belize there is a residency requirement of three days and a waiting period of five days; if you go on a planning trip within three months of the wedding, you can stay in the country for three days, then apply for the license. The license is valid for three months, meaning that you have up to three months to get married in Belize. This way, you can reserve the date for your civil service ahead of time, and the license will be waiting for you when you arrive.

RELIGIOUS REQUIREMENTS

If you are planning a religious wedding ceremony, the officiant at your destination may require additional documentation, such as baptismal or confirmation certificates, annulment papers, or proof that you have completed premarital counseling. Discuss your plans with your religious or spiritual leader at home to be sure that marriage outside of the parish or community will be recognized. If your leader is open to traveling for the event, you might consider inviting her to officiate the religious ceremony at your destination. The advantage of hiring local religious officiants, however, is that in addition to officiating your ceremony, they are often able to assist you with fulfilling their country's legal requirements.

© DAVID BECKSTEAD

You may have questions about a specific marriage law or legal issue. For marriage laws in the United States and other countries, you can consult the Marriage Laws Web site (www.usmarriagelaws.com). If you feel uncertain about the legal aspects of any marital issue, be sure to clarify what the law is before you proceed. Cousin marriages, for example, are allowed in many cultures and countries but not in others; if this was of concern to you, it would be vital to check the relevant laws.

Many countries, including the United States, are currently facing the issue of making same-sex marriages legal. There are two ways a country can acknowledge a same-sex marriage: A *civil union* is a legally binding agreement between two people and recognized by the state, while a *commitment ceremony* is a public affirmation of a couple's commitment to one another. You might compare a commitment ceremony to a spiritual ceremony or celebration of a union that is not legally recognized. Several countries have ruled in favor of legal same-sex marriages. Denmark was the first country to allow same-sex marriage in 2000, and the Netherlands followed in 2001. Remember that even if you are legally married abroad, your union may not be legally recognized by your home country. Currently in the United States, same-sex marriages are only legally recognized in the states of Massachusetts and Vermont. This means that if you are legally married abroad and return to live in either one of these states, you will enjoy whatever rights the state gives a married couple joined in civil union. You will not, however, be granted any federal rights. If, down the road, the American government bans same-sex civil unions, the states of Vermont and Massachusetts will have to comply.

Research the laws currently in effect in your destination, and be aware of any disparity between what is legal there and what is legal at home. You can get the latest information on same-sex marriage by going to the International Lesbian and Gay Association's Web site (www.ilga.org). Additional information and articles regarding same-sex unions can be found on www.usmarriagelaws.com, www.free domtomarry.org, and www.gay-civil-unions.com.

GETTING IT DONE: STEPS TO TAKE

Now that you know what kinds of requirements you may be facing, keep yourself on track by establishing the steps you will need to follow. On pages 51–52 I've listed six basic steps that will carry you through the process; follow up with research to make sure you are aware of all the details. Anticipate deadlines, allow yourself ample time, and find out exactly where you need to go to file your documents.

1) VERIFY HOW TO HAVE A LEGALLY RECOGNIZED MARRIAGE

Once you have made an educated decision about where you want to be married, touch base with the destination's embassy/consulate in the United States and/or a registry office in the destination to verify the steps you will need to take to legalize your wedding. Remember, if the process seems overly complicated, you can seek professional help from a lawyer, your wedding venue, or a wedding planner at the destination. If you are planning a religious ceremony, ask your local religious leader what is required to validate a religious ceremony outside of the congregation.

2) GATHER YOUR DOCUMENTS

Once you know what your destination requires, immediately begin gathering and filing the necessary documents. The sooner you begin to gather these documents, the better off you will be. Remember that some documents may need to be duplicated, notarized, translated, and/or authenticated, and the sequence of these steps depends on your destination country. If you need to do some or all of the above, the process can take as long as a month and a half. Any incidental tasks, such as filing for a new birth certificate, can add time to an already lengthy bureaucratic process.

3) FILE THE NECESSARY DOCUMENTS AT HOME

You may have to present your documents and file for permission to marry in your destination at the country's consulate in the United States. If it is required that you do this in person, an appointment might be necessary. Find out if you need to bring witnesses to vouch for your single status. Or you may only have to send the documents, usually with a self-addressed, stamped envelope, to be processed and returned to you. To avoid frustration, always verify when government offices (both at home and in your destination country) are open.

4) DECIDE ON AN OFFICIANT

Decide well ahead of time who will be officiating your marriage ceremony. If you choose an officiant from your destination (as opposed to bringing one with you), she will most likely be familiar with the required legal process. In this case, she may be able to oversee the process for you. Some couples hire a lawyer from the destination who can both manage the legal steps and officiate the wedding. Be aware that the officiant may request your documents ahead of your trip.

5) MEET WITH YOUR OFFICIANT AT YOUR DESTINATION

You will want to meet with the officiant as soon as you arrive at your destination in case she needs to accompany you to a registry office, town hall, department of foreign affairs, or the American embassy in order to file documents or get a license.

6) GET MARRIED WITH WITNESSES AND FILE THE LICENSE

Your witnesses will have to sign the license and/or other legal documents in order to make your marriage legal. In most cases, the officiant will take responsibility for filing the paperwork after the ceremony, and you will receive a marriage certificate delivered to your home. Occasionally, you will be issued a marriage certificate on the spot. Make sure you know what you need to do to have an authenticated or certified marriage certificate, which you can use as proof of your marriage once you get home. The certificate may need to go through an authentication process at the destination, which may involve translation into your language and notarization. In some places, it is recommended that you send a copy to your own embassy in the destination country as a record of your marriage there. Once you return home, you do not have to file your license with the Department of Vital Records. However, if you are changing your name, you will have to go through the necessary steps with Social Security and the Department of Motor Vehicles, and you will need your marriage certificate to do so. If you are not changing your name, you do not have to file additional papers at home. The state will realize that you are married when you start filing your taxes as a married couple.

At this point, you no doubt understand why it is absolutely necessary to start the process as soon as possible. Try not to be overwhelmed. If you stay informed and get help as needed, you pave the way for a smooth and efficient process.

CHOOSING A (TENTATIVE) DATE

The perfect wedding date is just as important as the perfect wedding destination. Your first step is to make sure that the date you are considering falls during an ideal time of year in the destination. You can get this information on the tourism bureau's Web site. Consider climate, seasonal rates, national holidays, and perhaps political events. There are reasons for low seasonal rates, such as hurricane season in the Caribbean! Do not set the actual wedding date until you fall in love with a location *and* confirm that it is available on the day you desire.

GETTING FAMILY APPROVAL

If it is important to you to be surrounded by your loved ones on your wedding day, you will want to tell them your plans and see how they react to the destination you have chosen. Before you do this, make sure you are prepared to make a thorough presentation and answer any questions. Brace yourself if this is the first they have heard of your plans, as their initial reaction may not be as favorable as you had hoped. Remember that they may simply be reacting to the fact that the region is foreign to them, even if it is within the borders of their own country. Your family and friends may love the idea, in which case you can advance to the next step. Or they may present arguments for why it's not a good idea—Uncle Bob is in a wheelchair or your sister will be seven months pregnant—in which case you will have to reassess how important this destination is to you. Some couples faced with this dilemma compromise by planning a successive wedding, with a wedding ceremony and/or celebration both at home and away. If certain family members just cannot travel, consider the wonders that modern technology offers—perhaps a live feed on the Internet so they can witness the wedding as it is happening.

RESEARCHING LOCATION SITES

With your destination chosen and hopefully approved by the most important people attending your wedding, you can begin to gather the information you'll need to select locations for your ceremony and reception. For some couples, one location may serve both purposes. Even if you have a particular site in mind, research alternative venues in case there is a scheduling conflict or you find a site that is even more wonderful than your original choice.

Find out from tourism bureaus what venues have been used for wedding ceremonies and receptions in the past. Request brochures and photos; use these and any other resources to contact potential location sites. If you find a location that offers a wedding package, have them clarify exactly what they are offering and charging. Ask potential locations if they will assist you in getting your marriage license or at least review the steps with you. Also ask if they can provide references from people who have married there. Such references can be invaluable. Better than any brochure, an individual can provide all sorts of relevant details, including insight into any potential downsides or problems that you could address before you commit to the site.

I feel strongly that you should see a location in person before signing on the dotted line. Selecting your venue is best done after you have thoroughly researched your options and, if at all possible, seen them all firsthand on a planning trip (see chapter three). Whether or not you are able to go on a planning trip, it is essential at this stage to collect as much information as possible to make an informed choice later on. On pages 63–66 of the next chapter, you will find detailed lists of questions to consider when choosing your reception and ceremony location(s). For now, ask yourselves these basic questions as you consider potential venues:

- Does the site fit your wedding style?
- Is it a reasonable distance from the airport?
- Is it located in a nice area? Does it offer a pleasant setting and views?
- Is it large enough to accommodate your wedding celebration?
- Can the site be used for both the ceremony and the reception? If not, is the site close to other locations that could be used for the ceremony or reception?
- Does the site provide good food and a full bar?

- Does it provide any event planning services?
- Does it provide enough (or any) accommodations for your guests? If not, is it close to the lodging options?

This stage of planning does not involve committing to a location. In researching potential venues, you might be tempted to adopt the "grab-it-while-you-can" mentality and book a site quickly. Resist this temptation, at least until:

- You have seen it in person, if at all possible.
- You know how and where you will get your marriage license.
- You have confirmed that the location will be available on the date you want.
- You have confirmed that you understand the costs associated with the location and that those costs fit your budget.
- You have reviewed the more detailed lists of venue considerations in the next chapter (pages 63–66).

If you are worried you might lose the location before you are able to see it, ask them to reserve the date for you. Most locations are willing to "pencil you in" for a short time. You might offer to put down a small deposit in good faith to show that your interest is serious, but explain that you would like to see the site in person to be absolutely sure. Never sign a contract until you are certain you are ready.

LOOKING AHEAD

Now that you have found the perfect destination and potential sites for the ceremony and reception, you can begin to plan your wedding in earnest. You have the general setting and a tentative date, which will provide a context for the rest of the celebration details. Now ask yourself: *How well do I know this destination?* Is it somewhere that you and your fiancé have spent a lot of time? Do you know the restaurants, the attractions, the language, the people? Or is it someplace you have always wanted to visit but know very little about? The next phase of planning will take some effort—but if you stay on track, this part can be fun!

RESEARCHING THE HONEYMOON DESTINATION

While you're in the research mode, this may be a good time to start researching honeymoon possibilites. Many couples choose a destination wedding because they want to combine the two nuptial events into a "weddingmoon," celebrating their wedding and their honeymoon in the same wonderful location. Others desire a separation between the wedding celebration and the honeymoon; this can be as simple as moving your married selves to another town or city. You could get married in Venice, for example, and then honeymoon in Santorini. Or, like many of the couples with whom I've worked, you could get married on one Caribbean island, such as Anguilla, then go to another nearby island, such as St. Bart, for the honeymoon. If your destination wedding is within your own country, you might choose a more exotic destination for your honeymoon, even without having to travel abroad. A wedding in the Hudson Valley could be followed by a honeymoon in the Adirondacks, in Manhattan, or somewhere outside the state or region.

Selecting a honeymoon destination is different than choosing your wedding destination. When deciding on where you'll spend your honeymoon, you do not have to consider anyone else's opinions, comfort, or desires except your fiancé's and your own. Here are some questions for you to consider together:

- Do you want to depart for your honeymoon immediately after the reception or the following morning? Or would you like time to relax, collect your thoughts, visit with guests, and pack your bags?
- How much time do you have to spend on your honeymoon?
- How much money do you have to spend?
- How far from the wedding destination do you want to travel?
- Do you see your honeymoon as active or passive? In other words, do you see yourselves doing lots of activities or just kicking back and relaxing?
- Do you want your honeymoon to be an adventure and a learning experience? Or do you want to simply enjoy each other's company?
- Do you want to plan ahead, read maps, and follow road signs, or do you want to be adventurous and follow your nose to different sites and attractions?
- Do you want to be left to your own devices for meals, exploring markets and different restaurants each day? Or would you rather have meals available where you are staying, perhaps served to you in bed or at the same intimate table every night?
- What environment do you find to be the most romantic setting—land? Water? Mountains? Desert? Tropics? Would you rather frolic in the snow or play in the sun and sand?

{3} RESEARCHING YOUR *Destination's Resources*

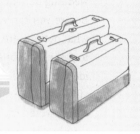

If you were getting married close to home, you would be well informed on your options for the ceremony and reception sites, caterers, flowers, and every other aspect of your wedding. You would devote weeks or months to research, meeting with potential service providers as many times as necessary to see, understand, and sample their wares before making your final selections. During this planning stage, you would also develop relationships with your service providers, building confidence in them professionally and personally.

In choosing to have a destination wedding, you've probably already realized that you will not be able to meet with your service providers on a regular basis. Nonetheless, you will still need to be well informed and make choices with confidence. Miscommunication can occur face-to-face, but it is much more likely to occur when your communication is by phone or fax and when there are language and cultural differences. It is difficult to visualize a reception site when you can't remember if, during your phone conversation, the manager said there was room for 20 *tables* or 20 *people*. While you might relish the discovery and excitement that come with destination weddings, you should also enjoy a sense of control and peace of mind during the planning process.

CAN YOU TAKE A PLANNING TRIP?

I urge all my clients to budget for and make a planning trip to their destination. Unless you are already well acquainted with the destination and its resources, a planning trip is the only way to be certain you will be happy with the destination, the sites and facilities, and the service providers. There is nothing like seeing a place and meeting the providers in person and nothing like face-to-face communication, especially in choosing and contracting services, to put your mind at ease.

Think of all the service providers you choose as your "dream team." On your wedding day, they will be providing everything from the menu to the photographs. Before you can assemble your dream team, you will need to thoroughly research what options are available at your destination, and a planning trip is an ideal way to gather that information firsthand. After all, the most effective way to choose an ideal location and dependable services is to do so in person. If you feel you cannot afford to make a planning trip and yet you do not know your destination extremely well, I would caution that you probably can't afford *not* to make one. Look again at your budget and reconsider the planning trip as a priority. One word of advice: The larger and more complicated the wedding, the more imperative the planning trip will be. If, after considering the financial and time commitment involved, you are absolutely certain that you can't make a planning trip to your destination, you have three alternatives:

+ **Consider a destination that is closer and less expensive.** I worked with a couple who lived in the Cayman Islands and wanted a wedding in Italy but decided that Italy would be too far for guests to travel and too expensive for them to plan. They settled on Trident Castle in Jamaica because it is much closer yet still removed from their home, plus it offered the European elegance they were seeking.

+ **Hire an experienced and trusted destination wedding planner to make the planning trip for you.** Because the planner will be acting as your scout and your advocate, you need to feel confident that she understands exactly what you are looking and hoping for. I once made a planning trip for a couple who had already contracted the reception site but were beginning to feel uneasy about it. My mission was to inspect all the locations and find a few additional quality vendors to provide services. I confirmed that their reception site was perfect and that the banquet manager was very capable and trustworthy. After discovering that a few of the hotels they had selected for accommodations were questionable, I visited others until I found some in the same price range that I could recommend. I also found an experienced independent coordinator who spoke English, a tour company for the guests, a good photographer, a reputable florist, and the best salon for the bride.

+ **Commit to doing the planning from home, via phone, fax, e-mail, and the Internet.** If you opt to plan from home, you have to be able to relinquish some control and resolve to "go with the flow." Because you will not be in command of every detail, you must be willing to accept whatever your team of service providers presents you with. It is possible that it will not be *exactly* what you thought you had requested. This approach to planning will work for those easygoing couples who love the adventure or spontaneity of it all. If you opt to forego the planning trip, I recommend you depart for your destination several days prior to the wedding so you can confirm everything in person with all of your service providers. Service providers in popular destination wedding regions are used to couples making final decisions only a few days before the wedding.

PLANNING: PRELIMINARY WORK

Once you decide how you will research your destination's wedding resources, it is time to get started. If you decide to go on a planning trip and do it in person, you will need to make travel arrangements; if not, you need to sit down in front of your computer and get started. Your first order of business is gathering the information you need to select a ceremony and reception site. After deciding on your locations(s), you'll shift your focus to researching and selecting service providers—officiant, caterer, coordinator, hair stylist, and so on. Whether you will be conducting the research process from home or at the destination itself, you can use the questions below to assess your potential destination resources:

- What are the options for a reception location?
- What options exist for a caterer, either associated with your location or not?
- What are the options for a ceremony location?
- Who will officiate your wedding?
- Who will help you obtain your license?
- Once in your destination, where will you have to go to file legal documents—the American embassy or consulate, the city hall, other government buildings?
- What options exist for guest accommodations?
- What are the location options for other aspects of your celebration, such as a rehearsal dinner?
- What options exist for other activities you may want to offer your guests, such as a tour or a local cultural event?
- What are the options for local assistance, such as professional wedding planners and/or coordinators?
- What are your local choices for florists?
- What are your local choices for photographers?
- What are the local options for the wedding cake?
- What are the local options for reception music and entertainment?
- What are your local choices for beauty and hair salons?
- What are your local choices for dry cleaners (for pressing)? Tuxedo rentals?
- What are the options at your destination for stationery? Rings? Possible gifts for your wedding party/guests?
- What are your local options for any ceremony- or reception-related rentals you may need, such as tents, linens, and lighting?
- What are your options for local transportation and/or escort services for your guests?

This list of questions might make even the most stalwart planner a bit nervous. I assure you that most, if not all, of this information can be gathered on a planning trip. If you are unable to arrange a planning trip or if you are still feeling apprehensive, this is a good opportunity to reassess whether or not you will be needing help. Keep in mind that, unless you anticipate a very simple wedding with limited guests, this research process can be the most time-consuming and rigorous part of the overall planning.

Did you work with a consultant in choosing your destination? If so, do you think you may need his continued help in researching the resources available there? If you have done the planning so far on your own, does it look like you might need some professional assistance at this point? If you are not going on a planning trip, I would strongly recommend you consider getting help at this point. You will have many questions to ask and much information to research and record. Plus, you will need much more visual documentation of your options since you won't be able to hop in the car and revisit the site to jog your memory.

Even those who *will* be making a planning trip should weigh the benefits of hiring professional help. You do not have to commit to the long-range services of a wedding planner; however, if you *are* going to need a planner's assistance throughout the process, it is best for him to be involved from the beginning. You can simply ask for help with the planning trip and reassess your needs for further assistance once you return. If you have a productive trip, you may feel confident that everything is falling into place; if not, you will surely be convinced that you need the efforts of more than one person to get everything in order.

THE PLANNING TRIP: WHO WILL GO?

I have to admit it—I love planning trips. A planning trip is a fun mission, a challenge, an adventure of discovery and learning with a purpose: to design the most romantic wedding you can imagine in a location far from home. Who will go on your planning trip? If you have contracted a wedding planner, she should be included. If you do not have the time to devote to a planning trip, you can send the planner by herself or with a trusted friend or family member. I caution you, however, that if you send someone in your stead, you must have confidence that she understands your wishes, as you will be handing over some of the decision-making responsibilities to her. I always ask couples to sign a waiver stating that they acknowledge this.

If both you and your fiancé want to have a say in the choices, or if you both want to meet the service providers in person, then you should go on the planning trip as a couple. In the event that only one goes, the other must be willing to accept whatever decisions are made. Finally, consider the person paying for the wedding. If it is anyone but yourselves, you may want to invite them to accompany you on the trip. With all the people involved in a planning trip, you can imagine what a costly expedition it can become. You may need to review your budget when you are deciding who will go.

REVIEWING YOUR MISSION

Review the list of questions on page 58 regarding your destination resources. Your mission, whether you are on a planning trip or not, is to decide on locations for your ceremony and reception, confirm your date with those sites, decide on the wedding trip itinerary of events, and gather information on potential service providers. Customize a written "planning mission," and establish the means by which you will test the services. At your destination, you will probably be able to see, taste, and hear the possibilities; this will be a little more challenging if you are not taking a planning trip. For example, you will want to hear the caterer's menu ideas and, if possible, taste the food; find out where to bring your legal documents and, if possible, go there to clarify and confirm the process; and meet with photographers and musicians to see and hear their work.

RESEARCHING AND QUALIFYING SERVICE PROVIDERS

Ask the event managers at potential wedding locations if they have a list of preferred vendors. If they do, have them e-mail or fax it to you so you can contact the vendors and, if necessary, set up meetings. If they are unable to provide a list, contact tourism bureaus, major hotels, or resorts to request information on wedding service providers. You can also search the Internet for possibilities; the *Destination Bride* Web site (www.destinationbride.com) provides links to talented service providers around the globe. Try to make contact with the service providers you are considering and qualify each one before pursuing them further. Even if you think your referrals are coming from a trustworthy source, be sure to:

+ Check out their Web site.
+ Personally interview them over the phone or in person.
+ Ask to see their portfolio.
+ Ask them for a list of client references.

- Check their references.
- Check to see if they are on referral lists at the five-star resorts in the area.
- Ask everyone you deal with if they know the service providers you are considering, and ask for their opinion.
- Ask them if they are members of any professional associations.
- Confirm that their business is licensed and insured.

This process is important because pictures on Web sites and brochures do not always accurately reflect reality. A person may not be as trustworthy, enthusiastic, and professional as he seems. The more you know about your service providers, their work, and their reputation, the better off you will be.

SETTING UP MEETINGS

Once you have generated a list of all the service providers with whom you would like to meet, you can start setting up meetings. If you are going on a planning trip, make every effort to arrange the meetings before you go. You can always try to contact some when you arrive, and you will most likely get even more leads once you are there, so allow yourself time to follow up on those. If you are short on time, focus on accomplishing your priorities—not only the things that are most important to you but also the things that need to be seen, touched, and experienced firsthand, such as the location and the food. Your ceremony and reception venues are your most important choices; set up those meetings first, then set up your meetings with

service providers. If you are planning from home, you can conduct interviews and review the products or services in question by phone, fax, or Internet.

PLANNING: PUSHING AHEAD WITH THE LOCATIONS

With goals set, meetings planned, and photos, brochures, and other literature gathered, you are ready to push ahead with the planning. Begin your mission with the most important task: researching venues. If you plan on having two locations—one for the ceremony and one for the reception—ask yourself which is

MAKING THE MOST OF A PLANNING TRIP

Upon making your decision to take a planning trip, contact the wedding locations that interest you most to arrange for tours and tastings. Once you have set up meetings with the locations, make your travel arrangements. Avoid planning your trip during a holiday or a season when everything closes down. If any of the potential location sites offer accommodations, ask them if you can stay on-site. They may even insist that you do so and offer a rate you cannot refuse. You might also plan to stay at potential guest accommodations so you can ultimately refer them to friends and family with confidence.

Allow yourself as much time as you can afford for your planning trip. To accomplish everything in one trip, I suggest staying at least seven days. Plan for those days to be extremely busy. Remember, if you were planning a wedding close to home, you'd spend months working out the details. On a planning trip, you are doing the same work, but all within the time frame of a week or so. Capitalize on every minute of every day; use mornings to visit houses of worship, evenings to catch musical acts, and meals to test for potential caterers and recommendable restaurants. If you find you have free time, spend it shopping for rings, apparel, or favor ideas. Become familiar with the region and have a map handy so you can design an efficient meeting schedule. Look at your list and determine where your service providers are located. Does it make sense for them to come to you, or can you meet with several vendors located in the same area? Consider organizing the meetings by category—photographers and videographers one day, florists another.

Keep in mind that in some countries you will not be able to accomplish much on the weekends (and, in some areas, during the mid-afternoon, when businesses close for a few hours). I usually try to arrive on a Sunday so I can recuperate and be ready for work on Monday. To keep your schedule, confirm all your meeting appointments a week before you go. In addition to practical shoes, clothing, and the normal sundries, remember to pack:

* Necessary identification and travel documents
* Money and/or credit card to pay deposits if necessary
* Mobile phone with the proper coverage, and laptop computer
* Wedding binder
* Pictures of things you like, such as bouquets and cakes
* Swatches of the gowns (if you have them) for color matching
* Camera (preferably digital) and video camera to document everything
* Tape measure, ruler, and graph paper to measure for décor and to draw floor plans

either more important to you or more difficult to find. Your priorities should help you determine which you need to select first. Start with specific "must-have" location details—perhaps the wedding ceremony needs to be held in a church of a particular denomination or on a site that is significant to you. I recently worked with a couple who wanted me to recommend a castle or villa with a ballroom that was in close proximity to a beautiful Catholic church in Jamaica. I began by researching the churches first and found a list of possibilities in Montego Bay, Discovery

Bay, and Port Antonio. Sometimes couples have specific reception needs or ideas; they may request an ocean view, require enough space to accommodate a certain number of guests, or want the reception to be held in the same place where all the guests stay. In that case, start with the reception site.

CHOOSING YOUR RECEPTION LOCATION

In this section, I've included a list of general tasks to accomplish while exploring location venues as well as a comprehensive list of questions to consider. Some of these considerations will be very important to you; others might be less so. Touring a location in person is always the best way to answer these questions, but you can find the answers from home, too. The more questions you can answer and the more issues you can address, the more informed you will be as you proceed with your planning—and the more confident you will be making your final choices. Check off each item in the following task list as you investigate the reception site, and use the list of questions on page 65 for interviewing site managers. These tools should guide you through the decision-making process.

- Find out if the location is available on the date you want it.
- If it is a large location with multiple sites, view all the possibilities for your reception and/or ceremony.
- Meet with the banquet manager and/or other personnel to discuss their services.
- Clarify what services the location offers: Food and liquor? Decorating? Assistance with the marriage license? Event coordination? Also make sure you know what the location charges for each service.
- Be sure you understand exactly what is included in their event coordination services: Do they confirm the service providers? Do they assist with the ceremony? Do they oversee and orchestrate each course and event at the reception?
- Ask them about their concierge services, and ask yourself if you are confident that those services are excellent. If it is a large location with a lot going on, confirm that someone will be available to take care of your guests' every need.
- Take pictures and/or video of the location site, and collect or draw floor plans.
- Ask for the size and shape of the tables so you can determine layout and seating.
- Measure anything you think might need decorating.
- View and take photos of the china, cutlery, glassware, and linens they provide. You can plan the décor around them, or you can decide not to use what your location offers and find other options.
- Consider how the location will handle the order and flow of events.
- If possible, taste the food and wine they propose to serve.
- Ask them to draw up a contract for you to review.

Do not contract a location until all your important questions have been answered, you have toured the site in person and sampled the food to be served (or thoroughly investigated it from home), and you have developed a positive, confident feeling toward the people with whom you would be working. If necessary, you'll also want to be sure you have found an available ceremony location nearby. At this point, you should have a good sense of the location you'll be selecting, even if you do not contract the site immediately.

If you like what you've seen and feel ready to commit, ask the location to draw up a contract for you to review. In chapter five, pages 94–96, I discuss how to contract the site; refer to that section if you feel you must contract the site during your planning trip. Otherwise, ask the location to "pencil you in," and request enough time to review the contract and make your final decision. If you have not yet found any place that appeals to you, continue looking. Try a tourism office, a florist, or even the town hall as a resource. They may know where wedding parties go after the ceremony to celebrate.

CHOOSING YOUR CEREMONY LOCATION

If you are holding both the wedding ceremony and the reception at the same site, you are one step ahead. Even so, it is still important to clarify exactly where the ceremony will take place. If you are choosing separate locations for the ceremony and reception, investigate your options as thoroughly as you did for the reception site. Tour possible locations early in the planning trip and take several photographs when you visit. If you are considering an outdoor ceremony site, by all means plan a backup site in case of bad weather. Consider the following questions in your selection process:

- What are the available dates?
- What time of day can ceremonies take place?
- Are there any religious guidelines or restrictions, such as premarital counseling or conversion?
- What is the ceremony format? What are the ceremony rules and regulations?
- If applicable to your situation, can clergy from another church or even another religion perform the ceremony?

QUESTIONS, QUESTIONS, QUESTIONS

When choosing a reception site, you'll no doubt want to be sure it is the perfect place. Refer to this list of questions when making your selection:

* How far is it from the airport?
* Is it easy to find? Is it in a nice neighborhood? Does it have nice grounds and views? Does it have enough parking?
* Does it offer any ceremony sites, or is it close enough to one you can use?
* Does it provide any accommodations? If so, will there be enough for your guests? If not, is it close enough to other options for your guests?
* Is it your style? Will the décor match your plans, or is it simple enough that you can work with it to achieve the look you want?
* Is it large enough to accommodate your guests? Is it large enough for dancing?
* Do they have a room where the wedding party can dress or take a time out?
* Do they provide good food and a full bar? Do they have menu selections to choose from? Do they offer a tasting, and if so, when?
* Do they have a pastry chef? Can she provide the wedding cake? If so, do they charge a cake-cutting fee?
* Do they have a wine and champagne list, and can they special order if need be? Do they have a corkage fee?
* Do they provide any planning services?
* Do they have a list of service providers, including officiants?
* Will they help you obtain your wedding license?
* Are there enough bathrooms, or will you have to rent additional ones?
* Are they fully insured, or must you purchase insurance?
* What are the rules and regulations?
* What are the rental and payment policies?
* Do they include dishware, glasses, and utensils? Do you like them? If not, can they arrange for better quality?
* Do they include linens, including tablecloths, napkins, and chair covers? If so, what are your choices? Can you upgrade? To what, and how much will it cost?
* Do they provide any décor, such as centerpieces and candles?
* Do they have table numbers and stands, salt and pepper shakers, ashtrays, serving dishes, and utensils? (This is obviously only necessary to ascertain when you are considering a location other than a restaurant or banquet hall.)
* How do they charge, and what is included? Ask for the bottom line, including all fees: site fee, food, alcohol, corkage, cutting fee, gratuity, and tax—all items that can quickly add up. Many caterers and restaurants have a bad habit of quoting the menu price only—say $65 a person—but then deliver a bill that is closer to $125 per person. Avoid this shock by clarifying costs ahead of time.

- Can you have candles? An aisle runner? Rose petals, confetti, or rice?
- What parts of the site are you allowed and not allowed to decorate?
- Do they provide a coordinator?
- Do they provide or offer the services of any musicians, such as an organist? Are you allowed to hire other musicians?
- Do they use or allow the use of microphones? Can your videographer microphone the pastor or the couple?
- What is their policy on photography?
- Is there a place in which the wedding party can get ready or wait?
- Notice the layout to determine how you will make your entrance and departure. Is there a place for you to duck into before the ceremony begins, or will you be walking straight in and down the aisle?
- Are there bells that can be tolled at the end of the service?
- How is the lighting?
- Do you like the style of the site, and will the colors and décor work with your design?
- Can you hold a rehearsal at the site? If so, when?
- What are the fees for the site? For the officiant? When are they due?
- Will the officiant assist with the marriage license?
- What documents will be required by the site?

PLANNING: SELECTING SERVICE PROVIDERS

With your ceremony and reception location(s) chosen, you can now focus on selecting your dream team of service providers. To expedite any meetings or conversations with potential providers, have a list of questions prepared beforehand. Following is a list of general issues to consider for each service provider, regardless of their specialty. You can find specific questions tailored to each type of service provider on the *Destination Bride* Web site (www.destinationbride.com) and from just about any wedding planner. Ask all the service providers in a certain category identical questions so you will be able to compare the same information for each. Clarify what each one is offering and what they will charge for it.

- Are they available on your date?
- Do they speak English or another language you are fluent in?
- Can you see examples or try samples of their work? Do you like their style of work?
- Do you like their personality? Would you feel comfortable working with them?
- Do they customize their work, or do they offer packages? What changes can they provide if you want something different from their examples or packages? Do they offer demonstrations, samples, or trials before finalizing the order?
- What kinds of weddings have they done and for whom? Have they ever worked

with Americans or destination wedding couples before? Can they provide references and/or contact information for past clients?

- Are they accustomed to working with long-distance clients? Do they use the Internet regularly to communicate with clients? Can they open digital files?

- What can they provide within your budget? What are their fees? What is their payment policy? When and how do they need to be paid? Do they take credit cards?

As you are narrowing the field, continue to gather as much information as you can. If you are taking a planning trip, take plenty of photos. That way, if all the providers and their work later melt together in your memory, you can simply refer back to your pictures. Keep copies of any e-mail exchanges between you and the providers, and document your meetings by taking notes or even tape-recording them if permitted. Note the service providers that seem the most talented and professional, the easiest to work with, and the most understanding and supportive of your ideas. You may agonize over some of the choices, either because you're not pleased with your options or, more happily, because every provider seems equally appealing. Often you'll just *know* you're making the right decision through a combination of factors—who referred you to them, how you respond to their work, and how they strike you personally.

CATERERS

What will you and your guests be eating at the reception? A planning trip makes this decision much easier, as nothing compares to taste-testing food and wine. If the location you've chosen has catering services, request to set up a tasting. In most cases, you will first meet with the banquet manager to make your choices, then you will be served the selected menu for your approval. If you are choosing a caterer not affiliated with your location, the process of arranging a tasting will be the same. In choosing a menu, it is standard to choose a meat and either a fish or chicken dish, assuming a vegetarian dish will be provided to those who request it. If you know you will have a lot of vegetarian guests, you might consider choosing a vegetarian dish as one of your primary options. Ask to taste the wine as well and discuss champagne options for the toast.

Find out when the caterers will need the final guest count and if they also need to know the number for each different entrée. Many people object to preselecting entrées on invitations because they can't remember two months later what they chose. It is often more economical for the caterer to know in advance what people will be eating, so you may have to pay extra for the luxury of tableside ordering.

BUFFET VS. SIT-DOWN

Couples often ask me if buffets are less expensive than full-service meals. There is often no difference in cost, because although a buffet requires less staff, the caterer has less control over the size of the portions so they need to prepare a lot more food for a buffet. If there is no difference in cost, I would recommend that you choose for your guests the comfort of being waited on. Do not forget to ask the caterers or banquet managers what they will charge to feed children as well as your other wedding service providers or staff.

LOCAL WEDDING COORDINATORS

Will you be bringing someone from home—a professional planner, a friend, or a family member—to coordinate the events of the wedding day? (If you're still pondering whether or not this is necessary, I offer this thought: Why plan a gorgeous, memorable wedding celebration and not be able to enjoy it? A coordinator will allow you the freedom to forget the details and relax.) If a coordinator from home will not be accompanying you, consider meeting and/or interviewing local event coordinators in your destination. If your ceremony and/or reception location offers event coordination, interview the events manager to find out exactly what they offer. Ask any potential coordinators the following questions:

- Do you work alone, with an assistant, or with a team?
- Will you be the coordinator for this wedding, or will you assign someone else?
- Will we have the same coordinator throughout the duration of our stay?
- Do you meet guests at the airport?
- Do you escort guests on all of the tours, activities, and events?
- Will you handle all of the final payments at each event?
- Are you available to the guests if they have any questions or problems? If so, how and when?
- Will you attend to any problems our guests might have, including health problems and stolen or lost items?
- Will you confirm all of the service providers before each event?
- Will you assemble and deliver welcome packages and/or "Daily Ditties" (newsletters) to all of the guests?
- Will you take the gowns to be steamed or pressed?

- Will you pick up and return the tuxedos?
- Will you orchestrate the wedding rehearsal?
- Will you help set up the ceremony and attend to details such as musicians, candles, programs, rose petals, and aisle runner?
- Will you orchestrate the ceremony? Will you line up the wedding party, cue the music, assist the bride, and orchestrate the photos and/or the receiving line after the ceremony?
- Will you help set up the reception and attend to details such as seating cards, favors, and the guest book?
- Will you orchestrate the reception and attend to details such as seating, announcements, toasts, dances, food service, cake cutting, bouquet toss, and send-off?
- Will you gather the bride and groom's personal belongings, wedding mementos, and wedding gifts, and pack them in their car or take them to their room?
- How long do you stay? Will you oversee the cleanup?
- Do you arrange to have the wedding gown cleaned and preserved?
- Do you arrange to have the bouquet preserved?

If you cannot find one service provider to take care of all these tasks, you may want to divide the tasks between more than one coordinator, family member, or friend. While meeting with your location event manager or a local wedding coordinator, make sure you verify exactly what will be included in their services and what the costs will be.

WEDDING OFFICIANTS

If you haven't decided by now between a civil and religious ceremony, you need to do so as soon as possible. Hopefully, you have researched the requirements for each in your destination. You can often find a list of marriage officials on tourism or wedding Web sites, as well as on the destination's consular Web site. Your hotel, your wedding planner, or even your travel agent may be able to recommend a marriage officiant. Try to meet with the officiant(s) you are considering for the ceremony, whether civil or religious (or both). When you interview them, be sure to:

- Determine if you can have a legally binding civil or religious ceremony and if it is necessary to have both.
- Understand the marriage requirements and steps to having a legally recognized marriage. Inquire if the officiant will help you get your license and/or file the necessary documents at the appropriate offices after the ceremony, and ask for her assurance that you will receive a marriage certificate that is legally recognized in the destination and in your home country.
- Find out if the officiant speaks your language or if you'll need to hire a translator.

- Ask if the town hall or house of worship includes flowers, music, or any other details for the service.
- Discuss the options—music, readings, vows, rings—for the ceremony.
- Find out if she provides copies of the service.

LEGAL ASSISTANCE

Pages 43–52 of chapter two describe in great detail the measures you may need to take to get a legal marriage license. But even with this information, you would still probably appreciate somebody helping you through the process, especially if your destination is a foreign country. If the officiant does not help with filing for the

© CHARITY DE MEER

license, find someone who will. Ask your wedding planner, the local coordinator, or the venue's event manager if they can provide assistance. Even if you find somebody to help you, familiarize yourself with the filing procedure before you have to do it. You may need to go to the embassy, consulate, town or city hall, or other government buildings. Put your mind at ease by confirming and, if possible, visiting exactly where you'll have to go to apply for and file your license.

GUEST ACCOMMODATIONS

Have you ever chosen a hotel from a guidebook, only to arrive and discover it's not at all as you imagined? If so, you understand the benefit of being able to see and experience the lodging alternatives that you will be recommending to your guests. If you are not able to visit them firsthand, ask the tourism office or some of your service providers for advice. Plan on offering recommendations for at least one economical choice and one more deluxe option (see pages 78–79, chapter four), and make sure your choices are not too far apart so that transportation, especially group transportation, is easier. Inquire about policies regarding children and minimum night stays. Take note of the walking distance into town or to restaurants as well as what phone and computer services they offer. If you are experiencing the accommodations firsthand, also note the noise level.

PASTRY CHEFS

Sampling the wedding cake—yet another benefit of taking a planning trip! Show potential pastry chefs pictures of wedding cakes you like, and make sure they understand what you want, both in terms of the cake's appearance and flavors. Also confirm that the cake could be delivered to the reception site by the specific day and time. If the chef is not accustomed to baking a typical American wedding cake, ask if he or she would be willing to use a recipe that you supply. Keep in mind that you will have to translate the ingredients and convert the measurements and temperatures—and even then, since some ingredients may not be readily available, it may not taste quite the same. Consider adopting a "When in Rome..." attitude and try a local specialty for your wedding cake. You could even have a dessert table featuring local, seasonal pastries and sweets. If it is important to you, coordinate the design of the cake with the overall design of the wedding décor.

RENTAL COMPANIES

If you know that you will not need the basics like a tent, tables, and chairs, you may not need a rental company—but you never know about incidentals. It is always good to be aware of what options exist. A rental company might supply you with audio equipment, lighting, nice china, cutlery, and glassware if you do not like what the reception site offers.

FLORISTS AND DESIGNERS

Your reception location or wedding coordinator may take care of the flowers. If not, consider going to a local flower market to buy seasonal flowers. Then, with the help of a few friends, create simple arrangements for the wedding day. If this sounds a little too complicated, try to find the best florist (or the best florist you can afford) in town. Educate yourself on what will be in season on your wedding date. Then communicate your design ideas to the florist regarding theme, colors, favorite flowers, and preferences for vase arrangements and personal bouquets. Some florists offer broader decorating services such as table linens, props, and lighting for the reception. If you are interested, inquire about other items, too—candles, vases, and indigenous fabrics to be used for centerpieces. Buy samples and get ordering information if you find things you *must* have!

MUSICIANS

Selecting wedding musicians can be a difficult task. It is important to meet and hear the musicians before you hire them, and this can be quite challenging if you have not arranged a planning trip. In many countries, musicians do not have the means to cut a professional CD or develop a nifty Web site with sound bites. More often than not, you will have to rely on someone else's advice in choosing whom to hire. Do whatever possible to make sure the musicians you choose are highly recommended and professional. If you are visiting the area, you can go to nightclubs to hear local groups perform. However, club bands and the like may not always be the most reliable option. One of my clients tried to hire a subway entertainer in New York City, giving him a deposit in exchange for a phone number; the entertainer disappeared, never to be found again.

SALONS AND STYLISTS

Many upscale hotels have excellent salons on the premises. If not, the hotel staff will most likely be able to refer you to some. Check out the salons, look at their portfolios, and, if possible, set up trial sessions. When selecting a hairstyle, keep your veil or headpiece in mind. If you had a test run and liked the outcome, make

sure you get the same stylist for the actual wedding day. Before leaving, get the prices for the specific salon services in writing. The salon is one area where a language barrier may prove problematic; if necessary, rely on your wedding coordinator for effective communication.

PHOTOGRAPHERS AND VIDEOGRAPHERS

Always request to see a photographer's portfolio. And, as you are considering your options, ask yourself: Do you like his work, artistic sense, and personality? Can you afford the photographer? When you are interviewing a potential photographer, make sure you understand exactly *what* you will be getting (what is included in the package?) and *who* you will be getting (will the photographer himself be shooting or his assistant?). Also ask if and how you will get the photos before you go home and if you will be given the negatives.

Unless you can arrange for a friend or relative to videotape the event, consider hiring a local videographer. The same questions and issues for wedding photographers apply to videographers. Ask what format they shoot in; you will want their film to be compatible with your machine at home.

WEDDING TRANSPORTATION

Do you need local transportation for you and your guests? If so, what are your options—limousines, classic cars, trolleys, double-decker buses, carriages? Or perhaps something a little more adventurous that relates to the region—rickshaws, boats, camels, elephants, hot air balloons? In Greece, you could hire a donkey to carry you sidesaddle through the streets! If you need suggestions, ask around.

FAVORS AND WELCOME GIFTS

Favors and welcome gifts are one way to add local flavor to your wedding celebration. Destinations that are popular tourist spots often offer many kinds of regionally themed favors. If you go on a planning trip, don't be afraid to venture into the tourist traps to see what you can find and negotiate. If you do not want to buy the items then and there, ask if you can order them later and have them delivered to your hotel a few days before the wedding—but buy a sample or take a picture of the items for future reference. Have the vendors submit a quote to you in writing along with their contact information. Ask how and when you should order, especially if you choose something they will have to make. Be sure to note the location so you can find the same vendor again when you are ready to purchase.

JEWELERS

If you are looking for unique wedding rings, explore your destination for local resources. You may find something not only unique but also reasonably priced.

LOCAL RESTAURANTS AND EATERIES

Finding a few wonderful local eateries is a must, especially if you plan to host additional events, such as a welcome brunch. You may also want to provide your guests with a list of restaurants to patronize. Choose eateries that will add to the overall destination experience, be it through the menu, entertainment, or view. Check out pubs, bakeries, and options such as a cruise boat that offers dinner parties.

ACTIVITIES FOR YOUR GUESTS

Destination weddings, when held in a couple's own country, often take place over a weekend. However, for farther distances, it is not uncommon to plan a five-to-seven-day destination wedding. I recommend planning at least one event before the wedding. Understandably, some couples may not want to plan lots of events, either because the planning requires more work and money or because some groups would prefer to explore on their own. In my experience, though, the groups that do more together before the wedding day get acquainted early on and therefore have more fun. When the wedding rolls around, the guests have already shared adventures, formed friendships, and bonded as a group.

If you plan on offering activities, try to plan events that will give your guests the true local experience, such as eating in a beer garden or in a fish shack by the sea. Treat them to cultural spectacles, like a luau. If you want to provide an itinerary of events, tours, and/or activities, or even if you just want to provide your guests with a list of ideas, now is the time to investigate all your options. You can put together an itinerary yourself or hire a tour company. A tour company can provide you with a guide and a translator if you wish, and they can take care of all your transportation needs.

BANKS

As you choose your service providers, consider how you are going to pay them. The more exotic your destination, the less likely it is that all of the people you hire will accept credit cards. It may be advantageous to research local banks in your destination.

If you are making a planning trip, set aside some time to visit a local reputable bank and get some advice. You might even discuss the possibility of opening an account, which would give you the flexibility to get cash easily, write local checks, and wire money from your home bank. Most nice hotels have safes, but if you have any concerns about the safety of your or your guests' valuables, you can also ask the bank about a safety deposit box. Inquire about tipping customs, since they are governed by subtle cultural rules that are not often published anywhere. If you decide that getting an account is the way to go, you will have to complete the appropriate documents, which will be easier if you are on a planning trip.

Keep in mind that no matter what form of payment you plan to use for your service providers and incidentals, you will often be paying fees for the transaction and, if your destination is outside of the United States, you will also be paying a rate to exchange funds. Exchange rates change daily and are posted in most major newspapers as well as on Web sites, such as www.onanda.com. As you interview and select service providers, ask them which forms of payment they accept. The souvenir kiosk where you find wonderful wedding favors and the little village bakery making your cake may take cash only. Options for payment include:

- **Credit cards:** Consider some of the advantages to paying with a credit card: travel rewards, which may help pay for the wedding or honeymoon trips; recourse, if you have a dispute with authorization of a purchase; the best exchange rates at the time of transaction; purchase protection; and travel insurance.
- **Debit cards:** Because they allow you to spend only what you have in your bank account, debit cards prevent overspending yet still offer the benefits of long-distance payment and the best exchange rates at the time of transaction.
- **Draft:** A draft is like a money order. The funds are guaranteed so you cannot stop payment, and they are deposited in the vendor's account as soon as they clear.
- **Wire:** This is an electronic transfer sent from one account to another via the Federal Reserve Bank. The money can be wired from one bank account to another, from one United States Post Office to another, or from one Western Union or American Express office to another. Wired funds only take a day to clear, so it is the quickest way to pay for something short of using a credit card. However, you will pay the highest transaction fee to do this. When you wire money or receive wired funds, you pay a fee; these fees are higher to wire to foreign countries than to domestic destinations. The fee for receiving wired funds is nominal.
- **Cash:** Some vendors will insist on cash, so be sure you can access cash easily. The bank can tell you if and where ATM machines are available. Be cautious about walking around in any destination with a significant amount of cash.
- **Traveler's checks:** Traveler's checks are a safe way to carry funds in foreign countries, though the service provider has to be sure not to lose them since they are not replaceable once signed.

LOOKING AHEAD

Whether your planning takes place in person or over the phone and computer, you will probably find yourself exhausted as you're wrapping it all up. But hopefully you will also be excited about the things you have seen, the people you have met, and the ideas you have generated. With all your photos, notes, contact information, and samples, you can rest assured that you have accomplished the lion's share of your planning. Having done the legwork, you will be able to assemble your wedding "dream team" and put them in place to help you make your dream wedding a reality. You are now ready to start planning the big trip!

{4} PREPARING YOUR GUESTS AND
Preparing Yourselves

After researching options, interviewing service providers, exploring the destination, and making some decisions, your wedding plans are beginning to take shape. You have tended to several details at the destination itself; you can now switch your focus back home. It is time to start thinking about travel plans for the wedding and, finally, announcing your wedding plans to the world (or at least to your guests)! There are so many things to consider beyond just how you'll get to your destination and where you'll stay. For instance, how will you be communicating information to your guests? And what about your attire—have you thought about what you and your fiancé will wear on your wedding day? There's still some work ahead of you, so let's get started!

MAKING TRAVEL ARRANGEMENTS

Travel arrangements, specifically transportation and accommodations, may be the initial concern of your friends and family members when you tell them about your plans for a destination wedding. So prepare yourself for the questions "How will I get there?" and "Where will I stay?" by investigating all the possibilities. You are not obligated to make your guests' arrangements or pay their expenses. However, it is expected (and common courtesy) for you to research the options that will be available to them.

HOW TO GET THERE

There are many ways to find out about airfare to and from your destination. You can check official airline Web sites or general travel Web sites, such as Travelocity (www.travelocity.com), Expedia (www.expedia.com) or Cheap Tickets (www.cheaptickets.com). The Internet allows individuals to find and research options themselves, and it frequently offers excellent travel deals. This process, however, takes time and often involves a good deal of frustration. If you find this to be the case, it may be worthwhile to work through a travel agent, consultant, or destination wedding planner who offers travel services. Because they know how to find the best fares, consultants can save you valuable time and eliminate stress from the task of arranging travel plans. Some consultants will also coordinate all of your guests' travel needs, including hotel, rental cars, and airport transfers, and others will even offer their services as an escort for your group, facilitating travel and assisting with any problems that may occur while traveling.

TRAVEL INSURANCE

Do buy travel insurance for yourself. If you are offering your guests a travel package, you may want to include the price of travel insurance. In any case, encourage your guests to buy travel insurance through your travel coordinator, their own agent, or their credit card. You can also buy travel insurance at www.travelguard.com.

After researching the travel options, provide your guests with the information they will need to make their own plans. If you want to coordinate your guests' air travel as well as their ground transportation and transfers, I highly encourage arranging all their arrivals and departures at approximately the same time. If some of your guests would rather travel on their own itinerary, allow them the freedom to do so. Warn them, however, that you may not be able to arrange transportation to and from the hotel as you will with the other guests. In organizing your guests' travel, you have three main choices: independent travel arrangements, group travel fares, and charters. Try to determine what your guests would prefer and would utilize. I have set up wonderful group fares for destination weddings only to find that nobody takes advantage of them.

INDEPENDENT TRAVEL

Some couples decide to let their guests take care of their own arrangements. This works especially well if your guests are savvy travelers. There are many reasons why some people would rather make their own travel plans. Some people, feeling tied down by group travel arrangements, prefer the flexibility of making their own plans. Perhaps they want the freedom to choose when to arrive and depart. Some guests may want to use their frequent flier miles to book the trip, and they may have to do so independently of any group itinerary. It is also possible that some guests will take advantage of your wedding trip to do business or see more of the region on their own. If you opt to let your guests make plans on their own, at least provide them with a list of airlines and car rental companies that service your destination as well as a list of the hotels you recommend (and possibly have blocked).

You can organize a group package that includes airfare, accommodations, meals, and/or activities—a good option if you feel that your guests would rather have the *hows*, *whens*, and *wheres* of travel worked out for them in advance. If they are particularly busy people or inexperienced travelers, your guests may appreciate this option. One benefit of group travel is the opportunity for group rates and services. You can try to negotiate group rates yourself by calling airlines directly, or you can enlist the help of a travel consultant, who may be able to set up a group "conference" fare. To do this, the consultant will need to know from which cities all your guests are departing. He will then determine the airline that services all of those airports and negotiate a group rate directly with the airline. With group rates, your guests usually have to depart for your destination on the same date but can return at their leisure.

CHARTERS

It is possible to charter a plane for your entire group of guests. In order to do this, your guests will have to leave out of one airport, or sometimes two. Air Royale (www.air royale.com) can pick guests up in Los Angeles, then fly to New York to pick up more guests before flying to Europe or any other destination in the East. They can make the same stop in New York for the return flight before flying back to California, where they are based. You can research several other charter possibilities with JaxFax Travel Marketing (www.jaxfax.com).

Private charters are an expensive travel option, but they provide the most convenience, control, and fun. All the guests travel together as a group, so the party begins the moment everyone boards the plane! And because you are the only ones on the plane, you don't have to worry about lost luggage. Some companies even allow you to select the flight's menu, décor, and entertainment. Be aware (and make your guests aware, if they are paying) of the hefty cost involved. Charter flights are most feasible when transporting a large group.

WHERE TO STAY

Again, even if your guests are choosing their own lodging, you should still do them the service of researching and suggesting accommodations. There are usually many lodging options in any particular destination, ranging from dormitories, camps, motels, inns, and bed and breakfasts to chain hotels, boutique hotels, resorts, spas, apartments, houses, villas, and castles. Before you start researching and recommending hotels, honestly ask yourself what your guests will need, want, and be able to afford. Most guests will appreciate suggestions for a few different possibilities. Make sure your suggestions include something that everyone on your guest list can afford. If you have a diverse group of guests, try to suggest one luxury location and one that is more affordable. The general rule is to keep the number of properties as low as possible in order to facilitate group transportation.

As you are finding places that interest you, inquire about their group rates and reservation policies. Most hotels offer a group rate if you book a certain number of rooms or nights. Ask if you can block a group of rooms, and if so, ask what their blocking policy is. Some large hotels and resorts will allow you to block a certain number of rooms for a specific amount of time, usually until 30 to 60 days before the wedding. It often does not cost a thing to block rooms, although you may be asked to pay a deposit, which will be returned once the rooms are all reserved and paid for by the guests. The hotel may take a credit card number to guarantee the booking in case you do not release the rooms on time. Be sure you know the release date and mark this date on your calendar. In any case, make certain you understand each hotel's policies, get a contract, and keep track of the reservation progress so you do not lose money.

Stay in regular, friendly communication with the accommodations you will be using. Hotels and other lodging choices usually become your number-one resource for information and assistance at your destination. Make a genial connection with them so they'll take good care of you and your guests.

GROUND TRANSPORTATION

Will you be offering airport transfers, tours, or any other activities that necessitate ground transportation? If so, research ground transport companies that can provide you and your guests with comfortable transit, exciting tours, and knowledgeable guides. I would caution you not to cram too many activities into a tour itinerary. Also, be sure that your guests do not spend too much time on a bus—they shouldn't have to go far to find interesting things to do.

ACCOMMODATING YOUR GUESTS

Sometimes family politics or other group dynamics cause stress for the couple planning the wedding. If, for some reason, you want to keep certain segments of your party apart or together, you can be selective about the options you suggest to each segment. In general, it is nice for guests to be able to mingle, visit, and do things with each other during downtime. Be sure to consider places that allow children if you are expecting young guests to attend. Some couples with children plan to stay together so the kids can play and have fun while the parents socialize and have their own fun. Sometimes, depending on the rowdiness of the crowd, it is a good idea to keep the younger adults together, separate from the older generation. After all, some guests may not appreciate their fellow guests partying all night long in the room next door!

COMMUNICATING WITH YOUR GUESTS

If you plan to share your wedding celebration with friends and family, now is the time to broaden your decision-making process to include them. Your guests will need ample time to make their own plans to join you for the wedding, and they

DECIDING ON A WEDDING STYLE AND THEME

You and your fiancé have the nuts and bolts of your wedding in place, even if you haven't ironed out all of the details yet. Before you "go public" with your guests, consider the style and/or theme you want for your wedding.

Style refers to the overall feel of the wedding. Will it be casual, semiformal, or elegant? Modern or traditional? If you bought a chair, would you be drawn more to clean and modern Scandinavian lines, something ornate and formal, or a beanbag? When I consult with couples, I ask them to describe the serving pieces and flower containers they imagine using for their reception. Are they made of wood, ceramic, china, silver, brass, glass, raw metal, or something else? This always gives me a good sense of the tone they want to set.

The theme pulls everything together, making the event cohesive and memorable. It is like a scavenger hunt, capturing the guests' attention and leading them to the next detail. For a destination wedding, some aspect of the destination is often central to the theme—perhaps the culture (Caribbean, Italian, Spanish), the environment (desert, mountain, beach), or an image (dragonfly, tulip, leaf). Couples might also choose a theme that reflects their common interests or the story of how they met.

Some people perceive themes as restrictive and limiting. However, themes can generate lots of creative ideas and provide much-needed direction to the planning process. Let's say you are having an autumnal, country wedding, and your ceremony will take place on a footbridge over a babbling brook. Adopting a casual country theme, you might use purple grapes, apples, artichokes, and eggplants in your floral designs or as recurring images on printed materials. You could have a barn dance and a barbecue for the rehearsal/welcome party as well as a group hike, a pig roast reception with fireworks, and a farewell brunch in a one-room schoolhouse. Some couples do not want an overall concept theme, or they cannot agree on one that would reflect their very different styles and personalities. In this case, the theme can be as simple as a choice of colors. Used throughout the wedding design, a single color or color combination can add harmony and polish to the entire event.

Once you have agreed on your style, theme, and colors, you can begin to incorporate them into each component of your wedding's overall design, including your Web site, stationery, welcome gifts, flowers, décor, and activities. At this stage, do not worry if you haven't pinpointed any more specifics about your style and theme. The rest of the details will be finalized later. You might simply establish, for example, that your wedding will be informal, casual, and Caribbean in style, using the colors of azure blue, bright green, and sunshine yellow, with a tropical beach theme.

will need information from you along the way. Clear and regular communication with your guests is important; not only does it keep everybody abreast of your plans, it can build excitement and camaraderie among the group.

A PLANNING WEB SITE

You will be communicating with your guests regularly until you are all finally together at your destination. A terrific way to set the tone for your wedding *and* keep your guests up to date on all the details is to set up a wedding planning Web site. A Web site allows you to include fun graphics and details that you could never fit on the invitations without getting arrested by the etiquette police! It gives your guests a way to find out all they need to know at their convenience without much expense for you. It also builds the group dynamics of your wedding party, so that by the time everyone arrives at the destination, they already feel part of an online club that has been "meeting" for months.

You can design a Web site yourself, or find a free, basic one online at the Wedding Channel (www.weddingchannel.com) or The Knot (www.theknot.com). With the help of the *Destination Bride* Web site (www.destinationbride.com), you can tailor a Web site specifically for a destination wedding. No matter how you design it, protect your Web site with a password known only to you and your guests. Your site will be a work in progress as you plan your wedding, and guests will enjoy checking to see what has been changed or added. As you finalize details of the wedding, such as events and locations, you can post the information on the site. Even after the wedding, the Web site will be a great place to display photos of the trip. You might include any of the following items on the Web site:

+ Photos of you and your fiancé through the years, from childhood to today. You could even use a slide or PowerPoint presentation as a Web site introduction.
+ Stories of how you met and got engaged.
+ A schedule of events with dates, times, and locations, and a way to RSVP to the events. If you are collecting money for any of the scheduled events, such as a guided tour, you could collect the money online.
+ Directions to all the event locations.
+ Embassy and consulate information for your guests' reference.
+ Passport and visa application information, if applicable to your destination.
+ Destination information, including links to the tourism bureau, as well as fast facts on climate, voltage, and currency.
+ Money exchange information and/or a link to related Web sites that offer current exchange rates (www.onanda.com or www.xe.com).
+ Travel information, including a link to the person or company that is coordinating the travel reservations, flight, and hotel details.
+ Travel tips and packing suggestions.
+ An introduction to each member of your wedding party.
+ A guest book for Web site visitors to send messages.
+ Gift registry information, with links to pertinent stores or companies.
+ A place where guests can sign up for special needs, such as childcare or special dietary requirements.

- A live feed so guests who are unable to attend can still see the entire wedding celebration as it is happening.
- Wedding photos after the trip for everyone to enjoy.
- A link to the wedding photographer's Web site so all the guests may purchase copies of the wedding and trip photos.

A Web site affords a wide range of wonderful options. But if you don't feel comfortable communicating through technology or if you have a number of guests who do not use the Internet, you can certainly relay all of the same information by mailing out your wedding updates. Even if you have a Web site, you will most likely be updating certain guests—perhaps older relatives who do not have access to the Internet—with printed information sent through the mail. Web site or no, most people still send two things—the save-the-dates cards and the wedding invitations—by "snail mail," which is more personal and formal.

SAVE-THE-DATES NOTICES

You are finally ready to announce your intentions to the world! As soon as you have finalized the destination, date, location(s), and travel options, send out a save-the-dates notice so your guests can make their travel plans well in advance. (I call them save-the-*dates* notices because you are inviting your guests on a trip, not just a one-day affair.) The notices must clearly convey the most important information—the dates, the destination, the locations, the Web site address (and password) to your planning page, and contact information for the person making the travel arrangements. If you do not have a Web site, include an informational letter discussing travel options. Encourage your guests to make their travel arrangements as soon as possible, especially if you have reserved a block of rooms.

The save-the-dates notices not only announce your upcoming nuptials for the first time, they also introduce the tone, style, and theme of the wedding. You can buy ready-made save-the-dates notices, or you can have them designed to reflect your theme. If you plan to hire a designer to do the rest of the stationery, do so at this point. It is nice for this first communication with your guests to correspond with everything else that will follow.

As a preliminary announcement, the save-the-dates notice is, by nature, informal. So even if you are planning an elegant wedding, you can make the save-the-dates cards fun. I've seen all sorts of wonderful ideas—a magnet, a postcard from the destination, a message in a bottle, a fan that unfolds to reveal all the details. I have also seen CD save-the-dates, complete with much of the same information that you might put on a Web site; the CD cover was the actual notice, so even those without a computer received the basic information.

Most of all, save-the-dates cards should be simple, succinct, and enthusiastic. You do not want to convey a complicated, overly detailed message, suggesting that attending this wedding may be a major endeavor (and headache) for the guest. Also, be sure to address your save-the-dates notices as you would your invitations, so guests know if they are welcome to bring partners or children.

GIFT REGISTRY

I did not register for gifts when I got married, but I now know the value of doing so. You can do as I did and leave it up to your guests to decide what you need, but be prepared to receive dozens of mismatched wine glasses and 22 picture frames (all of which I have happily used)! A gift registry simplifies the process of buying a wedding gift by eliminating the guesswork. Destination wedding guests typically have more time between when they first learn about the wedding and the actual date, so they may want to ponder their choice of wedding gift early on.

It is a good idea to register for gifts early so the information can be included in your guest communications. The Web site, your save-the-dates notice, a wedding update, or a bridal shower invitation are appropriate places to relay registry information. Most major store chains have effective registry systems, both in the store and online, where guests can choose gifts and have them wrapped and shipped to the couple. The registry keeps track of what items have been purchased and what items still remain.

A destination wedding provides a perfect theme for wedding gifts. A couple who has everything and loves to travel or a couple who really wants a destination wedding but can't quite afford it might consider registering with a travel company for their trip or honeymoon. You can research the possibilities at The Big Day (800-304-1141 / www.thebigday.com), The Honeymoon (888-796-7772 / www.thehoneymoon.com), or HoneyLuna (800-809-5862 / www.honeyluna.com). Or, if you anticipate adventures across the globe in your future, register for luggage and

CREATIVE THEMES

I worked with one couple who, because they met in the theater, made *theater* their overall theme. This allowed for several creative and memorable design touches. We designed their save-the-dates notice as a marquee announcing their debut. Their updates included images of searchlight beams, the invitations looked like a stage with a curtain unveiling the information, the programs were playbills introducing the wedding party as the cast of characters, and the escort cards were tickets to the "main event"—the reception.

other travel accessories. You might also consider registering with a store at the destination that sells local treasures, such as pottery, linens, artwork, furniture, and crystal. If you are getting married in the Czech Republic, for example, you may want to take home their famous Bohemian crystal. Or, if your destination is Italy, perhaps you would like to outfit your living room with decorative inlaid furniture. Many of the larger stores that are accustomed to selling to tourists are willing and able to ship anywhere in the world. If you are concerned about being burdened with lots of gifts to carry home, remind guests to send gifts to your home, before or after the wedding, so you (and they) will not have to travel with the gifts.

INVITATIONS

There are three kinds of invitations: custom-designed invitations, predesigned invitations, and e-mail invitations. Regardless of the invitation type, they should be sent out two months ahead of time for a domestic wedding, with the RSVP date one month before the wedding. For an international wedding, invitations should be sent out three months in advance, with an RSVP date two months before the wedding. So, at least four months before the wedding, you will want to finalize your invitation design, whether custom-made or ready-made, and get them printed or ordered.

Custom-designed invitations are tailored to fit your style or theme; they can be as elaborate or creative as you wish. For custom-designed stationery, you may want to research resources both at your destination and closer to home. With global resources easily available through the Internet, it is not difficult to find and order whatever you want from wherever you want. An invitation should reflect your style, but it can also reflect something of the destination. Consider incorporating elements of your destination's culture and artistry into your stationery and/or invitation design. You may find preprinted papers, which could save you time and money. Carlson Craft (www.carlsoncraft.com) has some options, as do many stationery and office supply stores, such as Staples (www.staples.com). Or you may want to look for finer papers such as handmade papers, Italian marble paper, rice paper, or papyrus. Other personal touches can be added to your invitations with an embosser, a sealing stamp, or a Chinese chop carved with your names; you can get many of these items at Kate's Paperie in New York City (800-809-9880 / www.katespaperie.com). If you desire the very distinctive look of gold-foiled medieval invitations, complete with a wedding certificate in the same design, Alan Craddock of The Medieval Scribe (www.medievalscribe.com) offers gorgeous options for illuminated stationery in a medieval style. Or why not explore the possibilities of the local art of your destination? You may be able to commission a local artist to handpaint each invitation or paint an image of the wedding site, which could then be reproduced on your stationery and/or invitations.

If you would rather not create something from scratch, you can seek out the perfect premade invitations to go with your style and theme. This works best for couples who want something simple and traditional. If you are interested in having all your stationery correspond, inquire if the invitation supplier can also provide programs, seating cards, menus, and thank-you cards in the same design. Most stationery stores and some print shops have wedding invitation books to peruse. There are many companies from which to choose, but here are a few big suppliers that are online:

- Carlson Craft (800-545-4065 / www.carlsoncraft.com) is a large predesigned-invitation company offering a wide variety of items, sold online and by many retailers.
- The Wedding Invitations Store (888-364-6800 / www.wedding-invitations-store.com) has a selection of destination wedding designs.
- Anna Griffin (888-817-8170 / www.annagriffin.com) offers exquisite designs inspired by beautiful textiles and prints.
- Millie Rossman Kidd of Studio Mark Design (518-392-3689 / www.studiomark design.com) carries a cutting-edge line of designs, and she will also custom design wedding invitations.
- Hand Crafted Invitations (505-379-0768 / www.handcraftedinvitations.com) features several nifty invitation designs made of handmade papers.

If you are looking for something specific and unique, you may have to search many invitation books and Web sites before you find the right one. If you *do* find the perfect fit, predesigned invitations are usually quite reasonable, unless you go with a very high-quality package from Tiffany (800-843-3269 / www.tiffany.com), which you cannot buy online, or Crane & Co. (800-268-2281 / www.crane.com).

A small percentage of couples use evites, or e-mail invitations, for their wedding invitations. To invite guests to your wedding in this manner, you must be certain that everyone is online with an e-mail address. Explore this alternative by visiting the Evite Web site (www.evite.com), where you will find a selection of wedding invitation templates. You can add the pertinent wedding information to the template, then send it to your guests. E-mail invitations are the least formal and least expensive option, so they work well if you are having a casual, low-budget wedding for a small group of your closest friends and relatives. If you do opt for an evite, print one out on good quality paper to keep as a memento.

Of the three options, custom-designed invitations tend to cost the most, unless you or a friend does the design work. If you want to have custom-designed invitations and stationery for all your guest communications—save-the-dates, invitations, updates, welcome letters, programs, escort cards, menus, and thank-you cards—you'll need to choose a designer early. That way, the designer can develop a design that will be consistent for all of your correspondence, and you'll be able to save money by having all the stationery designed and printed at the same time.

Once you have decided on the style of your invitations, start thinking about who will address them. Do you feel comfortable with your own handwriting? Or would you rather have a professional calligrapher address the invitations artistically? If you are interested in hiring a calligrapher, research the possibilities. Calligraphers have different styles, so be sure to see samples of each candidate's script. Keep in mind, too, that calligraphers' prices vary dramatically. You can hire someone close to home, but if you want more choices, take a look at your options nationwide. In the past, I have used Gail Brill Design (www.gailbrilldesign.com) and Bernard Maisner (www.bernardmaisner.com). You can also find many resources at The Calligraphy Studio Web site (www.calligraphystudio.com).

REGULAR UPDATES

As you update your wedding planning Web site, e-mail your guests periodically to remind them to check the site for new information. If you are not using a Web site for regular communication with your guests, you may have to send out additional updates as things come up. If, for example, guests are not responding to your recommendations for travel arrangements, you might send out an update with a gentle reminder to finalize their plans. You can also use your wedding updates as an opportunity to build excitement. Printed updates can be designed to coincide with the theme or destination. For a wedding I planned in England, the bride's mother posted regular updates to everyone involved. She had great fun sending with each update a useful gift for the trip, such as an umbrella or a brand-new pound note.

It is very exciting when guests start responding to your invitations; somehow, the arrival of those RSVP cards makes it all very real. As your guests respond, you might send them the final update letter that contains travel and packing tips in addition to the final itinerary. If you have a Web site, update that with the same information. You can find suggestions for packing lists and travel tips on page 88.

Tell everyone to pack lightly because every ounce counts. You can always wash and iron clothes at the destination if you have to. Some people pack a change of clothing and personal hygiene items in their carry-on luggage, just in case (heaven forbid) their checked suitcase is lost. Suggest that your guests divide up their traveling funds and separate their traveler's checks from the receipts. That way, they will not be carrying all their money in one place. Also, advise everyone to always keep a record of credit card numbers and passport numbers in a journal or electronic organizer, or both, in case things get lost. Finally, caution against bringing valuable jewels, and suggest wrapping aerosols that may explode under pressure in sealable bags. It may seem as though you are preparing your guests to do battle, but a few friendly tips will help them be prepared rather than out of luck.

ON-SITE COMMUNICATIONS

The month or so before your departure, begin composing welcome letters for your guests. These letters will be waiting for your guests when they arrive at the destination. If you are planning to put together welcome packages or baskets for your guests, you can include the letters with those. In addition to welcoming your guests to your wedding and to the destination, the letters can include any information you want them to receive once they arrive, such as last-minute changes to the itinerary. If possible, ask the tourism bureau to deliver maps or brochures to your hotel so they'll be ready to be distributed with the welcome letters.

Another wonderful touch is to provide your guests with "Daily Ditties" each morning of their stay. These short notes are similar to the daily itineraries that cruise ships give their passengers, which include reminders about the day's activities and, if you choose, other more unusual information. A cultural or historical point of interest about the destination or a humorous "Did You Know...?" fact about the couple makes a good addition to the daily notes. For a consistent look, use your invitation stationery to create the Daily Ditties.

PACKING LIST AND TRAVEL TIPS

Provide your guests with a suggested packing list and a few travel tips.

Include on your packing list:

- Clothing appropriate for your destination's weather
- Traveler's checks, credit card, cash, and some local currency for tips, etc.
- Documents, such as passport, visa, and birth certificate, if applicable
- International medical card, if applicable
- Camera, film, and batteries
- Medical needs: prescription drugs, insect repellent (if appropriate), sunscreen, Dramamine, laxatives, and antidiarrheals
- Water purification tablets
- Bottle of water and inflatable pillow for the plane
- Luggage with wheels
- Fanny pack or money belt for valuables
- Any necessary electronics and adapter plugs

For travel tips, include specific information on:

- Passport and visa requirements, with information on how and where to get passports and, if necessary, visas
- Currency, including types of currency, exchange rate, best place to exchange money, how much cash to bring, whether to use credit card or traveler's checks, and standards for tipping (whom to tip and how much)
- Electrical voltage and whether adapters are needed for electronics
- Medical requirements, such as records of immunizations
- Communication to and from the area, including available phone and mail services, how guests will be able to phone home, how mail can be sent from the destination, and what address can be used for incoming mail
- Internet and e-mail, including any relevant e-mail addresses and Web sites
- Matters of safety, including issues regarding water, crime, or cultural attitudes toward women and/or Americans
- Security issues, with specific instructions to:
    - Arrive at the airport two hours in advance of a domestic flight and three hours before an international flight
    - Wear shoes that are easy to remove in the airport
    - Not pack any sharp or dangerous objects in your carry-on luggage
    - Pack items in plastic sealable bags so they can be easily inspected
    - Carry a photocopy of your passport in case the original is lost or stolen

Programs, seating charts, and menus—these are all options that you may choose to include on your wedding day. While it would be nice to have them all printed months before the event, these materials generally cannot be written until almost all the wedding details are finalized, such as your menu, guest list, and final order of events. I cover these items extensively in chapter five, pages 107–116.

POST-WEDDING COMMUNICATIONS

The common courtesy of sending thank-you notes to wedding guests is no different for a destination wedding. However, because you and your guests will have shared so much more than a few hours together, you will probably have a lot more to say than the standard thank-you note text. Thank them not only for their gift but also for making the effort to join the adventure. If you have a Web site, you can post photos and information about ordering prints as well as comments and reminiscences about your favorite moments. Be aware that even couples with a wedding Web site should send out personal thank-you notes. The stationery can be customized with your new monogram or a photograph of you or the destination. You could also include photos of the guests during the celebration or a copy of your wedding video.

WHAT TO WEAR

Many books, magazines, and consultants—not to mention designers and shops—are devoted to helping brides- and grooms-to-be choose what to wear for their big day. With all of these resources available, I'll just address bridal fashion as it relates to destination weddings. Your chosen destination will influence your choice of what to wear—and how you and your fiancé will look—at your wedding.

THE BRIDE'S GOWN AND TRAVEL WARDROBE

The wedding gown is the cornerstone of the bride's apparel, so begin by selecting a gown (or outfit) that fits the style of the wedding. Keep the destination in mind when making your selection. Many destination brides select simpler gowns or suits because they are easier to transport. This does not mean, however, that the logistics of transporting a "big" gown can't be worked out if that is what you want.

If you are planning a wedding in New York, Boston, Paris, Milan, London, or another fashionable, cosmopolitan city, you may want to visit designer shops and boutiques, such as Vera Wang or Priscilla of Boston, to see what kind of haute couture masterpiece they would dream up for you! Even if high design is not in your budget, do not discount the talent of local tailors and seamstresses. In many countries, including several African nations, it is commonplace to have all of your clothes made; not only can you find a good tailor on every corner, but their services are often very reasonable. Alternatively, you might consider buying lace or fabric from your destination and having a seamstress design your dress at home. Bear in mind that if you want a wedding dress custom made for you, you will need to give the designer *at least* six months.

If it interests you, research what local brides wear in your destination. In many cultures, a bride wears multiple outfits during her wedding. In Morocco, the

bride spends much of her time changing into as many as 17 jewel-laden outfits, which are often rented for the occasion. If nothing else, you could wear local attire for the rehearsal dinner, or you could change into a colorful ethnic costume later at the reception for dancing.

Pack your wedding garments very carefully. If you have purchased your gown from a salon, let them know that you are traveling for your wedding; they may have special packaging they can use to ensure the safety of the garment, and they also may be able to pack it in such a way that minimizes wrinkling. If you are flying to your destination, carry the gown with you on the plane so it is sure to arrive with you! The last thing you want is to face your wedding day without a gown because it was lost as checked luggage. When you arrive at your destination, have your gown pressed, preferably by a recommended professional cleaner. If this is not possible, you may be able to bring a small steamer in your suitcase and "press" the dress at your hotel. Or, if

© CHARITY DE MEER

you must, you can use the steam-from-the-shower method (hang your dress on a hanger in the bathroom; turn on the hot shower; and with the bathroom door closed, allow the room to fill with steam).

Because a destination wedding involves more than a ceremony and reception, you should also think about what else you will be wearing on your trip. Surely you will want stunning outfits for every day of your wedding trip and honeymoon, so avoid leaving your clothing choices to the last minute. With your destination firmly in mind, you can begin to gather clothes for the days before and after your big day and for the activities you have planned for your trip.

ACCESSORIES

Beyond the actual outfit or gown you will wear for your wedding, there are accessories to think about—shoes, the headpiece, jewelry, makeup, and perfume. There are so many details involved in any wedding, destination or not, but most brides enjoy the details of choosing accessories for their wedding attire. If buying African fabric for your gown is a little more than you are willing to do to make your destination wedding feel authentic, you can try to inject a little cultural flair with the accessories. For example, is there a scent indigenous to or widely used in your destination? If you like it, wear it!

WEDDING RINGS

While you're considering what jewelry to wear, don't forget your wedding rings. Investigate jewelry designs and designers from your destination. You may find interesting wedding bands that incorporate some of the gems native to that area. Do research to find which gems are mined in various regions of the world. Wherever you find your rings, be sure to select and order them in plenty of time to have them ready for your trip.

As every region and culture has its own colorful baubles and fine jewels, I recommend that brides accessorize with jewelry native to their destination. If you are planning your wedding in the Czech Republic, consider wearing crystals or garnets; think sapphires for Thailand, emeralds for South America, diamonds for South Africa, tanzanite for Tanzania. For a list of gems unique to each part of the world, visit the Web site for the International Colored Gemstone Association (www.gemstone.org) or Mt. Lily Gems (www.mtlilygems.com).

Shoes are an important accessory, so do not wait until the last minute to find matching shoes. You can find dyeable shoes at most bridal shops and on the Internet (www.dyeableshoesetc.com or www.dyeableshoestore.com). Some companies, such as Savvy Sneaks & Sandals (888-728-8980 / www.savvysneaks.com), specialize in decorative wedding sandals and even tennis shoes, which would be fun for a beach wedding. For other beach-related wedding apparel and accessories, check Beach Bride Guide (www.beachbrideguide.com) for resources. If you are having a western-themed wedding, consider fitting the part with wedding cowboy boots (216-798-3458 / www.westernweddingboots.com). Or, if you do not want to wear any shoes at all, you could still decorate your tootsies with special foot jewelry (www.foxyfeet.com).

BRIDESMAIDS' GOWNS AND ACCESSORIES

If you will be choosing gowns for your bridesmaids, give yourself enough time to find ones that will suit and please the women who will be wearing them. The most important factor, if you intend to coordinate outfits, is color. Even if the bridesmaids are choosing their own outfits for the wedding, let them know what color(s) you have in mind so they can make their choices accordingly. If you are not specific, you run the risk of a wedding party in a beautiful range of pinks, with one person wearing lime green from head to toe! This is why so many designers have introduced separates that women can mix and match. The bride is able to choose the designer, the color(s), and the fabric, and then leave it up to her bridesmaids to select their own separates. If you are ordering for the bridesmaids, warn them that they may have to hire a seamstress to make alterations once the dresses arrive. When you are ordering clothes for someone who is unable to be measured in person, it is always a good idea to order a size larger than she usually wears so alterations can be made for a perfect fit.

THE MEN'S ATTIRE

The simple solution to wedding party attire is to have all the men match, but there is no rule against the groom looking different from his groomsmen. If the men in your party need to rent tuxedos, inquire about renting them at your destination. Be sure to send the tuxedo shop pictures of the bridesmaids' gowns ahead of time so they can select the appropriate colors and styles to match. Also make sure that all the groomsmen send you their measurements with time to spare. They can have their measurements taken at any tuxedo shop or by any seamstress or tailor in their area. Most tuxedo shops at your destination will have options that are currently popular there. Island shops, for example, often have Hawaiian prints and tuxedo shorts, as well as cotton, linen, and silk suits. They may also have fun accessories that reflect the local culture. Whatever your groom will be wearing for the wedding, he too should give some thought to accessories. Perhaps there are some local touches he would like to add to his overall look, such as shoes, cuff links, a special tie, or distinctive cologne.

For quality clothing and excellent service, choose a tuxedo rental company that comes recommended by reputable establishments. Ask them when they will need all the measurements and what they will do if something does not fit when

© DAVID BECKSTEAD

the wedding party arrives. The tuxedos should be picked up immediately upon arrival so they can be tried on and, if necessary, altered in time for the wedding. If you decide it is easier to rent the suits from home and transport them to the destination, be sure to inquire about weekly rates and packing advice.

LOOKING AHEAD

You have already "traveled" far in your planning. You've researched your destination and your travel options, announced your upcoming wedding to your guests, and considered what you will wear for the big event and the rest of your wedding trip. Finally, you are ready to pull all the elements together and orchestrate the details of your dream-come-true destination wedding. Now begins the countdown to the big day—you can start by confirming all your contracts and choices.

PULLING IT ALL TOGETHER:
Contract, Confirm, and Coordinate

Over the past many months, you have researched and gathered information on countless details that will all come together for an incredible destination wedding—and, yes, the details *will* all come together. Your planning binder may be splitting at the seams, your budget full of cross-outs and arrows, and your desk littered with reminders, but rest assured you have done the bulk of your pre-wedding planning. In this last phase, you will finalize and contract your service providers, confirm (and reconfirm and even re-reconfirm) them, and on your wedding trip, coordinate them into the realization of your dreams—a romantic wedding and reception, and a fabulous trip for you and your loved ones.

FINALIZING AND CONTRACTING YOUR CHOICES

Once you have done your research, you will have to follow up with all the locations and service providers whom you contacted, whether it was during a planning trip or from your own home. If you have not already done so, review your options in each category—flowers, music, cake, and so on—and, with your fiancé (and wedding planner, if you have one), make your final choices. Once you make your decisions, inform your preferred service providers that you would like to hire them and would like them to send you a contract. Once the service provider accepts the job, let the others know that you have decided not to hire them so they do not hold the date for you. If you are working with a planner or another assistant of some kind, they can do some or all of this work for you.

As you receive the contracts, review them carefully and communicate any changes you want made before signing. Look for clauses that mention the use of your photos for promotional purposes. If you are not interested in letting the service providers use your images, you must tell them in writing. Sometimes you can specify how your pictures can be used or give them permission to use only certain photos. Also note their cancellation policy and any clauses about dissatisfaction (what happens if you are not happy with the end result?). Make sure you understand each service provider's payment schedule, including if and when they need a deposit. Deposits are usually required once services are formally contracted. Also inquire as to how each vendor wants to be paid. If necessary, review your payment options in chapter three, page 75. As you contract your service providers, update your budget with the actual figures for their fees and add each provider's contact information to your service provider list and/or your budget.

THE RECEPTION LOCATION

Choosing your reception location was perhaps the most difficult decision in your planning process. Review the list of questions you considered in making your choice (chapter three, pages 63, 65) to see if there are any details you need to iron out. Make sure you have covered your bases before signing the contract. Do you understand what the location will provide in terms of coordinating services? Decorating services? Assistance with the marriage license? Food and liquor? Personnel? Concierge services for your guests? Tables, linens, chairs, china? Also confirm what they are charging for each service. You do not want to be charged for something you will be contracting elsewhere, such as centerpieces that may be coming from an independent florist. This is also your opportunity to see if they can provide any service(s) that you have not found elsewhere. For example, if you are not satisfied with the cake designs you have received from local bakers, ask your location if their pastry chef can supply the cake.

© EMMANUEL VAUCHER

THE CEREMONY LOCATION

Whether you will be married in a church or on a grassy knoll overlooking the ocean, you will need to finalize your ceremony location. Are there any remaining details you need to address or requirements you need to meet to have your ceremony there? Are there functional items, such as tables or chairs, or décor elements, such as flowers and greenery, needed for your ceremony site? If so, take note of these items now so you will not forget to discuss them with your florist or designer. It is a good idea to review the list of questions and issues you considered in choosing your location (chapter three, pages 64–66) before signing a contract to finalize the choice.

THE MENU

Now is the time to finalize your caterer and menu choices if you haven't already done so. If you did not have the opportunity to sample your caterer's food before the reception, see if you can arrange a tasting during the days prior to the wedding. In making the menu selections for your reception, consider making the food part of your guests' destination experience—or even an adventure! It is a good idea to

© LONGUEVILLE HOUSE

have one "safe" dish that isn't the least bit scary for the picky eaters in the group. And remember, it is typical to offer one meat entrée, a fish or chicken entrée, and a vegetarian option. Once you make all of your decisions, verify that they are accurately reflected on the contract. If you will be printing menus for your guests, ask to be provided with the correct terms and/or descriptions of your choices.

THE WEDDING CAKE

From the pastry chefs you have researched, have you found the cake you want to serve? If the cake you are seeking is not available, have you found a chef who can work from a converted recipe? Once you are sure the cake will be perfect—either exactly as you envisioned it or something wonderful that you never even imagined—order it. Or, if you've decided to have a "local specialty" dessert table, order the pastries and sweets. Confirm the flavor(s) of the cake, and make sure that the chef has a picture of the cake you want and/or you have a picture of the cake the chef plans to make. Local flowers or artifacts can be used to decorate it, unless the pastry chef's decorative skills are tremendous, which is often the case in many European countries and metropolitan areas around the world. Finally, confirm that the cake will be delivered to your wedding location in time for the reception but not so early that it may not be properly refrigerated.

Now is the time to ask yourself who will be responsible for the reception and the ceremony décor—the banquet manager (or other location personnel), an independent florist, a designer? Or will you be pulling the décor elements together yourself? When you have selected the person for the job, you can discuss your style, theme, and color scheme with them and put it in their hands, trusting them to use their best judgment—a very common choice in international weddings. Or if you feel you have the time and interest, you can try to be involved in designing each detail of the wedding décor yourself. If you do want to have a say in every part of your wedding's décor, the best approach is to provide photographic images of details and arrangements you wish to emulate. A picture is worth a million poorly translated words! If the people with whom you are working are worth their weight in gold, they should be able to reproduce almost any photograph.

All the visual elements will be important in making the surroundings look spectacular. Are you clear on what the reception location will be providing? Do you have a list of all the decorative items needed for the ceremony? If you are working with an overall color scheme, do you know what kind of décor options the venue offers? Ask the location which, if any, of the following décor elements are available:

- Flowers (type and color?) and greens (type?)
- Containers (kinds—vases, baskets, ceramic?)
- Ribbons on the bouquets (size? type of fabric? complexity?)
- Fabric draping (where—on wedding arches or chuppahs, railings, tent poles?)
- Table linens (color? pattern? type of fabric? length?)
- Centerpieces
- Chairs (kinds—ballroom, wooden picnic chairs, metal folding?)
- Chair linens (kinds—chair covers, tassels, sashes, bows?)
- China (specific pieces? material—porcelain, glass, ceramic?)
- Silverware (style?) and glassware (style? specific types of glasses—water, low ball, high ball, champagne, red and white wine, cordials, martini?)
- Serving dishes (material—silver, wood, ceramic, woven, glass?)
- Lighting (types—spotlights, candles, luminaries, torches, strands, lanterns?)
- Props (types—artifacts, balloons, ice sculpture?)

If the location offers any of the above options, ask to see samples. Inquire about other décor issues, too. How do they fold the napkins and set the tables? Do you have any say in the centerpieces, if they are provided? Are candles placed on the tables? Do they supply menus or seating cards? What kind of serving dishes do they use to serve the food? How is the food displayed? If you absolutely do not like the items provided by the location, you can try to rent alternatives; in some countries it is actually more cost-effective to buy them.

If your location is taking care of floral arrangements, discuss the options

© CHARITY DE MEER

of in-season local flowers and ask if they might also suggest props, specialty linens, or lighting. If your venue is not providing the flowers for your reception, finalize your selection for florist and/or decorator services. Confirm that your florist understands how many flowers or arrangements you will need and where they are to be placed, both at the ceremony and the reception. If the flowers are to be coordinated with the overall décor, be sure your florist is familiar with your location(s) or at least has photographs of the space.

Explore what natural resources and seasonal flowers your destination has to offer, then use as many local items as possible to make the event colorful, cultural, and memorable. You may want to incorporate native flowers, fruits, or natural treasures like shells, sea glass, or gems into your décor as well as local cultural items, such as crafts, art, and textiles. In addition, you can create ambiance with candles or spot lighting, dramatic fabric draping, props, artifacts, and elegant or whimsical food displays. Once you have conveyed and confirmed exactly what you want, get a solid estimate on the costs of your flowers and the overall décor. Finalize your choices, then request a contract and send your deposit, which should be no more than 50 percent.

THE PHOTOGRAPHER AND VIDEOGRAPHER

Make your final choices for a photographer and, if you desire, a videographer. As with all your service providers, clarify what you want—formal portraits? candid shots? photos of the ceremony *and* the reception?—and review the fees and payment schedule. Verify exactly what services the package price includes. This can be tricky, as you may be charged for not only an album of photographs but also extraneous items like magnets and thank-you notes. Some photographers will give you the negatives in addition to the photos; ask the photographer if she provides this service. The best-case scenario is to get an album and the proofs along with the negatives. In the case of a destination wedding, it is desirable to get the product before you leave. But, because of time constraints, it is often unlikely that you will be able to return home with a finished album. As for the videographer, confirm that the wedding video will be shot in a format you can use at home.

If you are not being given the negatives, inquire if you will be able to purchase additional photos. Can the photographer post the proofs on her professional Web site or on your personal wedding Web site? You might also try to negotiate a good rate for reprints if you think your guests will be ordering a lot of photos after the trip. If you brought a photographer or a videographer from home, you will have time to breathe after the wedding, but you will still want to know exactly what to expect regarding package pricing and schedule.

THE MUSIC AND ENTERTAINMENT

There is no better way to liven up an event than with music. If everyone is already soaking in the wonders of the destination, they may be eager to dance to the native beat, whether that's calypso, merengue, oom-pa-pa polka, or zydeco. Do not be afraid to mix things up, too, and arrange for a variety of musical rhythms and influences. You may want a mandolin for the ceremony and a steel drum band for dancing at the reception.

If you still haven't found musicians, ask the banquet manager, wedding coordinator, or any other local resident for referrals. When you have found the group(s) you like, contract them for your ceremony and/or reception. Groups who are open to input may allow you to negotiate a song list. If there is something you just *have* to hear, send them the music—but don't go overboard with requests. Luckily, music is a universal language; given enough time, the musicians  should be able to learn your song(s). Communicate to them any special dances you have planned, such as your first dance and/or parent dances. If you really want a special song played but find it impossible to arrange, inquire about having a stereo and sound system in addition to your live music.

Are you planning any other form of entertainment? Are there performers who reflect your destination's culture and might add to your festivities? You may want to delight the children with a clown or a magician, or perhaps entertain the adults with dancers or a comedian. If so, choose the performer and contract their services as you have done with the musicians.

SPECIAL EFFECTS

Fireworks, sparklers, a giant bonfire, a biplane flying overhead, hot air balloons in the distance, kites, spotlighting, bubble or dry ice machines, a dove or butterfly release—all of these fall under the category of special effects. Any of these features will add an element of fun and creativity to your reception. If you are hiring a company to provide the special effects, make sure it is professional and well insured. You may need special permits, too, but most companies are aware of those regulations and will take care of obtaining any necessary permits.

LIABILITY INSURANCE

As the hosts of your wedding celebration, you will be responsible for the safety of your guests and the condition of the venue you rent. You may already have purchased wedding insurance that covers your financial outlay for the wedding. Now is a good time to consider liability insurance to cover any accidents that may occur at, or as a result of, your wedding ceremony and/or reception. You may want to talk to your insurance agent to see what he can offer. It is sometimes possible to get some coverage with a rider on your homeowner's insurance or get a one-day special event insurance policy. If you choose the latter, make sure it covers wedding-specific issues, such as injury to guests or staff, facility damage, property damage, and alcohol-related accidents. You can also contact R.V. Nuccio & Associates (800-364-2433 / www.rvnuccio.com) or WedSafe (877-723-3933 / www.wedsafe.com) to discuss and purchase wedding liability insurance.

ENSURING YOUR GUESTS' SAFETY

In addition to securing liability insurance, consider arranging your own "insurance policy" against drinking and driving at your wedding celebration. Make sure that taxis will be available during and after the reception, or hire a car and driver in case you need to get one or more of your guests back to their hotels safely.

THE MARRIAGE LICENSE

As you know, the particular requirements for getting a legally valid marriage license depend on your destination country and the type of ceremony you have planned. At this point, having reviewed chapter two and researched your own destination, you've gathered (or ordered) all the necessary documents. To be safe, make copies of all your legal documents and plan on bringing both sets. Regardless of the information provided in this book and the information you have researched, you should also contact the consulate of the country in which you plan to marry to check if any changes have been made to the marriage law requirements. Confirm with the consulate that your understanding of the requirements coincides with theirs.

You should now understand the entire process required to obtain and file your marriage license. (You may have decided to contract a lawyer or an on-site coordinator to help you navigate through the the steps.) Allot yourself enough time to complete this process once you arrive at your destination.

THE CEREMONY

Have you made final arrangements with someone to officiate your wedding? If not, do so now. Confirm the date and time of your wedding with the religious or civil official who will be marrying you, and double-check that you have met the legal and/or religious requirements necessary to have the ceremony you are planning. If you want to give the ceremony a personal touch, discuss different possibilities, such as special vows, songs, or readings, with your officiant. The officiant may also be able to suggest ways to add local cultural flavor to your ceremony through music, dance, or a traditional ritual.

If you are not able to get help from the religious officiant at your destination, consider consulting your spiritual leader or an interfaith minister near home. More and more interfaith ministers specialize in assisting with the design of wedding ceremonies. Taking your wishes into consideration, they can help you design a ceremony that reflects your values, priorities, and personalities.

If you need any ceremonial items for your wedding, arrange for them now, as you are finalizing your plans. Depending on your faith, these could include a unity candle, a ketubah, a talis, a chuppah, and/or a glass to break. Before you leave for your wedding trip, be sure any and all ceremonial items have either been prearranged at the destination or are gathered and ready to pack in your suitcase.

WEDDING TRANSPORTATION

You have probably already given some thought as to how you will get to the church (or other ceremony location). Now, with a clear sense of your wedding style, you can choose the mode of transportation that best suits you. Feel free to be creative. Why not arrive by horse and carriage, a hot air balloon, or maybe a bicycle for two?

Or go with a bang, as one of my couples did when they left the church in a 1968 Cadillac that backfired in unison with the ringing bells! Another couple departed from their island ceremony in a sailboat painted purple to match the gowns and flowers. In addition to transporting yourselves, don't forget about the wedding party. If flashy isn't your thing, you might coordinate a simple carpool. But if you want to go for the gusto, consider a trolley, limousine, or classic car to deliver the party in style. Nowadays you can get all kinds of limos, from Jaguars to Hummers. When you've made your decision, book the transportation service, confirming the date and time of their arrival and departure.

ATTIRE

Time will not be an issue if you buy your wedding dress at a department store, off the rack at a clearance sale, or at David's Bridal (located all over the United States). However, if you are ordering a gown or having one designed and made for you, you will need at least six months. If you are planning on wearing a designer or custom-made dress, make sure you have allowed enough time and confirmed your plans with the bridal shop or designer. Have you made your choices for the bridal party's attire? If you will be ordering bridesmaids' dresses, confirm those choices with the shop or designer as well.

If the men in your party will be wearing tuxedos, you have no doubt researched the options and are now ready to choose a shop that can supply rentals. Reserve the tuxedos and confirm when the shop will need exact measurements, then give the men in your party some time—perhaps a month—to get professionally measured, either by a seamstress, tailor, or tuxedo shop in their own town.

YOUR WEDDING COORDINATOR

There is no time like the present to reassess your manpower—or womanpower, as the case may be! By now, you should know exactly how much assistance and what kind of assistance you will be receiving from your reception venue and service providers. What sort of further help, referrals, guest coordination, decorating, and event orchestration do you need? To ensure that everything goes as planned on the big day, you will definitely need *somebody* to be in charge of coordinating your wedding ceremony and reception. Have you hired a professional for this job, either from home or at your destination? Or have you asked an organized friend to oversee the details and order the events?

As you are finalizing the plans for your wedding coordinator, keep all your trip events—not just the wedding reception—in mind, including any extra activities and off-site excursions. If your locations do not provide full service, determine what kind of help you will still need. Do you have one coordinator, or a whole team of helpers? Try to develop a plan for how you will tackle the tasks to be done. For example, your home-based team, perhaps consisting of a wedding planner, a travel consultant, friends, and/or family members, might coordinate all the guest reservations and communication before the event and help you with the preliminary details of the wedding, then turn over the coordination responsibilities to the local coordinator. If you opt for this plan, be sure to supply the events coordinator with copies of all of your service provider contracts and an order-of-events document that includes every minute detail. I also recommend that the wedding planner—or you, if you don't have a hired planner—make confirmation calls three weeks in advance and face-to-face confirmations within one week of the events.

Whether a professional or a trusted friend, the wedding coordinator should orchestrate every aspect of your ceremony and reception, from setup to cleanup, and deal with the service providers during the events. The coordinator might also direct the rehearsal, line the wedding party up for the procession, and help with photographs, seating, and the overall flow of the event. At the end of the night, the coordinator should gather up the gifts and mementos and store them safely in the couple's room or car. If you are hiring a planner, make sure you both agree upon the services for which he is responsible before signing a contract. If you are enlisting a close friend or relative for the job, review and confirm all her responsibilities.

Finally, this is a good time to revisit the question of what you will be wearing for the rest of your wedding trip. Remember to consider all the activities or events you have planned as well as your honeymoon.

FINALIZING YOUR TRAVEL PLANS

While you are busy contracting and confirming your service providers, do not forget to check on your guests' travel plans as well as your own. Believe it or not, I know a couple who meticulously planned every aspect of their destination wedding but forgot to make their own travel plans until very late in the game!

TRAVEL ARRANGEMENTS

Confirm all the travel options and arrangements that your guests have been offered, either on your own or through your travel consultant or wedding planner. If your friends and family are booking their travel independently, make sure the airlines and flight options you researched and suggested are still available and accurate. If you have arranged group or package rates or chartered a private flight, check that all the details are confirmed. Finally, make sure you and your fiancé have taken care of your own travel plans. I recommend arriving three to five days before your guests, depending on how many things you need to address before the wedding, including any legal or license issues. It may seem obvious, but be sure your own flights are booked!

GROUP ESCORTS

If the language and culture of your destination differ from your own, consider hiring a group escort. You can provide an escort for the entire trip, starting from your home base, or just for the destination itself. If you are working with a travel consultant or wedding planner, ask if she will act as an escort. A group escort will accompany your guests on tours, translate for them, suggest local restaurants and activities, and generally help them get around and enjoy themselves. If you are interested in hiring a group escort, research and review your options before contracting one. Even if you do not want to hire an escort, I still suggest exploring the options in case your guests would like to contract their own escort for activities during their stay.

ACCOMMODATION ARRANGEMENTS

Whether your guests will be making their own reservations directly or through a travel consultant, check that your lodging suggestions are adequate, with enough vacancies to accommodate your guests. If your guest accommodations are part of a package, confirm that the reservations and deposits are in order.

In the event that you reserved a block of rooms for your guests, you will probably have to release any unneeded rooms sometime between 30 to 90 days before the wedding. You will have a better sense of the appropriate number of rooms as people RSVP and make their plans. Make a note *now* to observe your reservation deadline and release any unnecessary rooms; otherwise, you may be charged for empty rooms. If you have a travel coordinator, ask if he will be responsible for this.

ITINERARY AND ACTIVITIES

You have dutifully attended to the 1,001 decisions to be made for your ceremony, reception, and travel plans, but have you considered the other events of your trip? If your destination wedding will be taking place over a long weekend, you might offer a welcome cocktail party the first night followed by a guided tour the next morning. A longer trip to a more distant destination might warrant even more activities. If you need to choose and reserve a space for a rehearsal dinner, post-wedding brunch, or farewell party, do so now. Finalize which activities you'll be offering your guests, then make sure all the locations, transportation, entertainment, and décor for these events are contracted.

If you haven't fully researched the other planned activities on your itinerary, follow up with this now. Ask your service providers, such as those at the reception site or at the hotel, for ideas of fun activities that can be arranged for your guests. If your planned events will require coordination, reservations, and transportation, have the guests sign up for each event in advance. This can be done over your Web site or through the updates you send out ahead of time. If you do not plan on paying for the extra events, ask the guests to pay in advance so you can provide an accurate count of participants.

THE HONEYMOON

Don't forget the honeymoon! If you are planning a honeymoon trip in another location, your wedding plans can easily overwhelm your "private getaway" plans. Tend to those details now. Make and confirm your honeymoon travel and accommodation reservations, and, if necessary, arrange for a friend or family member to take some of your wedding luggage and/or gifts home for you after the wedding.

GIFTS

How do you plan to thank the people who have made your wedding so memorable—your fiancé, your wedding party, your guests? A simple gift can go a long way in making someone feel appreciated. For a unique show of gratitude, look for gifts that reflect the destination or capture the spirit of the culture.

GIFTS FOR EACH OTHER

A wedding gift for your new spouse is certain to be cherished forever as a memory of your special day. For a destination wedding, it can be a memento of the trip, such as jewelry, china, a piece of furniture, a handcrafted coverlet or tablecloth, or an original painting from your destination. In some countries, these kinds of items can be very inexpensive. Many gifts can be either engraved or embroidered with a monogram—a sentimental touch, as the monogram symbolizes the new union of two people. You may not have had time thus far to purchase such a gift, but perhaps you've seen something wonderful, either on your planning trip or on a Web site, that you could order. If so, go ahead and place the order.

To start the trip out on the right note, some couples arrange for welcome letters and/or packages to be waiting for their guests upon their arrival. This is an opportunity to thank them for traveling so far and acquaint them with the destination,

perhaps with a list of local weekly happenings, a local newspaper, tourism brochures, maps, and a subway token or pass with directions on how to use the transit system.

If you like the idea of welcoming your guests with a gift package, you might include something unique to the region. Coins, stamps, flags, postcards, and compact discs of local music are always good choices, but feel free to explore other souvenir options, too. Just remember to allow enough time if you find anything that needs to be handmade or special ordered.

A basket of local products makes an excellent welcome gift. Ask local merchants (or your local wedding coordinator) if they can assemble their products for you. If not, recruit a friend to help you put the gift baskets together once you arrive in your destination. It is too much work to tailor gifts to individuals when you are assembling them right before the wedding, so avoid selecting items that are gender-specific. It is not necessary to give out gifts every day of the trip, as these gifts are meant to initially greet your guests, welcome them to the region, and give them a small slice of local life. Below is a list of some of the welcome packages I have assembled for destination weddings:

- **Hudson Valley, New York:** Shaker baskets filled with a bottle of Saratoga sparkling water, a bottle of local wine, apples, and maple sugar candies
- **Sorrento, Italy:** A bottle of limoncello liquer, two limoncello glasses, colorful pasta, and regional spice blends packaged in a colorful pottery bowl
- **Bohemia, Czech Republic:** A bottle of Moravian wine, two Bohemian crystal wine glasses, and a fine linen towel wrapped in lace

- **Montego Bay, Jamaica:** A calabash filled with Blue Mountain coffee, a little bottle of rum, fresh nutmeg, and chocolates
- **West Sussex, England:** Two teacups, some tea, local jam, and a package of scone baking mix wrapped in a tea towel

FAVORS

Wedding favors are not necessary if you are giving welcome gifts, but if your budget allows for favors, they do provide fun and festive nuances that can add to the overall reception décor. Favors, which are generally incorporated into the reception table settings, can be an extension of your wedding theme or a reflection of the region. I attended a wedding in England where they gave out Christmas crackers filled with silver charms. At the count of three, all the guests pulled them open to create a simultaneous festive crack!

GIFTS FOR THE WEDDING PARTY

For wedding party gifts, I suggest going to the closest artisan market in your destination and buying nice souvenirs, especially things that can be worn on the wedding day. You can give members of the bridal party accessories to match their gowns, such as a crystal choker, a brooch, or a brocade purse. For the men in the wedding party, consider money clips, cuff links or silk ties. Alternatively, you could buy items from home and pack them in your suitcase. Whatever gift you decide upon, make sure it is a genuine and lasting representation of your heartfelt thanks for being a part of your wedding celebration.

GIFTS FOR THE PARENTS

Your parents and your fiancé's parents are probably the most deserving of a thank-you gift as an expression of gratitude for their support and maybe even funding of your wedding. You may want to thank them with a day at the spa, a bottle of local champagne or cognac, or perhaps a piece of jewelry for mom and a tiepin for dad.

WRITING AN ORDER OF EVENTS

Having finalized and contracted your choices for the wedding ceremony, reception, and other events, you should have a clear sense of what needs to happen and when. If your destination wedding is to be a symphony, you (and/or your wedding planner) now need to orchestrate it. The order of events records everything you want to take place on your wedding day and during your trip. It may be many pages long, depending on the length of the trip and the number of events planned.

The master copy—a complete, detailed version—should be created by the person planning the wedding, whether that person is you or a professional planner. This copy is a daily itinerary that includes specific days and times along with a description of what is to happen and who is responsible for making it happen. The document will be filled in and perhaps altered as you continue to pull all the elements of your plans together.

From your master version, you can generate smaller versions that cover specific events. You may want to provide a version for your guests, outlining their itinerary for the trip. Create and print a version for the photographer and videographer, detailing the ceremony, reception, and any other events you want them to cover. Also make a ceremony version to be given to everyone involved in the ceremony; distribute this version to the service providers when you confirm their services a month before the wedding. At the rehearsal, give the ceremony version to all the members of your wedding party so they will be prepared for the flow of events and they will be aware of their responsibilities. Finally, create a reception version for the banquet manager, the musicians, and anyone else working at the reception.

By providing each "participant" with a written game plan, you ensure that everybody is on the same page in terms of where they should be and what they should be doing. On the wedding day, they will not have to be told what to do because they already know the details. When I am coordinating a wedding, the order of events is my most important confirmation and coordination tool. I keep it handy on a clipboard at all times, along with my list of service providers and the budget. You can certainly edit all three documents into one if you wish.

For a general guideline, I have created the following list of important elements to include when composing your order of events. Also take a look at the sample order of events on pages 110–113, which shows the amount of detail I typically incorporate into the document.

TIPPING

Tips are a kind of gift that you give your service providers. Familiarize yourself with the tipping policies in your destination, and be sure to review which tips are already included in the contracts. I have offered some tipping guidelines for each country reviewed in Part II; you can refer to your wedding planner, banquet manager, or hotel concierge to find out who, if anyone, needs to be tipped at the wedding. If your wedding is in the United States, plan to tip drivers, hair and makeup stylists, and the wait staff. In many countries, service people rely on tips for income; you do not want to contribute to negative feelings about foreigners by tipping incorrectly. If one of your service providers has gone beyond the call of duty, show your gratitude with a gift other than money. While money is nice, a gift is sentimental and heartfelt.

Feel free to create your own document, or use a blank form, as provided on the *Destination Bride* Web site (www.destinationbride.com).

- The number of guests expected for each event. Don't forget to include yourselves and your service providers.
- The name of your overall coordinator, if you have one, along with a mobile number or some sort of contact information in case of an emergency.
- A list of the items the couple is responsible for bringing, and another list of items the coordinator plans to provide.
- The names of each location, along with the contact information, the name of the person in charge, and directions for how to get there.
- The dates and times of each event.
- The time you expect each service provider to arrive and set up, perform their duty, and depart.
- The detailed instructions on setup and cleanup.
- The micro-events that are scheduled to occur during the course of an event, such as a toast, skit, or performance of some sort.
- A list of the procession and recession lineups for the wedding ceremony.

FINAL GUEST COMMUNICATIONS

Stay in communication with all your guests during the months and weeks leading up to the wedding. Your guests will no doubt receive their invitations with great anticipation, but the invitation, as lovely as it may be, should not be the last they hear from you. You can ensure that everything goes smoothly, particularly on the wedding day itself, by giving the issue of communication plenty of forethought.

INVITATIONS

As you wrap up the details for your wedding invitations, take time to finalize your guest list. You may have revised the list already, based on informal responses to your save-the-dates notices. Also consider what other stationery you want to add to the invitation order, such as programs, menus, and thank-you notes. Some items, like place cards, cannot be ordered until you get your RSVPs, but if you want to print them on coordinated stationery, you may have to order that now. For an efficient invitation operation, you'll need to:

APPROVE INVITATION DESIGN OR ORDER INVITATIONS
If you are working with a designer to customize your invitations, you will need to approve the design so your invitations can be printed. If you are ordering invitations from a printer, place your order.

ORDER OF *E*VENTS

FOR THE MARRIAGE OF   AND

ON

ARRIVALS AND NUMBERS

BRIDE AND GROOM ARRIVAL DATE:

BRIDE AND GROOM TO BRING:	○ GOWN AND TUXEDO	○ PAYMENT ENVELOPES
	○ RINGS	○ WELCOME LETTERS/GIFTS
	○ MARRIAGE LICENSE	○ WEDDING PARTY GIFTS

○ CEREMONY ITEMS (GUEST BOOK, PROGRAMS, ETC.):

○ RECEPTION ITEMS (SEATING CARDS, FLOOR PLAN, TABLE NUMBERS, ETC.):

○ OTHER:

WEDDING PLANNER ARRIVAL DATE:

| WEDDING PLANNER TO BRING: | ○ TOOL BOX | ○ FIRST-AID KIT |
| | ○ CEREMONY ITEMS: | |

○ RECEPTION ITEMS:

○ OTHER:

PARENTS ARRIVAL DATE(S):

GUESTS ARRIVAL DATE(S):

NUMBER OF GUESTS:

NUMBER OF SERVICE PROVIDERS TO EAT:

ACCOMMODATIONS

GUEST ACCOMMODATIONS:

(ADDRESS AND PHONE)

BRIDE'S QUARTERS: PHONE:

GROOM'S QUARTERS: PHONE:

PARENTS' QUARTERS: PHONE:

WELCOME LETTERS AND GIFTS:

WHAT WILL BE INCLUDED IN LETTER/GIFT:

WHO WILL ASSEMBLE:

WHO WILL DELIVER AND WHEN:

WEDDING REHEARSAL AND REHEARSAL DINNER

WEDDING REHEARSAL TIME AND LOCATION:

TO REVIEW AT REHEARSAL:

- ○ PARKING
- ○ FLOWERS
- ○ CEREMONY
- ○ OTHER:

- ○ SEATING
- ○ PROCESSION
- ○ RECESSION AND GET-AWAY

ITEMS TO GIVE WEDDING
PLANNER AT REHEARSAL:

- ○ PROGRAMS
- ○ FAVORS
- ○ GUEST BOOK
- ○ FLOOR PLAN
- ○ FINAL PAYMENT CHECKS IN ENVELOPES
- ○ OTHER:

- ○ SEATING ARRANGEMENTS
- ○ SEATING CARDS
- ○ CAKE TOPPER AND CAKE KNIFE
- ○ TOASTING GLASSES

REHEARSAL DINNER TIME AND LOCATION:

CEREMONY

CEREMONY TIME AND LOCATION:

CEREMONY DÉCOR SET UP:

FLORIST:	RENTALS:
WHEN:	WHEN:
WHAT:	WHAT:

DECORATOR:	RENTALS:
WHEN:	WHEN:
WHAT:	WHAT:

CEREMONY ARRIVALS:

THE WEDDING PARTY

BRIDE	WHEN:
	HOW:
BRIDESMAIDS	WHEN:
	HOW:
GROOM	WHEN:
	HOW:
GROOMSMEN	WHEN:
	HOW:
PARENTS	WHEN:
	HOW:

GUESTS	WHEN:
	HOW:

SERVICE PROVIDERS

    OFFICIANT: WHEN:

    MUSICIAN(S):   WHEN:

    PHOTOGRAPHER: WHEN:

        PRE-CEREMONY SHOTS:

            WHEN:

            WHERE:

        POST-CEREMONY SHOTS:

            WHEN:

            WHERE:

    OTHER: WHEN:

ORDER OF CEREMONY:

    PRELUDE MUSIC   WHEN:

    GROOM AND GROOMSMEN LINE UP   WHEN:

    BRIDE AND BRIDESMAIDS LINE UP   WHEN:

    PROCESSIONAL   WHEN:

    SEATING OF GRANDPARENTS, PARENTS, AND GUESTS OF HONOR   WHEN:

    PROCESSION OF BRIDAL PARTY

    CEREMONY

    RECEIVING LINE

        WHO:

        WHERE:

RECEPTION

    RECEPTION TIME AND LOCATION:

    RECEPTION DÉCOR SET UP:

        FLORIST: RENTALS:

            WHEN: WHEN:

            WHAT: WHAT:

        DECORATOR: RENTALS:

            WHEN: WHEN:

            WHAT: WHAT:

    RECEPTION ARRIVALS:

        CATERER: ENTERTAINMENT:

            WHEN: WHEN:

            WHERE: WHERE:

    WEDDING PARTY

        WHEN:

        WHO IS TO BE ANNOUNCED, IN ORDER:

COCKTAIL HOUR:

    WHEN:

    WHERE:

    ENTERTAINMENT:

    BEVERAGE INSTRUCTIONS: ○ OPEN   ○ CASH

WELCOME ANNOUNCEMENT:

    WHEN:

    WHO:

TOAST(S):

    WHEN:

    WHO:

BLESSING:

    WHEN:

    WHO:

DINNER:

    WHEN:

    DINNER MUSIC/ENTERTAINMENT:

DANCES:

    FIRST DANCE:

        WHEN:

        TITLE/ARTIST:

    FOLLOWING DANCES:

        FATHER/DAUGHTER DANCE:

        MOTHER/SON DANCE:

        WEDDING PARTY DANCE:

        OTHERS:

WEDDING CAKE CUTTING:

    WHEN:

BOUQUET TOSS:

    WHEN:

GARTER TOSS:

    WHEN:

BRIDE AND GROOM'S DEPARTURE:

    WHEN:

    HOW:

If you plan to hire a calligrapher, reserve his services early. Because of the additional preparation involved in a destination wedding, you will want to be ready to address and send your invitations the moment you receive them from the printer or designer. Get them in the mail two to three months in advance so guests have time to respond and you have time to finish planning with a final guest list in hand.

COORDINATE RSVPS

Set your RSVP date at least one month before the wedding—maybe two if you need your numbers well in advance. Do not wait on those stragglers who do not reply by the RSVP date; have someone call them to see what their intentions are. As people RSVP, make sure they have made their travel reservations. Once their travel plans are made, you can feel confident of their attendance. This may be your last chance to review your guests' accommodation plans. Confirm where people are planning to stay so you can coordinate welcome packages and transportation as necessary.

At this time, you can refine your guest list and draft your seating plan(s) for the wedding, which can be recorded in the guest database. Do not wait until the last minute to determine the seating arrangement. It may be one of the most tedious tasks, but you are the best judge of where, and next to whom, your guests should sit for the most lively and enjoyable results. Take care when drafting the arrangement; it can be quite embarrassing to realize you have forgotten to include a guest in the seating plans.

FINAL GUEST UPDATES

As guests respond to your invitations, send out a final update letter featuring the trip itinerary as well as travel and packing tips. (For a suggested list of tips, see chapter four, page 88.) If you have a Web site, update it with the same information. Do not wait too long to send and/or post the update, or you may find yourself inundated with questions from anxious guests. Also prepare welcome letters and any other correspondence you'd like to have waiting for your guests upon their arrival. Will you be giving your guests "Daily Ditties," brief memos outlining each day's activities? If so, print, copy, and pack these ahead of time. Or, to allow for any last-minute changes, you can plan to print the ditties on a daily basis at your destination; only choose this option if you have someone to do the work for you and you know for certain that the necessary equipment will be available for your use.

WEDDING DAY COMMUNICATIONS

With your finalized guest list, menu, and order of events in hand, you can finish any guest communications you are planning for your wedding day. Printed material, including programs, seating cards, and menus, will ensure clear communication and facilitate a smooth flow of events.

The program provides the details of your wedding ceremony. It should include the couple's names, date of the wedding, location, order of the ceremony events, readings, and music, as well as the names of the officiant, readers, and soloist(s). You can also include the names of the parents, grandparents, wedding party, and other musicians if you wish. Sometimes couples use the program to thank their guests, acknowledge special people who have lent a hand, or remember absent loved ones. In addition, you may want to mention the reception time and place with directions or instructions about transportation.

There are many ways to inform people where and with whom they will sit at the reception, the most common being seating charts and seating cards. Seating charts are most effective when they are organized in alphabetical order by last name, with printing large enough to read from a short distance. If you have a group of 50 to 100, make two identical charts to expedite the seating process. If you have even more guests, break up the alphabet and have two charts positioned apart from each other. Seating or escort cards come in all shapes and forms. These cards can be a nice way to present the guest favors as well. I have seen cards incorporated into little boxes of candy, silver bud vases, and miniature lanterns. If you set up the cards outside, attach them to a favor or affix them to the table so they do not blow away. Have the attendants or butlers assist with the seating process. Equipped with a printout of the seating arrangement and a copy of the floor plan, they can direct guests and deal with any problems. Also, give the tables names or numbers so guests can easily find the table you reference on the seating card or chart.

For the menus, allow the chef to give you the text; she is sure to provide mouth-watering descriptions of the day's fare. You can prepare one menu per table or one per person. Accent the menu with your monogram or some aspect of the wedding theme or, for a simple but elegant look, tuck the menu into folded napkins along with a sprig of thyme or lavender. (Some

INCORPORATING YOUR WEDDING THEME

The printed material for your wedding day can all be tied together using your chosen theme. A couple getting married in the Adirondacks might design the program, seating cards, and menu with a mountain theme and name each guest table at the reception for a mountain peak. Or, for an English country wedding, the theme might be an English garden, with each table named for an herb. The printed matter is all part of your unique wedding design, so be sure the photographer gets a shot of each, and save a few to frame or put in a memory book.

people wrap the tucked menus with ribbon and flowers; this is not necessarily the best option for a budget-conscious couple.) You do not need to include the hors d'oeuvres on the menu, since your guests will have already eaten those by the time they read the menu.

FINALIZING AND CONFIRMING YOUR ITINERARY

The process of confirming begins one month before the wedding, once you have determined the final guest count and established the final order of events. Proceed through this checklist to make sure you've taken all the final steps.

HAVE YOU FINALIZED ARRANGEMENTS TO OBTAIN A MARRIAGE LICENSE?

Check one last time with the consulate, wedding planner, or officiant to verify you are on track to get your marriage license. Pack all the necessary documents and extra photocopies of the documents to make the final application at the destination.

HAVE YOU CONFIRMED ALL TRAVEL PLANS?

Confirm your airline tickets, seat assignments, and time by which you need to be at the airport. If you are driving to your destination, make sure your directions are in order. Also confirm your accommodation reservations. If you negotiated a block on a group of rooms, make sure you've released the rooms you will not need.

HAVE YOU FINALIZED AND DISTRIBUTED THE ORDER OF EVENTS?

At this point, the order of events should include every detail from the moment you embark on your trip to the moment you leave for your honeymoon or return home. You should be able to identify any discrepancies in the order of events, with enough time to fix any problems. Keep the master copy for you and the wedding coordinator, and make sure service providers and pertinent guests are given finalized copies of their specific versions.

HAVE YOU CONFIRMED WITH ALL SERVICE PROVIDERS?

Three weeks before the wedding, begin confirming all the service providers via phone, e-mail, or fax. Provide them with the final guest count and their copy of the order of events. Be persistent, as it may take a week to make contact in some instances. Remember that the service is not confirmed until you make actual contact and they confirm receipt of that confirmation! Be sure to ask if they have any special needs, problems, or questions. You'll want to verify:

- The services you are expecting
- The date(s) and times of the events
- The address and phone number of the location as well as directions to it
- How and when they expect their final payment
- Their mobile phone numbers so you can reach them the day of the wedding

Update your service provider sheet with any notes you may have taken when confirming, then make the service provider list into one single sheet for easy reference on the wedding day. I find it helpful to enter each location and service provider number into my mobile phone before I depart as part of the confirmation process. Also tweak your budget and guest list with any updated information. Check to see that your planning binder is in good order, with all the contracts inside. (It's not a bad idea to bring copies of the contracts and leave the originals at home in case you lose the binder.) You might go through and lighten your load a bit by tossing papers, notes, and lists that are no longer relevant. Finally, make sure the information on your wedding Web site is accurate and up-to-date.

HAVE YOU FINALIZED THE SEATING PLAN?
Once you have heard from the last guest, submit your seating plan and floor plan to the banquet manager. He will be able to coordinate the table and chair arrangement with your plans. Make a point to handle this before you depart for the trip, or you and the coordinator will go mad trying to deal with it on-site.

FINAL DETAILS

Months and months of planning, design, and dreaming for the big day have passed. You've confirmed all your plans, and now you are approaching the finish line! Take some time to reflect on any final details that need attention, including your personal, home, and work concerns.

FINAL PAYMENTS

Before you depart, organize all your final payments in separate envelopes. You may not have final invoices for some of them, such as the florist or the caterer, but put an envelope aside with the estimated payment enclosed. Don't forget to include extra money for tips and incidentals, alloting extra cash for tipping in case someone goes out of her way to help. Although it might seem easier to pay in full in advance, I recommend waiting to make final payments until after the event, when you are sure that each service provider has delivered as promised.

PACKING FOR THE WEDDING TRIP

While I've made several suggestions for what to pack for the wedding trip, you will ultimately determine exactly what items you'll need. But, regardless of what you include in your bags and suitcases, do not forget these very important things:

 • The wedding gown. If possible, have the designer or salon pack the gown to fit in a small garment bag or box that can be carried onto the plane.

© THE ST. LUCIA TOURIST BOARD

• The marriage license documents. You can do without anything else, but you must have your documents if you want a legal marriage at the destination. If you forget them, stay calm—you can make it official when you get home.

• An international mobile phone, a first aid kit, a laptop computer, and printer, along with extra ink, paper, discs, and adaptor. If you have hired a wedding coordinator, she should be responsible for bringing these items.

YOUR ARRIVAL AT YOUR DESTINATION

The couple and/or the wedding coordinator should arrive a few days in advance of the guests to take care of business, confirm all of the service providers again in person, and go over the details one last time.

When you arrive at your destination you will want to conduct a final team meeting with the on-site wedding coordinator (if you have one), the location manager (or the rental company supplying the tent), the caterer or banquet manager, and possibly the floral designer or decorator. The most effective approach is to start at the ceremony location and progress to the reception location, following your vision of how the day should unfold. Walk through your plans for the ceremony and reception, making sure that each team member clearly understands your expectations. At this meeting you will verify arrival and setup times, setup tasks, the order of events, a backup plan for inclement weather, and cleanup instructions. This meeting is not only a final review of responsibilities but also a good preparation for smooth team dynamics, which will make the wedding day less stressful and more enjoyable for *everybody* involved.

Meet with your officiant right away to make sure all the steps have been taken to be legally married. In addition, you should also meet with, or at least call, the other service providers, including the photographer, the pastry chef, and the beauty stylist, to confirm the details.

If your gown needs steaming, take care of this task as soon as you arrive. Do not take your gown to just anyone; make sure they have been highly recommended as trustworthy and competent. Arrange and confim when to pick up your gown and any tuxedo rentals.

Before your guests arrive, assemble your welcome packages/baskets. If a few friends have arrived early, why not have a wrapping or basket-making party, complete with a nice bottle of wine to share? When you are finished, deliver the baskets and any welcome letters to your guests' rooms.

TAKING THE TIME TO RELAX

Remember what you first imagined your wedding might be? It was a lot of work to make your dream a reality, but the only task left now is to *enjoy* the fruits of your labor. Try to spend the day before the guests arrive relaxing and pampering yourself. Do whatever makes you look and feel your best. Some couples choose to spend a quiet afternoon alone together. You may want to get a massage, facial, manicure, and pedicure. During your wedding trip, take every opportunity you can to revel in the moment, knowing that your careful planning has paid off. It wasn't easy bringing all of the elements together, but you did it. And you've designed a remarkable, once-in-a-lifetime way to celebrate your wedding.

LOOKING AHEAD

I've tried to provide you with enough planning information to make your wedding trip and wedding day stress-free, as it should be. Some details may have seemed overwhelming along the way, but your thoroughness and attention to detail should now translate into confidence and relaxation.

The best advice I can give you now is to go with the flow. Offer your concerns, expectations, and worries up to the destination "wedding gods," and just enjoy whatever happens. You have done everything you could to make your wedding perfect; enjoy and appreciate the perfection that unfolds. Congratulations, and cheers!

part Two
THE DESTINATIONS

If you could be married anywhere in the world, where would you choose? Part II will not only help you determine the perfect destination for your wedding but will also provide you with all the resources you will need to make your dreams a reality. In this section, you will be introduced to a wide variety of destinations all across the globe. You will find popular destinations that are tried-and-true as well as exciting possibilities that remain relatively undiscovered. Be sure to use the resources offered in this section and in the Appendix (pages 370–375) to investigate the full range of locations and venues.

Part II is divided into six sections: North America; Central America, South America, and the Caribbean; Europe; Africa; Asia; and Oceania. Each section includes several countries, and each country features a few different regions. All the countries (and some regions) are broken down in the same manner with identical headings, so you can easily follow and compare information when trying to narrow down your choices. Every entry begins with a map and a brief description of the country, which typically includes a general comment on the climate. (For more in-depth information on the climate, consult the destination's tourism bureau.) After the map and description, there is an assortment of details broken down in the following manner:

COUNTRY OVERVIEW

Here you'll find information on the country's currency, tipping customs, international calling codes, and electricity.

CURRENCY: THIS SIMPLY GIVES THE NAME OF THE CURRENCY USED IN THE COUNTRY; TO FIND WEB SITES THAT PROVIDE THE LATEST CURRENCY EXCHANGE RATES, REFER TO THE APPENDIX. **TIPPING CUSTOMS:** BY FAMILIARIZING YOURSELF WITH THE COUNTRY'S TIPPING CUSTOMS, YOU WILL BE PREPARED WITH THE RIGHT AMOUNT OF CASH AND WILL AVOID OFFENDING ANYONE INADVERTANTLY. IN SOME COUNTRIES, SERVICE PROVIDERS RELY SOLELY ON TIPS FOR INCOME. THE LAST THING YOU WANT TO DO IS NEGLECT TO PAY THOSE WHO PROVIDE THE HELP YOU NEED ON YOUR WEDDING DAY. FOR ADDITIONAL INFORMATION ON TIPPING IN DIFFERENT COUNTRIES, VISIT HTTP://TRAVEL .DISCOVERY.COM/TIPS/INTERNATIONAL/TIPPING.HTML. **INTERNATIONAL CALLING CODE:** EVERY COUNTRY HAS AN INTERNATIONAL CALLING CODE. WHEN YOU ARE OUTSIDE OF THE COUNTRY, YOU NEED TO DIAL THE COUNTRY CODE AND THEN THE CITY CODE (AREA CODE) BEFORE THE NUMBER. IF YOU ARE CALLING FROM THE UNITED STATES, REMEMBER: WHEN CALLING THOSE COUNTRIES WITH AN INTERNATIONAL CALLING CODE OF "1," SUCH AS CANADA AND BERMUDA, SIMPLY DIAL 1 BEFORE ENTERING THE PHONE NUMBER. WHEN CALLING A COUNTRY WITH A CODE OTHER THAN "1," YOU MUST ALWAYS DIAL 011 BEFORE ENTERING THE INTERNATIONAL CALLING CODE AND SUBSEQUENT NUMBER. IF YOU NEED TO FIND A COUNTRY CODE OR CITY CODE, VISIT HTTP://COUNTRY

CALLINGCODES.COM. FOR ASSISTANCE, YOU CAN CALL THE INTERNATIONAL OPERATOR BY DIALING 00. WHEN MAKING PHONE CALLS TO OTHER PARTS OF THE GLOBE, CHECK THE TIME ZONE OF YOUR COUNTRY; THERE IS A MAP OF TIME ZONES AFTER THE APPENDIX. **ELECTRICITY:** ELECTRICITY IS EITHER 110/120V OR 220/240V. BE AWARE OF THE KINDS OF ELECTRICAL SOCKETS USED IN THE COUNTRY. MANY LUXURY HOTELS AND RESORTS PROVIDE HAIRDRYERS, BUT YOU MAY NEED TO BRING AN ADAPTER FOR OTHER APPLICANCES. BE CAREFUL—I HAVE A COUSIN WHO PLUGGED HER CURLING IRON INTO AN INCOMPATIBLE SOCKET AND SINGED HER HAIR!

PLANNING NOTES

In this section, you'll find information on the legal requirements for getting a marriage license as well as the options for wedding ceremonies.

SUGGESTED ASSISTANCE: Marriage laws range from simple and straightforward to complex and overwhelming. Check this section to see what kind of assistance, if any, is recommended in obtaining your marriage license and planning a ceremony in the chosen country.

SPECIAL REQUIREMENTS: Included in this section is the **RESIDENCY REQUIREMENT** and **WAITING PERIOD** for getting the marriage license. No matter where you plan to marry, you'll need to meet the country's entry requirements, provide identification, and prove you are free to be married. Some countries require a visa in addition to a passport, and sometimes you have to get specific immunizations. You can generally get this information from the consulate or embassy, either on their Web sites or by calling them directly. If you are divorced, you will have to show your divorce decree, and if you are a widow you will have to present the death certificate. You will most likely have to have these documents translated as well. Under the heading **SPECIAL NOTES**, there is additional information that couples need to know about other marriage requirements, such as blood tests or physicals.

CIVIL CEREMONIES: Some countries require civil ceremonies and others do not. Check here for this information and to find out what kind of restrictions are placed on civil ceremonies, such as those regarding location and officiants.

RELIGIOUS CEREMONIES: This section includes general options or local resources for major world religions, including Christianity, Judaism, Islam, Buddhism, and Hinduism, as well as nondenominational options. To research Buddhist resources worldwide, check www.buddhanet.net, a Buddhist information and education network. To locate mosques, officiants, and other Muslim resources, visit www.islamicfinder.org, a comprehensive Web site for Islam. And to find Hindu temples, look on the Temples Reference Center Web site, www.mandirnet.org. In general, it is advisable to contact your local religious leader or house of worship if you need help planning a religious ceremony abroad.

DESIGN IDEAS

Each destination has its own culture, customs, traditions, and cuisine, all of which can be incorporated into your wedding celebration. In this section, you'll find design ideas for planning a celebration that reflects the chosen destination, with inspiration for guests' welcome baskets, venue decorations, local wedding traditions and attire, the wedding meal, and reception entertainment.

PLANNING RESOURCES

This section provides the most important contacts you will need to research and plan a wedding. These include:

EMBASSY AND GOVERNMENT OFFICES: I recommend that you first contact the embassy or consulate to confirm entry and marriage requirements and to set up a meeting, if necessary. You can find contact information for United States embassies and consulates online at http://usembassy.state.gov or www.americanembassy.com.

TOURISM: Next, go to the tourism Web sites. Read through the sites thoroughly to learn everything you can about the country and its wedding options. Tourism Web sites often offer travel and itinerary ideas, locations, and occasionally, marriage laws and customs. The tourism site should also provide details about the climate, how to get there, ground transportation options, and perhaps even a list of marriage officiants and places of worship. Be sure to order any literature from the Web site, and call the tourism office to ask if they have any additional information on weddings. They might even be willing to give personal recommendations for locations, service providers, or other destination wedding material. It is always nice to talk directly to an expert, especially when they offer free information! When you call, ask if you can get a case of brochures or anything else that you can include in your guests' welcome packages. You can find a tourism bureau anywhere in the world by visiting the Tourism Offices Worldwide Directory (www.towd.com).

PARKS, MONUMENTS, AND HISTORIC SITES: State parks and historical commissions are valuable resources when looking for ceremony and/or reception locations. Not only are many of these sites beautiful, they can be a bargain; sometimes the site fee is a tax-deductible donation. Be sure to find out how to reserve the site, how to get a permit, what it will cost, and what the rules and regulations are.

WEDDING RESOURCES: The destination's wedding associations, publications, and Web sites can provide helpful information and assistance. If you are planning a wedding in the United States, check out the Wedding Zone Nationwide Wedding Planning Directory (www.weddingzone.net).

VENUES

In this section, you'll read about some of the most interesting wedding locations the destination has to offer. A brief introduction provides an overview of several hotel, resort, and site options, along with the relevant contact information. Following the introduction, there are a few reviews that highlight some of the most promising venues. It was very difficult to select which wedding locations to review because there are often so many wonderful choices in any given destination. My aim was to present options that represent a range of price, style, and atmosphere. For each review, I collected information from personal experience and from promotional materials provided by the venues. You'll find this information presented in the following format:

NAME OF VENUE

address

Web site

telephone number

SIZE: THE VENUE'S SIZE IS GENERALLY LISTED IN ACRES. **NUMBER OF ROOMS:** THIS INFORMATION IS ONLY LISTED FOR VENUES THAT PROVIDE LODGING, SUCH AS HOTELS, INNS, AND RESORTS; COMPARE THE NUMBER OF ROOMS WITH THE VENUE'S SIZE TO GET A SENSE OF HOW BIG THE PROPERTY IS. **WHEELCHAIR ACCESSIBLE:** THIS INFORMATION IS CRUCIAL IF YOU WILL BE HAVING GUESTS WHO ARE CONFINED TO A WHEELCHAIR. **RATES:** EACH VENUE HAS BEEN RATED A $, $$, OR $$$, BASED ON THE SCALE DESCRIBED ON THE NEXT PAGE. **SPECIAL NOTES:** THIS SECTION, WHICH

ADDRESSES THE ISSUES OF CHILDREN AND NONTRADITIONAL COUPLES, ONLY APPEARS WHEN WAR-
RANTED. VENUES HAVE DIFFERENT POLICIES ON CHILDREN. IF THERE ARE CHILDREN ON YOUR GUEST
LIST OR IN YOUR WEDDING PARTY, YOU WILL WANT TO KNOW UP FRONT IF THEY WILL BE WELCOME.
I NOTED ANY AGE REQUIREMENTS OR SPECIAL SERVICES FOR CHILDREN. SOME VENUES ARE OPEN
TO SINGLE-SEX UNIONS, WHILE OTHERS THAT ADVERTISE "COUPLES" REFER TO ONLY HETEROSEX-
UAL COUPLES. (SOME DO NOT EVEN ALLOW A MOTHER AND DAUGHTER TO STAY ON THE PROPERTY!)

REVIEW: The review provides a general overview of the property and what it has to offer.
CEREMONY OPTIONS: This section describes possible ceremony sites on the property.
RECEPTION OPTIONS: This section, sometimes combined with the "Ceremony Options"
 section, describes reception rooms and other locations on the property.
WEDDING SERVICES: This section gives you a sense of how much on-site assistance the
 venue provides, including planning, decorating, and coordinating the events.

There's a lot of information on the following pages, so fasten your seatbelt and prepare for a whirlwind tour of some of the most amazing wedding destinations and sites
the world has to offer! Open your mind, dream big, and enjoy!

THE RATING SYSTEM

Room rates are charged by inns and hotels. At some venues, they charge only for the rooms
and not separately for the site but, to do so, they may require full occupancy or a minimum
number of rooms to be taken. Rates below are per room, per night:
$ = $150 or less
$$ = $150 to $500
$$$ = more than $500

Site fees are charged to rent a private property, a public/nonprofit property, and sometimes, a
banquet room in a hotel. Often a location will charge a site fee for the ceremony site, primarily for the setup and breakdown costs.
$ = less than $1,500
$$ = $1,500 to $3,000
$$$ = more than $3,000

Catering fees might be the only fees charged in venues such as restaurants. The rates below
are per person.
$ = $75 or less
$$ = $75 to $150
$$$ = $150 or more

After analyzing each venue's rates and fees, I assigned them a $ bracket. In some instances,
I found that the season makes a drastic difference in the rates, which is something to consider if you want a luxury venue but cannot afford to pay their high-season rates. Some larger properties fall into all three brackets because they have accommodations for every price
range; these venues are worth considering, as they allow you to put up the entire wedding
party regardless of budget. Some of the properties charge room rates, site fees, and catering
fees, and sometimes all three fees fall into different brackets. Nevertheless, the rating system
should give you a general sense of prices.

north america

If there is one experience that is universally celebrated with great hope and joy, it is the moment when two people officially declare their love and pledge their commitment to one another. In North America, a continent characterized by diversity, you'll find endless ways and countless places to celebrate this experience. Destination weddings in North America are as unique and imaginative as the brides and grooms who plan them. You will find couples declaring "I do!" in helicopters and hot-air balloons, in regal hotels and romantic bed and breakfasts, in churches and drive-in chapels, in national parks and amusement parks. And you'll always find a wedding party celebrating the newlyweds' nuptials in true North American style— by noisily honking their car horns! There is boisterous honking from bustling Boston to hilly San Francisco, from majestic Niagara Falls to the colossal Grand Canyon, from Old Montreal streets to sleepy Texas border towns. If you are having trouble pinpointing the destination of your dreams, use the information on the following pages to decide how and where you want your wedding to take place.

"Ohhhhhh, Canada!..." Canada is definitely worth singing about, especially when you discover all it has to offer. There are high peaks, pristine lakes, natural wildlife, hot springs, impressive glaciers, gorgeous islands, Native American culture, historic castles, luxury hotels, cosmopolitan cities—the list goes on and on. Canada boasts European elegance, rugged natural beauty, and multicultural diversity, all within an international destination that is not too distant, foreign, or costly. It's no wonder Canadians are so friendly—they live in a wonderful land that is one of the world's best-kept secrets. If you are dreaming of an outdoor wedding celebration in Canada, plan on marrying between May and October.

COUNTRY OVERVIEW

CURRENCY: CANADIAN DOLLAR **TIPPING:** WAIT STAFF AND TAXI DRIVERS GET 15% AND PORTERS GET $1 (CANADIAN) PER BAG. **ELECTRICITY:** 110V **INTERNATIONAL CALLING CODE:** 1

PLANNING NOTES

SUGGESTED ASSISTANCE: It is important to know the marriage laws of the province in which you plan to marry, as the laws vary in complexity. Contact the Office of Vital Statistics in your chosen province or refer to the Canadian government's Web site (www.canada.gc.ca) for details.

SPECIAL REQUIREMENTS: RESIDENCY REQUIREMENT: None **WAITING PERIOD:** Some provinces have long waiting periods, which means you will have to plan on arriving early enough to accommodate the wait. **SPECIAL NOTES:** Call ahead to see if you need an appointment to get the license. The couple will have to prove their identity with a passport or birth certificate, and they will have to verify that they are free to be married with proof of age, a divorce decree, or former spouse's death certificate. On the wedding day, the officiant will complete the marriage registration form and, within 48 hours, send it to the Vital Statistics Agency, where the marriage is registered and a legal record is kept. The officiant may provide you with a statement of marriage, which can be used until the Vital Statistics Agency sends you the official marriage certificate. Canada is known for being one of the most liberal countries regarding same-sex marriage. Be aware that, although it is legal in some provinces, a same-sex marriage may not be legally recognized in your home country.

CIVIL CEREMONIES: Civil ceremonies are not required. In some provinces, there are restrictions on where civil ceremonies can be held. A list of all registered officiants is available from the Office of Vital Statistics in each province.

RELIGIOUS CEREMONIES: Religious ceremonies, while not required, can be performed by any registered religious officiant. You should be able to find what you are looking for in most large cities. A list of all registered religious marriage officiants is available at the Office of Vital Statistics in each province.

DESIGN IDEAS

Canada's identity is steeped in its Celtic, French, and Native American heritage, all of which may easily be adopted as a wedding theme. You can also design your wedding décor around the theme of nature or adventure. In the spirit of the adventurous daredevils who took the plunge over Niagara Falls in barrels, why not add a little fun and decorate your venue with wine and beer barrels of varying sizes? For your wedding florals, consider an indigenous bouquet with wild roses, dogwood, mayflowers, arctic poppies, lady's slippers, and violets. Ammolite, a lovely gem found only in Alberta, comes in a variety of colors—yellow, orange, red, and (rarely) blue—that change with the the light. It would be perfect for the groom's cuff links or the bride's jewelry.

The wedding celebration should include a menu of Canada's delectable local dishes. Two dishes of note are rapee pie, an Acadian dish made of chicken and potatoes, and smoked or planked salmon cooked on a cedar shingle. If you are a little more adventurous, incorporate a taste of caribou, venison, or bison. Your guests might be disappointed if you didn't provide Canadian beer—some of the best in the world—to wash down the meal. For entertainment, liven up the crowd with some French-Canadian folk music, sometimes referred to as Acadian music, or the beat of a Native American drum.

PLANNING RESOURCES

EMBASSY AND GOVERNMENT OFFICES:
Embassy of Canada (in the United States)
501 Pennsylvania Avenue NW, Washington DC 20001
www.canadianembassy.org
202-682-1740 / 202-682-7705

Embassy of the United States (in Canada)
490 Sussex Drive, Ottawa, Ontario, Canada, K1N 1G8
www.usembassycanada.gov
613-238-5335 / Consular Service: 613-238-5335

TOURISM:
Canadian Tourism Commission
55 Metcalfe Street, Suite 600, Ottawa, Ontario, Canada K1P 6L5
www.travelcanada.ca
613-946-1000

PARKS, MONUMENTS, AND HISTORIC SITES:
Kanada News / 1001 National Parks of Canada
301-315 Sherbrooke Street, New Westminster, BC, Canada V3L 3M4
www.national-parks-canada.com
604-517-1792

National Parks of Canada
25 Eddy Street, Gatineau, Quebec, Canada K1A 0M5
www.pc.gc.ca
888-773-8888

WEDDING RESOURCES:

HELPFUL PUBLICATIONS:
WeddingBells Canada: www.weddingbells.ca

WEDDING WEB SITES:
Canadian Bride: www.canadianbride.com
Canadian Rockies Wedding Planning:
   www.canadianrockies.net/weddings

© MALCOLM CARMICHAEL

NOVA SCOTIA

Nova Scotia, the easternmost province of Canada, has breathtaking shores, towering cliffs, peaceful beaches, and picturesque bays. It is easy to relax in the serene environs of Nova Scotia, especially if you enjoy outdoor activities such as hiking, biking, and whale- and bird-watching. Two islands worth visiting are Cape Breton, voted the most beautiful island in the world by *Condé Nast Traveler*, and Prince Edward Island. Avid golfers will no doubt want to make the trip to Cape Breton, where they'll find the best golf course in Canada, Highlands Links (800-441-1118 / www.highlandslinksgolf.com). And for literary fans, Prince Edward Island provided the rural, idyllic setting for the book *Anne of Green Gables*, whose main character is nothing short of a hopeless romantic. Nova Scotia is also home to Peggy's Cove, a small fishing village filled with charm and character. The quaint lighthouse, perched on a rocky shoreline, makes the village an ideal spot for wedding photographs.

PLANNING NOTES

SUGGESTED ASSISTANCE: Contact the Office of Vital Statistics (902-424-5200) for information on marriage laws in Nova Scotia.

SPECIAL REQUIREMENTS: WAITING PERIOD: Five days **SPECIAL NOTES:** You must obtain your license at least five days before the wedding. To do so, contact the deputy issuer of marriage licenses of the town in which you plan to marry. Deputy issuers are not located in government buildings; for a list of deputy issuers in Nova Scotia, go to www.gov.ns.ca. Two witnesses are required.

CIVIL CEREMONIES: To find a Justice of the Peace, ask the deputy issuer or go to www.gov.ns.ca.

RELIGIOUS CEREMONIES: There are several Christian churches throughout Nova Scotia. For a list of synagogues, check with the Atlantic Jewish Council (902-422-7491 / www.theajc.ns.ca). To find a Buddhist officiant, refer to http://buddhismcanada.com/ns.html. Couples from other faiths may find their options more limited in smaller towns and islands. To find an officant, you may have to seek help in Halifax.

PLANNING RESOURCES

TOURISM:
Novia Scotia Department of Tourism, Culture and Heritage
P.O. Box 456, Halifax, Nova Scotia, Canada B3J 2R5
www.novascotia.com
800-565-0000

VENUES

Whether you love the sea, wildlife, history or Celtic culture, you'll find a multitude of choices when selecting a venue in Nova Scotia. The region promises picturesque weddings, with its coastline and islands providing stunning scenery and beautiful backdrops. Nova Scotia, meaning "New Scotland," was once the gateway to Canada for Scottish immigrants, who found the sea islands and verdant highlands to be much like those of their homeland. Many of these immigrants arrived in Halifax at the **HISTORIC PIER 21** (902-

425-7770 / www.pier21.ca). Today, the pier is a national historic site and museum, offering a lovely wedding spot that overlooks the harbor. For those couples that can't resist the romantic call of the sea, **THE TALL SHIP SILVA** (902-429-9463 / www.tallshipsilva.com) hosts unforgettable wedding celebrations undersail from Halifax Harbour.

KELTIC LODGE ON CAPE BRETON ISLAND
Middle Head Peninsula, Ingonish Beach, Nova Scotia, Canada B0C 1L0
www.signatureresorts.com
800-565-0444 / 902-285-2880

SIZE: MAIN LODGE, INN, AND LARGE GUEST COTTAGES **NUMBER OF ROOMS:** 32 GUEST ROOMS AND 2 TWO-BEDROOM SUITES IN THE MAIN LODGE; 40 GUEST ROOMS, SOME WITH FIREPLACES, IN THE INN; 10 TWO- OR FOUR-BEDROOM COTTAGES **WHEELCHAIR ACCESSIBLE:** ALL FACILITIES BUT THE GUEST ROOMS IN THE MAIN LODGE **RATES:** $$ **SPECIAL NOTES:** ROOM COMPLIMENTARY FOR CHILDREN 17 YEARS AND UNDER WHEN SHARING THE ROOM WITH PARENTS. FOOD 50% OFF FOR CHILDREN AGES 4–12 YEARS AND COMPLIMENTARY FOR CHILDREN 3 YEARS AND UNDER

REVIEW: Perched on the cliffs of Middle Head Peninsula, the Keltic Lodge is a unique and beautiful resort overlooking the Atlantic Ocean. The lodge is located in Cape Breton Highlands National Park, neighboring the famed Highlands Links Golf Course. Charming rustic elegance characterizes the rooms, which are appointed with a double and a single bed or a queen-sized bed and, in some cases, a fireplace. Guests enjoy world-class cuisine featuring seafood delicacies and local gourmet delights. The Keltic Lodge has most recently been awarded the #3 Beach Hotel in North America by *Departures Magazine* and named one of the Top 700 Hotels and Resorts in the World by *Condé Nast Traveler*.

CEREMONY OPTIONS: Outdoor wedding ceremonies can be held in the gazebo, which overlooks the rugged coastline of Cape Smokey. An indoor ceremony for up to 200 guests can be held at the Ceilidh Hall.

RECEPTION OPTIONS: For a seated dinner, Ceilidh Hall accommodates a maximum of 140 guests.

WEDDING SERVICES: Provides catering and a list of preferred vendors.

QUEBEC

Many destination couples are attracted to the international flair of Quebec's cities. With their old-world charm and cosmopolitan style, Montreal and Quebec City offer visitors a decidedly European atmosphere. If you are unable to make a trip across the ocean but you've been hoping to capture the spirit of a European wedding, consider beautiful Quebec. Montreal, the second largest French-speaking city in the world, is actually an island located in the St. Lawrence River. There you can travel the cobblestone streets of Vieux-Port by horse-and-carriage and visit the quaint French restaurants and shops that line the old avenues. Or, if you prefer a more contemporary scene, you can explore the city's wide array of nightlife and entertainment options. Quebec City, situated on Cap Diamant overlooking the St. Lawrence River, is regarded as the cradle of French civilization in North America. Today, it is the capital of Quebec, a busy seaport, and a cultural hot spot. Quebec City is referred to as a natural citadel because of its location, and in 1985 it was declared a World Heritage Site by UNESCO as the only fortified city in North America. You can still walk the ramparts around the city and enjoy the view as you look down on the maze of narrow streets.

PLANNING NOTES

SUGGESTED ASSISTANCE: Contact the Office of Vital Statistics (418-643-3900) for information on marriage laws in Quebec.

SPECIAL REQUIREMENTS: WAITING PERIOD: 20 days SPECIAL NOTES: Ninety days prior to the ceremony, you must go to the court or place of worship where you intend to be married. There you must obtain a civil marriage form and interview with the Service des Marriages Civil or the officiant; the bride, groom, and a witness must attend the interview. Twenty days before the ceremony, the officiant must publish the banns, which entails posting a legal document at the intended ceremony site stating the couple's intention to marry; this ensures that nobody disagrees with the marriage. Two witnesses are required for the marriage ceremony. The marriage certificate must be in French or English.

CIVIL CEREMONIES: Civil ceremonies can be held only in the courthouse or the city (or town) hall.

RELIGIOUS CEREMONIES: Religious ceremonies may take place only in a house of worship. Christians and Jews should have no problem finding an officiant, and Muslims should be able to find an officiant easily in Montreal. For officiants and other resources, Buddhists can contact the Centre Bouddhiste Kankala (514-521-2529 / www.kankala.org/home.html).

© EMMANUEL VAUCHER

PLANNING RESOURCES

TOURISM:
Quebec Tourism / Tourisme Québec
P.O. Box 979, Montreal, Quebec, Canada H3C 2W3
www.bonjourquebec.com
877-266-5687 / 514-873-2015

VENUES

For an unforgettable experience in Quebec, plan a celebration at the **ICE HOTEL QUEBEC-CANADA** (877-505-0423 / www.icehotel-canada.com). Its unique wedding packages include nuptial ceremonies at an ice chapel—with fur cape and coat provided—followed by cocktails in the Absolut Ice Bar and festivities at the N'Ice Club. Another option is the elegant **FAIRMONT LE MANIOR RICHELIEU** (418-665-3703 / www.fairmont.com/richelieu), majestically perched on cliffs overlooking the St. Lawrence River. The Fairmont offers indoor and outdoor wedding ceremonies in a breathtaking and luxurious setting.

FAIRMONT LE CHÂTEAU FRONTENAC

1 Rue des Carrieres, Quebec City, Quebec, Canada G1R 4P5

www.fairmont.com/frontenac

800-257-7544 / 418-692-3861

SIZE: 18 FLOORS **NUMBER OF ROOMS:** 618 ROOMS, 21 SUITES, 55 "FAIRMONT GOLD" ROOMS **WHEELCHAIR ACCESSIBLE:** YES **RATES:** $$–$$$ **SPECIAL NOTES:** CHILDREN UNDER 18 FREE WHEN SHARING A ROOM WITH PARENTS

REVIEW: For over a century, Fairmont Le Château Frontenac has been the finest place to stay in Quebec City. Guests experience an unparalleled level of luxury, enjoying rooms with elegant chateau furnishings and regal décor reminiscent of historic Europe. Chef Jean Soulard, the first Canadian chef to receive the Maitre Cuisinier de France (Master Chef of France) award, presides over the hotel's legendary Le Champlain restaurant. Guests can also take in views of the St. Lawrence River from the two bars at the Château.

CEREMONY OPTIONS: The Salon Rose, located in one of the Château's many turrets, seats 80 guests. Outdoor ceremonies are often held at Governor's Park. The hotel's Web site provides a list of local churches, synagogues, and wedding officiants.

RECEPTION OPTIONS: You can choose from the Salon Rose or the Grand Ballroom, which seats up to 550 for dinner, bridal teas, and brunches. Alternative menus can be provided to accommodate guests with dietary restrictions.

WEDDING SERVICES: Wedding planning and coordinating services available.

ONTARIO

Ontario is home to Niagara Falls, a haven for honeymooners ever since 1804, when Jerome Bonaparte (Napoleon's younger brother) brought his new bride from Baltimore to see the natural wonder. Millions of visitors have chosen Niagara as their wedding or honeymoon destination, reveling in the majesty of the falls. With a "Cave of the Winds" tour (716-278-1730), visitors can climb down the sides and even walk behind the powerful cascading water. The Maid of the Mist (905-358-5781 / www.maidofthemist.com) offers boat rides into the horseshoe, where passengers find themselves surrounded by the thunderous falls. You can be married on the Maid of the Mist but you cannot reserve tickets, the boat, or space on the boat. For a bird's-eye view and a more unusual ceremony, couples can say "I do" as they fly over the falls aboard a helicopter (800-281-8034 / www.niagarahelicopters.com) or a tethered helium balloon (716-278-0824 / www.flightofangels.net). Niagara Falls are beautiful by night, when they are illumi-

nated by colored spotlights. Late-night vows can even be punctuated by a spectacular fireworks display over Horseshoe Falls, taking place on various evenings from May through September. Make time for a visit to Niagara-on-the-Lake, the "prettiest town in Canada," which outdoes itself each year with lovely flower displays.

PLANNING NOTES

SUGGESTED ASSISTANCE: Contact the Office of Vital Statistics (416-325-8305) for information on marriage laws in Ontario. For specific information regarding marriage at Niagara Falls, call Niagara City Hall (905-356-7521).

SPECIAL REQUIREMENTS: WAITING PERIOD: None **SPECIAL NOTES:** If you are planning a civil ceremony, you must apply for a marriage license by going to the municipal office in your chosen city or town. If you are planning a religious ceremony, you may be able to get married without a license, provided your officiant publishes the wedding banns. Be aware, however, that you can be married in a civil ceremony the same day you obtain the marriage license, while you must wait several weeks for the banns to be published before you can marry in a religious ceremony. If you are divorced and are not a Canadian citizen, you will have to hire a Canadian lawyer to assist in proving that your divorce is legal and in obtaining a marriage license; this may take some time, so plan accordingly. Two witnesses are required for the ceremony.

CIVIL CEREMONIES: Civil ceremonies must be performed either in the courthouse or in a clerk's office.

RELIGIOUS CEREMONIES: Ontario is extremely diverse, so you should not encounter any difficulties finding a religious officiant or church that suits you. For information on religious ceremonies in Niagara Falls, go to www.niagaraweddingscanada.com.

PLANNING RESOURCES

TOURISM:
OntarioTourism
Tenth Floor, Hearst Block, 900 Bay Street, Toronto, Ontario, Canada M7A 2E
www.ontariotravel.net
800-668-2746 / 416-326-9326

VENUES

Of the many wedding venues in Niagara Falls, one worth mentioning is the miniature **WAYSIDE CHAPEL** (866-645-1714), which claims to be the smallest operating church in the world with a maximum capacity of ten. It is a Christian Reformed church, but couples of other denominations are welcome.

NIAGARA FALLSVIEW WEDDINGS

Konica Minolta Tower Centre, 6732 Fallsview Boulevard,
Niagara Falls, Ontario, Canada L2G 3W6
www.niagara-fallsview-weddings.com
800-461-2492 / 866-325-5785

SIZE: 30 FLOORS (RAMADA PLAZA HOTEL FALLSVIEW); 15 FLOORS (RADISSON HOTEL & SUITES FALLSVIEW) **NUMBER OF ROOMS:** 42 (RAMADA); 232 (RADISSON) **WHEELCHAIR ACCESSIBLE:** YES **RATES:** $ **SPECIAL NOTES:** ASK ABOUT SPECIAL CHILD RATES

REVIEW: Panoramic Hospitality, Inc., the owner and operator of Niagara Fallsview Weddings, also owns the Konica Minolta Tower Centre, the Radisson Hotel & Suites Fallsview, and the Ramada Plaza Hotel Fallsview. The breathtaking views are what make their wedding packages so enticing, with accommodations, ceremonies, and receptions 525 feet above Niagara Falls. Worthy of note is the Ramada Plaza Hotel Fallsview, the sole boutique hotel in the Fallsview Resort district.

CEREMONY OPTIONS: A religious or nondenominational ceremony can be held in the chapel on Konica Minolta Tower's observation deck, which overlooks the falls.

RECEPTION OPTIONS: Receptions for up to 50 guests can be held in the Pinnacle Restaurant, located in the Konica Minolta Tower Centre. Cocktail receptions for up to 25 guests can be held in the Pinnacle Lounge.

WEDDING SERVICES: Complete wedding packages available.

THE NIAGARA PARKS COMMISSION

5881 Dunn Street, Niagara Falls, Ontario, Canada L2G 2N9
www.niagaraparks.com
877-642-7275

SIZE: THE COMMISSION MAINTAINS 4,250 ACRES OF PRISTINE PARK IN NIAGARA FALLS, INCLUDING 6 OUTDOOR WEDDING LOCATIONS **WHEELCHAIR ACCESSIBLE:** LIMITED **RATES:** $$

REVIEW: The Niagara Parks Commission puts the beauty of Niagara Falls at your fingertips. In addition to the Falls, the Commission oversees a butterfly conservatory, golf courses, and a heritage trail that features several historic sites.

CEREMONY AND RECEPTION OPTIONS: If you are planning an outdoor wedding, contact the Niagara Parks Commission to review your options. The Oakes Garden Theatre, which holds 30 guests, affords a view of Bridal Veil Falls. The lush Greenhouse Garden and the Botanical Gardens are both large enough for groups up to 150. Tucked away in a quiet corner of the gardens, Willow Pond accommodates 250. Two monuments, the Laura Secord Monument and the Mather Arch, provide nice backdrops for weddings. And for couples wanting a church wedding, Queenston Chapel is available for up to 100 guests. No reservations are needed for outdoor locations; however, a reservation and fee is required if you choose to have photos taken in the Greenhouse.

WEDDING SERVICES: The Parks Commission rents tents and chairs where possible.

ALBERTA

Alberta is Canada's mountain playground, dominated by the Canadian Rockies, glacier lakes, mountain streams, and massive ski resorts. It is where you can experience Native American culture, witness the largest herd of free-roaming bison, and spot many other species of mountain fauna. Alberta's mountain backdrops are awesome, providing picture-perfect scenery for an outdoor adventure or an elegant Alpine wedding.

PLANNING NOTES

SUGGESTED ASSISTANCE: Contact the Office of Vital Statistics (780-427-7013) for information on marriage laws in Alberta.

SPECIAL REQUIREMENTS: WAITING PERIOD: None **SPECIAL NOTES:** A marriage license can be purchased anytime before the ceremony (even the same day) from a registry

© THE FAIRMOUNT CHÂTEAU LAKE LOUISE

agent in your chosen town. Couples living outside of Alberta can make arrangements in advance through the Banff Bureau (403-762-2177 / www.banffbureau.com). Two witnesses over the age of 18 are required for the ceremony.

CIVIL CEREMONIES: There are no published restrictions on civil ceremonies.

RELIGIOUS CEREMONIES: In general, religious officiants are easily found; however, Buddhists, Muslims, and Hindus may have to look in Calgary and Edmonton.

PLANNING RESOURCES

TOURISM:
Travel Alberta Canada
P.O. Box 2500, Edmonton, Alberta, Canada T5J 2Z4
www.travelalberta.com
800-252-3782 / 780-427-4321

VENUES

For something a little out of the ordinary, contact **BANFF HUMMER BACKCOUNTRY TOURS** (403-760-4867 / www.banfflakelouiseweddings.com). Offering eco-adventure wedding options in the Rockies, Robin White and Karyn Faryna arrange and perform ceremonies and take care of the legal aspects. They transport you to the most picturesque (and unusual) wedding sites in southern Alberta, whether you want to arrive in a Hummer or helicopter, on horseback or motorcycle, by skis or dog sled, via Alpine hiking or white water rafting. They can even arrange a wedding at the Blackfoot Indian Reservation Village, complete with a campfire reception, Native American song and dance, and a blessing by the tribal elder.

FAIRMONT CHÂTEAU LAKE LOUISE
111 Lake Louise Drive, Lake Louise, Alberta, Canada ToL 1E0
www.fairmont.com/lakelouise
800-257-7544 / 403-522-3511

SIZE: 42 ACRES **NUMBER OF ROOMS:** 555 **WHEELCHAIR ACCESSIBLE:** YES **RATES:** $$–$$$ **SPECIAL NOTES:** CERTIFIED BABYSITTERS AND CHILDREN'S ACTIVITIES AVAILABLE. PLAYROOM AVAILABLE DURING WINTER MONTHS

REVIEW: The Fairmont Château Lake Louise is truly spectacular. Situated by a pristine lake and surrounded by dramatic mountains, its beauty seems almost mythical. The grand hotel, often referred to as a "Diamond in the Wilderness," offers pleasure without pretense to nature lovers, distinguished celebrity guests, snow worshippers, and seasoned travelers. Some guest rooms feature Alpine décor with carved wood and delightful details, while others are appointed with graceful nineteenth-century style furnishings. The Château was named to the *Condé Nast Traveler* Gold List for 2004, was awarded the 2003 AAA/CAA Four Diamond Award, and was voted one of the Top 100 Hotels in the United States and Canada by *Travel + Leisure*.

CEREMONY AND RECEPTION OPTIONS: Ceremonies and receptions can be held in your choice of rooms. The outdoor Victorian Terrace, overlooking Lake Louise, is ideal for wedding parties of up to 100 guests. The Alpine Room, which seats 60, is graced with Alpine décor. The Sun Room, seating 80 guests, has a large fireplace and three picture windows framing a view of Lake Louise. Accommodating 100, the Large

Lounge overlooks the lobby and offers mountain views. A former ballroom, the European-style Victoria Room seats 350.

WEDDING SERVICES: The Château's Conference Services and Catering Team specializes in events for 30 to 350 guests.

BRITISH COLUMBIA

Natural beauty abounds in British Columbia, where the mountains meet the Pacific Ocean. You will find rugged mountain ranges, dramatic canyons, rivers teeming with salmon, old-growth forests that are abundant in wildlife, and the Gulf Islands, which have lush rainforests, towering mountains, shell beaches, and secluded bays. Whether you want to relax in the tranquility of nature or revel in outdoor adventure, British Columbia is an appealing choice for wedding celebrations.

PLANNING NOTES

SUGGESTED ASSISTANCE: Contact the Vital Statistics Agency (604-660-2937) for information on marriage laws in British Columbia.

SPECIAL REQUIREMENTS: WAITING PERIOD: None **SPECIAL NOTES:** You can obtain the license at a marriage license issuer. For a list of issuers and officiants, call the Vital Statistics Agency. There is no published waiting period, which means you should be able to get married the same day you receive your marriage license; I recommend double-checking this first. Two witnesses are required.

CIVIL CEREMONIES: Civil ceremonies must be performed by an authorized marriage commissioner. Reserve their services well in advance as they book up early.

RELIGIOUS CEREMONIES: There are no restrictions on religious ceremonies, and you should have little trouble finding a religious officiant of your choice.

PLANNING RESOURCES

TOURISM:
British Columbia Tourism
www.hellobc.com
800-435-5622

Tourism Vancouver
200 Burrard Street, Suite 210, Vancouver, British Columbia, Canada V6C 3L6
www.tourismvancouver.com
604-683-2222

Tourism Victoria
812 Wharf Street, Victoria, British Columbia, Canada V8W 1T3
www.tourismvictoria.com
800-663-3883 / 250-953-2033

VENUES

One charmingly rustic venue in British Columbia is the **HISTORIC O'KEEFE RANCH** (250-542-7868 / www.okeeferanch.ca), an historic ranch settlement established in 1867. On the premises is St. Anne's Church, a popular site for weddings. Built in 1889, the simple, gray-sided structure is one of the oldest frame churches in British Columbia. A particularly enjoyable feature is St. Anne's antique pump organ, still used for services today. The church is nondenominational, and it can seat 50 to 60, with standing room in the back. For an outdoor wedding, a tented area can be set up among the rolling hills and heritage buildings. Or couples can celebrate at the restaurant, which seats up to 150. Although O'Keefe Ranch is only open to the public from May to October, weddings are permitted year-round. The staff can arrange for horse-drawn carriage service and guided tours, and they can provide a list of pump-organ musicians and wedding officiants.

FAIRMONT CHÂTEAU WHISTLER

4599 Château Boulevard, Whistler, British Columbia, Canada V0N 1B4

www.fairmont.com/whistler

604-938-8000

SIZE: 10.5 ACRES **NUMBER OF ROOMS:** 550 GUEST ROOMS AND SUITES **WHEELCHAIR ACCESSIBLE:** YES **RATES:** $$–$$$

REVIEW: The Fairmont Château Whistler is a landmark hotel that offers fun and relaxation on the spectacular slopes of Blackcomb Mountain. Guests can ski, sip hot chocolate by a roaring fire, relax in one of three outdoor hot tubs, gather at the poolside patio, or simply enjoy the mountain air. This location is in one of North America's favorite mountain resorts and will host the 2010 Winter Olympics. They say it offers "luxury on the doorstep of adventure." The Fairmont Château Whistler was also recently named #1 Golf Resort in Canada and the #1 Ski Resort Hotel in North America by *Condé Nast Traveler* magazine. Guests enjoy rooms that blend with the natural Alpine setting and a gorgeous Vida Wellness Spa.

CEREMONY OPTIONS: The Rooftop Chapel and Woodlands Terrace offer panoramic views of the surrounding mountains for 2 to 300 guests.

RECEPTION OPTIONS: Couples have a choice of the Rooftop Chapel and Woodlands Terrace or any of the three ballrooms. The Empress Ballroom offers a cozy, intimate setting of sage green, fabric-dressed walls and 13-foot ceilings, and is suitable for receptions of up to 200, but it can also be divided into smaller rooms for groups of any size. The Frontenac Ballroom (comprised of three sections) can seat as many as 530 in a bright, spacious atmosphere with 15-foot ceilings and fabric-covered walls. The MacDonald Ballroom (comprised of six sections) seats 910 and exudes warm elegance accented with red and gold carpet and fabric walls, grand chandeliers, 15-foot walls, and dark wood trim. Both ballrooms are accessed by a dramatic foyer (which may be used for cocktails) that lets the outside in via floor-to-ceiling windows. Several very nicely appointed hospitality suites are also available for small ceremonies and are well suited for bridal ready rooms or family rooms.

WEDDING SERVICES: Catering, and they provide a list of preferred vendors.

THE AERIE RESORT

P.O. Box 108, Malahat, British Columbia, Canada V0R 2L0

www.aerie.bc.ca

800-518-1933 / 250-743-7115

SIZE: 85 ACRES **NUMBER OF ROOMS:** 34 ROOMS AND SUITES AVAILABLE INCLUDING 6 IN THE VILLA CIELO **WHEELCHAIR ACCESSIBLE:** YES **RATES:** $$–$$$ **SPECIAL NOTES:** CHILDREN MUST BE 10 AND OVER TO ENJOY THE FINE DINING ROOM, BUT ARE WELCOME AT ANY AGE IN THE CASUAL RESTAURANT

REVIEW: Set high in the Malahat Mountains yet only 30km from Victoria is the world-renowned Aerie Resort. It is an elegant Mediterranean-style resort with unparalleled views over the Pacific Ocean, the San Juan Islands, and the Olympic Peninsula. There are acres of terraced gardens, bare rock cliffs, and bald eagles grace the skies. The rooms are luxuriously accented with goose-down duvets, striking Persian and Chinese silk carpets, Jacuzzi tubs, roaring fireplaces, and private decks where you can sip coffee in the morning and champagne in the evening. It is no wonder that *Condé Nast Traveler* named it the #1 resort in 2002. The Aerie is a perfect size for a small to medium wedding because the entire property can be rented for the group, making it feel as though it is truly your place for the duration of the stay.

CEREMONY AND RECEPTION OPTIONS: Choose from 12 beautifully sculpted acres of ponds, bridges, gazebos, terraced lawns, and waterfalls or the Cielo Gardens, which can accommodate up to 100. There is a particularly beautiful gazebo called the Cielo Chapel, which can accommodate 20 people. Indoor ceremonies and/or receptions can be held in the Summit Room, which overlooks the gardens, a pond, and the Olympic Mountains and holds up to 60, or in the Aerie Dining Room, which overlooks the Pacific Ocean and seats up to 80.

WEDDING SERVICES: Limited wedding planning services available.

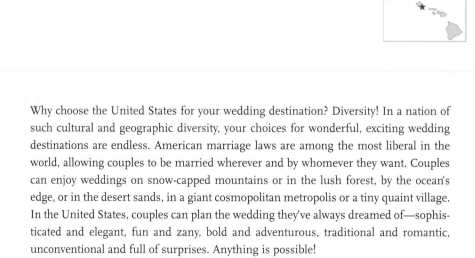

Why choose the United States for your wedding destination? Diversity! In a nation of such cultural and geographic diversity, your choices for wonderful, exciting wedding destinations are endless. American marriage laws are among the most liberal in the world, allowing couples to be married wherever and by whomever they want. Couples can enjoy weddings on snow-capped mountains or in the lush forest, by the ocean's edge, or in the desert sands, in a giant cosmopolitan metropolis or a tiny quaint village. In the United States, couples can plan the wedding they've always dreamed of—sophisticated and elegant, fun and zany, bold and adventurous, traditional and romantic, unconventional and full of surprises. Anything is possible!

COUNTRY OVERVIEW

CURRENCY: U.S. DOLLAR **TIPPING:** TIPS ARE EXPECTED BY TAXI DRIVERS, BEAUTICIANS, RESTAURANT WAIT STAFF, AND AIRPORT AND HOTEL SERVICE PEOPLE WHO HELP YOU WITH YOUR LUGGAGE. FOR WEDDING SERVICES, TIP CHAUFFEURS (LIMOUSINE AND COACH) AND WAIT STAFF; IT IS ALWAYS APPROPRIATE TO TIP ANY OTHER SERVICE PROVIDER WHO GOES BEYOND THE CALL OF DUTY TO MAKE YOUR WEDDING A SUCCESS. **ELECTRICITY:** 110V **INTERNATIONAL CALLING CODE:** (DIAL 1 BEFORE THE AREA CODE)

PLANNING NOTES

SUGGESTED ASSISTANCE: Each state has different marriage license requirements. You can find requirements state by state on www.marriage.about.com. Make sure you know what is expected before you go to get your marriage license, and be aware that, in most states, both the bride and groom must register in person.

SPECIAL REQUIREMENTS: RESIDENCY REQUIREMENT: None **WAITING PERIOD:** Some states require a waiting period between filing for a marriage license and getting married. The longest time needed to wait after filing for a marriage license is six days (in Wisconsin). Most states, however, allow you to get your license and be married immediately. A marriage license is valid for 30 to 90 days, depending on the state. (Nevada marriage licenses are valid for one year!) **SPECIAL NOTES:** Marriage licenses are obtained from a town, city, or county clerk of court in your chosen state. Most couples get the license in the town or city where they'll be getting married. Be sure to call the clerk's office ahead of time and confirm their hours of operation. Make an appointment if necessary, then verify what you need to bring and what the regulations are before you go to get the license. On the day of the wedding, have the officiant complete the license and the witnesses sign it, then file it back with the town or city clerk. The clerk will send you a marriage certificate in the mail. Some states, such as Massachusetts, require blood tests, and some states, such as Minnesota, require premarital education performed

© EMMANUEL VAUCHER

by a legal marriage officiant. Some states also require witnesses to sign the marriage license before it is filed. Translation is only necessary if a divorce decree or a death certificate is not in English.

CIVIL CEREMONIES: Civil ceremonies are an option for couples of no religious affiliation. If a couple is married in a religious ceremony, a civil ceremony is not required. If the couple wants to be married by a civil officiant, they can be married anywhere they wish—in- or outdoors unless the officiant requires that the ceremony take place at city hall. Current or retired judges are able to perform marriages. In some states, such as Massachusetts, a nonminister or non-justice of the peace, such as a relative or family friend, can buy a special one-time permission to perform a marriage.

If the officiant is not licensed in the state where the marriage will take place, be sure that he is authorized to perform the marriage. They may have to get a permit to do so. In such states such as Florida, notary publics can perform marriages.

RELIGIOUS CEREMONIES: Ceremonies of just about any religion can be performed throughout the United States. Just be sure your officiant is licensed in the region where you'll be married. The religious officiant is typically responsible for signing and filing the license after the ceremony. Alternatively, the couple or the wedding planner may file the license once the officiant and witnesses have signed it.

DESIGN IDEAS

Each state or region offers a multitude of design possibilities. I've provided design ideas for each individual state covered in the following pages.

PLANNING RESOURCES

EMBASSY AND GOVERNMENT OFFICES:

Each state, city, county, and/or town has its own civil offices responsible for dealing with marriage laws, ceremonies, and other related issues. If you have access to the Internet, it is quite easy to research and locate the contact information for these offices online.

TOURISM:

Each state, city, and/or town has a tourism, visitors, or convention center responsible for promoting its region and providing visitors with information. On the following pages, I've listed tourism-related information for each region.

HELPFUL WEB SITES:

The American Auto Association: www.aaa.com

PARKS, MONUMENTS, AND HISTORIC SITES:

HELPFUL WEB SITES:

American Bed and Breakfast Association: www.abba.com
National Park Service (United States Department of the Interior): www.nps.gov
National Register of Historic Places: www.nationalregisterofhistoricplaces.com

WEDDING RESOURCES:

HELPFUL PUBLICATIONS:

Bridal Guide: www.bridalguide.com
Brides: www.brides.com
Grace Ormonde Wedding Style: www.weddingstylemagazine.com
Martha Stewart Weddings: www.marthastewart.com
Modern Bride: www.modernbride.com
Perfect Wedding Guide: www.pwg.com

HELPFUL WEB SITES:

There are several national organizations that provide information on wedding-related products and services around the nation. In most cases, each region has its own local association. National organizations include those listed here:
The Association for Wedding Professionals International: www.afwpi.com
The Association of Bridal Consultants: www.bridalassn.com

The Association of Certified Professional Wedding Consultants: www.acpwc.com
The Bridal Association of America: www.bridalassociationofamerica.com
The Knot: www.theknot.com
June Wedding, Inc.: www.junewedding.com

REGION I: NORTHEAST

MASSACHUSETTS

Massachusetts is filled with wonderful wedding destinations, including Boston, Cape Cod, Cape Ann, and the Berkshires, but two stand out as favorites—Nantucket and Martha's Vineyard. Nantucket, affectionately known as "The Little Gray Lady of the Sea," is located 30 miles off the coast of Cape Cod. The island, a National Historic District, is characterized by soft sandy beaches, cobblestone streets, and seaside cottages covered with roses and hydrangea. Although it feels old-fashioned, the island offers the best of modern dining and shopping. And, with more than 36 percent of the island protected, Nantucket is a gem of environmental conservation. Larger in size and only seven miles from the mainland, Martha's Vineyard also mixes the old with the new. It has six towns, each with its own personality, as well as five lighthouses and 127 miles of beaches. During the religious revival of the 1800s, Martha's Vineyard was a Methodist campground, where thousands pitched tents to hear sermons in the outdoor tabernacle. The inhabitants eventually began building cottages, which became increasingly ornate as neighbors tried to outdo each other. More than 300 of these quaint gingerbread-style cottages still stand, many of which can be rented for events. With sites and services aplenty, Martha's Vineyard enjoys a booming wedding industry.

You can get to the islands by plane, private boat, or public ferry. Two reliable ferry companies are Hy-Line Cruises (800-492-8082 / www.hy-linecruises.com) and the Steamship Authority (508-477-8600 / www.steamshipauthority.com). The weather is best from May to October, but I advise against planning a wedding on either island through July and August, which is the peak tourist season. Most venues do not even offer weddings during these two months.

© MICHAEL GALVIN

PLANNING NOTES

SPECIAL REQUIREMENTS: WAITING PERIOD: Three days **SPECIAL NOTES:** Blood test required
CIVIL CEREMONIES: A civil ceremony is typically officiated by a justice of the peace. However, anyone, including a friend or relative, can obtain a one-time special appointment to solemnize a marriage. Contact the governor's office (617-727-5787) to request an application for permission. For a list of civil officiants in the state, contact the Massachusetts Justice of the Peace Association (800-663-8867 / www.mjpa.org).

RELIGIOUS CEREMONIES: While Massachusetts, particularly Boston, has a strong concentration of Irish Catholics, most other faiths and denominations are represented throughout the state. Considering the fact that Nantucket and Martha's Vineyard are islands, both offer a surprisingly wide variety of Christian churches. Both islands have interfaith churches that welcome couples from any religious backgrounds. Couples should contact the church of their choice as soon as possible to check on availability and fees. Some of the churches will not marry a couple unless they are members of the congregation or have a home on the island. Other churches will allow outside ministers to perform the ceremony. Note that Nantucket's rabbi is only there in the summer. One of the most popular chapels is the Siasconset Union Chapel (508-257-6616) because it is on the sea and it is nondenominational. Muslims and Buddhists will need to provide their own officiants. Regardless of your situation, make sure your officiant is registered with the state.

DESIGN IDEAS

For a wedding on Nantucket or Martha's Vineyard, an island theme offers all kinds of possibilities. Welcome your guests with Nantucket lightship baskets filled with local treasures—scrimshaw, seashells, and lighthouse-themed souvenirs. You could even extend the basket theme to your invitations, floral arrangements, and wedding cake! Roses and hydrangea, so vibrant and abundant on the islands, would make a beautiful and fragrant addition to the décor. The culinary bounty of New England makes for a delicious, locally flavored wedding menu. Cranberries, apples, and blueberries add taste and color to any feast, and baked beans, brown bread, and clam chowder are always favorites. For a real treat, host a traditional clambake right on the beach, complete with clams, scallops, lobster, and sweet corn. Wine from Nantucket would be a nice touch, especially if you are able to customize the labels.

PLANNING RESOURCES

TOURISM:
Martha's Vineyard Chamber of Commerce
P.O. Box 1698, Vineyard Haven, MA 02568
www.mvy.com
800-505-4815 / 508-693-0085

Massachusetts Office of Travel and Tourism
10 Park Plaza, Suite 4510, Boston, MA 02116
www.mass-vacation.com
800-227-6277 / 617-973-8500

Nantucket Island Chamber of Commerce
48 Main Street, Nantucket, MA 02554-3595
www.nantucketchamber.org
508-228-1700

WEDDING RESOURCES:
HELPFUL PUBLICATIONS:
Grace Ormonde Marriage: www.weddingstylemagazine.com
Island Weddings: www.nantucketonline.com
Southern New England Weddings: www.southernneweddings.com

Martha's Vineyard Online: www.mvol.com/weddings/
Nantucket Weddings: www.nantucketweddings.com
New England Bridal Guide: www.nebridalguide.com
New England Bride Online: www.nebride.com
New England Wedding Photography Network: www.newedding.net
New England Wedding Planner: www.newenglandweddingplanner.com

VENUES

Venues on Nantucket and Martha's Vineyard are sure to be wonderfully charming. You might consider finding the perfect private property to rent for a week (usually Thursday to Thursday for weddings), so you can marry and celebrate in the privacy of "your own home." Contact any local real estate company for information. On Nantucket, try **WEST-BROOK REAL ESTATE** (508-257-6206 / www.westbrookrealestate.com), and on Martha's Vineyard, try Martha's Vineyard Vacation Rentals (800-556-4225 / www.mvvacation rentals.com). Both islands boast many lovely bed and breakfast inns. One inexpensive option is **THE CAPTAIN R. FLANDERS HOUSE** (508-645-3123 / www.captainflanders.com), located in the town of Chilmark on Martha's Vineyard.

© MICHAEL GALVIN

Lighthouses make memorable sites for wedding ceremonies. For information regarding **BRANT POINT LIGHTHOUSE** on Nantucket, contact the Coast Guard Station (508-228-0388), and for information on the **GREAT POINT LIGHTHOUSE**, contact the Trustees of Reservations (508-228-3359). All five lighthouses on Martha's Vineyard are available for special events. For permission to use the lighthouses, call the **MARTHA'S VINEYARD HISTORICAL SOCIETY** (508-627-4441). If you are captivated by the Vineyard's history, have your ceremony in **THE TABERNACLE** of Martha's Vineyard Campmeeting Association (508-693-0525 / www.mvcma.org). This historical church, which made Martha's Vineyard what it is today, is a large open-air building located in the center of a manicured village green and surrounded by colorful cottages. Another interesting historical site on Martha's Vineyard is **THE DR. DANIEL FISHER HOUSE AND THE OLD WHALING CHURCH** (508-627-4440 / www.mvpreservation.org). This house, one of the most elegant options on the island, features a large porch and spacious grounds. Outdoor ceremonies can be held in the garden or, if you prefer a church setting, at the Old Whaling Church right next door. The mansion can accommodate parties up to 250 with the use of the porch and a tent in the yard.

If it's an island celebration, how about a wedding afloat? For small weddings off the coast of Nantucket, there are 4 boats that can accommodate approximately 20 passengers each. The best resource for Nantucket boat information is the **NANTUCKET BOAT BASIN** (800-626-2628 / www.nantucketboatbasin.com). The Vineyard's harbors are full of vessels available for private charter. **MARTHA'S VINEYARD CHAMBER OF COMMERCE** (508-693-0085 / www.mvy.com/islandinfo/index.html) has information on all the island's marinas, whose sailing and motor yachts can accommodate groups of varying sizes.

Either island is perfect for an outdoor celebration. If you are interested in using the public beaches of Nantucket, contact the **BOARD OF SELECTMEN** (508-228-7255) to request a list of rules and regulations. A noise ordinance forbids loud music past 10:00 P.M. and bonfires are not allowed, though permits for fireworks can be obtained. Martha's Vineyard has many conservation sites that are simply stunning. If you would like more information about the areas that allow weddings, contact **THE VINEYARD CONSERVATION SOCIETY, INC.** (508-693-9588 / www.vineyardconservationsociety.org).

THE NANTUCKET LIGHTSHIP
P.O. Box 3185, Waquot, MA 02536
www.nantucketlightship.com
617-821-6771

SIZE: 128 FEET **NUMBER OF ROOMS:** 5 STATE ROOMS, EACH WITH ITS OWN BATH **WHEELCHAIR ACCESSIBLE:** POSSIBLE BUT DIFFICULT **RATES:** $$$

REVIEW: The Nantucket Lightship is a cornerstone of the island's history and culture. A lightship is like a lighthouse on the water, warning boats to stay clear of a nearby dangerous shoal. Sailors were stationed on a lightship for three months at a time, and it was during their watch that they designed and fabricated the Nantucket lightship baskets, so famous today. The Lightship, which has recently been refurbished, is a metal-hulled motor yacht with a mahogany and rosewood interior. It is docked in Nantucket and rented out for special events and overnight accommodations. Guests have a choice of renting on a nightly or weekly basis. If a group wishes the boat to be moored instead of docked, you must hire a crew at your own expense.
CEREMONY OPTIONS: Ceremonies can take place on deck.
RECEPTION OPTIONS: The boat can accommodate 149 guests for dinner and dancing. Receptions cannot be held under sail because there are not enough lifeboats.
WEDDING SERVICES: No services offered, as the Lightship simply provides the space. Caterers are welcome.

THE SUMMER HOUSE
Box 880, Siasconset, MA 02564
www.thesummerhouse.com
508-257-4577

SIZE: COMPLEX OF 13 COTTAGES AND A RESTAURANT **NUMBER OF ROOMS:** 34 **WHEELCHAIR ACCESSIBLE:** NO **RATES:** $$$

REVIEW: Hidden away on a bluff overlooking the sea, the Summer House is a charming complex in the heart of historic Nantucket. The complex features ten rose-covered cottages, a main building for the office and the formal restaurant, and an oceanside luncheon restaurant. Each cottage has a Jacuzzi, some have galley kitchens, and one has a fireplace. The main restaurant, housed in a white clapboard building, offers dining *al fresco* on the porch or inside by a cozy fireplace on cool nights. The Summer House is located eight miles east of downtown Siasconset (known locally as "Sconset"), which has been a thriving theater and arts community since its inception. In town, you'll find two other wonderful Summer House properties—the Summer House Fair Street, which has a Shakespearean garden and 12 lovely rooms, and the Summer House India Street, a restored mansion with ten rooms.

CEREMONY OPTIONS: Weddings are permitted on the oceanside patio on Siasconset Beach, where one of the House's restaurants is located. The Summer Houses in town are quite close to St. Paul's Church, which has beautiful original Tiffany stained-glass windows.

RECEPTION OPTIONS: The dining room at the restaurant can accommodate 120 people. A tented wedding on the beachside patio can accommodate 200 plus.

WEDDING SERVICES: The location and food is supplied, but no planning or coordinating services are available.

THE JETTIES PAVILION
One Bathing Beach Road, P.O. Box 546, Nantucket MA 02554
www.jettiespavilion.com
508-228-2064

SIZE: N/A **NUMBER OF ROOMS:** NO LODGING **WHEELCHAIR ACCESSIBLE:** YES **RATES:** $$

REVIEW: If you'd like a beautiful beach wedding with a casual atmosphere, consider the Jetties Pavilion, a venue with kitchen and bathroom facilities. Note that you cannot have loud music past 9:30 P.M., so you'll need to plan an early celebration.

CEREMONY AND RECEPTION OPTIONS: The deck under the Pavilion accommodates up to 132 guests. Because the beach area is unlimited, it is ideal for larger weddings—they have accommodated as many as 6,000! If you anticipate a smaller wedding, keep in mind that the Jetties Pavilion prefers not to do parties for fewer than 40 guests. You have the option of hiring the Pavilion to provide food or arranging for your own caterer. They supply a top-shelf bar, and they do so at less cost than any other venue on the island.

WEDDING SERVICES: Provides catering and bar services for groups interested in casual, buffet-style beach barbecues.

JARED COFFIN HOUSE
29 Broad Street, P.O. Box 1580, Nantucket, MA 02554-1580
www.jaredcoffinhouse.com
508-228-2400

SIZE: COMPLEX OF 6 HISTORIC BUILDINGS **NUMBER OF ROOMS:** 60 **WHEELCHAIR ACCESSIBLE:** NO **RATES:** $$

REVIEW: The Jared Coffin House, a stately three-story brick mansion, is the main house in an historic inn complex. It is an elegant, traditional New England home featuring high ceilings, chandeliers, antiques, and old oil paintings. Five other historic homes complete the complex and offer very comfortable overnight accommodations.

CEREMONY OPTIONS: The meticulously manicured gardens at the Jared Coffin House are very popular for wedding ceremonies and photography. In case of inclement weather, the ceremony can be moved inside to the Grand Parlor and Library in the Main House of the complex. If you prefer a church ceremony, there are several churches in town.

RECEPTION OPTIONS: The Main Dining Room, measuring 41 feet by 28 feet, can accommodate up to 80 guests for dinner. The adjacent Eben Allen Room offers room for an additional 30 guests or room for entertainment.

WEDDING SERVICES: The staff is willing to help with any of your planning needs.

THE WINNETU INN & RESORT
31 Dunes Road, RFD 270B, Edgartown, MA 02539
www.winnetu.com
508-627-4747

SIZE: 11 ACRES **NUMBER OF ROOMS:** 50 SUITES; 3-BEDROOM TOWNHOUSES AVAILABLE AT NEARBY SISTER RESORT **WHEELCHAIR ACCESSIBLE:** YES **RATES:** $ (SPRING/FALL)–$$ (SUMMER) **SPECIAL NOTES:** NONTRADITIONAL COUPLES WELCOME

REVIEW: The Winnetu is a lovely New England resort offering tennis, spa services, a heated pool, and comfortable, contemporary accommodations. One of the inn's unique features is their collection of classic cars, available for special events. A 1931 open-sided model-AA bus, a 1929 Woodie Wagon, and a 1945 fire engine can all be used to transport wedding parties.

CEREMONY OPTIONS: You can exchange vows on the beach or on the resort's beautiful, sweeping lawn with the surf as a backdrop.

RECEPTION OPTIONS: The Winnetu accommodates receptions for up to 145 guests. Its indoor reception area features a fireplace and an adjacent outdoor deck. The deck can be used with the indoor reception area, or it can be tented to the lawns.

WEDDING SERVICES: An event professional is available to help with planning.

© MICHAEL GALVIN

LAMBERT'S COVE INN
RR1, P.O. Box 422,
Vineyard Haven, MA 02568
www.lambertscoveinn.com
508-693-2298

SIZE: 7 ACRES **NUMBER OF ROOMS:** 15 **WHEELCHAIR ACCESSIBLE:** YES **RATES:** $

REVIEW: The lovely English gardens, orchards, barn, and carriage-house guest rooms make Lambert's Cove one of the most romantic venues on Martha's Vineyard. The inn, an elegant farmhouse dating to 1790, is made all the more picturesque by the 150-year-old vine-covered stone walls that border it. Fireplaces add plenty of coziness, while French doors and a grand piano in the formal library lend grace and charm.

CEREMONY OPTIONS: Ceremonies can be held in the English garden, in a garden gazebo, on a nearby private beach, or on the inn's huge deck, which can be tented.

RECEPTION OPTIONS: For an indoor reception using the inn's two dining rooms, 60 guests can be accommodated. A tented, outdoor reception is suitable for up to 250.

WEDDING SERVICES: Lambert's Cove has been hosting weddings for 20 years. The inn provides the food, and a wedding coordinator helps plan the details.

INN AT BLUEBERRY HILL

74 North Road, Chilmark, MA 02535

www.blueberryinn.com

800-356-3322 / 508-645-3322

SIZE: 56 ACRES **NUMBER OF ROOMS:** 24 **WHEELCHAIR ACCESSIBLE:** YES **RATES:** $$ **SPECIAL NOTES:** CHILDREN OVER 12 ARE ALWAYS WELCOME, AND YOUNGER CHILDREN ARE WELCOME WHEN THE ENTIRE PROPERTY IS RENTED FOR THE WEDDING

REVIEW: The Inn at Blueberry Hill is an authentic New England farm, offering a natural spa-like retreat in the more rural part of Martha's Vineyard. Located in Chilmark, the smallest town on the island, the inn offers spa services, tennis and croquet, fine cuisine, and access to the local beaches. There is also a pool, hot tub, and fitness room for guests to enjoy. The inn's pastures, stone walls, and gardens are surrounded by vast tracts of conservation land and hiking trails. This is the perfect location for a couple wanting to celebrate in an exclusive and secluded location.

CEREMONY OPTIONS: A ceremony tent can be set up anywhere on the property. Most couples choose to hold their ceremony near the woods and the stone walls.

RECEPTION OPTIONS: For a small, intimate dinner reception, the dining room in Theo's, the inn's restaurant, can be used. For a larger reception complete with dinner and dancing, the inn can set up a tented area outdoors for a maximum capacity of 200.

WEDDING SERVICES: Provides food as well as a list of service providers.

NEW YORK

From big-city buzz to small-town tranquility, New York never ceases to "wow" brides and grooms with its many possibilities. New York brings to mind any number of destinations—Long Island, the Hudson River Valley, the Finger Lakes, the Catskills, the Adirondacks, Cooperstown, and of course, Niagara Falls—but perhaps the most obvious is New York City, mecca of metropolitan energy, fashion, and sophistication. There is something for everyone in the Big Apple—fine food, dramatic architecture, world-renowned museums, Central Park, Times Square, Broadway. New York City weddings are some of the most expensive in the world, but if you are willing to think outside the box, it is possible to create a masterpiece out of very little. After all, the city is teeming with talented (and often undiscovered) artists, designers, and entertainers.

While New York City is indeed exciting, you'll be shortchanging yourself if you neglect the rest of the state. Home to 3,000 lakes and ponds and 30,000 miles of stream, the Adirondacks boast crystal-clear water at every bend, often against a dramatic backdrop of mountains blanketed by evergreens. There are 105 towns in the Adirondacks, many of them small and quaint, as well as many prominent cultural and commercial centers, such as Lake Placid and Saratoga. The Finger Lakes region remains relatively undiscovered, despite its stunning lakeside manors and fruitful vineyards. The wine of the Finger Lakes is very special, with 80 percent of it being made from native grapes such as Catawba, Concord, and Delaware. Route 20 is lined with farmland and several lake towns, each offering Norman Rockwell-esque beauty.

© IRIS CHALIT

Unless they are baseball fans, most couples do not think of Cooperstown as a wedding destination, but this town is well worth considering for your big day. Birthplace of baseball and home to the National Baseball Hall of Fame and Doubleday Field, Cooperstown is abuzz with golf, shopping, art, history, theater, and famous breweries! If you wish to celebrate outdoors, plan your wedding between mid-May and mid-October. Because mid-summer can be quite hot, the most popular months are June and September. If you want a winter wedding with snow, consider January and February; winters in the Adirondacks begin a little earlier and last longer.

PLANNING NOTES

SPECIAL REQUIREMENTS: WAITING PERIOD: 24 hours after the purchase of the license
CIVIL CEREMONIES: A civil ceremony can be performed by the mayor or former mayor of a city or village, a city clerk, a marriage officer, a judge, or a justice of the peace. Ship captains are not authorized to perform civil ceremonies in New York state. Anyone performing a marriage in New York City must be registered in the city to do so. If you are planning a ceremony in New York City, whether civil or religious, be sure to contact the Office of the City Clerk (212-669-2400 / www.nycmarriagebureau.com)

to see if an appointment is required to get your marriage license. The office may be able to provide a list of civil officiants.

RELIGIOUS CEREMONIES: Christian and Jewish venues and officiants are readily available throughout the state. Other religions are represented in the larger cities, especially in New York City, where you can find every faith and philosophy imaginable. New York City's famous St. Patrick's Cathedral is only available to members of the diocese (212-753-2261). It is relatively easy to locate nondenominational chapels and interfaith ministers in New York. Nondenominational options of note include The Wedding in the Country Chapel (518-882-6773 / www.aweddinginthecountry.com), near Saratoga Springs, and Temple Shabbat Shalom (518-893-0808 / www.rabbi weddings.com), where Rabbi Alpern and his wife welcome couples of all faiths.

DESIGN IDEAS

A New York wedding is the perfect opportunity to be creative! Getting married in New York City? You might take your inspiration from Broadway, incorporating marquees, opening curtains, playbills, tickets, titles, and songs into the overall design. These days patriotism is a popular theme. What could be more fitting than a ceremony on Liberty Island and a reception on Ellis Island, with red, white, and blue décor, images of Old Glory and the Statue of Liberty, and a menu of American favorites?

Consider a camp theme for weddings in the Adirondacks. A fishing creel could greet your guests, holding a compass, a sachet of balsam, trail mix, bug spray, sunscreen, and a few bottles of Saranac beer. Enhance the outdoorsy atmosphere with Adirondack furniture, birch bark baskets, and forest-inspired floral arrangements of evergreen branches, trillium, and ferns. Guests are certain to enjoy grilled trout, bass, and venison and perhaps a "woodsy" wedding cake as well as a campfire, complete with songs and s'mores.

A grape harvest theme works well in the Finger Lakes region, especially for a fall wedding. Welcome packages could be romantic, with two wine glasses, a personalized bottle of wine, a special corkscrew, cheese and crackers, and bunches of purple and green grapes. Grapes or grapevines make gorgeous embellishments for bouquets, cake decorations, and interior décor. Impress your guests with an autumnal meal of roast turkey or ham, garnished with raisins and grapes, accompanied by a squash bisque, and highlighted with the best local wines.

A Cooperstown wedding begs for a baseball theme. Hit a home run with your welcome baskets, stuffing them with baseball cards, Cracker Jacks, bubble gum in a pouch, and beer from one of the local breweries. Plan a baseball game for the day before the wedding—bride's side versus groom's side, each with their own uniforms! For a culinary twist, offer a make-your-own hot dog station, stocked with gourmet dogs, sausage, kielbasa, peppers, sauerkraut, cheese, chili, mustard, horseradish, and relish. Don't forget to include "Take Me Out to the Ball Game" on your reception playlist!

PLANNING RESOURCES

TOURISM:
Adirondack Regional Tourism Council
P.O. Box 2149, Plattsburgh, NY 12901
www.adk.com
518-846-8016

Cooperstown / Otsego County Tourism
242 Main Street, Oneonta, NY 13820

www.visitcooperstown.com
800-843-3394 / 607-643-0059

Finger Lakes Tourism
309 Lake Street, Penn Yan, NY 14527
www.fingerlakes.org
800-548-4836

Finger Lakes Visitors Connection
25 Gorham Street. Canandaigua, NY 14424
www.visitfingerlakes.com
877-386-4669 / 585-394-3915

New York City Convention and Visitors Bureau
810 Seventh Avenue, New York, NY 10019
www.nycvisit.com
212-484-1200

New York State Tourism
30 South Pearl Street, Albany, NY 12245
www.iloveny.state.ny.us
800-225-5697 / 518-474-4116

Wine Country Tourism Association
P.O. Box 452, Hammondsport, NY 14840
607-569-2989

PARKS, MONUMENTS, AND HISTORIC SITES:
New York City Department of Parks and Recreation
The Arsenal, Central Park, 830 Fifth Avenue, New York, NY 10021
www.nyc.gov/parks
212-639-9675

The New-York Historical Society
170 Central Park West, New York, NY 10024
www.nyhistory.org
212-873-3400

New York State Adirondack Park Agency
P.O. Box 99, Route 86, Ray Brook, NY 12977
www.apa.state.ny.us
518-891-4050

WEDDING RESOURCES:
  HELPFUL PUBLICATIONS:
  Grace Ormonde Marriage: www.weddingstylemagazine.com
  Locations Magazine: www.locationsmagazine.com
  Manhattan Bride: www.manhattanbride.com
  Modern Bride Connection New York: www.modernbride.com/local/newyorkmetro
  Wedding Sites and Services: www.weddingsitesandservices.com

© LAURIE RHODES

HELPFUL WEB SITES:
Central New York Weddings: www.cnyweddings.com
Long Island Weddings: www.liweddings.com
NYCity Weddings: www.nycityweddings.com
Special Event Network: www.specialeventnetwork.net

VENUES

In New York City, wedding venues abound, promising couples the opportunity to marry in grand style. Contact **WORLD YACHT** (212-630-8100 / www.worldyacht.com) or **SPIRIT CRUISES** (212-727-7735 / www.spiritcitycruises.com) if the idea of exchanging vows while cruising around Manhattan appeals to you. Offering a fleet of boats for parties of all sizes, both companies have on-staff wedding planners, food services, and disc jockeys. New York City is known for its historic luxury hotels, which boast dedicated wedding staffs, spacious facilities, gourmet food, and impeccable service. Among the best are **THE PLAZA HOTEL** (800-527-4727 / www.fairmont.com/theplaza), **THE WALDORF ASTORIA** (212-355-3000 / www.waldorf.com), **THE PIERRE NEW YORK** (212-838-8000 / www.fourseasons.com/pierre), **THE CARLYLE** (888-767-3966 / www.thecarlyle.com), and **THE REGENCY** (212-759-4100 / www.loewshotels.com). For more intimate affairs, consider the city's smaller boutique hotels, such as **THE ST. REGIS** (212-753-4500 / www.stregis.com), the only five-star, five-diamond property in Manhattan. St. Regis weddings are most often held on the top floor in the rooftop ballroom. An option for couples seeking a cozier venue with big city sophistication is **THE ALGONQUIN HOTEL** (888-304-2047 / www.algonquinhotel.com). The hotel is a literary landmark, having attracted the likes of Sinclair Lewis and William Faulkner—and it is one of the best deals in town. If you are planning a small, private, and elegant celebration, look into a mansion, loft, or penthouse, which typically charge a site fee separate from the services and fees of the caterer. The **OTTO KAHN AND JAMES BURDEN MANSIONS** (212-722-4745 / www.cshnyc.org/rentals.htm) are unique properties owned and run by the Sacred Heart Convent. These impressive mansions flaunt exquisite and elegant details with a Renaissance feel. The **MANHATTAN PENTHOUSE ON FIFTH AVENUE** (212-627-8838 / www.manhattanpenthouse.com), located in one of New York's tallest turn-of-the-century buildings, occupies an entire floor, with 12-foot arched windows that provide grand city vistas. If you want to make the most of a Big Apple theme, why not tie the knot at a famous New York City landmark? You can marry at the feet of Lady Liberty on **LIBERTY ISLAND** (212-363-3200 / www.nps.gov/stli), 86 stories high on the promenade of the **EMPIRE STATE BUILDING** (212-736-3100 / www.esbnyc.com), or at the center of **THE BROOKLYN BRIDGE** (212-788-1703 or 718-802-0603).

© SPIRIT CRUISES

Many museums, including the **AMERICAN MUSEUM OF NATURAL HISTORY** (212-769-5350 / www.amnh.org) and the **METROPOLITAN MUSEUM OF ART** (212-650-2600 / www.metmuseum.org), accommodate private events. In the heart of Broadway, the historic **GOTHAM HALL** (212-244-4300 / www.gothamhallevents.com) monumentalizes Art Nouveau. The hall's ballroom, its crowning glory, would be a dramatic setting for any wedding.

If you want to bask in the beauty of the Adirondacks, there's the **SUN CASTLE RESORT** (518-668-2085 / www.suncastleresort.com), a recently renovated stone castle overlooking Lake George. Or look into the lake boats provided by the **LAKE GEORGE STEAMBOAT COMPANY** (800-553-2628 / www.lakegeorgesteamboat.com).

Just outside the Adirondacks is Saratoga Springs, famed for high society, horse racing, and healing waters. **SARATOGA SPA STATE PARK** (518-584-2535 / www.saratogaspa statepark.org), a National Historic Landmark, is home to a performing arts center, a petrified forest, miles of trails, and wonderful wedding sites. One such site is the **HALL OF SPRINGS** (518-583-3003 / www.glensandersmansion.com), a ballroom with marble columns and crystal chandeliers. **THE GIDEON PUTNAM RESORT AND SPA** (800-732-1560 / www.gideonputnam.com), located in the heart of the park, is an elegant hotel option. In Saratoga, you'll also find **THE NATIONAL MUSEUM OF DANCE** (518-584-2225 / www.dance museum.org), a spacious Arts and Crafts-style building with a lovely courtyard.

In the Finger Lakes region, **MID-LAKES NAVIGATION** (800-545-4318 / www.mid lakesnav.com) offers romantic cruises on Lake Skaneateles and the Erie Canal. **GENEVA ON THE LAKE** (800-343-6382 / www.genevaonthelake.com), the grand dame of Seneca Lake, specializes in outdoor weddings, with lush formal gardens and old-world elegance. High on a hill overlooking Keuka Lake sits **ESPERANZA MANSION** (866-927-4400 / www.esperanzamansion.com), an historic Greek revival mansion that is sure to impress. You may also want to consider **WATKINS GLEN STATE PARK** (607-535-4511), famous for its gorge trails that wind along 200-foot cliffs and 19 waterfalls.

Cooperstown-bound baseball fans will be thrilled to learn they can be married at **DOUBLEDAY FIELD** (888-766-0060 / www.friendsofdoubleday.org). To obtain permission, contact both the Baseball Hall of Fame (607-547-7200 / www.baseballhalloffame.org) and the Village of Cooperstown (607-547-8344). Or, for something different, how about exchanging vows before the bridal altar in **HOWE CAVERNS** (518-296-8900 / www.howe caverns.com), surrounded by illuminated stalactites? **THE FARMERS' MUSEUM** (607-547-1412 / www.farmersmuseum.org), located on land once owned by American writer James Fenimore Cooper, is a museum venue that documents life on a nineteenth-century farm.

CENTRAL PARK

14 East Sixtieth Street, New York, NY 10022

www.centralparknyc.org

212-310-660 / Department of Parks and Recreation (for permit): 212-408-0226 / Central Park Conservancy (wedding hotline): 212-360-2766

SIZE: 843 ACRES **NUMBER OF ROOMS:** NO LODGING **WHEELCHAIR ACCESSIBLE:** YES **RATES:** $

REVIEW: Everyone has heard of Central Park, one of the most romantic destinations in New York City. There are seven bodies of water, seven beautiful fountains, a lovely carousel, and lots of green space—136 acres of woodlands, 250 acres of lawn, and 58 miles of walking trails. In addition to being a natural playground, it is also the hub of the community. The park is always alive, whether there's a concert, a carnival, or just a collection of individual entertainers. Central Park Zoo is a favorite for animal lovers, with polar bears, penguins, tamarins, and more.

CEREMONY OPTIONS: There are numerous ceremony locations in Central Park; the park's Web site lists some of the more popular ones. Wedding parties in the park are limited to 100 people. The Conservatory Gardens, which are always in high demand, offer three distinct formal gardens spanning six acres. Tents are not permitted, so you'll need a backup plan for rain. To use any site in the park, you'll need a permit, which can be obtained for a nominal fee by applying online or calling 212-408-0226. It will take a month to get the permit, so be sure to apply early. Note that an additional $50 permit fee is required for photographers.

RECEPTION OPTIONS: Among other reception locations in the park, **TAVERN ON THE GREEN** (212-873-3200 / www.tavernonthegreen.com), surrounded by giant topiaries and illuminated trees, has hosted many notable weddings. **THE BOATHOUSE IN CENTRAL PARK** (212-517-2233) is a Victorian boathouse on the largest lake, where you can arrange for a romantic gondola ride. **THE GARDEN PAVILION CAFÉ** (212-988-0575), accommodating up to 500 guests, is tented and heated for year-round entertaining.

WEDDING SERVICES: None

ELLIS ISLAND

Ellis Island Immigration Museum, New York, NY 10004

www.ellisisland.com/indexevents.html

212-363-3200

SIZE: 200,000 SQUARE FEET NUMBER OF ROOMS: NO LODGING WHEELCHAIR ACCESSIBLE: YES
RATES: $$–$$$

REVIEW: Part of the Statue of Liberty National Park, Ellis Island is one of the most historic and patriotic wedding sites you could choose. Its 162-million-dollar renovation in 1990 made it an amazing wedding venue, perfect for large celebrations. Transportation to the island is provided exclusively by the Ellis Island Ferry, as no other boats are allowed to access the island.

CEREMONY OPTIONS: For your ceremony, take advantage of the waterfront, where you'll enjoy breathtaking views of the Statue of Liberty and the Manhattan skyline.

RECEPTION OPTIONS: Receptions are held in the monumental Registry Room, where over 12 million immigrants were welcomed into the United States. When illuminated, the extraordinary vaulted ceilings transform the space into an elegant ballroom for groups of up to 1,000. The lighting on the exterior of the building is also spectacular, leaving a lasting impression as you and your guests depart on the ferry.

WEDDING SERVICES: Catering and full-service planning assistance are provided by Aramark (212-344-0996). Fireworks can be arranged as your ferries depart Ellis Island—a memorable sight with the Statue of Liberty in the background.

ANGEL ORENSANZ FOUNDATION CENTER FOR THE ARTS

172 Norfolk Street, New York, NY 10002

www.orensanz.org/center

212-529-7194

SIZE: 10,000 SQUARE FEET NUMBER OF ROOMS: NO LODGING WHEELCHAIR ACCESSIBLE: YES
RATES: $$$

REVIEW: This neo-Gothic building was built in 1849 as the first reformed synagogue in New York City. The congregation abandoned the building in 1973 and, in 1986, the Spanish artist Angel Orensanz saved the landmark by transforming it into his studio and an exhibition space. It has recently been discovered as a wedding venue by many celebrities, including Sarah Jessica Parker. The space has the feel of an old theater, with a wide-open main hall surrounded by a second-floor balcony.

CEREMONY OPTIONS: Though it is no longer a religious space, the beautiful gilded alter area still remains, serving as the perfect stage for wedding ceremonies.

RECEPTION OPTIONS: Typically, after the ceremony, guests move upstairs to the balcony and studios, where they enjoy a cocktail hour while the first floor is reset. Dinner then takes place on the first floor in what used to be the sanctuary. Up to 300 guests can be accommodated if both floors are set with tables, a viable option because the openness of the balconies keeps the second-floor guests from feeling excluded.

WEDDING SERVICES: The site provides linens, chairs, tables, and custom-designed, professional theater lighting for the event. If you check out the space during the day, don't be daunted by its lackluster appearance; once the lighting is set, the space is glorious. They do not offer planning services but can suggest service providers.

© ELKE ROSTHAL, WWW.ELKEPHOTO.COM

CAPITALE

130 Bowery, New York, NY 10013

www.capitaleny.com

212-334-5500

SIZE: 10,000 SQUARE FEET; SEATS OVER 500 **NUMBER OF ROOMS:** NO LODGING **WHEELCHAIR ACCESSIBLE:** YES **RATES:** $$$

REVIEW: Built in 1893, Capitale was once the home of the Bowery Savings Bank in the heart of Chinatown. Today the newly renovated building is one of New York City's finest venues for elegant functions. The stunning interior features Corinthian columns, a 75-foot decorated ceiling, an art glass skylight, and an enormous bronze vault. Overhead hangs a state-of-the-art sound system, designed to blend with the venue's classic architecture.

CEREMONY OPTIONS: The beautiful ballroom is ideal for both the ceremony and the reception. The ceremony can be set facing the bronze vault.

RECEPTION OPTIONS: The cocktail hour can take place in the expansive foyer, where the focal point is a full-service alabaster bar. Dinner is usually held in the ballroom, which can accommodate 500 for dinner. Also on the first floor are two executive rooms that can accommodate dinners for 30. Winding stairs lead up and around the ballroom to a balcony, providing a view of the festivities below. Upstairs, there are two smaller function rooms that can accommodate 60 people.

THE SAGAMORE

110 Sagamore Road, P.O. Box 450, Bolton Landing, NY 12814

www.thesagamore.com

800-358-3585 / 518-644-9400

SIZE: 72 ACRES ON ISLAND, PLUS OFF-ISLAND GOLF COURSE **NUMBER OF ROOMS:** 350 **WHEELCHAIR ACCESSIBLE:** YES **RATES:** $$–$$$

REVIEW: The Sagamore is the gem of Lake George, which is considered to be one of the most beautiful lakes in the United States. Built in 1883, the resort has long enjoyed its status as the social center of Millionaire Mile and Green Island. As a result, The Sagamore is listed in the National Register of Historic Places and is an Historic Hotel of America. It is situated high on a point of land on its very own island, which is unique for the Northeast. The hotel's recently renovated rooms and suites combine the elegance of bygone years with the modern style. In the summer, guests relax by the lake, on the Donald Ross Championship Golf Course, or in the new sailing school, and in the winter, guests enjoy an indoor pool and a European-style spa.

CEREMONY OPTIONS: Any bridal entrance is sure to be grand on the Sagamore's distinctive outdoor staircase aisle. Lined with trees bedecked in white lights, the aisle descends toward the water until it reaches a stone terrace, where the mountains and the lake provide a backdrop. There is also a balcony off the main hotel—a perfect vantage point to view the expansive scape of Lake George and its many islands.

RECEPTION OPTIONS: The Sagamore's newly constructed, glass-enclosed ballroom overlooks the lake and mountains. The room, which accommodates up to 175 guests, opens onto a garden area. The Sagamore Dining Room, located in the main hotel, holds up to 225. The Trillium Dining Room, with a capacity of 150, is an elegant setting with lovely terraces and garden areas. There is also the *Morgan*, a 72-foot replica of a nineteenth-century touring boat, which can accommodate up to 80 guests.

WEDDING SERVICES: The Sagamore has a wedding coordinator on staff.

THE WAWBEEK ON UPPER SARANAC LAKE

553 Hawk Ridge, Tupper Lake, NY 12986

www.wawbeek.com

800-953-2656 / 518-359-2656

SIZE: 40 ACRES NUMBER OF ROOMS: 36 BEDROOMS WITHIN 14 BUILDINGS WHEELCHAIR ACCESSIBLE: YES RATES: $$

REVIEW: The Wawbeek is a century-old camp on the inviting shores of Upper Saranac Lake. The compound includes several cabins and three larger buildings that can be used for gatherings. The original "eating cabin" is the site of the Wawbeek Restaurant, a space evocative of a great hall or lodge. It promises comfort, with dark hardwood floors, two floors of open entertaining space, a giant stone fireplace that warms up both floors, and a second-floor screened-in porch overlooking the lake.

CEREMONY OPTIONS: Outdoor ceremonies can be lakeside on the beach, or indoors in the Lake House, Mountain House, or Carriage House. There is also a chapel on the small island located a few hundred yards offshore.

RECEPTION OPTIONS: The restaurant is best suited for larger affairs. An outdoor tent can be set up to augment the restaurant space or to function alone as a reception space.

WEDDING SERVICES: The Wawbeek's event planner can help plan and coordinate.

LAKE PLACID LODGE

Whiteface Inn Road, P.O. Box 550, Lake Placid, NY 12946

www.lakeplacidlodge.com

877-523-2700 / 518-523-2700

SIZE: 15 ACRES **NUMBER OF ROOMS:** 17 ROOMS AND 17 CABINS (ALL CABINS SLEEP AT LEAST 2, AND SOME CABINS HAVE MORE THAN 1 BEDROOM) **WHEELCHAIR ACCESSIBLE:** YES **RATES:** $$$
SPECIAL NOTES: CHILDREN 14 YEARS OLD AND OLDER WELCOME; YOUNGER CHILDREN ONLY PERMITTED IF YOU BOOK THE ENTIRE RESORT

© EMMANUEL VAUCHER

REVIEW: Upon arrival at Lake Placid Lodge, you will realize you have discovered one of the most exclusive mountain retreats in North America. With hot tubs and stone fireplaces in every cabin and room, this Relais & Châteaux property is guaranteed to soothe the senses. Adirondack antiques, local art, Oriental rugs, and eclectic furniture add character to the accommodations. The highly acclaimed restaurant combines classic French with New American cuisine, using locally produced organic bounty. For outings, the Lodge has a boat that can accommodate 25 guests. If you love Lake Placid Lodge, you might also want to look into **THE POINT** (800-255-3530 / www.thepoint resort.com), another wonderful Relais & Châteaux property.

CEREMONY OPTIONS: You can be married anywhere on the grounds, including the beach.

RECEPTION OPTIONS: Receptions can be held in the Lodge's dining room, which features an enchanting woodsy décor. The ceiling is sculpted with local trees and branches, giving guests the feeling that they are comfortably perched somewhere in the Adirondack canopy. Combine wonderful food with this unique environment, then add the stunning views of Lake Placid and Whiteface Mountain—and you have the ultimate dining experience.

WEDDING SERVICES: Wedding service available.

POINT O' PINES
7201 State Route 8, Brant Lake, NY 12815
www.pointopines.com
518-494-3213

SIZE: 550 ACRES **NUMBER OF ROOMS:** 75 **WHEELCHAIR ACCESSIBLE:** YES **RATES:** $

REVIEW: Point o' Pines, an upscale summer camp for girls, allows private events when camp is not in session. It occupies a picturesque peninsula on the eastern shore of Brant Lake. Guests become "campers," staying in rustic bunkhouses, complete with sturdy bunk beds. There is no need to worry about your guests "roughing it" in the wild, however, as they are welcome to use the Har-Tru tennis courts, outdoor basketball courts, and softball field. The main lodge, which sometimes doubles as a restaurant, is a huge room with 40-foot cathedral ceilings and a west wall made almost entirely of glass, permitting views of Brant Lake. Both the boathouse and the main lodge have lakeside decks, and between the two is a spacious white sand beach, complete with canoes, volleyball nets, a campfire pit, and Adirondack chairs. Horseback riding is available at the nearby farm, which features a barn that can be used for parties.

CEREMONY OPTIONS: Ceremonies can be held in the boathouse, on the beach, or on the grassy knoll among huge pine trees overlooking the lake.

RECEPTION OPTIONS: For receptions, the boathouse accommodates 175, the main lodge accommodates 300, and a tent on the beach accommodates as many as you wish.

WEDDING SERVICES: A very capable on-site banquet manager can arrange for a variety of services and rentals.

© BELHURST CASTLE / PHOTOGRAPHY BY NEIL SJOBLOM

BELHURST CASTLE
4069 Route 14 South, Geneva, NY 14456
www.belhurst.com
315-781-0201

SIZE: 23 ACRES **NUMBER OF ROOMS:** 11 ROOMS IN THE CASTLE (ALSO 20 ROOMS IN THE VINIFERA INN; 13 IN THE WHITE SPRINGS MANOR; 3 ROOMS IN THE DYER HOUSE; 1 SUITE IN THE CARRIAGE HOUSE; 1 LOFT IN THE ICE HOUSE) **WHEELCHAIR ACCESSIBLE:** YES **RATES:** $$

REVIEW: Belhurst, which was built over a period of four years beginning in 1885, is an inviting castle constructed of red Medina stone in the "Richardson Romanesque" style. Its sprawling green lawns extend to the shores of Seneca Lake. The castle's warm, spacious interior features rich woodwork and beamed cathedral ceilings. Antiques, fine art, and Oriental rugs give the guest rooms plenty of charm. The property also includes the luxurious White Springs Manor, a Georgian Revival farm mansion close to the castle, as well as the Vinifera Inn, with rooms offering Jacuzzis, lake views, and fireplaces. In June of 2004, Belhurst became the newest winery to join the Seneca Lake Wine Trail, meaning they can provide their own wine for wedding receptions.

CEREMONY OPTIONS: Outdoor ceremonies can be held on the castle's front lawn, overlooking the lake. Ceremonies can also take place on the lawn outside White Springs Manor, which overlooks the vineyards and Seneca Lake Valley.

RECEPTION OPTIONS: The castle's ballroom, which accommodates up to 250, boasts breathtaking views of Seneca Lake and the gardens. The Meritage Ballroom holds up to 200 and also provides spectacular lake views.

WEDDING SERVICES: Wedding coordinator on site.

CAYUGA NATURE CENTER
1420 Taughannock Boulevard. Ithaca, NY 14850
www.cayuganaturecenter.org
607-273-6260

SIZE: 125 ACRES **NUMBER OF ROOMS:** 75 DORMITORY-STYLE BUNKS **WHEELCHAIR ACCESSIBLE:** YES **RATES:** $

REVIEW: Located six miles from Ithaca, the Nature Center sits on a gentle slope overlooking beautiful Cayuga Lake. There are five miles of marked trails for all non-motorized recreation, and the trail system includes a self-guided tour of the local vegetation and birdlife. You can find areas for a variety of other outdoor activities, including volleyball, horseshoes, archery, winter tubing, and tobogganing. The lodge is a four-season facility rentable by the hour, day, weekend, or week. It includes a kitchen with an adjoining dining room, a multipurpose room equipped with a fireplace, and a spacious enclosed porch overlooking the lake. Seventy-five dormitory-style bunks are available, with showers and bathrooms.

CEREMONY OPTIONS: Ceremonies can be held anywhere on the 125-acre property.

RECEPTION OPTIONS: A large courtyard on the property accommodates receptions for 50. The Great Room, which has high ceilings and a glass-enclosed porch, accommodates up to 70. There are also many fields for larger, tented weddings.

WEDDING SERVICES: None

LETCHWORTH STATE PARK

One Letchworth State Park, Castile, NY 14427

www.nysparks.state.ny.us/parks

585-493-3600

SIZE: OVER 14,000 ACRES **NUMBER OF ROOMS:** THE PARK MAINTAINS 82 CABINS, 270 CAMPSITES, THE GLEN IRIS INN (12 ROOMS AND 4 DELUXE SUITES), PINEWOOD LODGE (7 LUXURY EFFICIENCIES), CAROLINE'S COTTAGE (3-BEDROOM HOUSE AVAILABLE FOR RENT), AND THE STONE HOUSE (4-BEDROOM HOUSE AVAILABLE FOR RENT) **WHEELCHAIR ACCESSIBLE:** DIFFICULT ON THE TRAILS. SOME ROOMS AT THE INN AND THE CABINS ARE ACCESSIBLE **RATES:** $

REVIEW: Letchworth Park's 66 miles of trails can be explored on foot, bike, snowmobile, skis, or horseback. If that's not enough to keep you busy, the park features nature, history, and performing arts programs as well as two swimming pools, guided walks and tours, whitewater rafting, kayaking, hot air ballooning, ice skating, snow tubing, and horse-drawn sleigh rides. Sometimes referred to as "The Grand Canyon of the East," the gorge is 600 feet deep in parts, having been carved out by the Genesee River. There are a variety of guest accommodations in the park, including cabins and campsites (named among the top 100 in the nation), the Glen Iris Inn, the Pinewood Lodge, Caroline's Cottage, and the Stone House. Worthy of note is the **GLEN IRIS INN** (585-493-2622 / www.glenirisinn.com), formerly the country estate of William Pryor Letchworth. This inn, which overlooks Middle Falls, has been hosting guests since 1914, and although it is a historic building, it offers the modern luxury of air-conditioned rooms.

CEREMONY OPTIONS: Take your pick of ceremony settings—under the trees, next to a waterfall, or over the falls in a hot air balloon (www.balloonsoverletchworth.com). At the Glen Iris Inn, you can be married in front of the inn at the Middle Falls overlook; this is only an option if the ceremony is held in conjunction with a reception.

RECEPTION OPTIONS: Glen Iris Inn can host tented receptions for as many as 250. The inn also accommodates up to 100 in the Terrace Dining Room and 30 in the Letchworth Room. Other options include the large picnic pavilions in the park, which vary in size and can handle up to 180 people. Note that every car will be charged a one-time fee of $12 at the gate to gain entrance to the park.

WEDDING SERVICES: The Glen Iris Inn has a wedding coordinator on staff. No assistance is provided for weddings in the park.

THE COOPERSTOWN AND CHARLOTTE VALLEY RAILROAD

Leatherstocking Railway Historical Society, P.O. Box 681, Oneonta, NY 13820

www.lrhs.com

607-432-2429

SIZE: OFFERS A TOTAL OF 3 PASSENGER CARS, 1 COMBO CAR, 1 DINING CAR, 1 GONDOLA, AND A CABOOSE **NUMBER OF ROOMS:** NO LODGING **WHEELCHAIR ACCESSIBLE:** YES (THERE IS A LIFT TO THE TRAIN) **RATES:** $ **SPECIAL NOTES:** CHILDREN ARE WELCOME AND DOGS ARE INVITED!

REVIEW: The Leatherstocking Historical Society restores vintage rail cars from the 1800s and then keeps the romance of train travel alive by offering scenic 16-mile tours through the Upper Susquehanna River Valley. The train crosses the river twice over two steel-truss bridges and travels through a variety of landscapes.

CEREMONY OPTIONS: Ceremonies can be held in a restored 1869 train station in Milford, New York. You can also stop along the way to exchange vows or say "I do" in Cooperstown, where there's a makeshift station in an old rail postal car.

RECEPTION OPTIONS: The train can accommodate as many as 210 guests for a casual cocktail party in several cars and 40 guests for a sit-down dinner in the dining car. A band can set up on the open-air gondola car, giving guests the rare opportunity to dance under the stars as the train makes its way through forests and farmland.

WEDDING SERVICES: The venue can provide casual food and/or make recommendations for local caterers and services.

THE OTESAGA RESORT HOTEL AND THE COOPER INN

60 Lake Street, Cooperstown, NY 13326-0311

www.otesaga.com

800-348-6222 / 607-547-9931

SIZE: MORE THAN 200 ACRES (INCLUDING GOLF COURSE) **NUMBER OF ROOMS:** 136, INCLUDING 20 SUITES IN THE OTESAGA AND 15 ROOMS AND SUITES IN THE COOPER INN **WHEELCHAIR ACCESSIBLE:** YES **RATES** $$

REVIEW: The Otesaga, selected as a member of the Historic Hotels of America by the National Trust for Historic Preservation, is a grand Federal-style hotel resort. Choose from the hotel, a AAA Four-Diamond property with newly renovated guest rooms, or the Cooper Inn, an historic inn dating back to 1813. From the immense veranda or the expansive lawn, guests can enjoy Lake Otsego, which James Fenimore Cooper fondly referred to as "Glimmerglass." *Condé Nast Traveler* named the resort's Leatherstocking Golf Course one of the Top 50 Golf Resorts in the United States.

CEREMONY OPTIONS: The Otesaga does not allow on-site wedding ceremonies. Most couples choose to be married in a church or at the Farmer's Museum, the Fenimore Art Museum, or Doubleday Field.

RECEPTION OPTIONS: The Otesaga has 13 reception rooms of varying sizes and styles. Several of them open onto the 180-foot white-columned veranda that runs the expanse of the hotel. You can have a dinner reception for up to 200 guests in the ballroom, which has lovely French doors and soaring coffered ceilings. Another option is the main dining room on the west wing, which, when coupled with the Fenimore Room, accommodates up to 300 for dinner.

WEDDING SERVICES: The Otesaga has an on-site wedding coordinator.

RHODE ISLAND

Rhode Island may be the smallest state in the Union, but don't let that fool you. This state has much to offer destination couples, especially those seeking quaint seaside venues. Rhode Island proudly lays claim to Block Island, a wonderful wedding destination with water so blue and sand so soft, you might mistake it for the Caribbean. The crown jewel of the state is Newport, a city of colonial heritage, sailboats and yachts, beautiful beaches, lively waterfront festivals, and Gilded Age mansions. Many of these magnificent turn-of-the-century mansions, once summer "cottages" of the rich and famous, are available for weddings. From 1930 to 1983, Newport hosted the celebrated America's Cup race, and today, Newport remains one of the great sailing capitals of the world. Its harbor is full of gorgeous sailing yachts, many of which can host wedding celebrations as well. Couples planning a wedding will find the visitors bureau in Newport remarkably helpful and its Web site very user-friendly. An online request form makes the research process easy, leaving the bureau the task of gathering and sending information on locations and service providers. If you hope to make sailing part of the celebration, plan your wedding between May and October. Don't rule out the rest of the year, however, as Newport is an excellent winter destination.

© JOHN CORBETT, WWW.CORBETTPHOTOGRAPHY.NET

PLANNING NOTES

SPECIAL REQUIREMENTS: WAITING PERIOD: None. You do, however, need to get your license in the town where you plan to marry.

CIVIL CEREMONIES: Civil ceremonies can be performed by judges, justices of the peace, and court clerks.

RELIGIOUS CEREMONIES: Newport has dozens of Christian churches, among them St. Mary's Catholic Church, where John F. Kennedy and Jacqueline Bouvier were married in 1953. Newport is also home to Jewish synagogues as well as a Baha'i community. Be sure to confirm the availability of your religious officiant and house of worship well before your wedding date.

DESIGN IDEAS

There's no better place for a nautical nuptial theme than Newport. Sailing-related images could adorn everything from the invitations to the cake. In the welcome baskets, place a map, a compass, a sailor's hat, sunscreen—and maybe even some Dramamine! Why not go all out and celebrate with a traditional clambake on the beach? The man to contact is T.R. at **MCGRATH CLAMBAKES, INC**. (401-847-7743 / www.riclambake.com), whose family has been serving traditional clambakes since 1969.

The movie *The Great Gatsby*, starring Robert Redford and Mia Farrow, was filmed at Rosecliff in Newport. If you find inspiration in the Roaring Twenties, have a Gatsby gala. Such a celebration calls for display and decadence, with lots of fountains, flowers, and pearls. The guests' welcome packages could hold a small bottle of cognac, two cognac glasses, a long cigarette holder, and a package of candy cigarettes. Ask your guests to dress in flapper fashion from the 1920s, and be sure they have the chance to dance the Charleston. In the spirit of indulgence, serve caviar and oysters on the half shell, and have champagne flow throughout the evening. Top off the night with fireworks or, like in the movie, a swim-fest in the fountain!

PLANNING RESOURCES

TOURISM:
Newport County Convention and Visitors Bureau
23 America's Cup Avenue, Newport, RI 02840
www.gonewport.com
800-976-5122

Rhode Island Tourism
One West Exchange Street, Providence, RI 02903
www.visitrhodeisland.com
800-556-2484 / 401-222-2601

WEDDING RESOURCES:
HELPFUL PUBLICATIONS:
Newport Weddings: 401-849-3300

HELPFUL WEB SITES:
Rhode Island Weddings Resource: www.riwedding.com
Weddings and Events in Rhode Island: www.weddingsri.com

VENUES

Yachts can be chartered for nearly any purpose—ceremonies and receptions, bachelor parties, rehearsal dinners, and accommodations. **THE NEWPORT YACHTING CENTER** (401-846-1600 ext. 218 / www.newportyachtingcenter.com) offers boats such as *Adirondack II*, a 78-foot schooner, for ceremonies. The Center can also host tented receptions in the heart of Newport Harbor. **ALDEN YACHTS** (401-683-4200 / www.aldenyachts.com) represents over 600 yachts, including *The Aurora*, an 80-passenger, 101-foot classic schooner, and *Enticer*, a 50-passenger, 85-foot powerboat, for events. Some waterfront properties, such as the **HERRESHOFF MUSEUM** (401-253-5000 / www.herreshoff.org) in Bristol, have a dock where the boat can tie up while the wedding party gets ready on it. After the reception, the couple can depart on the boat for their honeymoon night. **VIKING TOURS** (401-847-6921 / www.vikingtoursnewport.com) is able to transport guests aboard the 140-passenger *Viking Queen* (which can be used for dinners) and aboard coaches and old-fashioned trolleys. If you'd like a beachfront celebration, consider **EASTON'S BEACH ROTUNDA BALLROOM** or **THE KING PARK GAZEBO** (401-845-5800 / www.cityofnew port.com/ dept/parks/weddings.html). For an elegant venue, look into the Louis XIII-style **BELCOURT CASTLE** (401-846-0669 / www.belcourtcastle.com). Its 60 rooms include a chapel, library, music room, grand ballroom, and banquet hall, called "the most beautiful dining room in America" by First Lady Mrs. Dwight D. Eisenhower. **THE ASTORS' BEECH-WOOD MANSION** (401-846-3772 / www.astorsbeechwood.com) is the venue of choice for couples who want to marry in style. Sites include the grand mansion's lawn, veranda, and mirrored ballroom, and services include butlers to escort the bridesmaids and fluff the bride's train! **THE EISENHOWER HOUSE** (401-847-6740 / www.eisenhowerhouse.com) is an historic Victorian, used by the Eisenhower family as a "summer White House." The property, now a state park, hosts weddings on the large lawns overlooking the sea.

OCEANCLIFF

65 Ridge Road, Newport, RI 02840

www.newportexperience.com/oceancliff.htm

401-848-0795

SIZE: 10 ACRES **NUMBER OF ROOMS:** 24 GUEST ROOMS AND SUITES **WHEELCHAIR ACCESSI-BLE:** YES **RATES:** $$$

REVIEW: Couples are sure to be inspired by this magnificent oceanside mansion, which is situated on ten acres by beautiful Narragansett Bay. If you have enough guests, consider booking the entire estate for your wedding party—you will feel spoiled, having the luxury of enjoying Oceancliff's gorgeous views, oceanside tennis, and indoor pool all to yourselves.

CEREMONY OPTIONS: OceanCliff offers a ceremony site right on the water. In the case of inclement weather, the upper deck can be tented for a ceremony that overlooks the bay. It may also be possible to have a ceremony aboard the 101-foot, 80-passenger *Aurora*, which is the largest wooden schooner in Newport.

RECEPTION OPTIONS: Accommodating 250, the spacious waterfront ballroom has bronze period-style chandeliers and floor-to-ceiling windows looking out onto the bay.

WEDDING SERVICES: Provides planning assistance and food for all events, including weddings, rehearsal dinners, and post-wedding brunches.

ROSECLIFF

The Preservation Society of Newport County, 424 Bellevue Avenue, Newport, RI 02840

www.newportmansions.org

401-847-1000

SIZE: 9 ACRES **NUMBER OF ROOMS:** NO LODGING **WHEELCHAIR ACCESSIBLE:** YES **RATES:** $$$

REVIEW: Rosecliff, fashioned after the Grand Trianon at Versailles, is home to the largest ballroom in Newport, with full-length French doors that open to a stone terrace overlooking the Atlantic. The heart-shaped staircase makes for a dramatic bridal entrance.

CEREMONY OPTIONS: Ceremonies can take place on the gardens, lawns, or terrace. The rose garden is an especially lovely site for a ceremony or photography.

RECEPTION OPTIONS: The ballroom accommodates 220 guests for dinner and dancing, while the terrace holds up to 300 for cocktails. The salon accommodates 80 guests.

WEDDING SERVICES: Rosecliff offers planning assistance, security, custodians, parking attendants, tables, chairs, and tent rental coordination.

© NEWPORT HARBOR CORP.

CASTLE HILL INN & RESORT

590 Ocean Drive, Newport, RI 02840

www.castlehillinn.com

888-466-1355 / 401-849-3800

SIZE: 40 ACRES **NUMBER OF ROOMS:** 25 ROOMS AND SUITES **WHEELCHAIR ACCESSIBLE:** YES **RATES:** $$$ **SPECIAL NOTES:** CHILDREN 12 AND OVER MAY STAY IN THE MANSION ROOMS. YOUNGER CHILDREN ARE WELCOME IN THE CHALET, BEACH HOUSE, AND HARBOR HOUSE

REVIEW: Castle Hill welcomes guests to the Rhode Island seacoast with a variety of luxurious accommodations, ranging from an elegant Victorian mansion to a hip beachside house. The resort is situated on the entrance of the Narrangansett Bay, which offers dramatic views all through the day.

CEREMONY OPTIONS: Couples can exchange vows on the beautiful lawn terrace overlooking Narranganset Bay, in the chalet, or by the bay.

RECEPTION OPTIONS: The lovely ten-room mansion sets the scene for gourmet receptions featuring outstanding cuisine. Another option is the tented terrace and chalet, which can accommodate 450.

WEDDING SERVICES: The resort assists in planning and provides the food and rentals. It also offers rehearsal packages.

INTERNATIONAL TENNIS HALL OF FAME

194 Bellevue Avenue, Newport, RI 02840

www.tennisfame.com

800-457-1144 / 401-849-3990

SIZE: 6 ACRES **NUMBER OF ROOMS:** NO LODGING **WHEELCHAIR ACCESSIBLE:** YES **RATES:** $$

REVIEW: The International Hall of Fame is housed in what was the Newport Casino, a Victorian shingle-style building with an interior courtyard. Walking through the arched entrance, guests meet the stunning green grass tennis courts surrounded by latticework porches. This venue provides the perfect stage for an unforgettable event.

CEREMONY OPTIONS: Ceremonies are performed right on the grass courts.

RECEPTION OPTIONS: There are two large function areas and several smaller ones, all of which are connected in some way to either the museum or the courts. Museum galleries feature an extensive glass wall and doors that open onto the USTA Wing and Porch, a 100-foot porch overlooking the Casino's Horseshoe court. This area will accommodate 120 to 150 people, depending on the services being provided. Receptions for up to 200 guests can also be held on the Horseshoe Piazza, a curved, open-air porch just off the playing surface.
WEDDING SERVICES: Provides planning assistance.

REGION II: SOUTHEAST

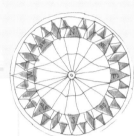

FLORIDA

Florida may be the only place where you can get married in Cinderella's Castle, but there's much more to Florida than Walt Disney World! There's sailing, scuba diving, and treasure hunting in the Keys, air boats, and gators in the Everglades, Art Deco and South Beach in Miami, and mansions in Palm Beach. Also worth exploring is the Destin area in the Panhandle, where you will find a relatively unknown paradise with pristine beaches and upscale yachting, as well as the Fort Myers area and the nearby islands of Amelia and Sanibel. Because transportation to Florida is relatively easy and affordable, it is a good destination if your wedding guests will be traveling from several locations throughout the United States. Florida is also an excellent option if you need or want a winter wedding but don't want the "wintery atmosphere." Another reason to consider Florida is that it is so close to many romantic honeymoon destinations. So once you tie the knot, you're already halfway to your honeymoon. The best time to plan a Florida wedding is during the fall, winter, or spring (except during spring break).

PLANNING NOTES

SPECIAL REQUIREMENTS: WAITING PERIOD: Three days, unless you take the four-hour state-sanctioned marriage course. The marriage license is valid for 60 days.

CIVIL CEREMONIES: There are no restrictions on civil ceremonies. Popular ceremony sites in Florida include hotels, gardens, yachts, beaches, and hotels.

RELIGIOUS CEREMONIES: Florida has a predominantly Christian and Jewish population; larger cities have a greater representation of other faiths.

DESIGN IDEAS

Florida evokes images of seashells, sand, palm trees, and gators, any of which would make a festive "fun-and-sun" theme. For a fairytale wedding theme, call the experts at Walt Disney World (321-939-4610 / www.disneyweddings.com). Their wedding team can help you plan the personalized event you've always dreamed of. Because Florida's inhabitants hail from all over the United States—and all over the world—there is rich cultural diversity. With a strong Cuban, Caribbean, and South American influence in Miami, it is easy to incorporate diverse and delicious cuisine into your menu. Seafood is plentiful, as is alligator meat, which would certainly provide a little culinary adventure for the out-of-towners. And for dessert, don't forget to offer your guests a slice of key lime pie. As a special treat, consider highlighting your cocktail hour with the services of a cigar roller, who will roll a variety of cigars in all sizes and flavors for the guests.

PLANNING RESOURCES

TOURISM:
Visit Florida
661 East Jefferson Street, Suite 300, Tallahassee, FL 32301
www.flausa.com
888-735-2872 / 850-488-5607

PARKS, MONUMENTS, AND HISTORIC SITES:
Florida State Parks
3900 Commonwealth Boulevard, Tallahassee, FL 32399
www.dep.state.fl.us/parks
850-245-2118

WEDDING RESOURCES:
HELPFUL PUBLICATIONS:
Florida Weddings and Parties: www.floridasmart.com/business/weddings
Orlando Wedding Guide: www.orlandoweddingguide.com

VENUES

You'll find countless hotel and resort venues for your wedding in Florida. If you want your wedding to be the thrill of a lifetime, consider pledging your undying love in a hot air balloon (866-454-3373 / www.miamiballooning.com) or in a sailplane (786-243-7640 / www.miamigliders.com)!

THE FISHER ISLAND HOTEL & RESORT

One Fisher Island Drive, Fisher Island, FL 33109

www.fisherisland-florida.com

800-537-3708 / 305-535-6080

SIZE: 216-ACRE ISLAND **NUMBER OF ROOMS:** 65 **WHEELCHAIR ACCESSIBLE:** YES **RATES:** $$$

REVIEW: The privately owned resort of Fisher Island is a favorite spot for celebrities (such as Julia Roberts and John Cusack) seeking a quiet, nearby tropical escape. The island is a short ferry ride from downtown Miami, but you must be on the list of expected guests if you plan to disembark on the island. The palatial Mediterranean-style villa, built in 1926 as William and Rosamund Vanderbilt's winter home, has been restored and transformed into The Fisher Island Club. Housed in the mansion is The Vanderbilt Room, one of six restaurants on the island, offering formal dining and elegant service. Guests stay in a variety of accommodations, from courtyard villas with sitting rooms, private patios, and hot tubs to spacious seaside villas. Everything on the island is within walking distance, but if you are short on time or energy, all cottages and villas come with the use of a private golf cart.

CEREMONY OPTIONS: For couples who want an outdoor ceremony, Fisher Island Club offers various possibilities. The Vanderbilt Mansion boasts a gorgeous pool area fac-

© VIZCAYA MUSEUM AND GARDENS

ing the Beach Club and the Marina & Yachting Center. This can be used for smaller ceremonies and receptions, but to accommodate larger crowds, it also includes a sizable outdoor patio facing the water. The club's most famous outdoor area is the Aviary, which surrounds one of the world's largest banyan trees.

RECEPTION OPTIONS: Indoor weddings are held in the Vanderbilt Mansion's Ballroom, which accommodates 150 guests comfortably. Elegant lighting and hand-painted walls with ornate floral details evoke a romantic mood. The doors to the ballroom open up, allowing guests to enjoy their cocktail hour or dessert while taking in city views.

WEDDING SERVICES: An on-site banquet manager provides some planning services, and a list of highly recommended local wedding vendors is provided.

THE BILTMORE HOTEL
1200 Anastasia Avenue, Coral Gables, FL 33134
www.biltmorehotel.com
305-445-1926

SIZE: 15–16 ACRES **NUMBER OF ROOMS:** 280 GUEST ROOMS AND 39 SUITES **WHEELCHAIR ACCESSIBLE:** YES **RATES:** $$–$$$

REVIEW: After undergoing a ten-year, 40-million-dollar refurbishment, the four-star, four-diamond Biltmore Hotel has never looked better. The facelift of the Mediterranean-style hotel gave special attention to improving guest rooms and enlarging suites. There are 39 luxury suites from which to choose, including several bridal suites. Designated a National Historic Landmark in 1996, the Biltmore has long been a luxury getaway for notable guests, from the dignified to the infamous. Knowing that the Duke and Duchess of Windsor were once guests here, as was Al Capone, one can't help but feel a part of this grand hotel's rich history.

CEREMONY OPTIONS: Couples can choose from a variety of spectacular settings. Outdoor venues include the Country Club Courtyard as well as several terraces and gardens. For indoor ceremonies, there are three grand ballrooms and the two-story Danielson Gallery, which accommodates 200.

RECEPTION OPTIONS: Three gorgeous ballrooms offer the ultimate in European opulence. The Granada, framed by an arched ceiling and accented with rich golden colors and dark wood, accommodates up to 250 guests. The Alhambra Ballroom, which also holds 250, features a majestic ceiling, antique mirrors, and a fireplace. The room also has French doors, which open onto a terrace overlooking the swimming pool. The Country Club Ballroom is the largest of the three rooms, measuring 6,200 square feet and accommodating up to 420 guests. With 46-foot ceilings and stone columns, it has served as an impressive stage for many celebrity weddings and other notable events, such as the welcome reception for the 1994 Summit of the Americas Conference, attended by President Bill Clinton and 33 other world leaders.

WEDDING SERVICES: Staff available for planning assistance.

VIZCAYA MUSEUM & GARDENS
3521 South Miami Avenue, Miami, FL 33129
www.vizcayamuseum.com
305-250-9133

SIZE: MORE THAN 10 ACRES OF FORMAL GARDENS **NUMBER OF ROOMS:** NO LODGING **WHEELCHAIR ACCESSIBLE:** YES **RATES:** $$–$$$

REVIEW: In the early twentieth century, industrialist James Deering built this Mediterranean-style villa overlooking Biscayne Bay. He named it *Vizcaya*, a Basque word meaning "elevated place." Today, this grand palazzo is a meticulously maintained museum owned by Dade County. It can be rented during the evening hours for special events. With spectacular sculpture and immaculate formal gardens, the museum makes a marvelous wedding venue.

CEREMONY OPTIONS: The museum is available for weddings only after 6:30 P.M. The extensive formal gardens provide many options for ceremony sites. You can also be married in the courtyard, located inside the house, which can accommodate up to 100 people.

RECEPTION OPTIONS: The courtyard can accommodate 100 guests or less for a dinner reception. For larger events, a tent can be set up over the front terrace, which overlooks Biscayne Bay.

WEDDING SERVICES: Provides a list of preferred vendors.

© VIZCAYA MUSEUM AND GARDENS

THE BREAKERS

One South County Road, Palm Beach, FL 33480

www.weddingsbythebreakers.com

561-659-8415

SIZE: 140 ACRES **NUMBER OF ROOMS:** 560 RECENTLY RENOVATED GUEST ROOMS, INCLUDING 57 SUITES **WHEELCHAIR ACCESSIBLE:** YES **RATES:** $–$$

REVIEW: This former heavyweight champion of the South Florida resort world is back in buff shape after receiving a ten-year, 145-million-dollar revitalization. Listed on the National Register of Historic Landmarks, the AAA Five-Diamond resort is sure to impress. There are eight world-class restaurants, including L'Escalier, the flagship featuring modern French cuisine. For relaxation, the hotel offers four heated oceanfront pools overlooking a half-mile private beach, a 20,000-square-foot luxury oceanfront spa, two fitness centers, 36 holes of championship golf, and ten tennis courts.

CEREMONY OPTIONS: Outdoor ceremonies (and receptions) can be held in a beautiful courtyard or on an oceanfront lawn and terrace.

RECEPTION OPTIONS: Featuring crystal chandeliers hung from 24-foot ceilings, the Ponce de Leon Ballroom can be divided into six sections and can seat as many as 1,100 guests. Accommodating 700, the recently renovated Venetian Ballroom is a cream and gold room with a marble floor and a breathtaking view of the Atlantic. The Mediterranean Ballroom accommodates 300 and features a magnificent hand-painted ceiling, elegant arches and columns, and a marble floor. The Magnolia and Gold Rooms are perfect for more intimate affairs of up to 100.

WEDDING SERVICES: Full service.

GEORGIA

With Georgia comes Southern hospitality, expansive plantations, elegant mansions, and majestic trees dripping with Spanish moss. One of the most popular destinations is beautiful Savannah, known as the "Jewel of the South." The city is full of romantic possibilities, with several cultural attractions, 22 historic squares, and over 1,100 historic buildings, inns, and restaurants. Savannah enjoys a subtropical climate, which makes the months of July and August very hot. The best time to get married is late spring and early fall. Also in Georgia are the Barrier Islands, covering 150 miles from

Ossabaw Island down to Cumberland Island. Cumberland, which is still under development, is the newest National Seashore. The Golden Isles begin at Brunswick and Little St. Simons Island and include Sea Island, St. Simons, and Jekyll Island. A year-round destination, the islands feature miles of secluded beaches, over 300 species of birds, and acres of primeval forests. Springtime weather is pleasant, and in the summer, when the water is warm, coastal breezes temper the heat and humidity. Autumn is crystal clear with mild temperatures and low humidity, and winter is both mild and brief.

PLANNING NOTES

SPECIAL REQUIREMENTS: WAITING PERIOD: None, but Georgia does require a blood test. Both applicants must submit a valid blood test on Georgia Form 3411, which must be signed by a licensed physician or the County Health Department. Blood tests are valid for 30 days. The bride must also be tested for rubella.
CIVIL CEREMONIES: Civil ceremonies may be performed by a justice of the peace.
RELIGIOUS CEREMONIES: Jewish and Christian options are readily available. There is an Islamic center in Savannah. Buddhists may have to go to Atlanta to find an officiant.

DESIGN IDEAS

Why not celebrate a Georgia wedding with a Southern hospitality theme? You could go all out with period dress à la *Gone With the Wind*, or keep it simple with a horse and carriage, parasols, a traditional "Down South" menu, mint juleps, and southern dance music. Your welcome packages might include a tin box of Byrd Company Key Lime Cooler cookies, pralines, sugar and spice pecans, a copy of *Gone With the Wind*, and if you are planning an island wedding, a box of saltwater taffy. For a truly cultural experience, hire the Georgia Sea Islands Singers, a wonderful group who sings in Gullah and Geechee, a dialect derived from that of coastal slaves.

PLANNING RESOURCES

TOURISM:
Georgia State Tourism
www.georgia.org/tourism
404-962-4000 / 800-847-4842

River Street Hospitality Center
1 River Street, Savannah, GA 31401
www.officialsavannahguide.com
912-651-6662

Savannah Convention & Visitors Bureau
101 East Bay Street, Savannah, GA 31401
www.savannah-visit.com
877-728-2662 / 912-644-6400

HELPFUL WEB SITES:
The Georgia Coast: www.visitcoastalgeorgia.com
Golden Isles Navigator: www.gacoast.com
Savannah Georgia Visitor Information: www.savannahgeorgia.com

PARKS, MONUMENTS, AND HISTORIC SITES:
Georgia State Parks and Historic Sites
2 MLK Jr. Drive, Suite 1352 East, Atlanta, GA 30334
www.gastateparks.org
404-656-2770

National Park Service, Cumberland Island
P.O. Box 806, St. Marys, GA 31558
www.nps.gov/cuis
877-860-6787 / 912-882-4335

WEDDING RESOURCES:
HELPFUL PUBLICATIONS:
The Wedding Planner. www.savcvb.com / 877-728-2662
(available through the Savannah Area Convention & Visitors Bureau)

HELPFUL WEB SITES:
The Georgia Bride: www.georgiabride.com
Golden Isles Weddings: www.gacoast.com/weddings.html
Savannah Weddings Planning Guide: www.savannahconcierge.com/
savannah/wedding.php

VENUES

Savannah has an abundance of lovely historic churches, many of which can be viewed at www.georgiamagazine.com/counties/chatham/tour/churches.htm. The city's many public squares and parks are also popular sites for weddings, requiring only a nominal security deposit for use. For details, check with the **CITY OF SAVANNAH, DEPARTMENT OF**

LEISURE SERVICES (912-351-3837 / www.savannahga.gov). If the river inspires you, why not plan a wedding aboard a riverboat? Savannah's **RIVER STREET RIVERBOAT COMPANY** (800-786-6404 / www.savannahriverboat.com) has the Georgia Queen and the Savannah River Queen, which can accommodate as many as 600 passengers. No matter what venue you choose, consider the possibility of arriving the old-fashioned way—in a horse-drawn carriage! For more information, contact the **PLANTATION CARRIAGE COMPANY** (912-201-0001 / www.plantationcarriage.com).

THE TELFAIR MUSEUM OF ART

121 Barnard Street, Savannah, GA 31401

www.telfair.org

912-232-1177 ext. 16

SIZE: 64,000 SQUARE FEET NUMBER OF ROOMS: NO LODGING WHEELCHAIR ACCESSIBLE: YES
RATES: $$$

REVIEW: Located in Savannah's historic district, the Telfair Museum of Art is made up of three impressive buildings. The Telfair Academy Mansion, now the fine arts museum, was built in 1819 by English architect William Jay and is today a National Historic Landmark. The South's oldest public art museum, it combines world-class art with historic architecture. Jay also designed the Telfair's Owens-Thomas House, another National Historic Landmark from 1819. This house museum is considered the finest example of English Regency architecture in the United States. In October 2005, the Telfair will also include the Jepson Center for the Arts, a 64,000-square-foot, state-of-the-art building near the Academy on Telfair Square.

CEREMONY AND RECEPTION OPTIONS: If you'd like to celebrate amidst world-class art and historic architecture, hold your wedding ceremony and/or reception at the Telfair Academy. The Academy features a soaring, three-story rotunda housing works from the museum's collection, a classic sculpture gallery, smaller galleries, and charming period rooms. It can accommodate up to 200 for cocktails and as many as 130 for a sit-down dinner. Ceremonies and small receptions may also be held outdoors in the lovely parterre garden at the Owens-Thomas House, which can accommodate up to 100 guests. Surrounded by plant-covered walls, the garden makes a wonderful setting for photographs. Overlooking the garden is the mansion's porch, an ideal spot for musicians to perform. The Telfair's Jepson Center, designed by acclaimed architect Moshe Safdie, promises to be Savannah's most impressive new event venue. The Center will feature a grand staircase leading to expansive galleries as well as a three-story atrium with views of historic Telfair Square. The Jepson Center will accommodate very large groups, and, unlike the other facilities, it will have a full-function kitchen.

WEDDING SERVICES: None. Provides list of service providers.

THE CLOISTER AT SEA ISLAND

100 First Street, Sea Island, GA 31561

www.seaisland.com

800-732-4752 / 912-638-3611

SIZE: 2,750 ACRES **NUMBER OF ROOMS:** 210 **WHEELCHAIR ACCESSIBLE:** YES **RATES:** $$$

REVIEW: The Sea Island Company has been cultivating Sea Island as one of the premiere vacation destinations in the world since opening in 1928. It played host to the 30th G8 Summit in June 2004, during which international leaders gathered to discuss world issues. It is also where President George Bush and Barbara Bush spent their honeymoon in 1945. The Cloister at Sea Island offers a beautiful and secluded setting, featuring Spanish-style architecture, a relaxed atmosphere, and gracious hospitality. Guests have access to five miles of private beach, stables, a shooting school, a world-class spa, children's activities, and plenty of leisure sports, including tennis, biking, sailing, windsurfing, and 54 holes of golf. Lucky guests may spot a loggerhead turtle coming to shore to nest, as the island averages 66 nests a year. The restaurants at Sea Island, which may be as famous as the hotel itself, promise fine dining experiences.

CEREMONY AND RECEPTION OPTIONS: If you are inclined to having a dawn ceremony, you can marry at sunrise on Sea Island's Beach Club lawn. Located right next to the beach, the site is tented and has no guest limit. The Ocean Room is part of the Beach Club, accommodating up to 90 for dinner. It is an open-air, pergola-style room with a Spanish floor, beamed ceilings, and mahogany windows and doors overlooking the Atlantic. Or you may want to select one of the 150 mansion "cottages" that are available for rent through Sea Island Cottage Rentals. Another option is Rainbow Island, where a pavilion can accommodate 60. More are welcome to spill out and enjoy a casual picnic-style event as long as the weather is agreeable. The Retreat Club on St. Simons Island is a beautiful "low country" style clubhouse that sits on the Retreat Golf Course designed by Sea Island's touring pro, Davis Love. The rustic and historic Corn Barn, an original plantation building, looks out on Sea Island's Seaside Course and can accommodate 120 for a sit-down dinner. In the spring of 2006, The Cloister will open the hotel's brand-new main building overlooking the Black Banks River, styled after the original 1928 hotel. It will offer romantic river walks, verandas perfect for entertaining, a state-of-the-art spa, and private butler services for all guests. If you do not want to get married on the Sea Island grounds, a few chapels and churches are located nearby on St. Simons Island and in Brunswick.

WEDDING SERVICES: Wedding coordinator on staff.

© COURTESY OF SEA ISLAND COMPANY

GREYFIELD INN, CUMBERLAND ISLAND
Office: 8 North Second Street, P.O. Box 900, Fernandina Beach, FL 32035
www.greyfieldinn.com
866-410-8051 / 904-261-6408

SIZE: 200 ACRES **NUMBER OF ROOMS:** 17 ROOMS; INN ACCOMMODATES 34–44 GUESTS **WHEEL-CHAIR ACCESSIBLE:** YES (THE CHURCH COULD BE DIFFICULT) **RATES:** $$$

REVIEW: Cumberland is Georgia's largest barrier island, accessible by ferry from St. Marys. The island has 36,415 acres, 16,850 of which are mud flats, salt marshes, and tidal creeks. As a wildlife preserve, it is famous for its dunes, maritime forests, sea turtles, wild horses, and abundant bird life. About half of Cumberland Island is public land, and the rest is private. With only 100 residents on the island, communication is limited to mobile phones. Greyfield Inn is a turn-of-the-century mansion built by Lucy Carnegie for her daughter, Margaret, as a wedding gift. Guests not staying at the inn can be taken to the island by private boat from Fernandina Beach, Florida.

CEREMONY OPTIONS: Most people choose to get married at the Greyfield Inn. When John F. Kennedy Jr. and Carolyn Bessette married on Cumberland Island, however, they chose to exchange their vows at the First African Baptist Church, founded in 1893. The church does not have electricity and is quite small, with four pews on one side and five pews on the other, each seating about four people. The only access to the church is a 14-mile long, single-lane dirt road from the south end of the island—a challenge in itself, since only island residents are allowed to drive on the island. However, if you follow in the footsteps of John and Carolyn, The Greyfield Inn will drive you and your guests to the church. To hold a wedding on Cumberland Island National Seashore, request an application for a special use permit from the National Park Service (877-860-6787 / www.nps.gov). You may also choose to be married on either a pristine beach or under a canopy of famous Georgia oak trees.

RECEPTION OPTIONS: A reception for up to 75 people can be held at the Greyfield Inn.

WEDDING SERVICES: Wedding coordinator on staff.

LOUISIANA

The most popular destination in Louisiana is New Orleans, one of the few places in the United States where you can feel like you're in another country. If you would like your wedding to have an international flair without having to leave the mainland, "The Big Easy" may be your choice. New Orleans appeals to people for a wide variety of reasons. It could be the mouth-watering food, the vibrant music scene, the charming architecture, the laid-back Delta lifestyle, the ceaseless festive spirit of the French Quarter—or a combination of everything—that makes the city so irresistible. Whatever it is, "N'awlins" has it in spades. Considering the heat and humidity of a Louisiana summer, the best time to plan a wedding is April through May or September through November.

PLANNING NOTES

SPECIAL REQUIREMENTS: WAITING PERIOD: 72 hours **SPECIAL NOTES:** Marriage license is valid for 30 days. Louisiana offers a covenant marriage; applicants must undergo premarital counseling.

CIVIL CEREMONIES: There are no published restrictions on civil ceremonies.

RELIGIOUS CEREMONIES: Christian, Jewish, and Muslim ceremonies can be arranged. In addition to most major religions, Voodoo is also practiced in parts of Louisiana. If you are interested in a Voodoo wedding, contact the Voodoo Spiritual Temple in New Orleans (504-522-9627 / www.voodoospiritualtemple.org).

DESIGN IDEAS

When most people think of New Orleans, they think of Mardi Gras, with its festive parades, fancy floats, and flashy costumes. So why not give your wedding a carnival atmosphere with masks, beads, and a purple, yellow, and green color scheme? Be sure to also use magnolias, the state flower, which are not only evergreen but wonderfully fragrant. Indulgence defines Mardi Gras festivities, so go all out with a delicious menu of Cajun cuisine. New Orleans, home of famed chef Emeril Lagasse, is known for its great

© BRIAN K. CRAIN, WWW.BKCPHOTO.COM

food—jambalaya, gumbo, andouille sausage, grillades, etouffee, muffaletta, po'boys, beignets, café au lait, and of course, locally harvested crawfish and oysters. And a New Orleans wedding would not be complete without big band and Dixieland jazz, with musicians wearing red suspenders and white hats.

PLANNING RESOURCES

TOURISM:
The Louisiana Office of Tourism
P.O. Box 94291, Baton Rouge, LA 70804-9291
www.crt.state.la.us/crt/tourism.htm
225-342-8119

New Orleans Convention & Visitors Bureau
2020 St. Charles Avenue, New Orleans, LA 70130
www.neworleanscvb.com
800-672-6124

New Orleans Online: www.neworleansonline.com

WEDDING RESOURCES:
HELPFUL WEB SITES:
Bob Walker's Official New Orleans Area Wedding Guide:
www.walkerpub.com/5_enter.html

VENUES

The splendid venues of Louisiana give couples ample opportunity to celebrate in true Southern style. **BOURBON VIEUX** (888-855-8438 / www.bourbonvieux.com) is a New Orleans icon, famous for having one of the longest balconies in the French Quarter. Guests can indulge in their own reception revelry while taking in a great view of Bourbon Street's nightly festivities. If you are charmed by the historic Garden District of New Orleans, you might consider the elegant **VAN BENTHUYSEN ELMS MANSION** (504-895-9200 / www.elmsmansion.com), which has a lovely outdoor garden for weddings. For a nostalgic riverboat wedding, celebrate with a private party aboard **THE CREOLE QUEEN** or **THE CAJUN QUEEN** (504-587-1794 / www.neworleanspaddlewheels.com).

There is more to Lousiana than New Orleans, so venture into the heart of the state and check out **LOUISIANA CASTLE** (958-839-9988 / www.louisianacastle.com) in Franklinton. This replica of an English-Norman keep castle is perfect for Renaissance-style weddings. In Lafayette, **THE VERMILIONVILLE CAJUN/CREOLE HERITAGE AND FOLKLIFE PARK** (337-233-4077 / www.vermilionville.org) is an interesting living history museum, where an evening wedding can include a ferry ride across Le Petit Bay.

THE RITZ-CARLTON NEW ORLEANS

921 Canal Street, New Orleans, LA 70112

www.ritzcarlton.com/hotels/new_orleans

504-524-1331

SIZE: 20,694 SQUARE FEET **NUMBER OF ROOMS:** 527 GUEST ROOMS   **WHEELCHAIR ACCESSI-BLE:** YES **RATES:** $$–$$$

REVIEW: Known as the Crown Jewel of the Crescent City, New Orleans' Ritz-Carlton is the only hotel in Louisiana awarded a Five-Diamond rating by AAA. It is located on the edge of the Vieux Carre (French Quarter) in the historic Maison Blanche building. The hotel houses a 20,000-square-foot European-style day spa and fitness center, and the lavish rooms reflect timeless Southern elegance. Pamper yourself by staying on the Club Level, where you will have your own dedicated concierge.

CEREMONY OPTIONS: Couples can say "I do" on a rooftop terrace overlooking the city or in a grand rotunda with a beautiful fountain in the center.

RECEPTION OPTIONS: The Ritz-Carlton's Mercier Terrace is a traditional French Quarter courtyard, complete with native plants and a fountain. It accommodates 80 seated and 125 standing. The Grand Ballroom is, in a word, opulent, with lush draperies, Czech crystal chandeliers, and luxurious paneling and carpeting. This is the perfect spot for a large wedding, as it will hold 500 for a seated dinner or 770 for cocktails. Receptions can also be held in the penthouse, the courtyard, or one of the 16 additional meeting rooms.

WEDDING SERVICES: Has a dedicated wedding staff.

MAGNOLIA MANSION

2127 Prytania Street, New Orleans, LA 70130

www.magnoliamansion.com

888-222-9235 / 504-412-9500

© FRED PLUNKETT / MAGNOLIA MANSION

SIZE: 12,000 SQUARE FEET **NUMBER OF ROOMS:** 9 UNIQUELY THEMED ROOMS **WHEELCHAIR ACCESSIBLE:** MANSION: NO; COURTYARD: YES **RATES:** $–$$$ **SPECIAL NOTES:** CHILDREN ARE NOT ALLOWED IN GUEST ROOMS, BUT MAY ATTEND WEDDINGS AND RECEPTIONS

REVIEW: Romantic, elegant, and enchanting, Magnolia Mansion is one of New Orleans' most treasured and most photographed antebellum structures. The mansion, built between 1857 and 1858, epitomizes Southern style and grandeur. Guest rooms are uniquely decorated, with themes ranging from "Gone With the Wind" to "Cinderella's Boudoir." Live oaks and magnolia trees surround the mansion's beautifully landscaped grounds, making it a truly authentic Southern Belle wedding location. Magnolia Mansion's history is rich and interesting; past owners include prominent New Orleans families. From 1938 to 1954, it served as the New Orleans Chapter of the American Red Cross. The mansion is known to be home to a few friendly resident spirits, who occasionally provide the guests with ghostly encounters.

CEREMONY OPTION: Wedding ceremonies can take place in the Grand Hallway or in the mansion's courtyard.

RECEPTION OPTIONS: There are several options for your reception. If the entire mansion and grounds are rented, there is space for 1,000 people. The Pardi Gras Courtyard accommodates 250 guests seated and 500 for cocktails or buffet. The mansion and the veranda hold 350 people, and the Big Easy Spirit Gathering accommodates 300 guests. For slightly smaller receptions, celebrate with 100 guests in the Garden Courtyard or with 40 guests in the mansion's foyer. To maintain its historic beauty, the mansion does not allow lit candles, red wine, or Bloody Marys inside; you can, however, have these items in the courtyard.

WEDDING SERVICES: Specializing in elopement packages, the hotel offers wedding planning, an on-site minister, and a list of preferred vendors.

NEW ORLEANS CITY PARK

One Palm Drive, New Orleans, LA 70124

www.neworleanscitypark.com/weddings.php

504-482-4888

SIZE: 1,500 ACRES IN THE HEART OF NEW ORLEANS **WHEELCHAIR ACCESSIBLE:** FOR THE MOST PART, IT IS WHEELCHAIR ACCESSIBLE. HOWEVER, THE PARK MAY NEED TO MAKE SOME SPECIAL ARRANGEMENTS **RATES:** $–$$$

REVIEW: The New Orleans City Park is one of the oldest and largest city parks in the United States, the first parcel of land having been purchased in 1854. Once the site of the Allard Plantation, the park is now home to the New Orleans Museum of Art as well as the largest collection of live oak trees in the world (over 14,000). The New Orleans Botanical Garden and the Besthoff Sculpture Garden can also be found within the park's boundaries. If you're looking for a romantic setting in the heart of New Orleans, the park fits the bill. Your wedding can be set amidst oak trees, beautiful gardens, and Art Deco fountains. The New Orleans City Park offers seven different venues for special events, providing a wide range of settings, from whimsical to sleepy bayou to neoclassical.

CEREMONY AND RECEPTION OPTIONS: Many of the park's locations will work well for both ceremonies and receptions. The Pavilion of the Two Sisters may be rented alone or in concert with the 12 acres of botanical gardens in which it sits. The main room can accommodate up to 400 for cocktails or 300 seated. If the gardens are rented as well, up to 2,000 guests may be accommodated. The pavilion, modeled after a traditional European orangery, has lovely views of the Azalea and Parterre Rose Gardens. The Garden Study Center, one of the grounds' original buildings, is reminiscent of an English cottage. The center holds 60 guests for seated dinners and luncheons, and 50 to 75 guests for cocktail parties. If you use the Lath House as well, you can invite up to 175 guests for a cocktail reception. Overlooking Bayou Metairie, the Parkview Terrace Room features hardwood floors and French doors, which open out to a 2,400-square-foot balcony. This room is located on the second floor of a mission-style building; it accommodates 150 guests for a cocktail reception, 100 for seated dinners. The Popp Fountain, built in 1937 and restored in 1999, provides an elegant, dramatic, and private setting for your vows. With 11 acres surrounding the fountain, there is no limit on the number of guests. Originally built in 1907 as a dancing pavilion, the Peristyle is a neoclassical structure that holds up to 300 guests. Four concrete lions stand guard at the Peristyle's steps, which lead down to the Bayou Metairie, as the park's inhabitants—swans, ducks, and geese—swim by in the bayou. The Lupin Foundation Carousel Building houses an antique wooden carousel that is listed on the National Register of Historic Places. With its carnival-like atmosphere, the building can accommodate 200 guests for cocktail parties or 120 for seated dinners. For a whimsical wedding and reception, celebrate in Storyland, a play area that features 26 storybook vignettes. This fanciful setting holds 300 guests.

WEDDING SERVICES: Catering, tent coordination, and wedding packages available.

REGION III: WEST

ARIZONA

Experience nature at its best in Arizona, where you'll find stunning landscapes in the northern plateaus, central mountains, and southern deserts. In the western part of the state, the Colorado River flows from the Grand Canyon down to Mexico. The Canyon's South Rim, with its awesome vistas, is one of the most visited places on Earth. The remote, less-traveled North Rim offers summer wildflowers, breathtaking views, and solitude. Not far from the Grand Canyon are more of Arizona's natural treasures, the Painted Desert and Petrified Forest. If you're looking for unusual ways to tour the Arizona terrain, explore the Sonoran Desert's Organ Pipe Cactus National Monument from the comfort of a hot air balloon. (You can even be married as you float over the spectacular scenery!) Head to the stars with a visit to Kitt Peak National Observatory, or experience the old West with a trip to Tombstone or Bisbee, where the spirit of bygone days still lingers. Weddings are recommended in late spring, when Arizona's climate is cool and the desert flowers are in bloom.

PLANNING NOTES

SPECIAL REQUIREMENTS: WAITING PERIOD: None

CIVIL CEREMONIES: There are no restrictions on civil ceremonies. They may be performed by a judge, a magistrate, a clerk of the circuit court, a clerk, or a clerk-treasurer of a city or town.

RELIGIOUS CEREMONIES: Most world religions are represented in the cities. Couples can opt for a Native American wedding or choose to incorporate Native American traditions into their ceremony.

DESIGN IDEAS

For an Arizona wedding, you could choose a Grand Canyon, Mexican, or Native American theme—or you could combine aspects of all three. Your invitations might have an aged look, announcing an expedition to explore the Grand Canyon. Your welcome letters could resemble old trail maps leading the way to adventure, and the packages could include dream catchers or something made of turquoise, the abundant state gem. For wedding décor, use double-spouted pottery wedding vases or pots of flowering cactus with gold or silver nuggets at the base.

If you are interested in a Native American wedding, consider setting the tone with Native American flute music and an Apache or Cherokee blessing. You might also include a native wedding custom in your ceremony. In the Navajo tradition, for example, the bride and groom clean each other's hands and feed each other corn mush. To add a personal touch, honor each one of your guests with a Kachina doll that fits their personalities or lives. Get the reception going with Native American drums and dance, and feed your guests with Southwestern cuisine, including beans, green chili, wild rice, corn, and fry bread.

PLANNING RESOURCES

TOURISM:
Arizona Office of Tourism
1110 West Washington Street, Suite 155, Phoenix, AZ 85007
www.arizonaguide.com
866-275-5816

PARKS, MONUMENTS, AND HISTORIC SITES:
Arizona State Parks
1300 West Washington Street, Phoenix, AZ 85007
www.pr.state.az.us
602-542-4174

WEDDING RESOURCES:

HELPFUL PUBLICATIONS:
Phoenix Wedding Pages
(can be purchased at most Arizona bookstores)

HELPFUL WEB SITES:
Arizona Weddings: www.arizonaweddings.com
The Perfect Wedding Guide: www.thepwg.com/phoenix

VENUES

Yes, couples can be married in the majestic **GRAND CANYON NATIONAL PARK** (928-638-7888 / www.nps.gov/grca)! Call for details about sites, fees, officiants, and permits (which are required for outdoor weddings). Most sites remain open to the public even during wedding ceremonies, but visitors and passersby are generally respectful. Under good weather conditions, Shoshone Point can accommodate a reception for 85 people. The site, equipped with toilets, grills, and tables, is located at the end of a mile-long dirt road. Available from mid-May to mid-October, Shoshone Point is in high demand, so call early to reserve it. Other popular sites include Grandeur Point, Moran Point, and the West Rim Worship Site. Because it rains almost every afternoon between June and September, a morning ceremony is your best bet if you are planning an outdoor summer wedding. Indoor receptions can be held at the Shrine of the Ages, which has an auditorium that seats 280 people and a multipurpose room that accommodates 60; be aware that alcohol is not allowed on the premises. You may find your best options for indoor receptions through **XANTERRA PARKS & RESORTS** (www.grandcanyonlodges.com). In addition to banquet rooms at the Kachina and Thunderbird Lodges, Xanterra offers lodging at seven localities near the Canyon Rim.

Are you looking for some venue variety? **GRAND CANYON RAILWAY** (800-843-8724 / www.thetrain.com), which departs daily from Williams, Arizona, and makes its way to the Grand Canyon's South Rim, offers train weddings. Perhaps a helicopter flight through the Grand Canyon is your idea of romance. If so, make arrangements through **HELI USA** (800-359-8727 / www.heliusa.com) for an exhilarating and unforgettable "wedding flight ceremony." If you are still searching for the perfect ceremony site, explore the desert terrain by taking a **PINK JEEP TOUR** (800-873-3662 / www.pinkjeeptours.com) through Arizona's picturesque landscape.

© DAVID BECKSTEAD

The **COCONINO NATIONAL FOREST** (928-527-3600 / www.fs.fed.us/r3/coconino) in Sedona is home of Cathedral Rock, perhaps the most photographed monument in Arizona. A popular site for wedding ceremonies, Cathedral Rock is revered in Native American legend as the birthplace of the first man and woman. The couple, it is said, argued day and night; after appealing to the gods, they were placed together but back-to-back so as to remain joined but retain their own direction and vision. You can choose to marry directly at Cathedral Rock or in one of the many nearby chapels or churches. Built directly into a mountain, the **CATHOLIC CHAPEL OF THE HOLY CROSS** in Sedona is a unique structure; it is overseen by the Diocese of Phoenix (928-282-4069 / www.diocesephoenix.org).

THE ARIZONA BILTMORE RESORT & SPA
2400 East Missouri, Phoenix, AZ 85016
www.arizonabiltmore.com
800-950-0086 / 602-955-6600

SIZE: 39 ACRES **NUMBER OF ROOMS:** 738 GUEST ROOMS, INCLUDING 78 ONE- AND TWO-BEDROOM VILLAS **WHEELCHAIR ACCESSIBLE:** YES **RATES:** $$-$$$

REVIEW: The Arizona Biltmore is the only resort in the world with an interior reflecting the distinctive influence of Frank Lloyd Wright throughout. The hotel is appointed with unique mission-style furnishings and textiles in desert palettes of beige, sand, and ivory. You and your guests can escape to the Biltmore's spa to enjoy treatments derived from ancient cultures. There are many activities, including tennis, golf on a spectacular course, horseback riding through the mountain preserves, hot air ballooning, and touring the Grand Canyon by van, helicopter, or airplane.

CEREMONY OPTIONS: The Arizona Biltmore has three beautiful locations for wedding ceremonies. The Cottage Court, a unique circular lawn, is nestled within the spa's quaint cottages. The Paradise Garden has gorgeous rectangular flower gardens that resemble a cathedral aisle, affording the bride the procession of a lifetime. Grandest of the three is the Squaw Peak Terrace, a large octagon-shaped area of well-manicured lawns, gorgeous flower gardens, and fountains.

RECEPTION OPTIONS: The Aztec Room is the most popular space for weddings, accommodating 150 guests. Featuring the original gold leaf ceiling of the hotel, the Aztec Room has hosted many celebrity weddings, including those of Supreme Court Justice Sandra Day O'Connor and Senator John McCain. The elegant Gold Room, with a capacity of 300, has floor-to-ceiling windows and a 14-karat gold leaf ceiling. The circular Grand Ballroom, which holds 400, also has floor-to-ceiling windows. It allows easy access to a large terrace overlooking Squaw Peak Lawn, a perfect site for cocktails.

WEDDING SERVICES: Full service.

© PHOTO BY ISABELLE BOSQUET

FOUR SEASONS RESORT SCOTTSDALE AT TROON NORTH

10600 East Crescent Moon Drive, Scottsdale, AZ 85262
www.fourseasons.com/scottsdale/index.html
480-515-5700

SIZE: 40 ACRES **NUMBER OF ROOMS:** 210 CASITA GUEST ROOMS, INCLUDING 22 SUITES **WHEEL-CHAIR ACCESSIBLE:** YES **RATES:** $$–$$$ **SPECIAL NOTES:** A "KIDS FOR ALL SEASONS" ACTIVITIES PROGRAM IS AVAILABLE FOR YOUNG GUESTS

© PHOTO BY ISABELLE BOSQUET

REVIEW: Situated high in the Sonoran Desert of North Scottsdale, the Four Seasons Resort Scottsdale at Troon North is a AAA Five-Diamond Resort, named one of the Top 500 Hotels in the World by *Travel + Leisure* magazine. The resort features a full-service spa and fitness center, priority privileges on two of Arizona's finest golf courses, championship tennis facilities, distinctive cuisine, and doorstep access to hiking on Pinnacle Peak. Many of the suites include private plunge pools, outdoor garden showers, indoor and outdoor fireplaces, and telescopes for stargazing.

CEREMONY OPTIONS: At sunset, the Ironwood Terrace, Troon Lawn, and Fountain Terrace boast gorgeous views of the desert. Ironwood Terrace, which accommodates 350, consists of a flagstone-bordered lawn. Ceremonies can be held on the terrace's raised staging area, with its distinctive combination of water accents, an expansive fire pit, and a unique "wall of flames." The Fountain Terrace, accommodating 300, features a water fountain, vibrant bougainvillea-filled latilla, and stunning views of Pinnacle Peak. Large enough for 100 guests, Troon Lawn's tiered design includes a graduated boulder waterfall encircling an elevated fire pit. Each site promises unparalleled views, ambience for sunset ceremonies, and the perfect backdrop for wedding photos.

RECEPTION OPTIONS: Accommodating up to 350 guests, Ironwood Ballroom has ten-foot windows lining the entire south side, affording breathtaking views of the valley below. With spectacular 21-foot, desert-toned wooden ceilings, Pinnacle Ballroom also holds 350. Troon, overlooking the Fountain Terrace, is reserved for smaller parties of 90 or less.

WEDDING SERVICES: Provides some coordination, along with a list of preferred vendors.

THE BOULDERS RESORT & GOLDEN DOOR SPA

34631 North Tom Darlington Drive, P.O. Box 2090, Carefree, AZ 85377
www.wyndham.com/hotels/PHXTB/main.wnt
800-553-1717 / 480-488-9009

SIZE: 1,300 ACRES **NUMBER OF ROOMS:** 160 ADOBE CASITAS, 50 PUEBLO VILLAS **WHEELCHAIR ACCESSIBLE:** YES **RATES:** $$$

REVIEW: Located in the scenic Sonoran foothills, the Boulders Resort & Golden Door Spa is a dream-come-true for lovers of sports and nature. For the past 15 years, the Boulders has received AAA's Five Diamond Award. In 2000, it was awarded "Best Place for an Outdoor Wedding" by *The Wedding Chronicle* Readers' Poll. It is also one of the top tennis resorts in the United States. The property has two 18-hole golf courses designed by Jay Moorish, five restaurants, a full-service salon, and a 33,000-square-foot spa. (For a little pampering before or after the wedding, be sure to indulge in a Golden Door specialty hot rock massage!) Guest rooms feature natural woods, Mexican tiles, and private patios. The villas come with fireplaces, fully equipped kitchens, laundry facilities, and a garage.

CEREMONY OPTIONS: The most popular site for ceremonies is the Boulders' Duck Pond Lawn, a perfect location for parties of up to 250 guests. You can also choose from other lovely sites, including the Presidential Lawn near the Presidential Suite, the 19th Green Lawn near the Boulders Club, El Pedregal Courtyard, and the Tee Box on the golf course.

© PHOTO BY ISABELLE BOSQUET

RECEPTION OPTIONS: Holding up to 150 guests, the Sonoran Ballroom features 13-foot ceilings. It opens onto the Sonoran Patio, which offers spectacular views of the area. Both the ballroom and patio can be divided into smaller areas for a more intimate setting. With 16-foot ceilings, the Tohono Ballroom can hold up to 550 guests, or it too can be divided for a smaller affair. The Sunset Terrace fits 275 guests, while the Cocopeli Room accommodates 200. A reception in one of the clubhouses is suitable for 25 to 100 guests.

WEDDING SERVICES: Full service.

CALIFORNIA

When it comes to California, the question is not *What does it offer?* but *What doesn't it offer?* California has 1,264 miles of beach along the Pacific Ocean, 700 vineyards, and 420 lakes, including Lake Tahoe, which host thousands of destination weddings each year. It also offers 4.1 million acres of national park land, 1.3 million acres of state park land, 4,000 windmills, 45 snow resorts, and 21 historic missions. Everything seems larger than life in California, from its movie-star residents to its native Sequoia trees (so large, you can actually drive through some of them). There's a little something for everyone in California—the glitz of Tinsel Town, the over-the-top glamour of Beverly Hills, the old-world elegance of San Francisco. With desert, coastal, mountain, hill, and valley climates in the state, you can plan a wedding there any time of the year.

PLANNING NOTES

SPECIAL REQUIREMENTS: WAITING PERIOD: None **SPECIAL NOTES:** Call the city or town clerk's office for an appointment to apply for a marriage license; the license is valid for 90 days.

CIVIL CEREMONIES: Civil ceremonies can take place anywhere, including beaches, vineyards, and (of course) the town hall.

RELIGIOUS CEREMONIES: California does not set restrictions on religious ceremonies, as you can find just about any faith or denomination represented there. It is worth noting that San Francisco is home to Tien Hau Temple, the oldest Chinese temple in the United States.

DESIGN IDEAS

A wine-themed wedding would be appropriate in California, especially if you are marrying near Napa Valley. Decorate your venue with deep purple, burgundy, and green grapes as well as vines, vintage bottles, and wine casks, and of course, treat your guests to the local wine. California is also known for its wonderful produce, so fresh and beautiful it can be incorporated into both the menu and the décor. Citrus fruit, avocado, eggplant, and sweet potato make striking topiaries and vine arrangements.

With California being the home of Hollywood, you might focus on movie-star glamour and make the event your "debut" as husband and wife. A Hollywood theme lends itself to fun details, such as marquee invitations, costume attire, theater tickets for seating cards, and playbills for programs. A gold rush theme is another fun option. The wedding invitations could announce *Eureka!*, a Greek word meaning *I found it!* (Found what? True love, of course!) Welcome gifts could be presented in gold "pans" and all the décor could be gilded with gold. Even chocolate favors could be dipped in gold! This theme is versatile, as it can be fun and fanciful or lavish and elegant.

PLANNING RESOURCES

TOURISM:
California Tourism
P.O. Box 1499, Sacramento, CA 95812-1499
www.gocalif.ca.gov
800-862-2543

California Welcome Centers: www.visitcwc.com

PARKS, MONUMENTS, AND HISTORIC SITES:
California Department of Parks and Recreation
1416 Ninth Street, Sacramento, CA 95814
www.parks.ca.gov
800-777-0369

California Historical Society
678 Mission Street, San Francisco, CA 94105
www.calhist.org
415-357-1848

WEDDING RESOURCES:
Association for Wedding Professionals International
6700 Freeport Boulevard, Sacramento, CA 95822
www.afwpi.com
800-242-4461

HELPFUL PUBLICATIONS:
Coastal Weddings: www.coastalwedding.com
Sacramento Bride & Groom: www.sacbride.com
San Francisco Bay Area Wedding Guide: www.sfweddingguide.com

VENUES

There are so many wonderful hotels, inns, ranches, missions, and spas in California, you may have difficulty deciding on just one. I've tried to give you a sense of what the state has to offer by reviewing hotels in the most popular California destinations. If you are planning a fun, fanciful wedding, check out the wedding services offered by **UNIVERSAL STUDIOS** (800-959-9688 / www.universalstudios.com) or **DISNEYLAND** (714-781-4565 / www.disneyland.com). For a romantic castle wedding, contact **HEARST SAN SIMEON STATE HISTORICAL MONUMENT** (805-927-2020 / www.hearstcastle.com). If you are seeking a legendary venue for your wedding, look into the famous **BEVERLY HILLS HOTEL** (800-283-8885 / www.thebeverlyhillshotel.com), where Elizabeth Taylor spent all of her honeymoons but two!

THE FAIRMONT SAN FRANCISCO
950 Mason Street, San Francisco, CA 94108
www.fairmont.com/sanfrancisco
415-772-5000

SIZE: 1 CITY BLOCK; 8 STORIES **NUMBER OF ROOMS:** 529 ROOMS AND 62 SUITES **WHEELCHAIR ACCESSIBLE:** YES **RATES:** $-$$$

REVIEW: San Francisco's Fairmont Hotel, recognized by the National Trust for Historic Preservation as an Historic Hotel of the World, was designed by Julia Morgan, who also designed Hearst Castle. In 1945, the United Nations Charter was drafted in the hotel, and, since Harry Truman, every American president has been a guest there. The hotel is situated atop Nob Hill, where city views are spectacular. Fittingly, Tony Bennett first crooned *I Left My Heart in San Francisco* in the hotel's Venetian Room.

CEREMONY OPTIONS: The popular choice for ceremonies of 150 to 200 guests is the Pavilion Room, which overlooks the roof garden and provides a cityscape backdrop. The Grand Ballroom can accommodate both the ceremony and the reception.

RECEPTION OPTIONS: Twenty-four stories up, you can entertain 225 guests in the Crown Room, which offers the most wonderful views in San Francisco. For a larger reception, the Crown Room accommodates 350 people. Or, for an even larger affair, the Venetian Room and the Gold Room accommodate 800 each, while the Grand Ballroom accommodates up to 2,500.

WEDDING SERVICES: Provides an on-site event specialist.

THE MILLENNIUM BILTMORE HOTEL
506 South Grand Avenue, Los Angeles, CA 90071
www.millenniumhotels.com
800-245-8673 / 213-624-1011

SIZE: 11 FLOORS NUMBER OF ROOMS: 683 ROOMS, 56 SUITES WHEELCHAIR ACCESSIBLE: YES
RATES: $$–$$$

REVIEW: A celebrity haunt for notables from Will Rogers to Barbra Streisand, the Millennium Biltmore is the birthplace of the Oscar statuette. It is a glorious Spanish-Italian Renaissance-style hotel with a Romanesque swimming pool, spa amenities, and ceilings hand-painted by notable Vatican artist Giovanni Smeraldi. The hotel's cream-colored Classic guest rooms are decorated in a European style, while the richly decorated blue and gold Club rooms feature canopy beds, damask bedspreads, and mahogany armoires.

CEREMONY AND RECEPTION OPTIONS: The hotel has five ballrooms. The Emerald Room, which seats up to 180, features hand-painted ceilings, faux-travertine columns, and bronze chandeliers. Accommodating 250, the Gold Room is a two-level ballroom, accented by a curving balustrade and gold ceilings. The Crystal Ballroom seats 450 for dinner and is crowned with a 30-foot ceiling painted by Smeraldi. It also has a balcony, Austrian crystal chandeliers, and mirrored doors. The Tiffany, adjacent to the Crystal Ballroom, is an elegant venue for up to 200 guests. The Biltmore Bowl— the original venue for the Academy Award ceremonies—seats as many as 600 for dinner. It has recently been renovated in rich burgundy and gold tones.

WEDDING SERVICES: A wedding coordinator on staff oversees the catering only.

HOTEL CASA DEL MAR
1910 Ocean Way, Santa Monica, CA 90405
www.hotelcasadelmar.com
800-898-6999 / 310-581-5533

SIZE: 7 FLOORS NUMBER OF ROOMS: 129 GUEST ROOMS WHEELCHAIR ACCESSIBLE: 6 ROOMS
RATES: $$$

REVIEW: Hotel Casa Del Mar was once the grandest beach club in Santa Monica. Having undergone a 50-million-dollar facelift, it reemerged in October 1999 as one of the most luxurious historic hotels on the West Coast. The elegant brick building offers sophisticated European lodging right on the beach of Santa Monica Bay. The interior is tastefully decorated in shades of gold, blue, and apricot, and the rooms are appointed with gauzy drapery, fruitwood furnishings, hand-painted armoires, and Matisse-inspired art. Hotel Casa Del Mar is a member of The Leading Hotels of the World and a recipient of the Mobil Four-Star Award. Guests can enjoy the beach, the spa, the fitness center, or the fifth-floor pool that overlooks the ocean.

CEREMONY AND RECEPTION OPTIONS: There are no outside venues available. The ceremony can be held in the Colonnade Ballroom, where you and your guests will enjoy picturesque views of the beach, the Santa Monica Pier, and, if you time it right, the sunset. The Colonnade Ballroom has sculpted ceilings, Venetian glass chandeliers, and floor-to-ceiling windows.

WEDDING SERVICES: A team of professionals is available for ceremony coordination.

© DAVID BECKSTEAD

HOTEL DEL CORONADO
1500 Orange Avenue, Coronado, CA 92118
www.hoteldelcoronado.com
800-468-3533 / 619-435-6611

SIZE: 31 OCEANFRONT ACRES NUMBER OF ROOMS: 688 GUEST ROOMS AND SUITES IN 4 LOCATIONS: VICTORIAN BUILDING, TOWERS AND CABANAS, BEACH HOUSE, AND COTTAGES
WHEELCHAIR ACCESSIBLE: YES RATES: $$–$$$

REVIEW: The Hotel del Coronado, built in 1888, still reflects its Victorian roots, even after a 55-million-dollar renovation. It has been the backdrop for several films, including *Some Like It Hot* with Marilyn Monroe and Tony Curtis. Many of the rooms offer full ocean views or garden settings, and guests can enjoy 22 boutiques, two heated pools, and a spa and fitness center. There are many dining options, including the Sheerwater Restaurant, which serves coastal cuisine on expansive seaside terraces.

CEREMONY OPTIONS: Wedding ceremonies can take place in a garden setting (with a full ocean view) or right on the beach.

RECEPTION OPTIONS: The magnificent Crown Room, named for its unique crown chandeliers, is one of America's largest pillar-free rooms. It is an architectural marvel, with 30-foot panelled ceilings of sugar pine held together by wooden pegs. The Grande Ballroom, which holds 800 guests, has crystal chandeliers, rich tapestry draperies, and panoramic views of the ocean. Accommodating 350, the Garden Patio is a lovely option for an outdoor celebration.

WEDDING SERVICES: Full-service catering department. The hotel gives recommendations for wedding planning services.

THE QUEEN MARY
1126 Queens Highway, Long Beach, CA 90802

www.queenmary.com

800-437-2934 / 562-435-3511

SIZE: 1,000 FEET LONG **NUMBER OF ROOMS:** 365 ORIGINAL FIRST-CLASS STATE ROOMS **WHEEL-CHAIR ACCESSIBLE:** NO **RATES:** $–$$

REVIEW: Imagine getting married on one of the world's largest, most luxurious ocean-liners. The Queen Mary, built in the 1930s, made over 1,000 transatlantic crossings before retiring to Long Beach in 1967. With 12 decks and a 1,957-person capacity, this ship combines 1930s charm and style with modern conveniences. It has been the wedding and honeymoon choice for famous notables, including Elizabeth Taylor, who honeymooned on the ship with first husband Nicky Taylor in 1950.

CEREMONY OPTIONS: The Royal Wedding Chapel, located on the Promenade Deck, accommodates up to 300 guests. Candlelight ceremonies are popular.

RECEPTION OPTIONS: The Grand Salon, graced with 33-foot ceilings, a dance floor, and original artwork, holds up to 700 guests. The Queen's Salon accommodates 400 and features a stage and marble fireplaces. For groups of 160, the Royal Salon, adjoining with the King's View Room, is ideal for cocktails. The Capstan Club, seating 130, and the Britannia Salon, seating 480, each feature its own private ocean-view deck for indoor and outdoor affairs. The Verandah Grill is located on the deck at the stern. Parties of 100 can enjoy its waterfront views and whimsical décor. For events such as rehearsal parties and brunches, there are three harbor-view restaurants—Sir Winston's, The Chelsea, and the Promenade Café.

WEDDING SERVICES: On-site wedding coordinator available.

MISSION INN
3649 Mission Inn Avenue, Riverside, CA 92501

www.missioninn.com

800-843-7755 / 951-784-0300

SIZE: 1 CITY BLOCK **NUMBER OF ROOMS:** 239 GUEST ROOMS, INCLUDING 28 SUITES **WHEELCHAIR ACCESSIBLE:** YES **RATES:** $–$$$

REVIEW: The Mission, a National Historic Landmark, was built by an obsessive art collector over several decades, beginning in 1876 and ending in 1931. Today, the 6,000-piece art collection is displayed throughout the hotel. The Mission has dramatic architectural features, including flying buttresses, a rotunda, an Oriental courtyard, a cloister wing, and a music room. This eclectic architecture represents various styles and periods, from the Orient to Europe. Guests can bask in the sun by the California-style pool or relax in the brand-new spa, which opened in 2004.

CEREMONY OPTIONS: The Mission Inn has two chapels. The St. Francis of Assisi Chapel, which can accommodate up to 150 people, has a beautifully gilded eighteenth-century altar. With just enough room for 15 people standing, the St. Cecilia Chapel is appropriate for a more intimate wedding ceremony.

RECEPTION OPTIONS: Receptions can be held in the Atrio Courtyard, the Spanish Art Gallery, or the Galleria, which has a Tiffany stained-glass window.

WEDDING SERVICES: On-site wedding coordinator available.

MEADOWOOD NAPA VALLEY

900 Meadowood Lane, St. Helena, CA 94574

www.meadowood.com

800-458-8080 / 707-963-3646

SIZE: 250 ACRES **NUMBER OF ROOMS:** 85 **WHEELCHAIR ACCESSIBLE:** YES **RATES:** $$$

REVIEW: Meadowood is a Relais & Châteaux property, priding itself on hospitality and classic elegance. Located in the heart of the Napa Valley, it showcases the beauty of wine country at its best. Guests enjoy a variety of wine-related offerings, including a blending seminar, wine and food pairings for lunch or dinner, wine and croquet, discovery tastings, and wine-tasting games.

CEREMONY OPTIONS: Surrounded by woods and overlooking a golf course, Vintners Glen is an outdoor lawn area that can accommodate up to 250 people. Vintners Room, which is available in a package with Vintners Glen, can seat up to 150 guests. With this option, you can combine an outdoor ceremony (tented, if necessary) and an indoor reception.

RECEPTION OPTIONS: For a reception, Vintners Room (described above) can accommodate 250 guests for dancing. The Woodside Room, a smaller space for up to 70 people, is another possibility.

WEDDING SERVICES: On-site wedding coordinator available.

THE AHWAHNEE

Yosemite, CA 95389

www.yosemitepark.com

559-253-5635

SIZE: 6 FLOORS **NUMBER OF ROOMS:** 123 ROOMS, COMPRISED OF 99 HOTEL ROOMS, PARLORS, AND SUITES, AND 24 COTTAGES **WHEELCHAIR ACCESSIBLE:** YES **RATES:** $$–$$$

REVIEW: In the 1920s, visionaries wanted to build a hotel that would attract the affluent and the influential. Their hope was that the hotel guests would fall in love with Yosemite and, as a result, assist in the preservation of the natural treasure. And so the majestic, granite-and-timber Ahwahnee was built. The hotel was constructed with the idea of bringing the great outdoors inside, so the common rooms feature soaring ceilings and large windows that overlook Glacier Point and Sentinel Dome. Every room is unique—a visual delight, reflecting the beauty of the environment and Native American influence. Some of the rooms have terraces and others have fireplaces, and all the cottages have a patio. Consider visiting during the winter, when guests feel as though they have the hotel, forest, and mountains all to themselves. If you want to include activities and events, such as barbecues and guided tours, as part of your destination wedding, Yosemite is the perfect place.

CEREMONY OPTIONS: The Wedding Lawn, offering Yosemite Falls as a backdrop, is ideal for outdoor ceremonies. Indoor ceremonies can be held on the terrace overlooking Royal Arches and Washington Column or in one of the function rooms.

RECEPTION OPTIONS: The Solarium Room seats 90 people for dinner. The room is semi-circular, complete with a stone fountain, stone floor, iron chandeliers, and a balcony. The Mural Room, accented by a large mural on one wall, accommodates a more intimate group of 40 or less for dinner. It features hardwood floors, a fireplace, and its own patio. The Under Lounge, which also holds 40, may be used as an extra room to accommodate the buffet, the bar, and/or the dance floor.

WEDDING SERVICES: Event specialist on premises.

COLORADO

Colorado promises beauty, adventure, and excitement, with most of the state sitting at an elevation of nearly 7,000 feet or higher. Home to the Anasazi, Arapahoe, Cheyenne, and Commanche tribes, it offers a rich history and culture steeped in Native American lore. Colorado is also noted for its Wild West legends, such as "Buffalo Bill" Cody and Butch Cassidy. Evidence of this bygone era can be found in the many abandoned but well-preserved "Boomtowns" scattered about the picturesque backcountry. Colorado's adventure options—everything from class IV and V whitewater rapids to generously powdered ski slopes—entice many outdoor-enthusiast couples seeking a memorable wedding destination. If sunshine is a must on your wedding day, head to Colorado, where they enjoy 300 days of sun a year! Or, if snow is what you're after, look no further—Colorado gets fresh snow in the elevations every month except August! For a bright, warm summer wedding, stick to the months of June, July, and August. In Aspen, the temperature rarely gets near 80°F (27°C), so you can look forward to pleasant conditions there. Always plan on the possibility of cool weather, especially in the evenings.

© RODDY MACINNES

PLANNING NOTES

SPECIAL REQUIREMENTS: WAITING PERIOD: None

CIVIL CEREMONIES: A marriage is most often solemnized by a judge, a public official whose powers include solemnization of marriages, or an Indian tribal official. In Colorado, a ceremony is valid if performed in accordance with any mode of solemnization recognized by any Indian nation or tribe. For the ultimate "do-it-yourself couple," Colorado allow couples to officiate their own wedding. If you plan on solemnizing your own marriage, be advised that you will be responsible for acquiring, completing, and most importantly, returning your marriage certificate to the Clerk and Records Office within 60 days, or you will be fined.

RELIGIOUS CEREMONIES: Christian denominations are predominant in Colorado. Two interfaith chapels are the Vail Interfaith Chapel (970-476-3347) and the Aspen Chapel (970-925-7184), where The Aspen Jewish Congregation worships. For something a little different, consider joining as many as 100 other couples at the Loveland Ski Area's annual mass Mountaintop Wedding Ceremony on Valentine's Day, performed by a registered minister with the Universal Life Church (303-571-5580 ext.141 / www.skiloveland.com/wedding).

DESIGN IDEAS

For a Colorado wedding, take inspiration from outdoor adventure, the "Wild West," or nature. Two beautiful trees are the Colorado blue spruce, the state tree, and the aspen, similar to a birch with leaves that turn a lovely yellow in autumn. The Colorado state flower is the white and lavender columbine, perfect for delicate bouquets. And for jewelry, rhodochrosite, said to be the stone of love and balance, is a lovely pink, semiprecious stone found in Colorado.

For a Native American wedding theme, you could purchase artifacts to use as gifts and décor elements. Canoes can be hung over doors or fireplaces, or they can be used as a self-serve bar with bottles of soda and water inside. Miniature woven rugs make great table runners, placemats, and chair covers. Adorn the buffet table with vibrant Native American pots and baskets, and bedeck the bride and bridesmaids with elegant turquoise jewelry. You could highlight the evening with a bonfire and Native American song and dance.

© RODDY MACINNES

PLANNING RESOURCES

TOURISM:
Colorado Tourism Office
1625 Broadway, Suite 1700, Denver, CO 80202
www.colorado.com
303-892-3840

PARKS, MONUMENTS, AND HISTORIC SITES:
Colorado State Parks
www.parks.state.co.us
303-866-3437

Historic Hotels of the Rockies
1572 Race Street, Denver, CO 80206
www.historic-hotels.com/colorado.html
303-331-0629

WEDDING RESOURCES:
 HELPFUL PUBLICATIONS:
  Rocky Mountain Celebrations: 888-686-9333

VENUES

Colorado is a popular spot for adventurers and vacationers, so there are an overwhelming amount of destinations and venues from which to choose. Just in terms of ski resorts alone, there are hundreds of choices. If you are looking for a mountaintop celebration, look into **THE ASPEN MOUNTAIN CLUB** (970-925-8900 / www.aspenclub.com), located at the pinnacle of Aspen Mountain.

HOTEL JEROME

330 East Main Street, Aspen, CO 81611

www.hoteljerome.com

800-331-7213 / 970-920-2050

SIZE: 1 CITY BLOCK **NUMBER OF ROOMS:** 91 GUEST ROOMS AND SUITES **WHEELCHAIR ACCESSIBLE:** YES **RATES:** $$–$$$

REVIEW: The Hotel Jerome, built in 1889, has been elegantly restored and continuously updated to feature all the amenities and services expected of a world-class, twenty-first century luxury hotel. Located in the heart of historic downtown Aspen, the classic Hotel Jerome is the choice of most celebrities when they visit the city (Don Johnson and Melanie Griffith were married there). It is a charming, Victorian-style hotel constructed of terra cotta bricks and furnished with nineteenth-century antiques.

CEREMONY OPTIONS: Hold your ceremony in Jacob's Corner, a saloon-like setting perfect for an Old West style affair, or in the open air of the Garden Terrace.

RECEPTION OPTIONS: The Grand Ballroom, a stately salon with 16-foot ceilings, accommodates 500 guests. The Antler Bar, complete with antler chandeliers, holds 150. Jacob's Corner, with gilded mirrors, chandeliers, and a fireplace, has a capacity of 125. The Century Room, also capable of holding 125, offers casual elegance, and the Wheeler Room, accommodating 60, features mirrors and crystal. Outdoor dining decks are suitable for parties of up to 350.

WEDDING SERVICES: A list of recommended professionals is available upon request.

THE LODGE AT VAIL

174 East Gore Creek Drive, Vail, CO 81657

www.lodgeatvail.com

888-367-7625 / 970-476-5011

SIZE: 5 FLOORS **NUMBER OF ROOMS:** 169 GUEST ROOMS, INCLUDING 46 SUITES **WHEELCHAIR ACCESSIBLE:** YES **RATES:** $–$$$

REVIEW: Built in 1962, the Lodge at Vail was the first hotel built in Vail. Since then, the town has grown around the lodge, which has become the local hub. A member of Preferred Hotels & Resorts Worldwide, the Lodge holds a reputation for outstanding personal service and relaxed luxury. With its old-world elegance and warm hospitality, the Lodge has appeared on *Condé Nast Traveler*'s Gold List and *Travel + Leisure*'s list of the Top 500 Hotels Worldwide. Warm touches include antique armoires, high-backed leather chairs, woodburning fireplaces, and private walk-out balconies. Guests enjoy a heated outdoor pool, Jacuzzi, sauna, and two restaurants.

CEREMONY OPTIONS: The Lodge can help you arrange a ceremony on the outdoor wedding deck on top of Vail Mountain, at the Vail Interfaith Chapel, or at the Betty Ford Alpine Gardens. On the property, you can use any of the function rooms.

RECEPTION OPTIONS: For receptions, there are three options. The Wildflower Restaurant is the Lodge's signature eatery, offering fine dining in a floral atmosphere. The

Cucina Rustica, which seats 150, has a "mountainesque" style, complete with dark wood, a fireplace, and an outdoor patio. The International Ballroom, which accommodates 290, has 14-foot ceilings and a patio at the base of Vail Mountain.
WEDDING SERVICES: An on-site event coordinator can help with all your planning.

THE LITTLE NELL
675 East Durant Avenue, Aspen, CO 81611
www.thelittlenell.com
970-920-4600

SIZE: 1 ACRE **NUMBER OF ROOMS:** 92 **WHEELCHAIR ACCESSIBLE:** YES **RATES:** $$–$$$

REVIEW: This Relais & Châteaux gem is situated right at the base of Aspen Mountain. Warm and welcoming like a country inn and luxurious like a grand hotel, Little Nell has received much recognition for its exemplary service and culinary accomplishments. A recipient of the AAA Five Diamond Award and the Mobil Travel Guide Five-Star designation, Little Nell has been included in the *Condé Nast Traveler* 2004 Gold List. Little Nell's guest rooms are quite large and luxuriously furnished with over-stuffed chairs, plush down duvets, marble bathrooms, and fireplaces.

CEREMONY AND RECEPTION OPTIONS: Small ceremonies can take place in private suites, in the Alpine Room, or on the hotel deck. Larger ceremonies can be held in the Grand Salon, accommodating 130, or on the outdoor wedding deck. The deck, which sits on top of the mountain, offers a spectacular view of Aspen Mountain. Receptions are held in the mountaintop Sundeck, an enclosed space for up to 400. For receptions of 150, the exclusive Aspen Mountain Club, also perched on top of Aspen Mountain, can be used. Little Nell's restaurant, Benedict's, can host a party for 100.

WEDDING SERVICES: Full service.

NEVADA

Though most people associate glamour, glitz, and gambling with Nevada, there's a lot more to this state than just Vegas! With picturesque mountains, desert sunsets, historic sites, Lake Tahoe, and Native American culture, Nevada might surprise you with all it has to offer. Plenty of outdoor activities—skiing, fishing, hiking, horseback riding, bicycling, and even bathing in hot springs—can be worked into a destination wedding weekend. And, if you'd like to add some eco-adventure to your ceremony, why not exchange wedding vows in a Hummer, hot air balloon, helicopter, or gondola? When people think of weddings in Las Vegas, they automatically think of elopements, Elvis impersonators, and kitschy chapels. If you're a wedding-bound couple who wants full-blown fun and entertainment, the Vegas atmosphere is perfect. The city, home to some of the most amazing hotels, can transport you to almost any place in the world. With the exception of July and August, which are typically very hot, April through October are the ideal months for a Nevada wedding.

PLANNING NOTES

SPECIAL REQUIREMENTS: WAITING PERIOD: None

CIVIL CEREMONIES: There are no published restrictions for civil ceremonies. Most are performed by a justice of the peace.

RELIGIOUS CEREMONIES: Nevada is noted for having the most non-ecumenical chapels in the United States. Most religions have a presence in Las Vegas.

DESIGN IDEAS

If you're inspired by the kitschy side of Vegas, go with a "high-roller" wedding theme, complete with Elvis tunes, fuzzy die, roulette tables, and slot machines. A Vegas-style wedding, however, is not your only option. With ghost towns, old saloons, and the Carson Trail, Nevada is the heart of the Old West—a perfect place for an old-time Western wedding. To celebrate in cowboy fashion, wrap your welcome packages in bandanas and dress your tables with burlap, bandana napkins, and colorful cacti centerpieces. For entertainment, you might consider hiring a folk singer to croon cowboy songs during the cocktail hour or by a late night campfire.

Native American culture, which is very much alive in Nevada, could also provide some inspiration for décor. In Nevada, the "Silver State," you'll find beautiful Native American jewelry crafted from silver and turquoise. Why not use this combination to accent your wedding decorations, from your bouquets to your centerpieces?

PLANNING RESOURCES

TOURISM:
Nevada Commission on Tourism
401 North Carson Street, Carson City, NV 89701
www.travelnevada.com
800-638-2328

PARKS, MONUMENTS, AND HISTORIC SITES:
Nevada Division of State Parks
1300 South Curry Street, Carson City, Nevada 89703-5202
http://parks.nv.gov/
775-687-4384

WEDDING RESOURCES:
Lake Tahoe Wedding & Honeymoon Association
P.O. Box 14544, South Lake Tahoe, CA 96151
www.tahoeweddings.org
800-358-5683

HELPFUL WEB SITES:
Las Vegas Wedding Information: www.wedinvegas.com
Tahoe Weddings: www.tahoeweddings.com

VENUES

Its streets lined with flashy wedding chapels, Las Vegas welcomes brides and grooms like no other city. You certainly won't be at a loss for wedding sites in Vegas—in fact, you might be overwhelmed—but one that stands out is **A SPECIAL MEMORY WEDDING CHAPEL**

(800-962-7798 / www.aspecialmemoryweddingchapel.com). The staff can "service" a quickie wedding at their drive-up window, or they can perform a more traditional ceremony for up to 110 guests in a tastefully designed chapel room. They can also arrange all kinds of eco-adventure weddings, such as hot air balloon, horseback, helicopter, gondola, and Hummer weddings, in a variety of locations, including the Arch of the Great Spirit, the Valley of Fire, and the sacred lands of the Anasazi Indians. Lake Tahoe, one of the most beautiful lakes in the United States, offers several venue possibilities. If you want to simply get on the water, research your options on the **LAKE TAHOE BOATING GUIDE** (www.boattahoe.com), which lists just about every option, including large cruise boats that accommodate weddings and private parties.

THE WEDDING CHAPEL AT HARVEYS CASINO AND RESORT
P.O. Box 128, Lake Tahoe, NV 89449
www.harrahs.com/our_casinos/hlt/weddings/index.html
800-553-1022 / 775-588-2411

SIZE: APPROXIMATELY 25 ACRES **NUMBER OF ROOMS:** 740; MORE AT THE SISTER HOTEL, HARRAH'S **WHEELCHAIR ACCESSIBLE:** YES **RATES:** $–$$$

REVIEW: Harveys is a AAA Four-Diamond hotel with rooms designed for comfort. Guests enjoy six restaurants, a full-service health club, beach access, a pool and spa, cabaret theater, and of course, the casino.

CEREMONY OPTIONS: Harveys has its own wedding chapel that seats 50 guests or stands 100. The chapel is graced with 18-foot windows, allowing a view of the majestic Sierra Mountains. *The Tahoe Star*, the hotel's luxury yacht, accommodates parties of 36 for wedding ceremonies, which can be performed by the captain or one of the two interfaith ministers on staff. You can also arrange for a ceremony on the beach, at Logan Shoals Vista Point, or on the peak of Heavenly Mountain, which is accessed by gondola.

RECEPTION OPTIONS: In addition to The Tahoe Star, wedding receptions can be held in the hotel ballroom. When all sections of the ballroom are used, it can hold up to 1,000. Top of the Wheel, a premium reception room in what was once the original top-floor restaurant, offers gorgeous lake views and accommodates 120. Llewellyn's, which also affords fantastic views, is a restaurant located on the hotel's nineteenth floor. It can host a day wedding for 100.

WEDDING SERVICES: Full-service wedding services for "one-stop shopping."

GOLD HILL HOTEL
P.O. Box 740, Virginia City, NV 89440
www.goldhillhotel.net
775-847-0111

SIZE: N/A **NUMBER OF ROOMS:** 20 **WHEELCHAIR ACCESSIBLE:** YES **RATES:** $–$$

REVIEW: The Gold Hill Hotel is located in Virginia City, only minutes away from the Tahoe area. Staying in Virginia City is like stepping back in time. With the city's Old West saloons, museums, mines, and mansions, visitors can enjoy the sights and sounds of the gold- and silver-rush era. Gold Hill, Nevada's oldest hotel, boasts a large fireplace, Victorian décor, wood floors, authentic period accents, and an old winding staircase that leads into the Great Room. Set apart from the hotel's main house, the Guest House provides the perfect lodging for newlyweds.

CEREMONY OPTIONS: The winding staircase and Victorian furnishings make the hotel's Great Room a "great room" for wedding ceremonies. The Gazebo, able to hold 120, is also ideal, featuring landscaped grounds and a glorious view of the Sierras.

RECEPTION OPTIONS: The Crown Point Restaurant can seat up to 80 guests. Additional guests can be seated in the Great Room, with or without the use of the restaurant. A beautiful renovation has rescued the Gold Hill Hall, built in the 1870s, from decay. The hall now includes a service kitchen, bar, and room for 50 dinner guests. The Gazebo can also be used for a reception, accommodating up to 120.

WEDDING SERVICES: Provides a list of recommended service providers.

CAESARS PALACE

3570 Las Vegas Boulevard, Las Vegas, NV 89109

www.caesars.com

877-279-3334 / 877-427-7243

SIZE: 4.5 ACRES **NUMBER OF ROOMS:** 2,418 ROOMS; 5 WEDDING CHAPELS **WHEELCHAIR ACCESSIBLE:** YES **RATES:** $–$$$

REVIEW: The Garden of the Gods Pool Oasis is artfully fashioned after a Roman public bath, at the heart of which flow crystal waters of the circular Temple Pool. It is easy to imagine yourself in Julius Caesar's Rome as you stand amidst graceful fountains, imported marble statues, manicured gardens, swimming pools, and outdoor whirlpools, all rimmed with ancient mosaics. There are 24 restaurants and cafés, numerous shops, great entertainment, and larger-than-life spa and fitness centers. The spa has 28 treatment salons, where any pre-wedding jitters can be massaged away. With an abundance of amenities, the elegant, spacious guest rooms are fit for royalty.

© CAESARS PALACE WEDDING SERVICES

CEREMONY OPTIONS: Caesars' stunning gardens and chapels make for the wedding of your dreams. Decorated in warm gold tones, the Palace Chapel is elegant and intimate, able to accommodate up to 70. The chapel is located close to a choice of ballrooms, away from the bustle of the casino. Tropical palm trees, floral landscaping, and Roman architecture surround the Terrazza Lawn. Its garden, which seats 115 guests, features a Roman-style gazebo, a koi fish pond, and a fountain. The Intimate Garden is nestled in a private corner of Caesars Palace, with stone benches seating 150 guests. This garden is accented by a grand arched entry and a floral bordered aisle.

RECEPTION OPTIONS: The Bradley Ogden Restaurant offers American cuisine for up to 45. The

Terrazza, serving authentic Italian cuisine, accommodates up to 75. Overlooking the gardens, The Empress Court specializes in authentic Asian cuisine for up to 60. Cafe Lago offers an international menu and serves up to 70. It boasts a stone aqueduct, water walls, and a view of the Garden of the Gods.

WEDDING SERVICES: Full service.

LUXOR

3900 Las Vegas Boulevard South, Las Vegas, NV 89119

www.luxor.com

888-777-0188

SIZE: 30 FLOORS **NUMBER OF ROOMS:** 4,476 **WHEELCHAIR ACCESSIBLE:** YES **RATES:** $–$$$

REVIEW: Luxor is an awesome, 30-story, black glass pyramid. Egyptian accents within the hotel's warm, regal, and exotic décor provide a mystical sense of being carried through time to the ancient wonders of Egypt. Each guest room is designed as a luxurious experience in itself. Twin 22-story towers have spacious, inviting rooms with striking views of the city.

CEREMONY OPTIONS: There are two nicely appointed chapels, one that seats 60 guests and another that seats 100.

RECEPTION OPTIONS: Able to accommodate 50 to 1,000 guests, Luxor's lavish Egyptian Ballroom is adaptable for receptions of varying sizes.

WEDDING SERVICES: Full service; no outside professional services allowed.

THE VENETIAN

3355 Las Vegas Boulevard South, Las Vegas, NV 89109

www.venetianweddings.com

877-883-6423 / 702-414-4280

SIZE: N/A **NUMBER OF ROOMS:** OVER 4,000 SUITES **WHEELCHAIR ACCESSIBLE:** YES **RATES:** $–$$$

REVIEW: Have you always dreamt of a romantic wedding in Venice? Then head for The Venetian, where exquisite details will instantly transport you to the famous Italian city. Ornate paintings rival masterpieces, statues, and columns conjure up ancient times, and pools, gardens, fountains, and terraces evoke opulence. A fantasy wedding in Venice becomes reality along the Grand Canal, as gondolas pass by. With magnificent suites and service beyond compare, it is no surprise that *Travel + Leisure* magazine voted The Venetian one of the Top 100 Hotels in the World.

CEREMONY OPTIONS: There are three elegant and intimate chapels, each seating 40 to 50 guests, all housed under one grand chapel of 2,500 square feet, seating 150 if need be. A traditional Venetian wedding can take place in the marketplace, just below St. Mark's Square. The bridge, above the sparkling waters of the Grand Canal and under the glow of romantic street lights, provides a grand entrance for the bride. Couples can also exchange vows in a gondola, then be serenaded by the gondolier.

RECEPTION OPTIONS: Receptions can be held in the beautifully decorated Hospitality Parlors, which comfortably seat 40. The 17 privately owned restaurants, featuring such culinary celebrities as Wolfgang Puck, Thomas Keller, Emeril Lagasse, and Joachim Splichal, accommodate any taste. These restaurants can serve up to 200 guests.

WEDDING SERVICES: Full service, including tuxedo and gown rental!

BLISS MANSION BED AND BREAKFAST

608 Elizabeth Street, Carson City, NV 89703

www.blissmansion.com

775-887-8988

SIZE: N/A **NUMBER OF ROOMS:** 5 **WHEELCHAIR ACCESSIBLE:** YES **RATES:** $$

REVIEW: Built in 1879, Bliss Mansion stands directly across from the Governor's Mansion in the heart of Carson City's historic district. The mansion has been fully restored, and its suites feature such amenities as cozy fireplaces, large sunny windows, plush towels and robes, clawfoot tubs, and handmade herbal soaps, down pillows and comforters, and hand-carved mahogany beds with pillowtop mattresses. Victorian décor, marble fireplaces, warm wood accents, and glowing chandeliers create a magical setting. The grand staircase, which leads into the main parlor, promises every bride a dramatic entrance.

CEREMONY AND RECEPTION OPTIONS: The house can accomodate up to 65 guests for an indoor ceremony and/or reception. During the warmer months of June through September, events for up to 250 people can be held on the veranda and the mansion grounds. Sit-down dinners in the formal dining room are limited to 22.

WEDDING SERVICES: List of preferred vendors provided.

NEW MEXICO

New Mexico is known as the Land of Enchantment, and for good reason. From the fascinating formations of Carlsbad Caverns to the steep slopes of Taos, New Mexico is filled with enchanting natural wonders. Visitors enjoy relatively easy access to the state's 100 lakes and rivers and 13 national monuments and parks, 45 percent of which are on public land. Dotting the landscape are the unique mesas, which rise above the land in a surreal table-like formation. Native Americans built their pueblos on these mesas for security from their enemies. In New Mexico, there are 19 pueblos, all descendants of the ancient Pueblo cultures, which once inhabited Chaco Canyon, Mesa Verde, and Bandelier. Today's pueblos are the oldest tribal communities in the United States, and their vibrant culture is reflected in the beautiful pottery, jewelry, and weaving they produce today. The Sangre de Cristo Mountains endow the north with a dramatic landscape and give Santa Fe its claim as the highest state capital in the United States. Santa Fe, a favorite New Mexico destination, is renowned for being a mecca for the arts. If you are planning a wedding in Santa Fe, consider the months of May through October; winter is cold due to the city's high elevation.

PLANNING NOTES

SPECIAL REQUIREMENTS: WAITING PERIOD: None

CIVIL CEREMONIES: A civil ceremony can be performed by any kind of judge.

RELIGIOUS CEREMONIES: Santa Fe is an international city with many cultural and religious resources. If you cannot find the faith or denomination you are looking for, contact Irene Swain (505-983-1799 / www.santafenmweddings.com), who is an interfaith minister.

© MARK NOHL / COURTESY: NEW MEXICO DEPARTMENT OF TOURISM

DESIGN IDEAS

A wedding in New Mexico promises to be a colorful and festive occasion, whether your theme centers around desert beauty, Native American tradition, or Mexican culture—all significant components of the state's identity. To welcome your guests, fill a Navajo pot or basket with chili peppers, turquoise jewelry, and pecans (a major crop in New Mexico). Have fun creating a fitting color scheme for the wedding—perhaps soft desert sand tones punctuated by either turquoise or bright reds, oranges, yellows, and greens. You could dress up your tables with Navajo or Mexican table linens and brightly colored candles, then decorate the room with colorful paper lanterns. Cacti, such as yucca (the state flower), and brilliant blossoms, such as zinnias or gerbera daisies, can all give the wedding venue a distinctive look. For the menu, consider offering your guests gourmet Mexican fare. And to make the cuisine even more irresistible, use garlands of red and green chili peppers to accent the food displays. To incorporate a mix of New Mexican influences into your celebration, feature Navajo drums during your ceremony and a Mexican mariachi band during the reception.

PLANNING RESOURCES

TOURISM:
New Mexico Tourism Department
www.newmexico.org
800-733-6396 ext. 0643

PARKS, MONUMENTS, AND HISTORIC SITES:
New Mexico State Parks
P.O. Box 1147, Santa Fe, NM 87504
www.emnrd.state.nm.us/nmparks
888-667-2757

WEDDING RESOURCES:
HELPFUL WEB SITES:
Country Weddings: www.countryweddings.com/states/newmexico/index.shtml
New Mexico Wedding Professionals: www.nmwp.com

VENUES

If you are interested in a venue that combines natural beauty with Southwestern history, consider **PECOS NATIONAL HISTORIC PARK** (505-757-6414 / www.nps.gov/peco). Spanning 6,670 acres, it became a National Historic Park in 1990 in order to preserve 12,000 years of New Mexican history. The park incorporates the ancient pueblo of Pecos, two Spanish colonial missions, Santa Fe Trail sites, Kiva ruins, a Spanish mission church, the Forked Lightning Ranch, and the site of the Civil War Battle of Glorieta Pass. Ceremonies can be held in the old Spanish Mission Church. If you are planning a small wedding in Santa Fe, look into the **HACIENDA DEL CEREZO** (888-982-8001 / www.haciendadelcerezo.com), an exclusive property surrounded by mountains. To book a wedding there, you must book the entire inn (ten rooms) for a minimum of two nights, with no more than 40 people. If this fits your bill, prepare to enjoy all the Hacienda has to offer, from access to beautiful Arabian horses to the three gourmet meals—wine included—a day. Ceremonies can be held by the infinity pool or in the garden, and receptions can be held in the Great Room.

THE INN OF THE FIVE GRACES
150 East DeVargas Street, Santa Fe, NM 87501
www.fivegraces.com
505-992-0957

SIZE: 1 CITY BLOCK **NUMBER OF ROOMS:** 22 **WHEELCHAIR ACCESSIBLE:** YES **RATES:** $$

REVIEW: The Inn of the Five Graces, a Garrett Hotel Property, consists of a single-story adobe structure and a large two-story New Mexico river-rock building. So distinctive are the inn's architectural details that, in May of 2002, they captured the attention of *Architectural Digest*. Guests are sure to notice the details, too. The accommodations are decorated with artifacts from around the world, and the adobe walls are supported by ponderosa pine beams and cedar poles. In each suite, the rooms are divided by weathered green antique shutters with brass hinges, and the doors are all handcarved with inset glass panels. The Inn, located on the Santa Fe Trail, is next to the Santa Fe Playhouse and the famous Pink Adobe restaurant.

CEREMONY AND RECEPTION OPTIONS: Across the street from the inn is the Chapel of San Miguel, the oldest church in the United States. If the party reserves the entire inn, they can hold the ceremony and/or reception in the inn's two outside courtyards, which accommodate up to 100 people. There is no inside reception room, but inclement weather is not typically a concern in New Mexico.

WEDDING SERVICES: An on-site wedding coordinator helps with all the details.

BISHOP'S LODGE RESORT & SPA
P.O. Box 2367, Bishop Lodge Road, Santa Fe, NM 87501
www.bishopslodge.com
800-419-0492 / 505-983-6377

SIZE: 450 ACRES **NUMBER OF ROOMS:** 111 **WHEELCHAIR ACCESSIBLE:** YES **RATES:** $$

REVIEW: Bishop's Lodge welcomes you to Santa Fe with 15 lodges, all a beautiful blend of rustic and contemporary style. In addition to lots of tin work and painted wood, the décor features leather furniture and shades. Located only three miles from the center of Santa Fe, Bishop's Lodge is the best of both worlds—city-close yet country-quiet. Guests can rejuvenate at the ShaNah Spa and Wellness Center, which, in 2004, was named the *Condé Nast Johansens* "Most Outstanding Spa in North America." Guests also have access to tennis courts and a gorgeous pool, and they can partake in horseback riding, hiking, and skeet and trap shooting.

© COURTESY: NEW MEXICO DEPARTMENT OF TOURISM

CEREMONY OPTIONS: Bishop's Lodge offers several romantic ceremony locations. Lamy Chapel, an historic, adobe wedding chapel, accommodates only ten guests standing, but it is surrounded by the Portal of the Chapel, a terrace-like setting that fits another 30. Ceremonies for 50 can be held by the "wedding tree," an old crabapple tree on the lawn, if the weather permits. The Mesa Vista, an outlook on a small mountain with panoramic views, is a picturesque setting for larger ceremonies of 200. There is also a gazebo on the Little Tesuque Lawn, complete with tall pines and a little bridge spanning the Tesuque stream, accommodating 175.

RECEPTION OPTIONS: The Thunderbird and the adjoining El Charo Lounge accommodate 125 for a dinner reception. El Charo is an historic Western saloon featuring original tinwork and a copper-hooded fireplace. The largest and most elegant venue for receptions is the Tesuque Pavilion Ballroom, bedecked with carpet and flagstone floors, a large stone fireplace, and French doors leading out to a lawn portal, where there is a grass reception area equipped with an outdoor fireplace.

WEDDING SERVICES: Though the sales manager helps with general coordination, it is recommended that couples hire a full-service wedding planner.

INN OF THE ANASAZI

113 Washington Avenue, Santa Fe, NM 87501

www.innoftheanasazi.com

800-688-8100 / 505-988-3030

© JIM ORR / COURTESY: NEW MEXICO DEPARTMENT OF TOURISM

SIZE: 1 CITY BLOCK **NUMBER OF ROOMS:** 56 **WHEELCHAIR ACCESSIBLE:** YES **RATES:** $$

REVIEW: The Inn of the Anasazi is an architectural marvel, combining modern luxury with ancient Anasazi aesthetic. The inn's design, inspired by the Anasazi cliff dwellers, affords guests the opportunity to inhabit a dwelling built into the side of a cliff. With such unique character, this AAA Four Diamond inn has attracted recent recognition, earning itself a spot on *Condé Nast Traveler*'s Top 75 Hotels in North America and *Travel + Leisure*'s Top 100 Hotels in Continental United States and Canada. The rooms are appointed with hewn furniture, fireplaces, stonetop tables, Indian blankets, potted cacti, and artifacts.

CEREMONY AND RECEPTION OPTIONS: The inn's library opens up to a living room which combined can entertain 50 to 60 comfortably. The four-star restaurant can also be rented for affairs with 65 to 90 guests.

WEDDING SERVICES: Some wedding coordination is available.

WYOMING

The history of Wyoming—the "Cowboy State"—comes alive in its many historic forts, rodeos, mining towns, and dude ranches. Native American history and culture are also prevalent in this state, whose flag features the bison, once the main sustenance of the native people. If you want to celebrate amidst awe-inspiring surroundings, Wyoming is the destination for you. Its natural attractions—geysers, hot springs, Yellowstone, Grand Teton National, and the Rocky Mountains—boast beauty beyond compare. Destination couples will be impressed with the wide selection of luxury resorts, ranches, lodges, national parks, and adventure options. For a snowy wedding in Wyoming, plan your big day between December and March; to wed in warm, sunny weather, arrange for a celebration between June and August.

PLANNING NOTES

SPECIAL REQUIREMENTS: WAITING PERIOD: None

CIVIL CEREMONIES: There are no restrictions on civil ceremonies. They can be performed by a judge or a justice of the peace.

RELIGIOUS CEREMONIES: Wyoming offers a fairly diverse selection of Christian, Jewish, and Muslim resources. One nondenominational option is the historic Mammoth Hot

Springs Chapel (307-344-7430) in Yellowstone Park. Nonresident clergy officiants need to file for a permit from the Probate Court in the county where the marriage will take place.

DESIGN IDEAS

When designing your wedding, keep in mind that Wyoming mines yield diamonds, jade, moss agate, rubies, bloodstone, and peridot, all of which would add a lovely sparkle to the wedding. When pledging a lifetime of love and fidelity to each other, what could be more fitting than a ceremony by "Old Faithful"? You might adopt this as an overall theme, using postcards, etchings, or paintings of Yellowstone Park for invitations or favors. Welcome your guests with rucksacks holding a trail map, a compass, and gourmet trail mix. For wedding decor, let nature be your guide; when placed in old-fashioned baskets, bunches of native flowers, such as the vibrant Indian Paintbrush, lend a touch of understated beauty. Your wedding menu should include the best Wyoming has to offer—wild game and fish, lamb, and beef.

© DAVID BECKSTEAD

PLANNING RESOURCES

TOURISM:
Wyoming Dude Ranchers Association
P.O. Box 618, Dubois, WY 82513
www.wyomingdra.com
307-455-2084

Wyoming Travel & Tourism
www.wyomingtourism.org
800-225-5996

PARKS, MONUMENTS, AND HISTORIC SITES:
Wyoming State Parks and Cultural Resources
2301 Central Avenue, Cheyenne, WY 82002
http://wyoparks.state.wy.us
307-777-6303

WEDDING RESOURCES:
  HELPFUL PUBLICATIONS:
  A Grand Wedding & Event Planner. P. O. Box
    11233, Jackson, WY 83002

  HELPFUL WEB SITES:
  A Grand Wedding: www.jacksonholewedding.com
  Wyoming Brides: www.wyomingbrides.com

VENUES

Couples can be married in **YELLOWSTONE NATIONAL PARK** (307-344-7381 / www.nps.gov/yell), the home of Old Faithful and thousands of other geysers, steam vents, and hot springs. You must first obtain a special-use permit, whether you plan to marry at an outdoor site (307-344-2109) or in Mammoth Chapel (307-344-7430). Contact **XANTERRA PARKS & RESORTS** (307-344-7901 / www.travelyellowstone.com) to explore the park's accommodations and reception venues, from rustic to full service. One option is **MAM-**

MOTH HOT SPRINGS HOTEL (866-875-8456), which hosts buffet-style receptions in its Map Room. If you are planning a winter wedding, consider **JACKSON HOLE IDITAROD SLED DOG TOURS** (800-554-7388 / www.jhsleddog.com). Professional mushers and their canine partners guide you and your guests on sleds through the white wilderness, taking you to a hot spring for a pre-ceremony lunch, then to an icy waterfall for the exchange of vows. A tour specialist can customize outings for large groups, and brief lessons are provided for those wishing to drive a sled team.

AMANGANI

1535 North East Butte Road, Jackson, WY 83001

www.amanresorts.com

877-734-7333 / 307-734-7333

SIZE: 1,000 ACRES **NUMBER OF ROOMS:** 29 SUITES, 6 DELUXE SUITES, 4 AMANGANI SUITES, AND 1 GRAND TETON SUITE **WHEELCHAIR ACCESSIBLE:** YES **RATES:** $$$

REVIEW: Amangani, meaning "peaceful home," is the one and only Amanresort in the United States. Constructed with Oklahoma sandstone, Pacific redwood, Douglas fir, and cedar, the interior and exterior of Amangani were designed to be in tune with the natural surroundings. The rooms blend modern and rustic styles seamlessly, each with a fireplace; king-sized platform beds with down mattress pads and duvets; a balcony, deck or porch; and deep soaking tubs with window views. Guests keep themselves busy with hiking, fishing, skiing, snowmobiling, snowboarding, dogsledding, and more. The resort's health center and gym offer exercise and spa services and a 35-meter, 80°F (27°C) outdoor swimming pool. Massage, yoga, steam rooms, and seaweed wraps are just a taste of the pampering that guests can receive.

CEREMONY AND RECEPTION OPTIONS: Couples can choose from the cozy redwood-paneled special occasion room with regional artwork and a large black slate fireplace, the library with dramatic mountain views, or the lounge with a cathedral-like redwood ceiling and a perfect stairway for the bride's entrance. Each location has a capacity of 75 guests. Exclusive use of Amangani is an option—one that would provide more space and flexibility. The resort can arrange horse-drawn sleighs or carriages if the couple wishes.

WEDDING SERVICES: Full service.

THE WORT HOTEL

Glenwood and Broadway, P.O. Box 69, Jackson, WY 83001

www.worthotel.com

800-322-2727 / 307-733-2190

SIZE: 1 CITY BLOCK **NUMBER OF ROOMS:** 60 GUEST ROOMS, INCLUDING 3 SPACIOUS LUXURY SUITES **WHEELCHAIR ACCESSIBLE:** YES **RATES:** $$

REVIEW: Named one of "America's 54 Great Inns" by *National Geographic Explorer*, The Wort Hotel is Jackson Hole's premier boutique hotel, located just steps away from downtown galleries, shops, and eateries. Guests will delight in the hotel's spacious, wood-furnished rooms, two restaurants, Silver Dollar Bar, and fitness center.

CEREMONY OPTIONS: Ceremonies for up to 30 guests can be held by the Grand Staircase, where the lobby provides a lovely, intimate setting. Accommodating 70 people, the Goldpiece Room defines ambience, with 12-foot cast ceilings and a large fireplace.

RECEPTION OPTIONS: The Goldpiece Room, accented with antiques, remains the hotel's signature reception location. The largest reception location is the Jackson Room, a a sophisticated setting that holds 90. Both rooms may be utilized for a dramatic effect, joined by the hotel's historic main lobby; this option is restricted to certain time periods and to parties that meet minimum room block requirements.

WEDDING SERVICES: Full catering and wedding services. The hotel makes referrals for approved wedding planners and vendors. They can suggest off-site wedding sites in the shadows of the Teton and provide contacts for all the arrangements, including minister, catering, setup, transportation, and other needs.

© DAVID BECKSTEAD

SNAKE RIVER LODGE & SPA

7710 Granite Loop Road,
Teton Village, WY 83025
www.snakeriverlodge.com
866-975-7625 / 307-732-6000

SIZE: 2 ACRES **NUMBER OF ROOMS:** 88 GUEST ROOMS, 46 LUXURY CONDOMINIUMS **WHEELCHAIR ACCESSIBLE:** YES **RATES:** $$–$$$

REVIEW: Enjoy the grandeur of Jackson Hole Valley and the Grand Tetons in this luxurious AAA Four-Diamond lodge, which boasts posh guest rooms, superb service, gourmet dining, a full-service spa, an indoor/outdoor pool, and incredible scenery.

CEREMONY OPTIONS: You can tie the knot beside a waterfall cascading over granite boulders, at the peak of Rendezvous Mountain (accessed by a tram ride), or by the banks of the crystal clear Snake River. The lodge also offers beautiful indoor venues.

RECEPTION OPTIONS: There are five elegant reception spaces: the Apres Vous Room, suitable for 75; the Rendezvous Room, for 52; the Sundance Center, for 250; the Sundance North, for 100; and the Sundance South, for 100.

WEDDING SERVICES: On-site wedding coordinator and full-service catering. Weddings can be designed around skiing, fishing, canoeing, and other outdoor activities.

REGION IV: ALASKA

ALASKA

Alaska has drawn all kinds of adventurers over the years—first curious explorers, then hopeful gold prospectors, and now intrepid individuals in search of peace and solitude. If you are considering an eco-adventure wedding, take a careful look at what Alaska has to offer. One of the last states to join the union, Alaska boasts more than 550,000 square miles of excitement, from the rich Pacific coastline to the mountainous terrain rising over 12,000 feet. Its 3,000 rivers, 3 million lakes, and 5,000 glaciers make the state a popular choice for nature-loving couples. Combine Alaskan resources with the free spirit of its inhabitants and you get wedding opportunities like nowhere else in the world. In Alaska, couples can be married offshore on a fishing or tour boat, in a wilderness lodge, in an old gold-mining town, or on a train, or they can be transported via helicopter to a remote glacier with only Mother Nature as a witness. The best time to plan a wedding in Alaska is May through September. Dog sledding and winter weddings are best from November to March, but keep in mind that many places close during winter's deep freeze.

PLANNING NOTES

SPECIAL REQUIREMENTS: WAITING PERIOD: Three days

CIVIL CEREMONIES: In Alaska, civil marriages are solemnized by a marriage commissioner or by a member of the Salvation Army. Alaska allows any Alaskan to perform a wedding if she has been appointed to do so by a marriage commissioner from an Alaskan court; it is quite easy to obtain an appointment.

RELIGIOUS CEREMONIES: There are many options for Christians and Jews throughout the state. Hindu couples can find Dharma Centers in Anchorage and Juneau, and Muslim couples can find resources in Anchorage.

© GLACIER BAY LODGE & TOURS AND CHRIS AREND PHOTOGRAPHY

DESIGN IDEAS

For a native theme, incorporate the beautiful designs, music, and dance of Inuit culture into your wedding celebration. Or adopt a "gold rush" theme, with mining welcome baskets and gold nugget favors. The flora and fauna of Alaska will no doubt inspire any nature-enthusiast couple; invitations, programs, and even the cake could feature images of seals, polar bears, or arctic foxes, and floral décor could include wild Alaskan bouquets of lupine, blue iris, Queen Anne's lace, monty-casino, white caspia, multicolored daisy mums, and dark green ferns. Make the most of Alaska's resources to plan a mouthwatering meal; be sure to feature Alaskan salmon, halibut, trout, and/or caribou—the freshest you'll ever eat—on your reception menu.

PLANNING RESOURCES

TOURISM:
Alaska State Tourism Office
P. O.Box 110809, Juneau, AK 99811-0809
www.travelalaska.com
907-465-2012

PARKS, MONUMENTS, AND HISTORIC SITES:
Division of Parks and Outdoor Recreation
www.dnr.state.ak.us/parks

WEDDING RESOURCES:

HELPFUL PUBLICATIONS:
Alaska Bride & Groom: www.alaskabrideandgroom.com

HELPFUL WEB SITES:
Alaska Bride and Groom: www.alaskabrideandgroom.com
Alaska Wedding Vendors: www.alaskaweddingvendors.com
Anchorage Alaska Convention & Visitors Bureau Wedding Page:
www.anchorage.net/607.cfm

VENUES

The most famous park in Alaska is **DENALI NATIONAL PARK** (907-683-2294 / www.nps.gov/dena), which is approximately six million acres in size and home to Mount McKinley, North America's highest mountain at 20,320 miles in altitude. To be married in Denali, you must obtain a special-use permit by calling the chief ranger at the phone number listed above. The first 15 miles of park road are accessible to the public and their vehicles, so, logistically, it is easier to choose a site in this area. Beyond that point, the public must be on a tour or shuttle bus. Tents are not allowed for wedding celebrations, so be prepared for any kind of weather. Camping is permitted within the park on a reservation basis only; reservations for the year are taken beginning in December for mail and fax and in February for phone and Internet. For lodging and dog sledding in Denali, consider **EARTHSONG LODGE** (907-683-2863 / www.earthsonglodge.com). For larger groups, try **THE KANTISHNA ROADHOUSE** (800-942-7420 / www.kantishnaroadhouse.com) or **CAMP DENALI** (907-683-2290 / www.campdenali.com), which is much more than just a "camp." If you're seeking the perfect "compound" for a larger wedding party, consider **THE GRANDE DENALI LODGE**, **THE BLUFFS HOTEL**, and **THE APENGLOW RESTAURANT** (907-474-8555 / www.denalialaska.com), all located just outside the entrance of the park.

   HOLLAND AMERICA (206-281-3535 / www.hollandamerica.com) and **PRINCESS CRUISE LINES** (800-774-6237 / www.princess.com) offer popular Alaskan wedding packages, including helicopter glacier weddings and romantic cruises, rail, and wilderness lodge experiences. Helicopter glacier weddings can also be arranged through **COASTAL HELICOPTERS, INC**. (907-789-5600 / www.coastalhelicopters.com). With Alaska being host to the Iditarod, an annual dog sled race that covers 1,150 miles, what could be more fitting than a dog sled-themed wedding? If this interests you, call the **ALASKA DOG MUSHERS ASSOCIATION** in Fairbanks (907-457-6874 / www.sleddog.org); for a nominal fee, the association rents out its lodge, Mushers Hall, for special events.

HATCHER PASS LODGE
Box 763, Palmer, AK 99645
www.hatcherpasslodge.com
907-745-5897 / 907-745-1200

SIZE: 10 PRIVATE ACRES NEXT TO 761-ACRE INDEPENDENCE MINE STATE HISTORICAL PARK **NUMBER OF ROOMS**: 3 ROOMS IN MAIN LODGE, PLUS 9 CABINS (ACCOMMODATIONS FOR 40 PEOPLE IN ALL) **WHEELCHAIR ACCESSIBLE:** TERRAIN IS ROUGH; LODGE WORKS WITH HANDICAPPED GUESTS ON A CASE-BY-CASE BASIS **RATES:** $

REVIEW: The area around Hatcher Pass Lodge is a training site for the United States Cross Country Ski Team. Not a pro skier? Don't worry—the Talkeetna Mountains provide varied terrain for backcountry skiers of all abilities, with miles of groomed trails, some as high as 4,000 feet. Lodge guests can indulge in a delicious mountain-fare breakfast (from hotcakes and warm maple syrup to omelets) as well as lunch and dinner (fondue, homemade soups, smoked halibut, and more). At the bar, guests can enjoy a selection of gourmet beer, wine, and hot specialty drinks, including a local favorite, The Hatcher Pass Steamer. The lodge's cabins have half baths, while the lodge itself has showers. There is also a sauna house on the grounds.

CEREMONY OPTIONS: Wedding ceremonies are performed here year-round, and the sky is the limit. A short walk dawn a path brings you to The Knoll, which gives way to the magnificent backdrop of the Matanuska Valley. If you would like to hike to your mountaintop ceremony, a higher peak can be reached within an hour. Some people snowcat to the remote backcountry and ski, snowshoe, or hike to their selected spot. In the case of inclement weather, the lodge can also be used for ceremonies.

RECEPTION OPTIONS: The lodge can accommodate up to 40 guests. For outdoor receptions, tent rental is available.

WEDDING SERVICES: The lodge provides a list of recommended service providers and handles food and beverages; specialty and vegetarian menus are available on request.

GLACIER BAY LODGE

Office: 241 West Ship Creek Avenue, Anchorage, AK 99501

Lodge: P.O. Box 179, Gustavus, AK 99826

www.visitglacierbay.com

(reservations) 888-229-8687 / (office) 907-264-4600 / (lodge) 907-697-4000

SIZE: GLACIER BAY NATIONAL PARK COVERS 3.3 MILLION ACRES NUMBER OF ROOMS: 56 WHEELCHAIR ACCESSIBLE: LIMITED RATES: $$

REVIEW: Offering pristine natural beauty, Glacier Bay National Park (907-697-2230 / www.nps.gov/glba) is a remote venue in Alaska. Glacier Bay Lodge, 1,000 miles from Anchorage and 60 miles from Juneau, provides the only lodging within the national park. Open during the summer months and accessible solely by plane or boat, the lodge is located right on the water, surrounded by Sitka spruce in an old-growth rainforest. From the deck, you can watch whales pass by all summer long. The Fairweather Dining Room serves fresh seafood, delivered right to their dock.

CEREMONY OPTIONS: If the weather is nice, the deck is a beautiful spot for a ceremony —and whales might even attend! Inside, you can have a cozy ceremony in front of the large stone fireplace.

RECEPTION OPTIONS: The Fairweather Dining Room can seat 84, the deck can seat 70, and a smaller private dining room seats 25 or less. All reception rooms have windows overlooking the water. The lodge's whale-watching tour boat can be used for wedding reception dinners, accommodating up to 150.

WEDDING SERVICES: Provides some assistance.

ALASKA NATIVE HERITAGE CENTER

8800 Heritage Center Drive, Anchorage, AK 99506

www.alaskanative.net

800-315-6608 / 907-330-8000

SIZE: 26 ACRES NUMBER OF ROOMS: NO LODGING WHEELCHAIR ACCESSIBLE: YES RATES: $

REVIEW: In the late 1980s, the Alaskan Federation of Natives established the Heritage Center to preserve and celebrate native Alaskan culture. In the Center, you'll find many aspects of native traditions and customs represented in all forms. Located just 12 minutes from downtown Anchorage, this multifunction site is based around the 26,000-square-foot Welcome House, with demonstration areas, a theatre, a café, a gift shop, and a large, open circular hall for gatherings and performances. Outside, along a trail around a two-acre lake, there is a village site, five traditional village exhibits, and a talking circle.

CEREMONY OPTIONS: There are many ceremony options outdoors, including exhibit sites along the lakeside trail and a deck off the main building. Indoor ceremonies are held in the Gathering Place, which accommodates up to 440 guests

RECEPTION OPTIONS: Receptions can be held outside on the deck or inside at the Gathering Place. This setting provides an ideal space for entertainment such as native dancers and performers.

WEDDING SERVICES: The Center is happy to help you plan your event, large or small. An on-site catering manager can arrange food and beverage details.

KACHEMAK BAY WILDERNESS LODGE

P.O. Box 956, China Poot Bay, Homer, AK 99603

www.alaskawildernesslodge.com

907-235-7915

SIZE: 20 ACRES   NUMBER OF ROOMS: 5 SEPARATE ACCOMMODATIONS FOR 10 INDIVIDUAL COUPLES OR 19 PEOPLE "FAMILY STYLE"   WHEELCHAIR ACCESSIBLE: NO   RATES: $$$

REVIEW: If you're dreaming of "getting away from it all" for your wedding, Kachemak is the place for you. Kachemak has all the benefits of civilized hospitality and all the excitement of the wilderness. If more guests are invited than they can accommodate, the lodge works out additional accommodations at Land's End Resort in Homer. From there, your guests can board the luxury vessel, *The Rainbow Connection*, and take a 20-minute trip to Kachemak Bay, arriving in style for your big day.

CEREMONY OPTIONS: There are several beautiful locations on the lodge's grounds.

RECEPTION OPTIONS: The lodge can accommodate up to 40 people for a reception, providing all the food and beverages and, if desired, a tent. *The Rainbow Connection* is also available to take guests on a journey they won't soon forget, winding through bays and fjords and offering views of wildlife and natural beauty not seen anywhere else in the world.

WEDDING SERVICES: Full service.

REGION V: HAWAII

HAWAII

Long the number-one wedding destination, Hawaii is greatly responsible for making destination weddings so popular. To many, Hawaii is a paradise on earth, with sunny weather, fabulous sandy beaches, luxury hotels, beautiful terrain, breathtaking views, and delicious fruits of the earth. Because there is so much to see and do on each of the six main islands—Hawaii, Maui, Molokai, Oahu, Kauai, and Lanai—you may want to marry on one of the islands and then honeymoon on one or two of the others.

Hawaii, "The Big Island," is unmatched in natural diversity, with volcanoes (including the massive Mauna Loa and still-active Kilauea), black lava fields, snow-capped mountain peaks, alpine meadows, a glacial lake, underwater caves, waterfalls, rainforests, deserts, and beaches of gold, black, and green. Kauai, often referred to as the "Garden Isle," is the most tropical and probably the most romantic, featuring Wailua Falls, Fern Grotto, and Waimea Canyon. Maui, "The Valley Isle," is perfect if you love golf, hiking, windsurfing, tennis, and water sports. According to legend, Maui captured the sun and secured the promise of long days for the enjoyment of the islands' people and visitors. In Oahu, meaning "The Gathering Space," tourists enjoy the attractions of Waikiki Beach, surfers take on the 25-foot waves of the Banzai Pipeline, cliff divers plummet from 60-foot heights above Waimea Falls, and plant lovers find the largest variety of tropical botanical life. Molokai, the "Friendly Isle"—the least developed and the most "Hawaiian" of all the islands—boasts sand dunes, coral reefs, and rain forests, the state's highest waterfall and longest white-sand beach, and the world's highest sea cliffs. Lanai, Hawaii's unspoiled "Secluded Island," is a new yet very desirable wedding destination, especially since Bill and Melinda Gates were married there. No matter which island you choose, I recommend planning your wedding during "low season" in the spring or fall. Prices and crowds decrease, but the weather remains gorgeous.

PLANNING NOTES

SPECIAL REQUIREMENTS: WAITING PERIOD: None **SPECIAL NOTES:** Two forms of identification are required, and you must pay for the marriage license in cash. The marriage license is valid for 30 days.

CIVIL CEREMONIES: There are no restrictions on civil ceremonies in Hawaii.

RELIGIOUS CEREMONIES: Weddings of almost any denomination can be arranged, and interfaith ministers can be hired to work with anyone. There are many beautiful churches in Hawaii, but the state's oldest, Mokuaikaua Church (808-329-0655), is located on the Big Island. Situated on land given to missionaries by King Kamehameha III, Mokuaikaua was constructed of coral in 1837. You can view more interesting churches at www.hawaiiweb.com. For Catholic weddings, contact the Catholic Diocese of Hawaii (808-533-1791). Jewish couples may want to contact any of the following synagogues on Oahu: Chabad (808-735-8161), Sof Maarav (808-595-3678), or Emanuel (808-595-7521).

DESIGN IDEAS

Hawaii, greatly influenced by Polynesian culture, is the perfect place for an exotic, tropically themed wedding. For welcome gifts, package chocolate-covered macadamia nuts, Kona coffee, and Niihau shell jewelry in handcrafted koa or milo wooden bowls. A lei ceremony can also give your wedding a decidedly Hawaiian flavor. During this ceremony, the bride and groom exchange fragrant flower leis as a symbol of their everlasting love. Pineapples, seashells, and tropical flowers could accent the décor, and the bride could wear a floral wreath instead of a veil.

Why not celebrate with a luau? Traditional luau fare consist of a pig wrapped in ti leaves, then baked in an imu (underground oven) until succulent. You can also opt for lomi lomi (salmon), ahi (tuna), opakapaka (blue snapper), or mahi mahi (dolphin fish). Accompaniments include poi, a kind of taro paste, and of course mai tais to wash it all down. For authentic entertainment, hire a ukulele player to serenade you and your guests. Fire dancers or hula dancers also make great evening entertainment, and it might be fun to provide hula lessons for your guests.

PLANNING RESOURCES

TOURISM:
Hawaii Visitors & Convention Bureau
2270 Kalakaua Avenue, Suite 801, Honolulu, HI 96815
www.gohawaii.com
800-464-2924

HawaiiWeb, Inc.
91-6416 Kapolei Parkway, Honolulu, HI 96706
www.hawaiiweb.com
866-268-7459

Lanai Tourism
P.O. Box 630310, Lanai City, HI 96763
www.islandoflanai.com

PARKS, MONUMENTS, AND HISTORIC SITES:
National Park Service (United States Department of the Interior)
www.nps.gov

WEDDING RESOURCES:
HELPFUL PUBLICATIONS:
Pacific Rim Weddings Magazine: www.pacificweddings.com

HELPFUL WEB SITES:
Hawaiian Wedding Shop: www.hawaiianweddingshop.com

VENUES

Because it is such a popular wedding destination, Hawaii offers an endless number of wedding locations and services. You can plan virtually any kind of wedding there, from the traditional to the exotic. Couples who love history and nature might want to check out **PARKER RANCH** (808-885-7311 / www.parkerranch.com), a 175,000-acre cattle ranch on the big island of Hawaii. On the island of Molokai, you can find another working ranch, **THE MOLOKA'I RANCH** (888-627-8082 / www.revacommsb.com/~molokai2). Here, guests stay in a 22-room luxury lodge or in a "tentalow," a unique 40-tent platform beach village. In Kauai, you can take a river cruise down the only navigable river in Hawaii, the Wailua River, to the **FERN GROTTO**, another popular wedding site. Covered with tropical ferns, the Fern Grotto is a natural amphitheatre with excellent acoustics. For a picturesque ceremony, trek (by car or foot) 10,000 feet up to the peak of Maui's **HALEAKALA**, one of the world's largest dormant volcanos. An exchange of vows at sunrise or sunset is sure to be unforgettable. Also in Maui, you can have a ceremony (free of charge) at the **KEPANIWAI PARK AND HERITAGE GARDENS**, a showcase of gardens and Hawaiian dwellings. Oahu is home to the **DIAMOND HEAD CRATER**, where you can drive inside, climb 760 feet up, and exchange your vows overlooking Waikiki and the Pacific Ocean.

On Lanai are three venues, the Lodge at Koele, the Manele Bay Hotel, and the Lanai Conference Center, which share wedding services and a reservation line (800-450-3704). Self-described as a "bastion of old-world elegance and Hawaiian grace" and named by *Condé Nast Traveler* as the #1 place to stay in the United States, **THE LODGE AT KOELE** (808-565-7300 / www.lodgeatkoele.com) stands among the world's most elite resorts.

The lodge has magnificent ceremony locations, but it cannot accommodate more than 50 for indoor receptions. The luxurious Mediterranean-style **MANELE BAY HOTEL** (808-565-7700 / www.manelebay.com), which overlooks Hulopoe Bay, accommodates small groups for indoor affairs and larger groups of 100 by the pool. A ceremony at either hotel can be followed with a reception at the **LANAI CONFERENCE CENTER**, which is perched on a knoll above the Manele Bay Hotel. The center has more than 12,000 square feet of reception space, including the Kaunolu Ballroom and the Moana and Kumulani Terraces.

FOUR SEASONS RESORT MAUI AT WAILEA
3900 Wailea Alanui, Wailea, HI 96753
www.fourseasons.com/maui
808-874-8000

SIZE: 11 ACRES **NUMBER OF ROOMS:** 377 ROOMS, INCLUDING 75 SUITES **WHEELCHAIR ACCESSIBLE:** YES **RATES:** $$–$$$ **SPECIAL NOTES:** CHILDREN ARE WELCOME AND WELL CARED FOR IN THE 'KIDS FOR ALL SEASONS' PROGRAM

REVIEW: Perfect for a tropical wedding, the Four Seasons Resort in Maui features a palatial, open-air design with reflecting pools, fountains, waterfalls, and gorgeous views. The resort boasts 36,229 square feet of function space, including an outdoor, oceanfront location for beach weddings. Most guest rooms look out at the Pacific Ocean, while others overlook tropical hillsides and landscaped gardens. Guests can partake in water sports, tennis, spa amenities, and golf, and when hunger strikes, they can choose from three of the finest restaurants on Maui. Ferraro's Bar e Ristorante offers authentic cucina rustica beneath the stars, Spago prepares Wolfgang Puck's California fusion cuisine, and Pacific Grill specializes in surf 'n turf dishes.

CEREMONY OPTIONS: The resort has several outdoor settings that are ideal for wedding ceremonies. Set in a sculpture garden, the Ku'uipo Point Gazebo surrounds you with bougainvillea and affords stunning ocean and mouintain views. The manicured Oceanfront Lawn, which overlooks Wailea Beach, is lined by coconut palms and thatched-roof hales. From the Kaimana Lawn and its plantation-style gazebo, you can see both the ocean and Mount Haleakala. For the most intimate location, the secluded Seasons Lawn is hidden amidst a garden of tropical foliage and sacred palms.

RECEPTION OPTIONS: There are 13 indoor facilities that can accommodate 100 to 700 guests and three outdoor locations that can accommodate 80 to 500.

WEDDING SERVICES: Offers wedding packages and on-site coordinator.

© DAVID BECKSTEAD

KONA VILLAGE RESORT

P.O. Box 1299, Kailua-Kona, HI 96745

www.konavillage.com

800-367-5290 / 808-325-5555

SIZE: 82 ACRES **NUMBER OF ROOMS:** 125 THATCHED HALES (GRASS HUTS) **WHEELCHAIR ACCESSIBLE:** YES **RATES:** $$$ **SPECIAL NOTES:** CHILDREN'S PROGRAMS OFFER EDUCATIONAL AND ENTERTAINING ACTIVITIES FOR YOUNG GUESTS

REVIEW: Kona Village is located on the site of an ancient fishing town at the base of Mount Hualalai. The village consists of hales (grass huts), which reflect nine Polynesian cultures. All guests sleep in the hales; for extra luxury, you can choose one with a private, outdoor whirlpool spa. Kona Village is a retreat from phones, television, and the bustle of everyday life. The grounds offer ponds, manicured lawns, peaceful lagoons, lava flow formations, and black-and-white beaches. Guests are often treated to the spectacle of manta rays swimming by the dozens at night and outriggering canoe trips during the day. Tradition inspires the meals served at the resort, including one of Hawaii's most authentic luaus. A recipient of several awards, the resort is hailed for its preservation and protection of Kona culture and history. In 2002, *Travel + Leisure* named Kona Village one of the Top 50 Romantic Getaways.

CEREMONY OPTIONS: For an outdoor ceremony, you have your choice of lagoons, private beaches, oceanfront areas, and Kona Village's very own coconut grove.

RECEPTION OPTIONS: There are several outdoor areas for wedding receptions, most of which accommodate up to 300 people.

WEDDING SERVICES: Provides full-service coordinator.

INTER-ISLAND HELICOPTERS

449 Kuiloko Road, Hanapepe, HI 96716

www.interislandhelicopters.com

800-656-5009 / 808-335-5009

SIZE: N/A **NUMBER OF ROOMS:** N/A **WHEELCHAIR ACCESSIBLE:** NO **RATES:** DOUBLE THE COST OF AN AVERAGE LIMOUSINE RENTAL, BUT THE FEE ALSO INCLUDES THE SITE FEE

REVIEW: If you want an intimate yet exhilarating wedding ceremony *and* you want a private tour of the island of Kauai from above, a helicopter ceremony is for you. No more than four passengers will fit in a helicopter—don't forget to save a seat for the officiant and the photographer! If you plan to invite more guests, you will have to hire more than one helicopter. Both civil and religious ceremonies can be arranged as well as any other wedding services you may desire, such as music, flowers, and food. Inter-Island Helicopters will transport you anywhere that they have permission to land. Or you can be flown to their very own private Puu Ka Ele Waterfall, which is so remote it can only be reached by helicopter. While this option is exciting, it is not for those that are weak at heart, stomach, or nerves!

central america, south america, and the caribbean

This area of the world wears many faces, which is what makes it so exciting. The people of Central America, South America, and the Caribbean share a passion for romance, music, food, and dance—all the ingredients you need for a perfect wedding. No matter which country you choose as your destination, you are sure to find breathtaking venues—remote islands, pristine beaches, tropical rainforests, bustling metropolises, majestic mountains and glaciers, and more. Consider the Caribbean islands covered in this section, and then explore others—the Cayman Islands, the Dominican Republic, the Virgin Islands, Turks and Caicos, St. Vincent and the Grenadines—as honeymoon possibilities. Moving South, you'll be tempted by more wonderful locales—the amazing Machu Piccu Sanctuary Lodge, the great wilderness of northern Patagonia, the beautiful Isla de Margarita off the coast of Venezuela, the cosmopolitan communities of Uruguay. To help narrow down your choices, contact the Latin American Travel Association (www.lata.org) and the Caribbean Tourism Organisation (www.doitcaribbean.com).

Bermuda and the Caribbean

Bermuda and the Caribbean Islands are by far the most popular wedding destination for couples from the East Coast of the United States. (I have grouped Bermuda with the Caribbean Islands because, even though the country is not located in the Caribbean Sea, it offers many wonderful similarities to its Caribbean neighbors.) What draws so many couples to the islands? Close proximity and frequent direct flights make the area easily accessible. English is widely spoken on the islands, and the residency requirements for marriage are generally quite lenient. But beyond the pragmatic reasons, Bermuda and the Caribbean lure couples with their luxury hotels and resorts, quaint churches, fruitful plantations, incredible sunsets, and soft powder beaches on the bluest water you can imagine. In addition to being endowed with natural beauty, the islands are historical and multicultural, with a wonderful blend of Latin American, African, and European cultural influences. Visitors enjoy the warm and welcoming islanders, who offer the best of the region, from scuba diving and sailing to calypso music and cuisine (think rum, coffee, jerk chicken, and Caribbean spices!).

Though I've selected only a few countries to review in this section, I strongly encourage you to investigate the possibilities on *all* the islands. Though the hurricanes of 2004 ravaged some parts of the Caribbean, including the Cayman Islands, Grenada, Jamaica, and Cuba, these areas are all recovering nicely, and they are very eager to host destination weddings. For more information on the Caribbean, especially those islands not covered in this book, try the following resources: the Caribbean Wedding Association (407-566-8000 / www.caribbeanweddingassociation.com), the Caribbean Tourism Organisation (246-427-5242 / www.doitcaribbean.com), the Caribbean Hotel Association (787-725-9139 / www.caribbeanhotels.org), and Villas Caribe (800-645-7498 / http://villascaribe.com).

BERMUDA

Bermuda is one of the smallest, most densely populated countries in the world, but don't let that stop you from considering this island of world-class resorts and soft white-sand beaches. A British territory, Bermuda is one of the most affluent places in the world, where people are educated, sophisticated, and very respectful of privacy. Many couples find the island hospitality, with its touch of genteel British influence, very inviting. The country's most popular pastimes—golf, tennis, and yachting—are indicative of the Bermudians' quiet way of life. The speed limit is 20 mph, restaurants are very expensive, and casual attire in public is frowned upon. Bermuda is noted for its unique and almost surreal look, created by pastel homes, quaint churches, and pink sand. The mild climate has few extremes, except during the hurricane season, which runs August through September. During the summer, public beaches never close. The pace slows during the winter months from November to March, when temperatures range from 55° to 70°F (13° to 21°C); if you are hoping to save money, this is a good time to go.

COUNTRY OVERVIEW

CURRENCY: BOTH BERMUDIAN AND U.S. DOLLARS **TIPPING:** SERVICE CHARGE OF 10%, IF NOT 15% (MORE FOR EXCEPTIONAL SERVICE) IS STANDARD FOR EVERYTHING FROM BAGGAGE HANDLERS TO BEAUTICIANS. MOST RESTAURANTS WILL ADD A 15% SERVICE CHARGE; IF NOT, A 15% TIP IS CUSTOMARY AT RESTAURANTS. PORTERS AT THE AIRPORT EXPECT $1 PER BAG. TAXI DRIVERS USUALLY RECEIVE 15% OF THE FARE. **ELECTRICITY:** 110V **INTERNATIONAL CALLING CODE:** 1

PLANNING NOTES

SUGGESTED ASSISTANCE: Minimal assistance necessary, as the process is quite easy.

SPECIAL REQUIREMENTS: WAITING PERIOD: None, once you have obtained the license
RESIDENCY REQUIREMENT: None

CIVIL CEREMONIES: Civil ceremonies are optional. A "Notice of Intent Form" must be submitted and posted two weeks prior to the ceremony. Couples may choose to have the registrar general (or a minister of religion) preside over a civil ceremony in a specially decorated "Marriage Room" at the Registry General offices; advance notice of one week is needed to reserve the room.

RELIGIOUS CEREMONIES: Christianity is the dominant religious choice of Bermudians; the majority are Protestant, but there are several other denominational and non denominational churches. On the island, there is also a strong Jewish community (441-291-1785) and a Muslim community (441-292-5986). You may invite your own spiritual leader from any faith to serve as officiant as long as you obtain permission from the Department of Immigration (441-297-7940) and the registrar general. Most churches will only offer religious ceremonies to residents or members of the congregation; for that reason, most weddings in Bermuda are civil ceremonies.

DESIGN IDEAS

You can welcome your guests to Bermuda with any number of little surprises (www.bermudagiftideas.com)—perhaps a "Bermuda Triangle" pendant made from local sea glass or a handmade trinket box of indigenous cedar. Many jewelers offer necklaces created from sand dollars or replicas of early Spanish coins once found throughout the many coves and inlets in Bermuda. Be sure to also include some of Bermuda's many culinary treats, such as Black Seal Rum, honey, or rum cake.

Couples who choose a Bermuda wedding often wed under a "moongate," an ancient stone arch found throughout the island. A walk through a moongate promises a life of

© MOXLEY ASSOCIATES

everlasting happiness. Another popular custom is to wear Bermuda dress shorts—the universal attire in Bermuda. Bermuda shorts, which come in a variety of colors and fabrics, are worn with dress shirts, jackets, and loafers with tassels. At wedding receptions, two cakes are usually served; the groom's cake is a plain pound cake wrapped in gold leaf and the bride's is a fruitcake wrapped in silver. Your menu could include Bermuda lobster, or shark and fish chowder with sherry, peppers, and rum. For native entertainment, you might hire the Bermuda Gombey dancers, a source of great pride on the island. Gombey dance, derived from the island's African slaves, incorporates West African, Caribbean, and Native American influence.

PLANNING RESOURCES

EMBASSY AND GOVERNMENT OFFICES:
Embassy of Great Britain (in the United States)
3100 Massachusetts Avenue NW, Washington, DC 20008
www.britainusa.com/embassy
202-588-7800 / Consulate General (New York): 212-745-0202

Consulate of the United States (in Bermuda)
P. O. Box HM 325, Crown Hill, 16 Middle Road, Devonshire DV 03, Bermuda
441-295-1342

Registrar General's Office of Bermuda
Government Administration Building, 30 Parliament Street, Hamilton HM 12, Bermuda
441-297-7706 / 441-297-7707

TOURISM:
Bermuda Department of Tourism
Bermuda: P.O. Box HM, 465 Hamilton, HM BX, Bermuda
United States: 205 East Forty-second Street, New York, NY 10017
www.bermudatourism.com
800-223-6106 / 212-818-9800

PARKS, MONUMENTS, AND HISTORIC SITES:
Bermuda National Trust
P.O. Box HM 61, Hamilton, HM AX, Bermuda
441-236-6483

WEDDING RESOURCES:
HELPFUL WEB SITES:
Bermuda.com Limited: www.bermuda.com/weddings

VENUES

Bermuda has many upscale hotels and resorts fashioned around golf, tennis, and water sports; some even include boats that can be chartered for special events. On the island, you'll find many cottage colonies, which typically feature a main clubhouse with a main dining area surrounded by separate cottages nestled in private corners of the property. **AUNT NEA'S INN** (441-297-1630 / www.auntneas.com), considered to be one of the most romantic inns on the island, is a lovely old manor centrally located in Olde Towne of St. George's. If a nautical wedding is what you seek, contact **CHARTER BERMUDA** (441-335-9522 /

www.charterbermuda.com) for a catamaran that accommodates up to 80 guests or a glass-bottom boat that holds up to 100 passengers.

CAMBRIDGE BEACHES

30 Kings Point Road, Somerset MA 02, Bermuda

www.cambridgebeaches.com

800-468-7300 / 441-234-0331

SIZE: 30 ACRES **NUMBER OF ROOMS:** 94 ROOMS AND SUITES IN COTTAGES **WHEELCHAIR ACCESSIBLE:** LIMITED **RATES:** $$–$$$ **SPECIAL NOTES:** WEDDING GROUPS ARE LIMITED TO 50 PEOPLE UNLESS THE ENTIRE PROPERTY IS BOOKED WELL IN ADVANCE. CHILDREN UNDER 5 NOT ALLOWED.

REVIEW: Cambridge Beaches is a highly acclaimed, hidden-away cottage colony resort that considers romance their specialty. Every cottage is different, each with unique décor. They offer an on-site marina, three tennis courts, croquet, indoor and outdoor pools, five beaches, water sports, an ocean spa, and golf nearby.

CEREMONY OPTIONS: Most ceremonies are performed outdoors on the lawn overlooking the cliffs, beach, and sea. In inclement weather, the beachside Aquarium Bathhouse is luxuriously decorated with flowers and floating candles on the pool.

RECEPTION OPTIONS: Most receptions are held in the Aquarium Baths, which overlooks the ocean, but there are also two restaurants on the property available for parties of 50 or more. No matter where you opt to hold your celebration, you will not be disappointed by the food. According to *Food & Wine*, Cambridge Beaches' Tamarisk Room is one of the best restaurants in Bermuda.

WEDDING SERVICES: Some assistance provided. Facilitates marriage license. Full range of wedding and honeymoon packages available.

THE REEFS

56 South Shore Road, Southampton SN 02, Bermuda

www.thereefs.com

800-742-2008 / 441-238-0222

SIZE: 6 ACRES **NUMBER OF ROOMS:** 106 ROOMS, 20 SUITES **WHEELCHAIR ACCESSIBLE:** NO **RATES:** $$–$$$

REVIEW: Hugging the cliffs surrounding Christian Bay, The Reefs is a small, luxury hotel that offers unparalleled southshore views of the ocean. It has been decorated with awards from *Condé Nast Traveler*, *Travel + Leisure*, *Gourmet*, and *The Bermudian*. The suites are spacious, and the room rates include breakfast, afternoon tea, and dinner. With one of the nicest beaches on the island, guests can enjoy snorkeling, kayaking, and tennis as well as chartered sailing and horseback riding.

CEREMONY OPTIONS: Caso's Point, a special two-tiered outdoor wedding terrace, is available for up to 80 guests. Beachside weddings are limited to 12.

RECEPTION OPTIONS: There are three restaurants from which to choose. For an outdoor reception, Grill 56 accommodates 60 guests. Directly off Grill 56, Ocean Echo Terrace provides alfresco dining for 50 guests and a spectacular clifftop view. Coconuts offers an eclectic treehouse atmosphere for up to 90 guests.

WEDDING SERVICES: Full service. Facilitates marriage license and helps secure officiants.

WATERLOO HOUSE

P.O. Box HM 333, Hamilton HM BX, Bermuda

www.waterloohouse.com

800-468-4100 / 441-295-4480

SIZE: 3 ACRES **NUMBER OF ROOMS:** 23 ROOMS, 6 SUITES **WHEELCHAIR ACCESSIBLE:** LIMITED
RATES: $$ **SPECIAL NOTES:** CHILDCARE AVAILABLE

REVIEW: Waterloo House, a Relais & Château property, is an example of a typical Bermuda cottage colony. Multicolored cottages and beautiful common rooms make Waterloo House a perfect location for small, elegant weddings. The hotel is appointed with antique and Victorian-style furnishings, large fireplaces, and a spacious outdoor terrace used for fine dining and entertaining. Waterloo House also boasts a wine list that has been recognized by *Wine Spectator* as one of the world's most outstanding five years running.

CEREMONY AND RECEPTION OPTIONS: Wedding ceremonies and receptions for up to 80 guests may be held outdoors on grass terraces overlooking the harbor. Indoor events can be held in the Poinciana Terrace, which seats 100 for dinner, or the Wellington Room, which accommodates 80 comfortably.

WEDDING SERVICES: Some assistance available.

© CHARITY DE MEER

ANGUILLA

Modern Bride readers recently named Anguilla one of the best wedding locations in the world, and over 200,000 viewers chose Anguilla for NBC's first "*Today Show* Destination Wedding Contest." Anguilla is a magical island in the British West Indies known for its undulating dunes, gentle terrain, and beautiful, secluded beaches. The 16-mile-long island is home to more goats than people, making it seem worlds apart from civilization. Be prepared to enjoy fine dining, meet friendly people, and explore fascinating places, including caves and caverns. And if you're lucky, you may even catch a glimpse of one of the island's cherished sea turtles. Some couples choose to get married in the tranquil beauty of Anguilla, then honeymoon on one of the nearby islands, such as St. Martin or St. Bart, where they can experience a more cosmopolitan atmosphere.

The climate is fairly constant with temperatures that range from 78°F to 88°F (26°C to 31°C). The rainy season, which consists of brief showers interspersed with sunshine, occurs in the autumn, when the occasional hurricane blows through. Peak tourist season runs from mid-December to mid-April. To enjoy the best snorkeling and scuba diving, visit the island during May, June, or July.

COUNTRY OVERVIEW

CURRENCY: EASTERN CARIBBEAN DOLLAR (U.S. DOLLAR WIDELY ACCEPTED) **TIPPING:** A 10% SERV-
ICE CHARGE IS ADDED TO ALL HOTEL BILLS; CHECK WITH THE CONCIERGE OR HOTEL MANAGER TO
FIND OUT WHO IS COVERED. A 15% SERVICE CHARGE IS ALSO ADDED TO MOST RESTAURANT BILLS.
TIP DRIVERS 10%. **ELECTRICITY:** 110V **INTERNATIONAL CALLING CODE:** 1

PLANNING NOTES

SUGGESTED ASSISTANCE: Minimal assistance necessary, as the process is quite easy.
SPECIAL REQUIREMENTS: WAITING PERIOD: Two days **RESIDENCY REQUIREMENT:** Two
days
CIVIL CEREMONIES: A civil ceremony is not required, but it is an option. For more information, call the Office of the Magistrate (264-497-2377).
RELIGIOUS CEREMONIES: A wedding performed by a religious officiant is legally binding
as long as the officiant files the license after the ceremony. There are over 40
churches represented on the island, which is remarkable for its size. The island is predominantly Christian, so spiritual leaders from other faith traditions will most likely
need to come from other locales. You can bring your own or you may be able to find
what you are looking for on either St. Martin or St. Bart. Catholics generally need to
give their priest three to six months' notice. The Anguilla tourist bureau can provide
recommendations for religious officiants, including a nondenominational minister.

DESIGN IDEAS

Anguilla is home to many artists, including potters, sculptors, painters, and woodworkers.
For welcome gift ideas, check out the local crafts at the Anguilla Arts and Crafts Center.
You might also welcome your guests with local flowers, such as the ever-present bougainvil-
lea and hibiscus (which would also make beautiful bouquets).

Salt, fish, and lobster are some of Anguilla's natural resources, so it is only fitting that
a wedding feast feature lobster—and lots of it! In addition to lobster bisque, traditional
favorites include saltfish and johnnycakes, tamarind balls, bull's foot soup, oxtail and conch
stew, sweet-corn chowder, and rice and peas. Talented musicians are available throughout Anguilla, playing everything from saxophones to steel drums. For more island entertainment, you might include a Jumbie dancer or Mocko Jumbie performer in your festivities.
The Jumbie dance, which originated in Ghana, once took place following Christian rituals,
such as baptism or weddings. Mocko Jumbie, meaning "good god" or "good spirit," is
the art of stilt walking, always popular at Carnavale.

PLANNING RESOURCES

EMBASSY AND GOVERNMENT OFFICES:
Embassy of Great Britain (in the United States)
3100 Massachussetts Avenue NW, Washington, DC 20008
www.britainusa.com
202-588-7800 / Consulate General (New York): 212-745-0202

Consulate of the United States *(none in Anguilla; use phone numbers provided)*
Consular Section (Barbados): 246-431-0225 / Consular Agency (Antigua): 268-463-6531

Magistrate's Court
The Valley, Anguilla, British West Indies
264-497-2377

TOURISM:
The Anguilla Tourist Board
Coronation Avenue, The Valley, Anguilla,
    British West Indies
www.anguilla-vacation.com
800-553-4939 / 914-287-2400

PARKS, MONUMENTS, AND HISTORIC SITES:
The Anguilla National Trust
P.O. Box 1234, The Valley, Anguilla,
    British West Indies
www.ant.ai
264-497-5297

WEDDING RESOURCES:
HELPFUL WEB SITES:
Anguilla Wedding: www.anguillawedding.com

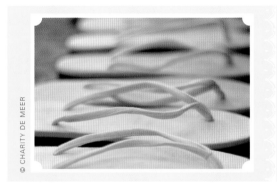

© CHARITY DE MEER

VENUES

If your idea of the perfect wedding venue involves peace and quiet, pampering, and beaches aplenty, you'll find Anguilla full of tempting options. There are several highly acclaimed beach resorts and villas on the island. If you have a passion for gourmet food, consider the **CUISINART RESORT & SPA** (264-498-2000 / 212-972-0880 / www.cuisinart resort.com), where organic, hydroponic fruits and vegetables are grown and incorporated into mouthwatering cuisine. Another smaller gourmet option is the **ALTAMER RESORT** (264-498-4000 / www.altamer.com), whose award-winning chef creates culinary masterpieces in the beachside restaurant. If you are seeking other villa options, you might try networking with **LUXURY VILLAS** (264-497-3575 / www.luxuryvillas.com). Though it is a beach resort, **ANGUILLA GREAT HOUSE** (264-497-6061 / www.anguillagreathouse.com) feels more like an old estate. It would provide a unique backdrop for any wedding. **THE ARAWAK BEACH INN** (877-427-2925 / 264-497-4888 / www.arawakbeach.com) is a fun and colorful venue, particularly appealing if you are looking for something a little less expensive. Those who love modern architecture will love the private and luxurious **COV-ECASTLES** (800-223-1108 / 264-497-6801 / www.covecastles.com), featuring an ultramodern design that has been praised in *Architectural Digest* twice. Situated right on the beach and shaped like domed sandcastles, the 2-, 3-, and 4-bedroom villas have seascape views from every room. Covecastles offers intimate weddings for up to 25 guests, and the new 5–6 bedroom grand villa, called The Point, would make a perfect wedding hub.

MALLIOUHANA HOTEL & SPA

Box 173, Meads Bay, Anguilla, British West Indies

www.malliouhana.com

800-835-0796 / 264-497-6111

SIZE: 26 ACRES NUMBER OF ROOMS: 34 DOUBLES; 19 SUITES WHEELCHAIR ACCESSIBLE: NO
RATES: $$–$$$ SPECIAL NOTES: CHILDREN OF ALL AGES ARE WELCOME; HOWEVER, CHILDREN
ARE NOT PERMITTED IN THE MAIN RESTAURANT AFTER 7:00 PM. THE HOTEL HAS A SUPERVISED CHIL-
DREN'S PLAYGROUND, FEATURING A PIRATE SHIP WITH WATER CANNONS AND A WATER SLIDE.

© MALLIOUHANA PUBLIC RELATIONS USA

REVIEW: A 2004 reader's survey by *Condé Nast Traveler* named Malliouhana the "Best Resort in the Caribbean." Malliouhana reflects a blend of Mediterranean design and French Riviera style—all wrapped up in warm Anguillan sunshine and smiles. The resort sits on a bluff overlooking the Caribbean Sea, which affords guests a breathtaking view from their private balconies and terraces. The distinctive rooms are remarkably large (the smallest at 720 square feet) and feature handsome walnut accents, rattan furnishings, marble bathrooms, and vivid Haitian artwork. Michel Rostang, a notable two-star Michelin chef, supervises outstanding menus at the main restaurant and the beachside Le Bistro. And wine lovers will appreciate the 25,000-plus bottle wine list, which has been recognized by *Wine Spectator*. In addition to a state-of-the-art, 15,000-square-foot, oceanfront spa, the resort offers complimentary recreational activities, including windsurfing, waterskiing, sailing, and snorkeling. **CEREMONY AND RECEPTION OPTIONS:** Your ceremony and reception can be held just about anywhere on the property, including any one of the open-air dining rooms or restaurants, the semiprivate beach, the garden, or the pool villa. Most locations offer views of the sea and sunset. Le Bistro and the main dining room can accommodate up to 120 guests, while the pool villa is perfect for smaller groups of 50 to 70.

WEDDING SERVICES: Full service. Facilitates marriage license.

CAP JULUCA

P.O. Box 240, Maundays Bay, Anguilla, Leeward Islands, British West Indies
www.capjuluca.com
888-858-5822 / 264-497-6666

SIZE: 179 ACRES **NUMBER OF ROOMS:** 58 LUXURY ROOMS AND JUNIOR SUITES, 7 SUITES, AND 6 POOL VILLAS **WHEELCHAIR ACCESSIBLE:** NO **RATES:** $$$ **SPECIAL NOTES:** CHILDREN 2 YEARS AND OLDER ARE WELCOME

REVIEW: Cap Juluca, a Caribbean favorite for years, has been highly decorated with awards from all the leading travel publications, including *Andrew Harper's Hideaway Report,* which rated it the Best Caribbean Resort and the #3 International Resort Hotel. If the thought of inhabiting a Moroccan castle appeals to you, you're bound to be impressed. Among Cap Juluca's captivating features are its Moorish parapet and domes, reminiscent of the Arabian Nights, and its two miles of pristine, sugar-white beach. The rooms and suites, all of which are beachfront, are grand in size but minimalist in design. They have outdoor solariums, king-sized beds, Brazilian walnut accents, white Italian tile floors, and marble bathrooms, many with double tubs. North African artwork, inlaid mirrors, and area rugs give each room a distinct flavor. Guests can enjoy tennis, swimming, croquet, fitness, waterskiing, kayaking, scuba diving, sailing, spa and holistic services, and an aqua golf driving range.

CEREMONY OPTIONS: With sea and mountain views, a sunset wedding ceremony at Cap Juluca epitomizes romance, whether it is held on the powder-white crescent of Maundays Bay beach, beneath the Moorish arches of a villa, or under a gazebo perched on a sand dune. The beach can accommodate any number of guests, the wedding lawn and gazebo can accommodate up to 200, and the villas are limited to smaller groups.

RECEPTION OPTIONS: Tented receptions can be held on the beach for as many guests as you wish. If you prefer to be indoors overlooking the sea, Pimms, the open-air restaurant, sits a mere six feet from the edge of the sea. It accommodates up to 80 guests, but if your group exceeds 80, you can use an additional room in Pimms called Kemia. For more casual beach dining, George's accommodates 90.

WEDDING SERVICES: Full service. Facilitates marriage license.

THE BAHAMAS

The Bahamas, just off the coast of Florida, is a nation of 700 diverse islands and uninhabited cays just waiting to be explored. The Bahamas have long been celebrated islands. San Salvador is where Christopher Columbus first set foot in the New World; Bimini is where Ernest Hemingway made his home away from home; and according to Bahamians, the crystal blue waters of the Bahamas were the only other thing beside the Great Wall of China that the Apollo astronauts saw from space!

© CHARITY DE MEER

The official motto of the Bahamas is "Forward, upward, and onward together"—an appropriate sentiment for any wedding. In the spirit of the motto, couples can take a stroll along a pink coral beach, an oceanside horseback ride, or a nocturnal swim among millions of bioluminescent organisms. They can also experience Bahamian nightlife, explore picturesque fishing villages, spelunk the islands' caves and underground rivers, dive among the ancient shipwrecks off Elbow Beach, and even swim with sea turtles, manta ray, and tarpons off Port Lucaya. Tourist season runs from November to May, when temperatures hover between 70°F (21°C) and 75°F (24°C). During the off-season months, you can expect to find bargains—as well as heat, humidity, and the chance of tropical storms. With beautiful beaches and summer temperatures year-round, it's easy to fall into the pace known as "island time," or "I'll-get-to-it-when-the-spirit-moves-me time." Just be sure to make your reservations well before you switch over to island time!

COUNTRY OVERVIEW

CURRENCY: BAHAMIAN DOLLAR **TIPPING:** TIP ACCORDING TO THE QUALITY OF SERVICE YOU RECEIVE, AND BE AWARE THAT MOST ESTABLISHMENTS INCLUDE GRATUITY IN THE BILL. A 15% TIP IS AVERAGE. **ELECTRICITY:** 110V **INTERNATIONAL CALLING CODE:** 242

PLANNING NOTES

SUGGESTED ASSISTANCE: Minimal assistance necessary, as the process is quite easy.
SPECIAL REQUIREMENTS: WAITING PERIOD: None, once you get the license **RESIDENCY REQUIREMENT:** 24 hours (You will be required to present a receipt, such as your passport, showing your date of arrival in the Bahamas.) **SPECIAL NOTES:** You may have to go to the American Embassy to obtain a notarized Affidavit of Single Status. The license can be obtained at the registrar general's office in Nassau or at a commissioner general's office on the specific island where you plan to marry.

CIVIL CEREMONIES: A civil ceremony is not required but it is an option, and it can take place anywhere you wish, even underwater! Call the Bahama Tourism Office or the registrar general for a list of government-certified civil officiants.

RELIGIOUS CEREMONIES: With the highest number of churches per capita in the world, the dominant religion of the Bahamas is Christianity. (You'll notice that cabdrivers drive with a Bible in their front seat.) There is, however, a synagogue in Freeport; for more information, contact the Freeport Hebrew Congregation (242-373-4025). Bahamian law dictates that you use one of the island's certified marriage officiants, whether your ceremony is civil or religious. To find a certified clergy member, interfaith minister, or nondenominational officiant, contact the island's registrar general. If you wish to bring your own religious officiant from elsewhere, he will have to work with a registered civil officiant to make the marriage legal.

DESIGN IDEAS

To find unique welcome gifts for your guests, explore Nassau's famous "Straw Market," where you will not only find handmade hats, mats, and baskets but also fabrics, jewelry, woodcarved objects, and local guava jams and jellies. Half the fun of shopping will be meeting and bargaining with the local merchants. You can also mix, bottle, and label your own wedding fragrance at the Perfume Factory on Andros.

Why not add local flavor to your wedding with some Bahamian traditions? Dress up your aisle with an authentic Bahamian Androsia print aisle runner, then line it with conch shells. You could even have your groomsmen wear Androsia shirts that match the aisle runner! With the islands' abundance of exotic flowers, you can create gorgeous bouquets, floral swags, and arbor decorations. To accent your arrangements, use seashells, palm fronds, sea grapes, raffia, wicker, or bamboo. Tempt your guests with a wedding menu of fresh fish (such as mahi-mahi or grouper), cracked conch, conch fritters, jerk chicken, and Caribbean lobster. For island entertainment, consider the traditional Bahamian music known as "Goombay," a synthesis of calypso, soca, and English folk songs, often featuring guitar, accordian, drums, and shakers. Steel drum bands are ever popular, as are the activities of fire dancing and doing the limbo!

PLANNING RESOURCES

EMBASSY AND GOVERNMENT OFFICES:
Embassy of the Commonwealth of The Bahamas (in the United States)
2220 Massachusetts Avenue NW, Washington, DC 20008
202-319-2660

Embassy of the United States (in The Bahamas)
P.O. Box N-8197, Nassau, The Bahamas
http://nassau.usembassy.gov
242-322-1181 / Consulate (New York City): 212-421-6420

Registrar General
P.O. Box H-5553, Nassau, The Bahamas
for weddings on Nassau and The Out Islands: 242-322-3316
for weddings on the Grand Bahama Island: 242-352-4934

TOURISM:
The Bahamas Ministry of Tourism
P.O. Box N-3701, Nassau, The Bahamas
www.bahamas.com
800-224-2627 / 242-302-2000 / Weddings and Honeymoon Unit:
   888-687-8425 / 242-302-2034

PARKS, MONUMENTS, AND HISTORIC SITES:
The Bahamas National Trust
P.O. Box N-4105, Nassau, The Bahamas
www.bahamasnationaltrust.com
809-393-1317

VENUES

With 700 islands come thousands of romantic wedding venues. For a nautical wedding celebration that won't break the bank, consider a sea cruise with **THE MAJESTY OF THE SEAS** (866-606-0994 / www.bahamacruiseweddings.com). Perhaps the best destination deal in the Bahamas is the **SANDALS ROYAL BAHAMIAN SPA RESORT** (888-726-3257 / www.sandals.com) on Nassau. With its own island, Sandals offers a free wedding if you stay a certain number of nights. **TIAMO RESORT** (242-357-2489 / www.tiamoresorts.com), located on Andros Island, is ideal for a small safari-like wedding. The 12-acre resort, accessible only by boat, has 11 beach bungalows and an indoor facility that accommodates up to 20 guests for dinner. On Grand Bahama Island, you'll find **PELICAN BAY AT LUCAYA** (800-852-3702 / www.pelicanbayhotel.com), a newer boutique hotel that was designated one of the "small treasures of the Bahamas" by the Ministry of Tourism. Another popular choice on Grand Bahama is the beachfront resort of **OLD BAHAMA BAY** (800-444-9469 / www.oldbahamabay.com). How does an underwater wedding sound to you? If you find this unique option irresistible, contact **GRAND BAHAMA SCUBA** (242-373-6775 / www.grand bahamascuba.com).

ONE&ONLY OCEAN CLUB

Paradise Island, Nassau, The Bahamas

www.oneandonlyoceanclub.com

800-321-3000 / 242-363-2501

SIZE: 65 ACRES **NUMBER OF ROOMS:** 3 VILLAS; 14 SUITES; 90 ROOMS; 4 COTTAGES **WHEELCHAIR ACCESSIBLE:** YES **RATES:** $$$

REVIEW: The One&Only Ocean Club, a member of The Leading Hotels of the World, has received numerous awards, including the 2004 *Condé Nast Traveler* Reader's Choice Award for the Best Resort in the Atlantic. Situated on miles of pristine beach, the club features tropical gardens designed with European elegance. The Versailles Gardens are terraced, punctuated with elegant statues of Carrera marble. Standing at the top of the gardens is a twelfth-century Augustinian cloister that was moved from France and now overlooks Nassau Harbor. The service is excellent and the rooms are opulent, with king-sized beds, hardwood floors, and marble bathrooms. Many rooms are beachfront or have private balconies, where you can take in the sea air and views. Guests enjoy a fresh-water pool, Har-Tru tennis courts, a state-of-the-art spa, and a Tom Weiskopf golf course as well as sailing, kayaking, and snorkeling on the property.

CEREMONY OPTIONS: Outdoor wedding ceremonies for up to 120 guests can take place on the hotel's beach or in the beautiful gardens, either by the lily pond or under the cloister arches.

RECEPTION OPTIONS: For parties with up to 120 guests, the reception can be held on the beach deck or the pool terrace. The Golf Club House is available for smaller groups of 60 or less.

WEDDING SERVICES: Full service. Facilitates the marriage license and suggests officiants.

ATLANTIS

Paradise Island, The Bahamas

www.atlantis.com

888-528-7155 / 242-363-3000

SIZE: 123 ACRES **NUMBER OF ROOMS:** 2,317 GUEST FACILITIES **WHEELCHAIR ACCESSIBLE:** YES **RATES:** $$–$$$

REVIEW: Atlantis, the world's largest island resort destination, is one of the few mega-properties that I find appealing because it offers such a unique travel experience. Inspired by its namesake, Atlantis is like an aquarium with accommodations. With approximately 50,000 animals on the property (most of which are native to the Bahamas), the island is home to an impressive marine habitat. The Dig, an imaginative, full-size depiction of the ruins of Atlantis, features a series of passageways that make you feel as if you are actually in the water with the marine life. This resort is a playground for all ages, with plenty of activities for adults *and* children. There are several theme swimming areas, including the Royal Baths and the Mayan Temple Waterslides and Pool. Atlantis also boasts the largest casino in the Caribbean and 35 restaurants, bars, and lounges with diverse menus. The rooms are complete with every amenity, including either a full or French balcony. Among the 120 suites is the 5,000-square-foot Bridge Suite, perched in an archway high above the resort.

CEREMONY AND RECEPTION OPTIONS: The 25,000-square-foot Atlantic Grand Ballroom, which can be divided into seven different sections, can hold groups of up to 2,700. The Junior Ballroom in the Coral Tower can be divided into three different sections. Couples can also choose from 18 outdoor venues that can accommodate groups of varying sizes up to 1,000. Atlantis recently announced its Phase III expansion project, scheduled to be completed in 2006. The expansion will add a new world-class conference facility, featuring a 50,000-square-foot Imperial Ballroom—the largest in the Bahamas and the Caribbean—to accommodate the needs of up to 5,000 guests.

WEDDING SERVICES: Full service. Facilitates the marriage license.

JAMAICA

If you're dreaming of sparkling white beaches, lush rainforests, dramatic mountain peaks, melodic rhythms, sweet fragrances, and spicy flavors, all combined with a "don't worry, be happy" attitude, then you're probably dreaming of Jamaica. There is a reason why couples from all over the world choose to marry in Jamaica. Besides its intoxicating natural beauty, friendly people, and rich culture, Jamaica offers many resources for making wedding dreams possible at any price. As one of the first countries to recognize the destination wedding market, Jamaica has a history of making every effort to accommodate couples. It is easy to be legally married there, and Jamaica's tourism Web site is one of the best, offering all the information a couple needs to plan a wedding.

Jamaica, the third largest island in the Caribbean, is an English-speaking country —which makes wedding planning from afar much easier! Its climate is tropical at sea

© LEN KAUFMAN

level and temperate toward the interior highlands. Generally, there is little temperature variation year-round, with the average ranging from 66°F (19°C) to 99°F (37°C). Between December and April, the weather is practically perfect for any activity on a daily basis. Be aware that Jamaica's hurricane season lasts from June to September.

COUNTRY OVERVIEW

CURRENCY: JAMAICAN DOLLAR **TIPPING:** UNLESS YOU ARE STAYING IN AN ALL-INCLUSIVE RESORT WHERE TIPS ARE INCLUDED, BE SURE TO TIP SERVICE PROVIDERS. MANY JAMAICANS DEPEND ON TIPS FOR THEIR LIVELIHOOD. **ELECTRICITY:** 110V **INTERNATIONAL CALLING CODE:** 876

PLANNING NOTES

SUGGESTED ASSISTANCE: Minimal assistance necessary, as the process is quite easy.
SPECIAL REQUIREMENTS: WAITING PERIOD: None **RESIDENCY REQUIREMENT:** 24 hours
CIVIL CEREMONIES: Civil ceremonies are not required, and they can take place just about anywhere you wish. You can find a list of marriage officiants on the embassy or the tourism Web sites (see pages 236–237).
RELIGIOUS CEREMONIES: On the whole, Jamaicans are a very religious people. According to the *Guinness Book of World Records*, Jamaica has more churches per square mile than any other country, so you'll have many choices! The majority are Christian; however, Islam and Judaism are also represented. Jamaica is also the birthplace of Rastafarianism, which celebrates African culture.

DESIGN IDEAS

Welcome your guests with a "taste of Jamaica" basket or calabash, filled with local nutmeg, jerk sauces, coffee, and rum. Nature provides several possibilities for wedding décor, such as sand, coral, conch shells, bamboo, palms, tropical fish, or flowers from the lignum vitae tree. This "tree of life" (so named for its medicinal quality) bears the national flower, a lavender-blue blossom, in spring and summer. If you are interested in orchids, contact **GREEN CASTLE ORCHID GROWERS** (876-382-7640).

There is nothing like Caribbean music to get a party going. The island is teeming with talented jazz musicians, whom you could hire for entertainment. And of course, no celebration in Jamaica is complete without a little calypso and some reggae. You could even adopt a Rasta theme for your wedding, featuring a red, yellow, and green color scheme and the music of Bob Marley. Celebrate the bounty of the sea and the flavors of the island with fresh seafood and spicy meats, ackee and salted cod fish, tropical fruits, coconut, yams, and chocolate. To top off the meal, serve rum punch and traditional Jamaican wedding cake. This dark and rich cake is made with rum-soaked dried fruits, such as raisins, dates, currants, and cherries, then finished with crisp white frosting and fresh flowers. Traditionally, slices of the cake are mailed in little boxes to friends and relatives who could not attend the wedding, and the top tier is kept for the christening of the couple's first child.

PLANNING RESOURCES

EMBASSY AND GOVERNMENT OFFICES:
Embassy of Jamaica (in the United States)
1520 New Hampshire Avenue NW,
Washington, DC 20036
202-452-0660

Embassy of the United States (in Jamaica)
2 Oxford Road, Third Floor, Kingston 5, Jamaica
http://kingston.usembassy.gov
876-929-4850

Department of the Registrar General
Twickenham Park, St. Catherine, Jamaica
www.rgd.gov.jm
876-984-3041

TOURISM:
Jamaican Tourist Board
Jamaica: 64 Knutsford Boulevard, Kingston 5,
    Jamaica
United States: 1320 South Dixie Highway, Suite
    1101, Coral Gables, FL 33146
www.visitjamaica.com
800-526-2422 / 800-233-4582

VENUES

© DAVID BECKSTEAD

Jamaica offers opportunities to wed nearly any-where—on river rafts, in caves, near waterfalls, and even underwater! If you'd like to marry amidst lush tropical gardens and waterfalls, try **SHAW PARK GARDENS** (876-974-2723 / www.shawpark gardens.com) in Ocho Rios. Or, to get married underwater, contact **ROSE HALL BEACH CLUB** (809-953-2341) or **MOBAY UNDERSEA TOURS** (876-940-4465 / www.mobayundersea tours.com). If you're daring, say "I do" in the buff at the famous **HEDO-NISM RESORTS** (877-467-8737 / www.super clubs.com)! For beautiful surroundings, consider **ROUND HILL RESORT** (800-972-2159 / www.roundhilljamaica.com), located on a former pineapple, allspice, and coconut plantation. If you are seeking elegance, your best bet is the **RITZ CARLTON MONTEGO BAY** (876-953-2800 / www.ritzcarlton.com/resorts/rose_hall_jamaica), home of the historic Rose Hall Plantation (known for its legendary voodoo-practicing "White Witch") and one of the island's best golf courses. With waterslides and pools, **WYNDHAM ROSE HALL RESORT & COUNTRY CLUB** (876-953-2650 / www.wyndham.com) is perfect if you have several children on the guest list. At **GRAND LIDO NEGRIL** (876-957-5010 / www.superclubs.com), you can marry at sunset aboard Princess Grace's honeymoon yacht! For a villa or private estate, contact **JAMAICA VILLAS BY LINDA SMITH** (301-229-4300 / www.jamaicavillas.com), and for the most eclectic and best boutique venues on the island, contact **ISLAND OUT-POST** (800-688-7678 / www.islandoutpost.com). **TRIDENT CASTLE** (876-993-2602) will satisfy couples who want European elegance in a Caribbean setting. Finally, for a hassle-free, all-inclusive wedding, take advantage of the WeddingMoon packages offered by **SANDALS ROYAL CARIBBEAN RESORT & OFFSHORE ISLAND** (888-726-3257 or 876-953-2231 / www.sandals.com). To accommodate the most private beach ceremonies, Sandals even has an offshore island, accessible by a 40-foot dragon boat.

HALF MOON

Half Moon P.O., Rose Hall, Montego Bay, Jamaica

www.halfmoon.com.jm

866-648-6951 / 876-953-2211

SIZE: 400 ACRES **NUMBER OF ROOMS:** 419 **WHEELCHAIR ACCESSIBLE:** YES **RATES:** $$

REVIEW: I am partial to Half Moon, because it was there that I met the editor who encouraged me to write this book—but I am not alone in my fondness for it. *Condé Nast Traveler* has voted it one of the Top 50 Tropical Resorts, and AAA has given Half Moon its Four-Diamond rating. With over 400 acres, the resort is set up like a neighborhood of white, Spanish-style villas. Each villa has seven guest rooms, living and dining rooms, balconies, and in the back, a large patio by a private pool. In addition, each villa is staffed with a cook, a housekeeper, and a butler to tend to the guests' needs. Guests get around the property on golf carts or in a regularly running jitney. Half Moon calls itself "The Complete Caribbean Resort" because it has two spectacular beaches, 36 stores, a world-class equestrian center, a championship golf course, tennis courts, spa facilities, and a gym. Best of all, guests can swim with dolphins in Half Moon's Dolphin Lagoon!

CEREMONY OPTIONS: The ceremony can be held at your own private villa. The seaside gazebo, the Hibiscus Lawn, the Royal Pavilion (which has a nice gazebo), and the Sugar Mill Restaurant are also available. You can even marry on horseback on the beach! The resort will transport you to any of the locations in a horse-drawn carriage if you so desire, and the on-site florist can provide floral arrangements.

RECEPTION OPTIONS: For the reception, you can choose from a full-service, cocktail, buffet, or formal dinner reception, a Jamaican-style beach barbecue, or a traditional afternoon tea. Banquets can be held at the semi-enclosed Royal Pavillion, which has an extensive lawn leading to the sea, or the Sugar Mill Restaurant, which overlooks the golf course. Receptions for small groups can be held in the villas.

WEDDING SERVICES: Full service. Facilitates marriage license.

GOOD HOPE COUNTRY HOUSE

P.O. Box 50, Falmouth, Trelawny, Jamaica

www.goodhopejamaica.com

876-610-5798

SIZE: 2,000 ACRES **NUMBER OF ROOMS:** 10 ROOMS IN A VARIETY OF COTTAGES **WHEELCHAIR ACCESSIBLE:** YES **RATES:** $–$$ **SPECIAL NOTES:** CHILDREN WELCOME; NANNIES AVAILABLE

REVIEW: Good Hope is an eighteenth-century Great House that sits high in the beautiful landscape of the Blue Mountains. Its lush 2,000 acres feature miles of hiking and horseback riding trails and a sanctuary for birds, including yellow- and black-billed parrots. Noted for its picturesque environs, Good Hope has been the setting for many photo shoots (*Vogue, Guess*, and *Travel + Leisure*, among others). Guests can meditate on the yoga deck, play tennis, swim, river tube, mountain bike, or simply lounge on the beautiful grounds enjoying the breathtaking views of the Queen of Spain Valley, the plantation land, the bamboo forests, and the meandering Martha Brae River. Accommodations include the Coach House (5 rooms), Bamboo (1), River Cottage (3), and Garden Cottage (1), each artfully and harmoniously designed.

CEREMONY OPTIONS: The most popular location for ceremonies is the Great House front lawn, but ceremonies can take place anywhere on the property—by the lily pond or the pool, in the garden terrace, in the yoga pavilion overlooking the mountains, on the raised sundial, or near any of the stone Buddhas that inhabit the grounds. In the event of inclement weather, the Great House, which has a large dining room and two living rooms connected by a 50-foot gallery, can accommodate up to 100.

RECEPTION OPTIONS: Receptions can be held on the grounds, on the terrace, or in the pavilion. Good Hope will provide custom-designed menus for parties of up to 200 people; the chefs combine the best of the island with innovative New Jamaican cuisine. Everything about Good Hope has a relaxed, simple elegance, and the service is simple and attentive without being overly formal or stuffy.

© LEN KAUFMAN

WEDDING SERVICES: Provides some assistance. Facilitates marriage license and recommends officiants.

THE CAVES

P.O. Box 3113, Light House Road, Negril, Jamaica

www.islandoutpost.com/caves/index.htm

876-957-0270

SIZE: 2 ACRES **NUMBER OF ROOMS:** 10 COTTAGES **WHEELCHAIR ACCESSIBLE:** NO **RATES:** $$$
SPECIAL NOTES: NO CHILDREN UNDER AGE 16 DUE TO THE DANGEROUS CLIFFS

REVIEW: Private and secluded yet close to the energy of Negril, The Caves promises exquisite romance. Situated in a garden on the edge of the sea are ten naturally ventilated, thatched-roofed, cliffside villas, described by *The New York Times* as "colorful wooden cottages (that) could have been designed by Matisse." The villas feature ocean views, verandas, and garden baths. The property is woven with cliffside paths, secret nooks, sundecks, and grottos—all remarkable sites for relaxing or dining. Guests can jump into the aqua-blue water from several points along the stonewall paths, or they can relax in the Jacuzzi that overlooks the ocean, in the saltwater pool, or in a cave hot tub. Guests can also raft, kayak, snorkel, and bike on the island.

CEREMONY OPTIONS: You can exchange vows in the cave, on any of the verandas or gazebos, or perhaps at the historic lighthouse next door.

RECEPTION OPTIONS: The chef, who takes pride in catering to guests' individual tastes, will work with you to prepare a casual or elegant wedding banquet. Banquets for up to 30 people can be held in the main dining room, which is housed in a thatched-roofed building. Receptions can also take place at The Sands, a sandy beach atop the cliffs. This area features a spectacular bar and a stone terrace with a cozy three-sided pavilion, a dance floor, and a stairway leading down to the sea.

WEDDING SERVICES: Provides assistance. Facilitates marriage license and finds officiant.

SILENT WATERS VILLA

Great River Private River Road, Montego Bay, Jamaica

www.jamaicavillas.net

(United States) 847-304-4700 / (Jamaica) 876-971-9119

SIZE: 18 ACRES **NUMBER OF ROOMS:** 5 GUEST VILLAS, PLUS OWNER'S VILLA (TOTAL OF 10 BEDROOMS) **WHEELCHAIR ACCESSIBLE:** YES **RATES:** $$

REVIEW: One of the most glamorous private homes in the Caribbean, Silent Waters is guaranteed to take your breath away. This mountaintop escape is an architectural gem, featuring a Balinese and Thai design that conveys peace and serenity. Beyond the front gate, a Zen garden with lily pads, grasses, and bridges awaits you. This opens up to a courtyard with an open-air bar, alfresco breakfast gazebo, and two open-air pavilions that serve as a separate living room and dining area. The buildings are surrounded by lush gardens, little ponds, and infinity pools, which look as though they drop off the edge of the mountain and into the sea. A waterfall cascades right through the master suite of each villa, and guests can dive out from the large indoor/outdoor shower into the attached private infinity-edge swimming pool. From any location on the property, there are views of either the sea or mountainous rainforest. A tennis court and helicopter pad rest atop the highest peak, making for a spectacular landing or an unforgettable tennis match.

CEREMONY OPTIONS: Ceremonies can take place in any of the gardens, by the infinity pool, or at the highest point on the helicopter pad.

RECEPTION OPTIONS: Though small and exclusive, Silent Waters has a first-class staff of 16 people, including two remarkable chefs. They can accommodate a sit-down dinner for up to 54 guests or a cocktail reception for up to 150.

WEDDING SERVICES: Provides some assistance.

PUERTO RICO

Puerto Rico, "The Island of Enchantment," is a tropical paradise that blends Latin American and European culture. When couples tell me they want to marry in Spain or Italy but are unable to make the trip, I suggest Puerto Rico. There, couples find beautiful architecture, with lots of plazas, paradors, and churches, and a colorful and festive culture, all steeped in a Spanish tradition. Puerto Rico has tropical rainforests, botanical gardens, 272 miles of coast, the world's largest underground river, and dramatic mountain ranges with great caves for spelunking. El Yunque, the Caribbean National Forest, is home to more than 400 species of trees, many of which are 100 feet tall. Imagine holding your marriage ceremony in a cathedral of towering trees! If solitude is what you seek, explore the offshore islands of Culebra, Vieques, Icacos, and Mona. Puerto Rico enjoys perpetual summer weather—perfect for tennis, golf, diving, snorkeling, and windsailing. The average ocean water temperature is 81° F (27°C), and underwater visibility is 10 to 60 feet. Peak season in Puerto Rico is mid-December to mid-April; plan to book popular resorts and destination locations months in advance.

COUNTRY OVERVIEW

CURRENCY: U.S. DOLLAR **TIPPING:** CHECK AHEAD, AS SOME HOTELS ADD A 10–15% SERVICE CHARGE TO THE BILL. OTHERWISE, TIP WAIT STAFF 15–20%, HOTEL PORTERS $1 PER BAG, MAIDS $1–$2 DAILY, AND TAXI DRIVERS 15–18%. TIP FLORISTS, PHOTOGRAPHERS, BAKERS, AND MUSICIANS ONLY FOR EXTRA SPECIAL SERVICES, UP TO 15%. **ELECTRICITY:** 110–220V **INTERNATIONAL CALLING CODE:** 1

PLANNING NOTES

SUGGESTED ASSISTANCE: Some assistance may be needed; start planning at least two months in advance. Contact the Demographic Registry for more information.

SPECIAL REQUIREMENTS: WAITING PERIOD: None RESIDENCY REQUIREMENT: None SPECIAL NOTES: Bride will need to have a blood test performed when she arrives.

CIVIL CEREMONIES: Civil ceremonies are not required. Weddings can be performed anywhere in Puerto Rico. For a list of registered officiants, contact the tourism office.

RELIGIOUS CEREMONIES: As the majority of Puerto Ricans are Christian, churches are quite easy to find. Jewish couples can contact the Jewish Center in San Juan (787-724-4157), and Muslim couples can contact the Islamic Center (787-751-6852). To research their options and resources, Hindu can call 787-723-2511 and Buddhists can call 787-722-7156.

DESIGN IDEAS

When you are ready to gather your welcome gifts, visit www.puertoricowow.com for ideas and call the tourism bureau for a Puerto Rican Crafts Route map. Plan to visit the two craft markets in Old San Juan, where you will find all kinds of local folk art to give as souvenirs. You may want to include a woodcarving from Jayuyya, handmade lace from Mundillo, and a bit of rich Puerto Rican coffee or Bacardi rum.

To give your ceremony a special touch, you could incorporate the traditional blessing of the coins. Once the coins have been blessed, the groom gives them to his wife as a symbol of good luck and prosperity. *Copias*, little bride dolls covered with these blessed coins, could be used as favors, on the cake, or in the welcome baskets. Puerto Rican cuisine uses a lot of rice, pork, chicken, and seafood and is flavored with *sofrito* (a mixture of onion, garlic, and cilantro) and *adobo* (salt, pepper, and garlic). The traditional wedding cake is a rum cake; other traditional desserts include coconuts, guava, flan, coconut bread pudding, *arroz con coco*, and *besitos de coco*. Because music is a source of national pride for Puerto Ricans (www.musicofpuertorico.com), guests might enjoy dancing to jazz, percussion, and other Latin beats, including salsa, merengue, flamenco, cha-cha, and rumba.

PLANNING RESOURCES

EMBASSY AND GOVERNMENT OFFICES:
Demographic Registry
P.O. Box 11854, Fernandez Juncos Station, San Juan, Puerto Rico 00910
787-728-7980

TOURISM:
The Puerto Rico Tourism Company
La Princesa Building #2, Paseo La Princesa, Old San Juan, Puerto Rico 00902
www.gotopuertorico.com
787-721-2400

© CHARITY DE MEER

PARKS, MONUMENTS, AND HISTORIC SITES:
San Juan National Historic Site
501 Norzagaray Street, San Juan, Puerto Rico 00901
www.nps.gov/saju
787-729-6960

VENUES

Puerto Rican venues include historic hotels and casinos, beach resorts, paradors, coffee and sugar plantations, ecolodges and exclusive spas. The **RIO GRANDE PLANTATION AND ECORESORT** (787-887-2779 / www.riogrande plantation.com), a former sugar plantation in the foothills of El Yunque rainforest, makes a lovely wedding site. **HACIENDA JUANITA** (787-838-2550 / www.hacienda juanita.com) is a parador set on a 24-acre farm located in the mountains. For a grand resort, consider **PARADISUS** (787-809-1770 / www.paradisus-puerto-rico.com), which offers elegant suites and villas with beautiful views of the ocean, the golf courses, or the mountains. Are you seeking a venue off the beaten track? You may enjoy the offshore island of Vieques, which is known for its Bioluminescence Bay, one of the most spectacular sites in the world. **VILLA QUINTA JACARANDA** (877-276-9763 / www.isla vieques.com/villa.html) and **THE CROW'S NEST INN** (787-741-0033 / www.crowsnest vieques.com) are the most luxurious options on Vieques, offering comfort, views, privacy, and décor that features commissioned artwork from well-known artists.

THE HORNED DORSET PRIMAVERA HOTEL

Apartado 1132, Rincon, Puerto Rico 00677
www.horneddorset.com
800-633-1857 / 787-823-4030

SIZE: 7 ACRES **NUMBER OF ROOMS:** 52 ROOMS; 53 SUITES **WHEELCHAIR ACCESSIBLE:** NO
RATES: $$–$$$ **SPECIAL NOTES:** CHILDREN OVER THE AGE OF 12 WELCOME,

REVIEW: The Horned Dorset, a Relais & Château property, is consistently voted one of the best hotels in the world by readers of *Condé Nast Traveler* and *Zagat*. The Spanish neo-Colonial-style hotel offers the luxurious feel of a private estate, with most of its guest rooms commanding panoramic views. Each of the 22 hillside suites has two floors, a wet bar, two bathrooms, and its own private plunge pool. The hotel's custom-designed teak furniture reflects the old world civility of its surroundings, where guests enjoy unparalleled French cuisine, kayaking, yoga, and swimming.

CEREMONY OPTIONS: Ceremonies for up to 100 guests are performed on the beach, on the hillside overlooking the sea, in the lush gardens, or by the pool.

RECEPTION OPTIONS: Informal rehearsal dinners, complete with steel band entertainment, can be held by one of three pools or on the seaside lawn. The formal dining room, a great house-style tropical dining room with a black-and-white marble floor reflecting overhead chandeliers, is available for receptions of up to 125 guests.

WEDDING PLANNING SERVICES: Full service. Facilitates marriage license and locates wedding officiants from many faiths.

EL CONQUISTADOR RESORT, LAS CASITAS VILLAGE, AND GOLDEN DOOR SPA

1000 Conquistador Avenue, Fajardo, Puerto Rico 00738

http://el-conquistador.wyndham-hotels.com

787-863-1000

SIZE: 500 ACRES **NUMBER OF ROOMS:** 750 ROOMS (452 NONSMOKING ROOMS); 16 SUITES **WHEELCHAIR ACCESSIBLE:** YES **RATES:** $$ **SPECIAL NOTES:** CHILDREN UNDER 16 STAY FREE; 2 ADULTS AND 2 CHILDREN PER ROOM

REVIEW: This Spanish-colonial Grand Hotel, built on a cliff overlooking the Caribbean, is modeled after the village of San Juan, with cobblestone streets, open-air plazas, gas lamps, and terra-cotta buildings. Rooms feature spectacular vistas, sitting rooms, spacious bathrooms, and stocked mini-bars. Guests enjoy a casino, a championship golf course, windsurfing, scuba diving, fishing, and massages at the fitness center.

CEREMONY OPTIONS: The Mirador, an outdoor terrace, is perfect for ceremonies with 50 to 150 guests. Many couples celebrate their ceremony at the Trellises, located on a bluff overlooking the Atlantic. Couples staying at Las Casitas Village may hold their ceremony in the privacy of their own casita. Another option is Parque Las Palmas, a large oceanside garden area surrounded by palm trees and natural flora.

RECEPTION OPTIONS: The elegant Magnolia Ballroom seats 80. Full-service banquet facilities can cater wedding receptions for 10 to 1,400 guests. From simple and casual to formal and elegant, the resort boasts exquisite cuisine and impeccable service. Tropical themes, with exotic floral decorations, are most popular.

WEDDING SERVICES: Full service. Facilitates marriage license and provides officiants.

EL CONVENTO

100 Cristo Street, Old San Juan, Puerto Rico 00901

www.elconvento.com

800-468-2779 / 787-723-9020

SIZE: 1 ACRE **NUMBER OF ROOMS:** 68 ROOMS; 8 SUITES **WHEELCHAIR ACCESSIBLE:** YES **RATES:** $$–$$$ **SPECIAL NOTES:** NONTRADITIONAL COUPLES WELCOME

REVIEW: Located in the historic Old San Juan district, this national landmark offers the unique charm of an intimate home away from home. El Convento, originally a Carmelite convent, is now a member of the Small Luxury Hotels of the World and the Puerto Rican government's official guesthouse for visiting heads of state and dignitaries. Handcrafted furniture, Andalusian tiles, marble bathrooms, and mahogany beams accent each room with old world style. Many of the guest rooms overlook the Plaza de las Mojas and the Cathedral of San Juan.

CEREMONY AND RECEPTION OPTIONS: For smaller weddings, choices include the Salon Paoli, perfect for a group of 50, and the Salon Zafiro, which accommodates 35. The Salon Oller seats 75 guests.

WEDDING SERVICES: Full service. Facilitates marriage license.

ST. LUCIA

St. Lucia is a lush tropical island gem, 27 miles long and 14 miles wide, with its eastern shore kissing the Atlantic Ocean and its western coast hugged by the calm Caribbean Sea. Located 21 miles south of Martinique and 90 miles northwest of Barbados, this independent democratic nation is part of the British West Indies. The island's orchards of banana, coconut, papaya, and mango trees give way to palm-fringed beaches and translucent waterways, while its rainforests house flourishing orchids, hot springs and flamboyant trees. St. Lucia is dotted with cultural heritage sites as well as historical and ecological landmarks, including the "drive-in" volcanoes of Gros Piton and Petit Piton. Visitors can do anything from cooking a meal of fresh crayfish on macambou leaves to exploring an old pirate hideout on Pigeon Island! Rich botanical gardens, old sugar plantations, small fishing villages, and plunging waterfalls create an enchanting tropical sanctuary that is perfect for romantic weddings and honeymoons. St. Lucia experiences temperatures ranging from 70°F (21°C) to 90°F (32°C) year-round, with a rainy season occurring June through November.

COUNTRY OVERVIEW

CURRENCY: EASTERN CARIBBEAN DOLLAR **TIPPING:** TIPPING IS NOT AUTOMATICALLY ADDED. IT IS CUSTOMARY TO TIP 10–12% OF THE BILL. TIPS ARE ACCEPTED BY HOTEL BELLHOPS, TAXI DRIVERS AND OTHER PERSONS PROVIDING SERVICE. **ELECTRICITY:** 220V **INTERNATIONAL CALLING CODE:** 758

PLANNING NOTES

SUGGESTED ASSISTANCE: Some assistance may be needed.
SPECIAL REQUIREMENTS: WAITING PERIOD: A waiting period of at least four to five business days is required once the application is processed. **RESIDENCY REQUIREMENT:** Two days
CIVIL CEREMONIES: Civil ceremonies are optional and can be held anywhere on the island. Once your required documents are in order and at least seven days before the ceremony is to take place, a local lawyer must apply for the license at the Attorney General's office, where a list of marriage officers (officiants) is available.
RELIGIOUS CEREMONIES: The island of St. Lucia is 80% Roman Catholic. Other denominations include Anglican, Methodist, Baptist, Seventh-Day Adventists, Church of the Nazarene, Christian Science, and the Salvation Army. Although there are Jewish, Hindu, and Muslim minorities in St. Lucia, it may be necessary for couples of these faiths to bring their own officiant; in these cases, the officiant would need to apply for permission to conduct the ceremony months in advance through the Office of the Attorney General.

DESIGN IDEAS

Welcome your guests to this tropical paradise with a variety of delicious native fruits, such as bananas, papayas, coconuts, and mangos, and a beautiful orchid bouquet. Consider using a rainforest theme for your décor; lush trees, ferns, and orchids, along with fountains of running water, are sure to give the wedding a peaceful and serene atmosphere. Hire a local baker to prepare a traditional Caribbean wedding cake—a fruitcake with rum and spices. And, if you want to add a uniquely St. Lucian touch, see if you can arrange for a Gros Piton-inspired volcano wedding cake. Bubbles might be more appropriate than confetti if the bride and groom are avid scuba divers, in which case an underwater theme may be in order (though you might want to stay clear of black rubber suits for the wedding party!). Don't forget to commence your wedding ceremony as they do every ceremonial event in St. Lucia—with a conch-blowing. For musical entertainment, your choices include reggae, jazz, calypso, soca, country, and hip hop. Why not incorporate a few of your favorites into different stages of the celebration? You can use one for cocktail hour, another for dinner, and yet another for dancing!

PLANNING RESOURCES

EMBASSY AND GOVERNMENT OFFICES:
Embassy of St. Lucia (in the United States)
3216 New Mexico Avenue NW, Washington, DC 20016
202-364-6792 / Consulate General (New York): 212-697-9360

Embassy of the United States (in Barbados, West Indies)
(The United States Ambassador to Barbados is accredited to Saint Lucia.)
P.O. Box 302, Bridgetown, Barbados, West Indies
246-436-4950 / Consular Section: 246-431-0225

Office of the Attorney General
Waterfront, Francis Compton Building, Castries, St. Lucia, West Indies
758-468-3200

TOURISM:
St. Lucia Tourist Board
St. Lucia: P.O. Box 221, Vide Bouteille, Castries, St. Lucia, West Indies
United States: 800 Second Avenue, Ninth Floor, New York, NY 10017
www.stlucia.org
(United States) 212-867-2950 / (St. Lucia) 758-452-4094

PARKS, MONUMENTS, AND HISTORIC SITES:
St. Lucia National Trust
P.O.Box 595, Castries, St. Lucia, West Indies
www.slunatrust.org
758-452-5005

VENUES

From beachfront resorts to secluded villas, St. Lucia is teeming with romantic wedding locations. **ANSE CHASTANET** (758-459-7000 / www.ansechastanet.com) is a 600-acre resort with beach units and gazebo cottages perched on a lush, tropical hill overlooking the sea and the Piton Mountains. The open-air rooms are individually decorated with original artwork and brightly colored madras prints. **REX CARIBBEAN** (758-452-9999 / www.rex caribbean.com) has several relaxing resort sites on the island, including the Royal Spa, which boasts award-winning restaurants and incredible sports facilities; the St. Lucian, where guests enjoy easy access to the Royal Spa and a shopping arcade; and Papillon, which features a fantastic butterfly-shaped pool. **STONEFIELD ESTATE VILLA RESORT** (758-

459-7037 / www.stonefieldvillas.com) offers a lovely poolside restaurant that can accommodate up to 50 guests for a dinner reception.

LADERA
P.O. Box 225, Soufriere, St. Lucia, West Indies
www.ladera.com
800-738-4752 / 758-459-7323

SIZE: 15 ACRES **NUMBER OF ROOMS:** 6 VILLAS; 19 SUITES **WHEELCHAIR ACCESSIBLE:** NO **RATES:** $$–$$$ **SPECIAL NOTES:** CHILDREN UNDER THE AGE OF 12 ARE DISCOURAGED BECAUSE THE HILLTOP LOCATION AND OVERHANGING BALCONIES CAN BE DANGEROUS.

REVIEW: Ladera, the location used for filming *Superman II*, offers unique mountainside accommodations and breathtaking views of the Piton Mountains. Imagine floating in your own private plunge pool just outside your villa, enjoying what *The Chicago Tribune* called the "most dramatic view in the Caribbean." Each guest room boasts panoramic views, an innovative open-air design, and an ambience of casual elegance created by polished woods, colorful madras linens, and ceramic tiles. Guests sip drinks by the edgeless pool, wander through the tropical gardens, and savor fine dining, spectacular sunsets, and spa treatments as well as swimming and snorkeling on the beach. They can also arrange for any kind of water sport, rainforest excursions, and trips to the nearby mineral baths.

CEREMONY OPTIONS: The most popular ceremony sites are the private villas, the gardens with a hilltop gazebo, and the wedding balcony, which accommodates 30 guests. The balcony affords an amazing view of the Piton Mountains and overlooks the azure Caribbean 1,000 feet below.

RECEPTION OPTIONS: Receptions for up to 80 guests can be held poolside, where guests can enjoy breathtaking views of the rainforest and mountains. The multilevel open-air bar/restaurant, which holds up to 100, is also an option for receptions.

WEDDING SERVICES: Full service. Facilitates marriage license. A justice of the peace is in residence for civil ceremonies. Staff can help locate officiants from several faiths.

WINDJAMMER LANDING
P.O.Box 1504, Castries, St. Lucia, West Indies
www.windjammer-landing.com
758-456-9000

SIZE: 60 ACRES **NUMBER OF ROOMS:** 248 VILLAS AND ESTATE VILLAS; 245 ROOMS **WHEELCHAIR ACCESSIBLE:** YES **RATES:** $$–$$$

REVIEW: The Windjammer Landing was designed after a Mediterranean village, with secluded villas and brick pathways that meander through more than 60 acres of gardens and waterfalls. The "village" encompasses 1,000 feet of white beaches, markets, a health spa, a fitness center, tennis courts, two pools, and several outdoor Jacuzzis. All the rooms have wonderful ocean views, and each villa has its own pool. In addition to the beautiful accommodations and impressive landscape, the five restaurants offer the best food on the island. In 2003, Chef Bob Bergstrom was named Chef of the Year at the Caribbean Culinary Federation's Taste of the Caribbean.

CEREMONY OPTIONS: The Gazebo and surrounding garden accommodates 60. Palm trees border this beautiful ceremony site, which affords a spectacular ocean view. The Estate Villas are wonderful for intimate weddings of up to ten people, whereas the Conference Center accommodates 40 to 50. Secluded beachside weddings for up to 60 are also possible.

RECEPTION OPTIONS: Accommodating 100, the Dragonfly Restaurant offers elegant dining with Caribbean flair. For a reception of 16 or less, there is an deck with a beautiful view. The Boardwalk Oceanside Dining Room can accommodate receptions for 100. A catered reception for up to ten guests can be held at the Estate Villas.

WEDDING SERVICES: Full service. Facilitates marriage license.

Argentina

Argentina is home to the Andes Mountains, the Patagonia glaciers, the Mendoza vine-yards, and the Pampas plains. You're bound to find something that strikes your fancy here, from elegant, old-world hotels to exciting eco-lodges. Remember that Argentina's seasons are the opposite to those in the northern hemisphere. To enjoy the beaches, go December through March; to ski, go July through October. Patagonia and the southern Andes are wonderful in the summer, with mild temperatures and long days, while the northern regions are best in the winter, with less rain and lower tropical temperatures. Because Argentina's Tierra del Fuego and Ushuaia (the world's southernmost city) form the gateway to Antarctica, you might even plan a honeymoon cruise to the South Pole!

COUNTRY OVERVIEW

CURRENCY: ARGENTINE PESO **TIPPING:** WAIT STAFF, DOORMEN, PORTERS, AND USHERS EXPECT A 10% TIP **ELECTRICITY:** 120V **INTERNATIONAL CALLING CODE:** 54

PLANNING NOTES

SUGGESTED ASSISTANCE: Assistance is a must unless you plan to arrive well in advance to apply for the license.

SPECIAL REQUIREMENTS: **WAITING PERIOD:** An administrative regulation requires you to apply for the marriage license as many as 28 days before the ceremony date. The exact number of days depends on the civil registry office you choose, so be sure to verify the office's guidelines. When you apply, you will have to submit all your documents in person; this can be done by another person, such as a wedding planner or a lawyer. **RESIDENCY REQUIREMENT:** None **SPECIAL NOTES:** A blood test must be done in a public hospital within one week of the ceremony.

CIVIL CEREMONIES: Only civil ceremonies are legally binding. They normally take place at the civil registry office in your chosen town. However, depending on the availability of the judge, you may be able to hire her to marry you at another more romantic location. For detailed information on the legal requirements and a directory of civil registry offices (in Spanish), check www.registrocivil.gov.ar.

RELIGIOUS CEREMONIES: Though predominantly Catholic, Argentina offers religious freedom to all. Resources for Jewish, Buddhist, and Muslim couples—and couples of almost any other religion—are easily found.

DESIGN IDEAS

Derived from the Latin word *Argentum*, meaning silver, the name *Argentina* refers to what early explorers found when they arrived in the country: native inhabitants bedecked with silver jewelry. With this in mind, you might choose silver as a wedding theme. Or adopt a location-based theme: a wine country celebration in Mendoza, an old-world soiree in Buenos Aires, or an outdoor ceremony by Iguaçu Falls. To welcome your guests, give silver jewelry decorated with *rodocrosita* (the national stone) or handpainted miniature *retablos* (altar boxes) and *chulucanas* (ceramic vases).

In Argentina, the bride often adds "something blue" to the traditional white dress by wearing a colored petticoat. And, in lieu of a maid of honor and best man, the groom's mother and the bride's father escort the couple down the aisle, then stand beside them during the entire church ceremony. In addition to adopting these traditions, you could create beautiful floral arrangements with Argentina's national flower, the red *ceibo*, a symbol of courage and fortitude. For entertainment, the tango is a must, as Argentina is said to be the birthplace of the sultry dance. (You might arrange tango lessons for your guests prior to the wedding.) Your menu could feature several traditional dishes, including *curantos* (shellfish, meat,

© FOUR SEASONS HOTEL BUENOS AIRES

and vegetables cooked on hot stones), venison, wild boar, lamb asados, fondue, and giant crabs from the Beagle Channel. A popular meal is *parrillada*, a mixed grill of steak prepared over charcoal and accompanied by *chimichurri*, a marinade served with salads and fried potatoes. For dessert, consider chocolate (over 130 types!) or *helado* (ice cream), which is considered a national delicacy.

PLANNING RESOURCES

EMBASSY AND GOVERNMENT OFFICES:
Embassy of the Argentine Republic (in the United States)
1600 New Hampshire Avenue NW, Washington, DC 20009
www.embassyofargentina-usa.org
202-238-6400

Embassy of the United States (in Argentina)
Avenida Colombia 4300, Buenos Aires, Argentina
http://buenosaires.usembassy.gov
54-11-5777-4533

Civil Registry Office
Uruguay 753,CP 1018, Buenos Aires, Argentina
www.registrocivil.gov.ar *(provides a list of Civil Registry offices throughout Argentina)*
54-11-4373-8441

TOURISM:
Argentina Tourist Information
12 West Fifty-sixth Street, New York, NY 10019
www.turismo.gov.ar
212-603-0433

PARKS, MONUMENTS, AND HISTORIC SITES:
Administration of National Parks
690 Santa Fe Avenue, Ground Floor, Buenos Aires, Argentina
www.parquesnacionales.gov.ar
54-11-4515-1365

VENUES

Awaiting you in Buenos Aires are the lovely and elegant **KEMPINSKI HOTELS** (54-11-6777-0400 / www.parkplazahotels.com). For an unforgettable experience, why not marry in Buenos Aires, the "Paris of the South," in March, during the city's Tango Festival? Outdoor enthusiasts seeking the thrill of a Patagonian wedding will enjoy **LOS NOTROS** (54-11-4814-3934 / www.losnotros.com), which sits on a glacier's edge near Los Glacieres National Park. **LLAO LLAO HOTEL AND RESORT** (54-11-5776-74450 / www.llaollao.com), near Nahuel Huapi Lake and Cathedral Ski Area, has an expansive terrace overlooking the lake and Tronador Volcano. **LAS BALSAS** (54-29-4449-4308 / www.lasbalsas.com), a member of the prestigious Relais & Châteaux chain, is located on the shores of Nahuel Huapi Lake, surrounded by snowcapped mountains. And one of the newest venues in Patagonia, **EOLO PATAGONIA'S SPIRIT** (54-11-4707-0539 / www.eolo.com.ar), is a mix between a villa and a mountain refuge.

ALVEAR PALACE HOTEL

Alvear Avenue 1891 (C1129AAA), Buenos Aires, Argentina

www.alvearpalace.com

54-11-4808-2100

SIZE: 1 LARGE CITY BLOCK **NUMBER OF ROOMS:** 85 ROOMS; 125 SUITES OF VARIOUS SIZES. **WHEEL-CHAIR ACCESSIBLE:** RESTRICTED **RATES:** $$$

REVIEW: For years, the Alvear Palace Hotel has been a home away from home for royals, emperors, and celebrities. Located in the Recoleta, the most elegant area of Buenos Aires, the Alvear Palace epitomizes luxury. When it was built in 1932, materials were imported from France to guarantee an impressive, genuine Louis XI neoclassical style. Numerous international awards, garnered from *Condé Nast Traveler*, *Travel + Leisure*, and other publications, herald this location as Top Hotel in Argentina and One of the Best Hotels in the World. The rooms, which combine romance and elegance, offer the most advanced technology and ultimate comfort, with personal butler service available 24/7.

CEREMONY AND RECEPTION OPTIONS: There are 12 meeting and entertaining rooms that can accommodate up to as many as 1,500. Several rooms are evocative of European castles, while others, such as the Alvear and the Emparatriz, are more modern in style. Many of the ballrooms are distinctly appointed with beautiful drapery, fine wood, chandeliers, mirrors, and antiques. The most interesting option is the Roof Garden Ballroom on the tenth floor, which accommodates 400 people.

WEDDING SERVICES: Provides some assistance.

FOUR SEASONS HOTEL BUENOS AIRES

Posadas 1086/88, C1011ABB, Buenos Aires, Argentina

www.fourseasons.com/buenosaires

800-819-5053 / 54-11-4321-1200

SIZE: 8,000 SQUARE FEET **NUMBER OF ROOMS:** 138 GUEST ROOMS, 27 SUITES **WHEELCHAIR ACCESSIBLE:** RESTRICTED **RATES:** $$ **SPECIAL NOTES:** MANY CHILDREN'S AMENITIES OFFERED, INCLUDING CHILD-SIZED BATHROBES, TOILETRIES, BEDTIME MILK AND COOKIES, AND SPECIAL MENUS. BABYSITTING SERVICES AVAILABLE WITH 24-HOUR NOTICE. COMPLIMENTARY CRIBS, ROLLAWAY BEDS, STROLLERS, DRAWING BOARDS WITH CRAYONS, AND MUCH MORE AVAILABLE FOR YOUNG GUESTS.

REVIEW: This Belle Epoque-style mansion has received numerous awards for excellence, including being named the 2003 Best Business Hotel by *Travel + Leisure* and one of the 2003 Top Ten Hotels and Resorts in Latin America by *Condé Nast Traveler*. It is centrally located in the upscale Recoleta district near the Obelisk, the Colon Theatre, and a marvelous selection of shops. The hotel, which offers the utmost in old-world elegance with modern amenities, is committed to supreme comfort. Guests enjoy gorgeous gardens, spa services, a fitness room, a beautiful pool, and even luxurious down duvets in each room.

CEREMONY AND RECEPTION OPTIONS: Anything from an intimate brunch to a sophisticated cocktail party can be arranged. The Mansion, from which the formal gardens are accessible, accommodates 150 guests, and the Grand Salon of the more contemporary Main Tower holds up to 450.

WEDDING SERVICES: Full service. Facilitates marriage license.

Belize

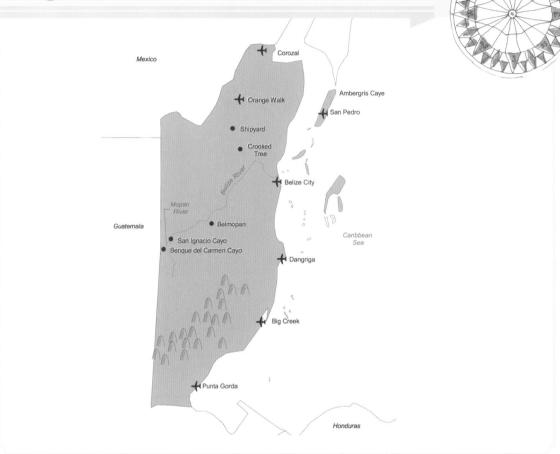

Only two hours away from three major U.S. gateways, Belize is a tempting subtropical destination with rainforests and mountains rich in wildlife, miles of beaches protected by coral reefs, and 200 cayes on the Caribbean coastline. Nature lovers will enjoy the waterfalls, caves, and granite riverbeds, and explorers will love the rainforest medicine trails and ancient Mayan cities (with ruins that make a great backdrop for photos). Belize's inhabitants, called *Sanpedranos*, speak their own island dialect, a combination of English, Creole, Mayan, and Spanish. November through January are the coolest months, with highs around 75°F (24°C), while May through September are the hottest at 81°F (27°C). The water temperature averages 82°F (28°C) year-round.

COUNTRY OVERVIEW

CURRENCY: BELIZE DOLLAR **TIPPING:** TIPS ARE NOT EXPECTED AND ARE RARELY ADDED TO THE BILL. HOWEVER, IT IS RECOMMENDED TO TIP 10–15% AT RESTAURANTS. THERE IS GENERALLY NO NEED TO TIP HOTELS, AS THEY TEND TO ADD A SERVICE CHARGE TO THE BILL. IT IS NOT CUSTOMARY TO TIP TAXI DRIVERS. **ELECTRICITY:** 110V **INTERNATIONAL CALLING CODE:** 501

PLANNING NOTES

SUGGESTED ASSISTANCE: Some assistance may be necessary.

SPECIAL REQUIREMENTS: **WAITING PERIOD:** Five days (Wedding coordinators in Belize can sometimes get around the five-day requirement.) **RESIDENCY REQUIREMENT:** Three days

CIVIL CEREMONIES: Civil ceremonies are required. They are performed by a justice of the peace or an official in the General Registry Office.

RELIGIOUS CEREMONIES: Catholicism is predominant in Belize. If you plan to marry in the Roman Catholic Church, don't forget that premarital counseling and copies of your baptismal certificates are required. Anglican and Presbyterian churches exist as do some other Christian denominations. Buddhist, Muslim, and Jewish couples may have difficulty finding officiants in Belize.

DESIGN IDEAS

If you love flowers, you have chosen the right destination! Belize is home to 300 species of orchids, so for a wedding theme, orchids are the obvious choice. Welcome your guests with a gorgeous bouquet of orchids and a basket filled with other local Belizean goods—wooden carvings, animals made out of coconuts, or replicas of Mayan artifacts—as well as edible treats.

For the wedding celebration, consider having a *Lazo* ceremony, during which a decorative garland is used to symbolically unite the couple for a lifetime of everlasting love. There are many interesting Mexican- and Spanish-influenced dishes that you could feature on your menu. Rice is a beloved dish in Belize—so beloved that some refer to the dinner hour as "rice hour." Also popular are fresh seafood, beans, hot peppers, and anything with a spicy kick. In every Belizean town, you can find vendors selling meat pies, corn fritters, or *dukunu* (corn and chicken tamales). For music, you may find it difficult to decide between punta, reggae, soca, salsa, merengue, cumbia, and traditional Mayan music; with so many choices, you could select a variety of tunes to entertain your guests over the course of the celebration.

PLANNING RESOURCES

EMBASSY AND GOVERNMENT OFFICES:
Embassy of Belize (in the United States)
2535 Massachusetts Avenue NW, Washington, DC 20008
www.embassyofbelize.org
202-332-9636

Embassy of the United States (in Belize)
29 Gabourel Lane, P.O. Box 286, Belize City, Belize
http://usembassy.state.gov/belize
501-227-7161

General Registry Department for License Information
Lower Flat of the Supreme Court Building, Regent Street, Belize City, Belize
501-227-7377

TOURISM:
Belize Tourism Board
New Central Bank Building, Level 2, Gabourel Lane, P.O. Box 325, Belize City, Belize
www.travelbelize.org
800-624-0686 / 501-223-1913

PARKS, MONUMENTS, AND HISTORIC SITES:
Belize Audubon Society *(grants permission for weddings in Belize's national parks)*
www.belizeaudubon.org
501-223-5004

VENUES

Belize boasts beach resorts, Mayan ruins, jungle lodges, haciendas, and luxury hotels. Ambergris Caye (www.ambergriscaye.com), one of the most popular destinations in Belize, is home to **CAPTAIN MORGAN'S RETREAT** (888-653-9090 / www.belizevacation.com), where you can stay in a thatched-roofed casita or in one of the beach villas (recently the location for Fox's *Temptation Island*). **RAMON'S VILLAGE** (800-624-4215 / www.ramons.com) is another great option on Ambergris, with authentic thatched-roofed cabanas, a lagoon-style pool, and a fabulous restaurant. Recognized as a PADI Gold Palm IDC Resort, Ramon's operates the largest scuba diving center in Belize. In San Pedro Town, just a few steps away from the azure Caribbean, lies **VICTORIA HOUSE** (800-247-5159 / www.victoria-house.com), an elegant boutique hotel. While smaller then some, this resort promises the casual elegance of a true Belizean experience. The peaceful casitas, plantation rooms, suites, and private villas are located amidst swaying palm trees.

FIVE SISTERS LODGE
P. O. Box 1731, San Ignacio, Cayo, Belize
www.fivesisterslodge.com
800-447-2931 / 501-820-4005

SIZE: 10.3 ACRES **NUMBER OF ROOMS:** 14 CABANAS **WHEELCHAIR ACCESSIBLE:** NO **RATES:** $$–$$$

REVIEW: Belizean-born Carlo Popper created the Five Sisters Lodge as an ecotourism facility to share with the world. The lodge, located in the largest protected area in Belize, sits in an immense rainforest and natural wildlife sanctuary, atop a hill overlooking the five rivers and waterfall for which it is named. Guests stay in one of 14 cabanas that are designed with local hardwoods, pimento sticks, traditional bay leaf, thatched roofs, and rich mahogany interiors. Outdoor activities include swimming, stargazing, bird-watching, caving, hiking, and horseback riding in the rainforest.

CEREMONY OPTIONS: Experience a rainforest ceremony at the newly constructed, non-denominational wedding chapel by the Five Sisters Waterfall.

RECEPTION OPTIONS: The reception (and the ceremony, if the couple prefers) can be held outdoors by the Five Sisters Waterfall, either in the open air or under a tent. The restaurant dining room is also an option if the weather isn't favorable or if the couple prefers to dine in the comfort of an indoor facility; however, the dining room is only available if the couple has reserved the entire property for the wedding party. The dining room, which accommodates 45, serves mouth-watering cuisine.

WEDDING SERVICES: Full service. Facilitates marriage license. The lodge will provide an officiant and will release two blue Morpho butterflies during or after the ceremony.

MOPAN RIVER RESORT
Riverside North, Benque Viejo del Carmen Cayo, Belize
www.mopanriverresort.com
501-823-2047

SIZE: 10 ACRES **NUMBER OF ROOMS:** 9 LUXURY CABANAS; 3 LUXURY SUITES **WHEELCHAIR ACCESSIBLE:** NO **RATES:** $$$ (ALL-INCLUSIVE) **SPECIAL NOTES:** CHILDREN UNDER 12 PERMITTED ONLY IF GROUP HAS BOOKED THE ENTIRE RESORT. RECOMMENDED MINIMUM AGE IS 16 YEARS.

© MOPAN RIVER RESORT, LTD.

REVIEW: Mopan River Resort features 12 luxury cabanas and suites on a grassy riverbank. Add to this the canopy of a mature coconut grove, along with avocado, mango, and citrus trees, colorful tropical plants, and singing birds—and you have a truly magical effect. A bird-watching tower, a swimming pool, local caves, Mayan ruins, and wildlife keep guests entertained. Many guests visit the nearby butterfly farm, the Aquacate Nature Reserve, and San Ignacio's Saturday market. There are tubes, inflatable kayaks, and an inflatable 12-person raft for trips down the Mopan. Each cabana and suite, constructed of Belizean hardwood, has unique thatched roofs, luxurious interiors, and all the amenities. The resort is closed July through October every year.

CEREMONY OPTIONS: The resort has its own wedding chapel, the Chapel of Angels, which seats up to 22 guests. Outdoor garden ceremonies are also possible.

RECEPTION OPTIONS: The reception is held in the resort's dining room, which accommodates 24 guests. This charming, thatched-roofed building is appointed with polished local hardwood furniture, complementing the interior and exterior walls.

WEDDING SERVICES: Full service. Facilitates marriage license. The minister, who is authorized to perform marriages in Belize, also acts as the on-site wedding planner. A local justice of the peace is also available for nonreligious services.

Brazil

Brazil enjoys a vibrant culture, a product of Native American, African, Japanese, and European roots. The Brazilian people, whose official language is Portuguese, live life with gusto and love a good celebration—best demonstrated during Carnival in Rio de Janeiro. Brazil claims cosmopolitan cities, sunny beaches, the largest rainforest in the world, and one of the most extensive river systems in the world. The country is rich in mineral deposits, including many precious gems. While there, you can purchase diamonds, topaz, amethyst, emeralds, tourmaline, and aquamarine. Think of the treasure you could bring home! In Brazil, you can find equatorial, tropical, semi-arid, highland tropical, and subtropical climates, with a rainy season between December and April.

COUNTRY OVERVIEW

CURRENCY: BRAZILIAN REAL **TIPPING:** RESTAURANTS USUALLY ADD 10% TO THE BILL, ASSUMING THAT YOU WILL LEAVE AN EXTRA 5% FOR GOOD SERVICE. IF THEY DO NOT ADD THE TIP TO THE BILL, YOU ARE EXPECTED TO LEAVE 15% FOR GOOD SERVICE. TAXI DRIVERS DON'T GET TIPS UNLESS THEY ARE IN RIO, WHERE THEY EXPECT 10%. **ELECTRICITY:**110V **INTERNATIONAL CALLING CODE:** 55

PLANNING NOTES

SUGGESTED ASSISTANCE: Assistance is a must. You can find a list of lawyers on the Web site for the American Embassy in Brazil (www.embaixada-americana.org.br), or you can call the embassy (55-21-292-7117) to request a list.

SPECIAL REQUIREMENTS: **WAITING PERIOD:** 30 days after applying for the license (You may be able to apply for a license on a planning trip.) **RESIDENCY REQUIREMENT:** None **SPECIAL NOTES:** There is a Civil Registry Office in every town and city; this is where you will apply for your marriage license once you arrive in Brazil. Contact the office ahead of time to be sure you understand what is expected of you. Contact information for the Civil Registry Offices is not readily available; if you are attempting to do this on your own, you may need to get the information from your hotel.

CIVIL CEREMONIES: Only civil ceremonies are legally recognized in Brazil. They usually take place in a Civil Registry Office and are performed by an official in the office.

RELIGIOUS CEREMONIES: Religious ceremonies may be performed outside the local civil registry, but they are not legally binding. Though Catholicism is dominant, most Western religions are represented in Brazil. There are several Jewish communities in the larger cities; you can find a list of rabbis in Brazil on www.kosherdelight.com. The Islamic community in Sao Paolo may be able to provide services to Muslim couples, and Buddhists can find resources in most of the large cities. Ten million Brazilians practice Macumba, a spirit worship influenced by African and Indian rituals.

DESIGN IDEAS

Welcome your guests with gifts of coffee, leather goods, jacaranda carvings, and jewelry made from semiprecious stones—packaged in a mahogany bowl, a handmade basket, or a woven hammock. For the most memorable and festive celebration, marry in Rio during Carnival, when the streets are alive with costumed revelers and samba rhythm—or just use a Carnival theme to liven up the party!

Brazilian cuisine, influenced by Portuguese, Native American, and African dishes, is delectable. Serve *churrasco*, a spicy meat skewered on a metal sword and cooked over an open fire; *vatapá*, a peppery fish, chicken, or shrimp stew seasoned with coconut milk and peanut oil; or *feijoada*, a dish consisting of beans, garlic, chile peppers, and up to 20 kinds of meat. Also offer *Cachaca*, a homemade whiskey often served with sugar and lime, or *Guaraná*, a soft drink made from tropical fruit. Don't forget to give each guest a *bem-casado* (meaning "well-married"), a shortbread cookie with chocolate filling. It won't be a truly Brazilian celebration unless there is plenty of music and dancing—samba, merengue, tango, and salsa. You might even arrange for a few pre-wedding lessons.

PLANNING RESOURCES

EMBASSY AND GOVERNMENT OFFICES
Embassy of Brazil (in the United States)
3006 Massachussetts Avenue NW, Washington, DC 20008
www.brazilemb.org
202-238-2700 / Consulate General: 202-238-2828

Embassy of the United States (in Brazil)
Avenida das Nações, Quadra 801, Lote 3, 70403-900, Brazil
www.embaixada-americana.org.br
55-61-312-7000

Civil Registry Office in Rio de Janeiro
Cartório do 1º Ofício de Notas , Av. Rio Branco nº 120,
Sobreloja 20, Centro, Rio de Janeiro, RJ 200021-120, Brazil, CEP
www.1oficionotas.com.br
55-21-2509-3006 / 55-21-2507-7610

TOURISM:
Brazil Tourism Office
www.braziltourism.org
800-727-2945

PARKS, MONUMENTS, AND HISTORIC SITES:
Ministry of the Environment
Esplanada dos Ministérios, Bloco B, 70068-900, Brazil, DF
55-61-317-1237

VENUES

Brazil offers a vast array of wedding venues! For a "wild-by-nature" wedding, the Amazon River Valley is home to several ecolodges. One of the most luxurious is the **TROPICAL HOTEL MANAUS** (800-701-2670 / www.tropicalhotel.com.br). Located on the Rio Negro, this colonial-style hotel features graceful arches and expansive patios. Other exciting eco-options in Brazil include: **ARIAU AMAZON TOWERS** (55-92-234-7308 / www.ariau towers.com), **GUANAVENAS POUSADA JUNGLE LODGE** (55-92-656-1500 / www.guanavenas.com.br), and **NATURE SAFARIS** (55-92-656-6033 / www.naturesafaris.com/ amazonlodge.php).

© EMBRATUR

To take advantage of Brazil's sunny beaches, head to one of the country's newest and most luxurious beach resorts, **NANNAI BEACH RESORT** (55-81-3552-0100 / www.nannai.com.br). Located in Porto de Galinhas, the resort sits amidst 3,000 coconut palms on a white sand beach. It is Polynesian in style, with palm-roofed bungalows surrounded by pools and gardens. Or consider a wedding in grand fashion at the **FERRADURA INN EXCLUSIVE** (55-21-2259-5465 / www.buziosonline.com.br/ ferradurainn) on the popular island of Búzios (www.buzios online.com.br). The inn offers four exclusive mansions facing the Búzios Sea and beaches. If you find mountains romantic, nothing beats the **HOTEL E FAZENDA ROSA DOS VENTOS** (55-21-2644-9900 / www.hotelrosados ventos.com.br). This mountaintop Relais & Châteaux hotel and restaurant is located on 250 acres in the heart of the Serra dos Orgaos National Park.

JUMA LODGE
Lago do Juma, S/N, Lado Esquerdo, Brazil
www.jumalodge.com
55-92-232-2707

SIZE: 3,500 ACRES **NUMBER OF ROOMS:** 8 BUNGALOWS WITH A FOREST VIEW; 3 BUNGALOWS WITH A LAKE VIEW **WHEELCHAIR ACCESSIBLE:** NO **RATES:** $$–$$$ **SPECIAL NOTES:** CHILDREN AGE 5 AND UNDER FREE; CHILDREN AGES 6–11 HALF-PRICE

REVIEW: After flying into Manaus, you will be transported by motor boat and van into the heart of the rainforest, where Juma Lodge awaits your arrival. There, rising above Juma Lake on stilts, are bungalows made from rich local timber and thatched with leaves from the native babaçu tree. Each room has a fan, mini-bar, private bath, and a veranda, complete with a hammock for quiet meditation or slumber. Guests can trek through the rainforest, canoe, fish, watch alligators, and enjoy the wildlife. A bungalow restaurant overlooking the lake offers both international and local cuisine.

CEREMONY AND RECEPTION OPTIONS: Juma Lodge is able to accommodate small wedding parties of up to 33. Ceremonies can be held outside in the gardens surrounding the lodge or in the dining room, which offers spectacular views of Lake Juma.

WEDDING SERVICES: Provides wedding planning service.

COPACABANA PALACE
Avenida Atlantica 1702, Rio de Janeiro, CED 22021-001, Brazil
www.copacabanapalace.com.br
55-21-2548-7070

SIZE: 36,000 SQUARE FEET **NUMBER OF ROOMS:** 225 APARTMENTS; 118 SUITES **WHEELCHAIR ACCESSIBLE:** YES **RATES:** $$–$$$ **SPECIAL NOTES:** CHILDREN UNDER 12 FREE

REVIEW: Located on the famous Copacabana Beach, Copacabana Palace is an Orient Express Hotel, a member of the Leading Hotels of the World and one of Rio's most famous landmarks. Over the years, this Mediterranean-style hotel has been the meeting place of kings and presidents. Princess Diana, Robert DeNiro, Orson Welles, Eva Perón, Marlene Dietrich, and Igor Stravinsky have all stayed there. Guest rooms are stylish, elegant, and comfortable, many with seaside views, and the hotel's restaurants are two of Rio's finest. Cipriani's is elegant, serving classic Italian cuisine, while Pergula offers afternoon tea and alfresco dining. In addition to the semi-Olympic sized pool, there is a rooftop tennis court and fitness center. The Saturday *feijoada* is a social event that rivals the gala Carnival Ball held there each year.

CEREMONY OPTIONS: Ceremonies are performed regularly in a number of beautiful meeting rooms, the most popular being the Salao Nobre and the Golden Room.

RECEPTION OPTIONS: The hotel offers a wide variety of options for receptions, meeting the needs of 60 to 250 guests in their luxurious restaurants. With an illuminated glass dance floor and a beautiful crystal chandelier, the opulent Salao Nobre and the Golden Room are ideal for cocktails and wedding parties up to 250.

WEDDING SERVICES: Wedding arrangements are coordinated through the hotel's events department, which provides the names of local officiants available to perform civil ceremonies. Honeymoon packages include an eight-minute panoramic helicopter flight through the locale.

Costa Rica

Many couples cannot resist the call of Costa Rica, a country rated "best adventure destination" and "top value" by bridal publications. A Costa Rican itinerary could include everything from witnessing volcanic eruptions to taking a trip through the rainforest canopy. Over one-quarter of Costa Rica consists of environmentally protected areas, including national parks, reserves, refuges, marine sanctuaries, and conservation and biological reserves. The country has a wonderfully diverse animal and plant population, with 857 species of birds, 9,000 species of plants, and 1,200 varieties of orchids. Costa Ricans, or *Ticos*, boast a 96 percent literacy rate, honor civil liberties and human rights, and treasure strong family traditions, which include warm hospitality to strangers.

Costa Rica is characterized by microclimates, making generalizations difficult. There is no winter or summer, as such; most regions have a dry season from December to April and a rainy season from May to November. Expect brief rainfall daily, except during *veranillo*, a relatively dry period that occurs along the Pacific coast between July and September. Temperature, which varies with elevation, averages 72°F (22°C) in the central valley, 82°F (28°C) on the Atlantic coast, and 89°F (32°C) on the Pacific coast.

COUNTRY OVERVIEW

CURRENCY: COSTA RICAN COLON **TIPPING:** RESTAURANTS GENERALLY ADD A 10% SERVICE CHARGE, THOUGH EXCELLENT SERVICE MAY WARRANT MORE. TOUR GUIDES ARE GENERALLY TIPPED ANY-WHERE FROM $3 TO $20. PORTERS AND BELLHOPS GET AROUND 75 CENTS PER BAG. HOTEL MAIDS AND TOUR DRIVERS ARE SOMETIMES TIPPED, WHILE TAXI DRIVERS ARE RARELY TIPPED. COSTA RICANS GENERALLY DO NOT TIP, SO THE AMOUNT IS UP TO YOU, DEPENDENT ON THE LEVEL OF SERVICE YOU RECEIVE. **ELECTRICITY:** 110V **INTERNATIONAL CALLING CODE:** 506

PLANNING NOTES

SUGGESTED ASSISTANCE: Assistance is a must. Everything needs to be translated and authenticated every step of the way. After the ceremony, you will need help getting your marriage certificate authenticated.

SPECIAL REQUIREMENTS: WAITING PERIOD: None; however, if the bride has been previously married, she must wait 300 days after her divorce or the death of her husband. **RESIDENCY REQUIREMENT:** None **SPECIAL NOTES:** Both the bride and the groom must provide a copy of their police record.

CIVIL CEREMONIES: Civil ceremonies are performed by local attorneys or judges. There are no published restrictions on civil ceremony locations, but they typically take place in the General Registry Office.

RELIGIOUS CEREMONIES: Costa Rica is a largely Roman Catholic country, though other faiths are welcome. There are several options in San Jose for Jewish couples, and Muslim couples can call the Al Markaz (Dawa-e-Tabligh) Centro Islamico (506-272-878) in San Jose for information. Buddhist resources are more difficult to locate.

DESIGN IDEAS

Costa Rica is known for its coffee, cocoa, and hardwoods that are used to make trinkets, canes, and furniture. For welcome gifts, package some local treasures in *carretas*, beautifully painted miniature oxcarts that have become a national symbol. For other gift ideas, check out www.costaricanmarket.com. There is no shortage of gorgeous tropical flowers in Costa Rica. The *guaria morada* is the national flower, and its symbolism is perfect for a wedding. According to Costa Rican tradition, the flower brings fortune, good luck, union, and family understanding; evokes peace, love, and hope for the future; and channels the best cosmic experiences.

Be sure to include local dishes in your wedding menu, including coconut-ginger *ceviche* (pieces of marinated fish served in a coconut), fresh lobster-artichoke crepes, and rice and beans cooked in coconut milk. Entertain your guests with the native music, which is influenced by Spanish, Caribbean, African, and indigenous cultures. Costa Rican rhythms include cumbia, lambada, marcado, merengue, salsa, soca, sinkit, and marimba (xylophone) music. Your guests might also enjoy dancing the *punto guanacaste*, the national dance of Costa Rica, and the *cuadrille*, which is very much like a maypole dance.

PLANNING RESOURCES

EMBASSY AND GOVERNMENT OFFICES:
Embassy of Costa Rica (in the United States)
2114 S Street NW, Washington, DC 20008
www.costarica-embassy.org
202-234-2945 / 202-234-2946

Embassy of the United States (in Costa Rica)
Calle 120 Avenida 0, Pavas, San José, Costa Rica
www.usembassy.or.cr
506-519-2000 / Consulate: 506-220-3050 or 506-220-3939

Registro Civil
Apartado Postal 10218, San José 1000, Costa Rica

TOURISM:
Costa Rican Ministry of Tourism
www.visitcostarica.com
800-343-6332

PARKS, MONUMENTS, AND HISTORIC SITES:
The Costa Rica Tourism and Travel Bureau
www.costaricabureau.com/nationalparks.htm
506-296-7074

© HOTEL VILLA CALETAS

VENUES

Costa Rica is home to several luxury resorts, ecolodges, and villas. **PUNTA ISLITA RESORT AND SPA** near San Jose (506-231-6122 / www.hotelpuntaislita.com) is an elegant resort situated on a 500-acre mountain outpost overlooking the Pacific Ocean. The resort, recognized as one of the best small luxury hotels in the world, features a spa that offers native, natural treatments based on ancient healing arts. Surrounded by small primitive villages, it is an ideal romantic hideaway, and the hotel's private horseshoe-shaped beach is a picture-perfect wedding location.

If you love the rainforest, consider the **LAPA RIOS ECOLODGE** (506-735-5130 / 506-735-5281 / www.laparios.com). While this ecolodge does not coordinate weddings, it is a wonderful location for marriage celebrations. You may also want to visit the Guanacaste region, one of only three places in the world where the leatherback sea turtle comes ashore to nest. A 1998 *New York Times* article likened the **HOTEL VILLA BAULA** (506-653-0644 or 506-653-0493 / www.hotelvillabaula.com) to "Swiss Family Robinson—with electricity." Several nearby churches and restaurants could accommodate an intimate wedding. **LAKE COTER ECOLODGE** (506-289-6060 / www.ecolodgecostarica.com), known for its breathtaking view of the Arenal Volcano, is located on a 300-acre forest reserve in the mountains near the Lake of Arenal. There, visitors have the rare opportunity to interact with the local Maleku Indians.

COSTA RICA TREE HOUSE OF THE IGUANAVERDE ASSOCIATION

30-7304 Puerto Viejo, Talamanca, Limon, Costa Rica

www.costaricatreehouse.com

506-750-0706

SIZE: 10 ACRES **NUMBER OF ROOMS:** THE TREEHOUSE HAS 2 ROOMS (SLEEPING UP TO 5); THE BEACH HOUSE HAS 1 (SLEEPING UP TO 4) **WHEELCHAIR ACCESSIBLE:** NO **RATES:** $

REVIEW: The Costa Rica Tree House is located on oceanfront property owned by the Iguanaverde foundation (www.iguanaverde.com), which is dedicated to protecting the green iguana. Built in and around a Sangrillo tree, the Tree House consists of two levels, with a veranda overlooking Punta Uva beach, considered one of Costa Rica's most beautiful beaches. The upstairs room has a private bath and double bed, and the downstairs room has a double bed and space for an additional single bed; both levels share a living room and kitchen. A second building, the Beach House, features one open room, which includes a fully equipped kitchen, living area, and sleeping area with a king-size bed, as well as a veranda that overlooks the Caribbean. Located within the Gandoca Manzanilla Wildlife Refuge, it offers hiking, water sports, and local attractions, like the Butterfly Museum and a cacao farm. Guests can also enjoy dolphin-watching boat rides and the services of experienced guides who are familiar with indigenous medicinal plants and native wildlife.

CEREMONY OPTIONS: The large gardens make a superb ceremony setting for up to 100 guests. Gorgeous oceanside locations are also available for varied numbers of guests.

RECEPTION OPTIONS: There are restaurants nearby, many within a five- to ten-minute walking distance. House recommendations include the Puerto Viejo Salsa Brava, Selvin's, and The Helena. A catered reception can also be arranged in one of the beautiful gardens surrounding either the Tree House or the Beach House.

WEDDING SERVICES: Provides some assistance.

VILLA CALETAS MOUNTAIN AND SEASIDE RESORT

Jacó Central Pacific, Punta Arenas, Costa Rica

www.villacaletas.com

506-637-0505

SIZE: 150 ACRES **NUMBER OF ROOMS:** 5 STANDARD ROOMS; 13 VILLAS; SUITES: 2 MASTER, 5 DELUXE, 2 REGULAR, 2 SUPERIOR, AND 6 JUNIOR **WHEELCHAIR ACCESSIBLE:** YES **RATES:** $–$$$

© HOTEL VILLA CALETAS

REVIEW: Villa Caletas, a distinguished member of the Small Distinctive Hotels of Costa Rica, sits high on a cliff overlooking the ocean and surrounded by rainforest. Inspired by French colonial and Victorian architecture, its spacious guest rooms are filled with art and antiques. All beautifully appointed, the accommodations range from standard rooms to luxurious master suites. Guests can enjoy the resort's two restaurants, which offer exquisite cuisine. They can also relax in the gardens, filled with exotic plants and wildflowers, or in the nearby Carara Preserve, home to rare scarlet macaws. There are also opportunities to experience a "canopy tour" of the rainforest, explore the countryside by horseback, go on a crocodile observation trip by boat, or take a tour of nearby coffee plantations.

CEREMONY OPTIONS: Wedding ceremonies can be held outdoors in the magnificent Greek amphitheater located on the resort property or indoors on one of two terraces, all of which seat 10 to 150 guests. Each location overlooks the ocean.

RECEPTION OPTIONS: Three meeting rooms are available for the ceremony and/or reception. The Amphitheatre Restaurant and Terrace seats approximately 120 guests and offers beautiful ocean views. The Mirador Restaurant and Terrace, which seats up to 60, can be used individually or in combination with the Amphitheatre. Located above the Amphitheatre, it too offers outstanding ocean views. Small receptions can also be held in the Martiguez Lounge, which accommodates up to 40 guests.

WEDDING SERVICES: Provides some assistance.

CALA LUNA HOTEL AND VILLAS

Playa Tamarindo, Costa Rica

www.calaluna.com

506-653-0214

SIZE: 3 ACRES **NUMBER OF ROOMS:** 5 THREE-BEDROOM VILLAS; 16 TWO-BEDROOM VILLAS; 20 DELUXE HOTEL ROOMS **WHEELCHAIR ACCESSIBLE:** YES **RATES:** $–$$ **SPECIAL NOTES:** CHILDREN UNDER AGE 12 FREE

REVIEW: Cala Luna is a luxury hotel nestled in a charming fishing village (population 1,000) on the northwestern shoreline of Costa Rica. The site features traditional

Central American architecture, with grass-topped buildings reminiscent of structures built by indigenous people. A mecca for adventure lovers, the Cala Luna offers jungle boat safaris through giant mangrove swamps as well as trips to the National Marine Park and the active volcano at Rincon De La Vieja. Leisure activities include surfing, snorkeling, waterskiing, windsurfing, and horseback riding. And for avid fishing enthusiasts, the Cala Luna has a 26-foot boat complete with skipper and gear. With each villa comes a private pool, parking, two or three fully equipped baths, and a fully equipped kitchen that even includes an espresso machine.

CEREMONY OPTIONS: Beachside and sunset weddings are available.

RECEPTION OPTIONS: The hotel restaurant, Cala Moresca, overlooks the pool and seats 60. Catering to sophisticated tastes, the restaurant features international cuisine (including specialties from the Guanacaste region) and uses fresh, local products (including fresh lobster caught just outside the hotel). Another restaurant, La Caleta, offers a more informal dining environment, with a capacity of 40.

WEDDING SERVICES: Provides some assistance. When requested, staff will suggest local area officiants to conduct services.

XANDARI RESORT & SPA

APDO 1485-4050, Alajuela, Costa Rica
United States Office: Box 1449, Summerland, CA 93067
www.xandari.com
800-686-7879 / 506-443-2020

SIZE: 40 ACRES (COFFEE AND FRUIT PLANTATION) **NUMBER OF ROOMS:** 21 VILLAS **WHEELCHAIR ACCESSIBLE:** NO **RATES:** $–$$ **SPECIAL NOTES:** CHILDREN UNDER AGE 3 FREE

REVIEW: Xandari is a tropical paradise with 21 private palm-roofed villas, all secluded on a coffee plantation amidst waterfalls, streams, fountains, and gardens. The *Star Report* rates Xandari as one of the seven most unique architectural resorts in the world. The villas, private terraces, furniture, and gardens are designed with great attention to detail. Each villa boasts original works of art, a private-view terrace, a walled-in sun area, a bar kitchen, either a king bed or two full beds, and its own private Jacuzzi tucked under a *jalapa* (palm-roofed pavilion). The facilities include a spacious art studio and an organic greenhouse with a hydroponic garden, where vegetables are grown for the restaurant. Guests can indulge in exotic facial and body treatments and a swim in the heated lap pool.

CEREMONY OPTIONS: Xandari will help arrange ceremonies conducted by priests, rabbis, lawyers, or lay people. The favored location is poolside, with a dramatic backdrop of hills and sky. Many couples choose to be married near one of the five natural waterfalls or in the artist's studio. Any of these locations can accommodate up to 40.

RECEPTION OPTIONS: Receptions can take place in the dining room or poolside, where tables for the bridal party can be set up on a viewing platform, accessible by a flower-strewn bridge that spans the reflecting pool. With advanced notice, the entire resort can be rented for weddings. Small private ceremonies can be held in the villas.

WEDDING SERVICES: Full service. Facilitates marriage license.

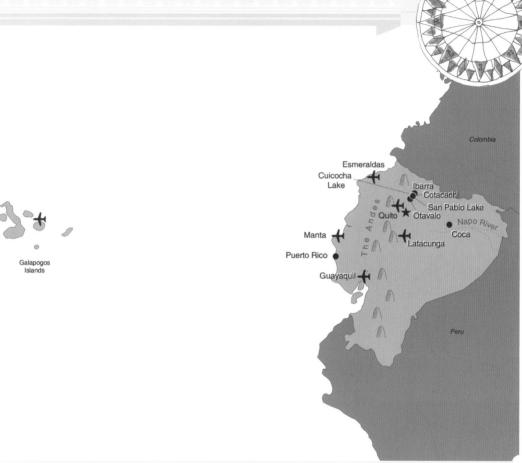

Ecuador offers myriad cultures and climates, nicely packaged in one beautiful, friendly, and easily accessible country. Where else can you visit a colonial city high in the Andes, hike in a misty forest, canoe down an Amazon tributary, paddle through a mangrove forest, *and* escape to the Galapagos Islands—where you can swim with sea lions, dolphins, manta rays, penguins, and turtles? Though tourist season runs December through January and June through August, the best time to visit depends on the region. The beaches are wonderful from May to December, the highlands June to September. Year-round, you'll find spring-like weather in the Central Valley and rain in the East. January to April, while unpleasantly hot, is a good time to snorkel in the Galapagos.

COUNTRY OVERVIEW

CURRENCY: U.S. DOLLAR (THE DOLLAR REPLACED THE SUCRE IN 2000) **TIPPING:** TIP WAIT STAFF, DOORMEN, PORTERS, AND THEATER USHERS 10%. QUALITY RESTAURANTS ADD 10% TAX AND A 10% SURCHARGE TO THEIR BILLS; IF YOU WANT TO TIP WAITERS, HAND IT TO THEM DIRECTLY RATHER THAN LEAVING IT ON THE TABLE. **ELECTRICITY:** 120V **INTERNATIONAL CALLING CODE:** 593

PLANNING NOTES

SUGGESTED ASSISTANCE: Assistance is helpful, especially if you don't speak Spanish.
SPECIAL REQUIREMENTS: WAITING PERIOD: None **RESIDENCY REQUIREMENT:** None
CIVIL CEREMONIES: Civil ceremonies are required and take place at the Registro Civil office of the city in which you plan to marry. A judge or official from the office usually performs the ceremony.
RELIGIOUS CEREMONIES: Though mostly Catholic, Ecuador does have other faiths and denominations in the larger cities. Jewish couples can call the Asociacion Israelita de Quito (593-2502-734), and Muslim couples can contact Quito's As Salaam Mosque (593-223-7654). Buddhist and Hindu resources are not readily available.

DESIGN IDEAS

Welcome your guests with colorful woven wool bags filled with Ecuadorian ponchos, sweaters, jewelry, ceramic figurines, and bead dolls—and don't forget to include a Panama hat, which despite its name, originated in Ecuador, and a woodcarving from San Antonio de Ibarra. The Andean market in Otavalo, north of Quito, is a fun resource for these items.

Indulge your guests by spicing up your wedding menu with delicious Ecuadorian cuisine. Include *ceviche*, a refreshing seafood soup served with popcorn and onion, *patacones* (fried plantain chips), and *aji*, a spicy Ecuadorian salsa. You might also serve *lechon* (a roasted pig)—or be very adventuous and try *cuy* (roasted guinea pig). Give the celebration Ecuadorian flair with native fold dancers and Andean drums and pan flutes.

PLANNING RESOURCES

EMBASSY AND GOVERNMENT OFFICES:
Embassy of Ecuador (in the United States)
2535 Fifteenth Street NW, Washington, DC 20009
www.ecuador.org
202-234-7200 / Consulate: 202-234-7166

Embassy of the United States (in Ecuador)
Avenida 12 de Octubre y Patria, Quito, Ecuador
www.usembassy.org.ec
593-2-2562-890

Consulate General of the United States (in Ecuador)
9 de Octubre y Garcia Moreno, Guayaqui, Ecuador
593-4-2323-570 / 593-4-2322-756

Registro Civil (in Quito)
Mejia y Guayaquil, Quito, Ecuador
593-2-2955-222

TOURISM:
Ecuador Ministry of Tourism
Eloy Alfaro N32-300 Carlos Tobar, Quito, Ecuador
www.vivecuador.com
593-2-2507-559 / 593-2-2507-560

Galapagos Chamber of Tourism
Avenida Charles Darwin y Charles Binford, Puerto Ayora, Isla Santa Cruz, Galapagos
www.galapagostour.org

HELPFUL WEB SITES:
The Best of Ecuador: www.thebestofecuador.com
Ecuador Explorer: www.ecuadorexplorer.com

PARKS, MONUMENTS, AND HISTORIC SITES:
Ministerio del Ambiente
www.ambiente.gov.ec
593-2-2529-845

VENUES

Ecuador's venues are as varied as the country's terrain. One option in the Amazon region is **LA SELVA JUNGLE LODGE** (593-2-2550-995 / www.laselvajunglelodge.com), a winner of the World Congress on Tourism and the Environment's Ecotourism Award. Colonial hotels abound in Quito and throughout smaller cities in the Andes. **THE SAN JORGE ECO-LODGE** (877-565-2569 / www.eco-logesanjorge.com), just outside Quito, is a lovely, traditional eighteenth-century Ecuadorian farm. For memorable wedding cruises around the Galapagos Islands, contact Lenin Villacis at **NAUTICA GALAPAGOS CIA LTDA** (593-2-2503-608 / www.galapagosandmore.com).

HOSTERÍA HACIENDA PINSAQUÍ

Panamericana Norte km. 5, Otavalo, Ecuador

www.haciendapinsaqui.com

593-6-2946-116

SIZE: 30 ACRES **NUMBER OF ROOMS:** 17 **WHEELCHAIR ACCESSIBLE:** NO **RATES:** $ **SPECIAL NOTES:** CHILDREN UNDER AGE 6 STAY FREE

REVIEW: One of the grandest Spanish colonial hotels in Ecuador, Hostería Hacienda Pinsaquí is located in Otavalo, a beautiful Andean town famous for its Indian market. The property epitomizes old-fashioned country charm, with antiques decorating every room. Guests can enjoy horseback tours through local eucalyptus groves to the Peguche Waterfall, a once-sacred Incan site that is still used today for baptisms.

CEREMONY: The 200-year-old hacienda, surrounded by gardens that have been cultivated for centuries, provides a beautiful ceremony location for up to 300 guests.

RECEPTION OPTIONS: A reception can be held outdoors under tents and canopies or indoors in the hosteria's restaurant.

WEDDING SERVICES: Provides some assistance.

HACIENDA CUSÍN

San Pablo del Lago, Imbabura, Ecuador

www.haciendacusin.com

800-670-6984 / 593-6-291-8013

SIZE: 30 ACRES (10 ACRES OF GARDENS) **NUMBER OF ROOMS:** 44 GUESTROOMS, GARDEN COTTAGES AND FAMILY SUITES **WHEELCHAIR ACCESSIBLE:** NO **RATES:** $

REVIEW: Recognized by *Martha Stewart* and *Gourmet* magazines, Hacienda Cusín has been hosting wedding parties in their lush garden sanctuary for over 25 years. The antique wall tapestries, chandeliers, and fireplaces set a warm, welcoming tone in the dining area and adjoining luxurious Salon Bolivar. Many of the rooms feature beamed ceilings, fireplaces, and balconies. The affordable rates include all meals, an Internet café, a video library, horseback riding, and the use of sports facilities.

CEREMONY OPTIONS: A horse and carriage can carry the bride through the seventeenth-century courtyard, down a rose-petal-covered path to the garden, where up to 200 guests (and Andean musicians, if you like) await under an old cedro tree.

RECEPTION OPTIONS: After the ceremony, the couple leads a procession across the wooden bridge to the central courtyard of El Monasterio for reception festivities.

WEDDING SERVICES: Full service. Facilitates marriage license.

HOSTERÍA LA BARQUITA

Puerto Rico, Manabi, Ecuador

www.labarquita-ec.com

593-4-2780-051

SIZE: ½ ACRE **NUMBER OF ROOMS:** 11 ROOMS FACING THE SEA, PLUS 3 BUDGET ROOMS (ACCOMMODATES UP TO 42 GUESTS IN ALL) **WHEELCHAIR ACCESSIBLE:** RESTRICTED **RATES:** $ **SPECIAL NOTES:** CHILDREN UNDER AGE 2 STAY FREE; CHILDREN AGES 2–12 HALF-FARE

REVIEW: Located on the jungle's edge close to the Machalilla National Park, this small but magical resort is like a rainforest village on its own private beach. Here you can enjoy bird- and whale-watching, horseback riding, surfing, and snorkeling. You can also spend time taking Spanish classes as well as tours of the Galapagos coastline. Guest rooms are "rainforest rustic," designed with indigenous woods, hammocks, and verandas overlooking the coastline. The restaurant offers fresh Ecuadorian, international, and vegetarian cuisine.

CEREMONY OPTIONS: You can marry in the small bamboo church in the village of Puerto Rico or in the Olon sanctuary, a small cliffside church overlooking the ocean.

RECEPTION OPTIONS: The Galleon, the hosteria's restaurant built to look like a boat, holds receptions for up to 50, offering magnificent menus, music, views, and sea breezes.

WEDDING SERVICES: Full service.

Mexico offers a broad palette of possibilities for fabulous destination weddings. Many couples are beckoned by Mexico's crystal white beaches, desert landscapes, and mystical jungles as well as its wealth of architectural and archeological sites—all possible locations for a storybook wedding. Others are drawn to its vibrant color, culture, folklore, arts and crafts, music, food, dance, and pageantry, which make the country an irresistible celebration of the senses. Mexico's climate varies according to altitude. The coastal areas and lowlands are hot and humid, the central plateau is temperate even in winter, and the inland highlands are mostly mild. Rainfall varies greatly from region to region, but generally speaking, the dry season runs from October to May.

COUNTRY OVERVIEW

CURRENCY: MEXICAN PESO **TIPPING:** WITH THE EXCEPTION OF RESORTS, MOST RESTAURANTS DO NOT ADD A SERVICE CHARGE TO THE BILLS; A 10–15% TIP IS CUSTOMARY. PORTERS AND BELLHOPS ARE GENERALLY TIPPED 9–10 PESOS, WHILE TAXI DRIVERS RECEIVE 5–10 PESOS. **ELECTRICITY:** 120V **INTERNATIONAL CALLING CODE:** 5

PLANNING NOTES

LEGAL REQUIREMENTS: Some assistance may be needed. You will need translation services, chest x-rays, and blood tests once you arrive, and you will want to get your marriage certificate legalized after the ceremony before you return home.

SPECIAL REQUIREMENTS: WAITING PERIOD: None; however, previously married brides/grooms must verify one year's time lapse since the death of former partner or since divorce decree. **RESIDENCY REQUIREMENT:** None

CIVIL CEREMONIES: Most Mexicans have both a religious and civil ceremony, but only civil ceremonies are recognized in Mexico. The civil marriage is legally binding in both Mexico and your country of origin, whereas the religious marriage is merely ceremonial. Contact the Civil Registry (Oficina del Registro Civil) in the town nearest your planned destination to determine legal requirements.

RELIGIOUS CEREMONIES: Mexico is a predominantly Catholic country, though other faiths are represented in smaller numbers. Most Christian denominations are represented in Mexico. There is a fairly strong Jewish community; go to to www.maven.co.il to find out more about Jewish resources in Mexico. Muslim couples will find many Islamic centers and communities, especially in Monterey and Guadalajara. There are Dharma centers in both Chiapas and Mexico City; however, Hindu temples are not readily found in Mexico.

DESIGN IDEAS

Mexico's folk art makes the perfect welcome gift for your guests. Look for onyx sculptures, handcrafted silver jewelry, Tarahumara basketry, handpainted pottery from Puebla, and Papel Amate paintings by the Otami Indians. For a celebration as colorful as the folk art, spice up your ceremony with some Mexican wedding customs. Traditionally, the groom wears a wedding shirt called the *guayabera*, and he gives his wife 13 gold coins, representing Christ and the apostles, which the priest blesses during the ceremony. Following the vows, the priest wraps a lasso, a large rosary, or a band of flowers, ribbons, or gold in a figure eight around the couple to symbolize their eternal unity. During the reception, guests encircle the couple in a large heart-shaped ring to bless their union. To learn more about these and other Mexican wedding traditions, check out www.muy bueno.net/articles/mexicanwedding.htm.

Though it varies from region to region, Mexican cuisine is always mouthwatering. Characteristic of the country's diverse influences, dishes incorporate French, Spanish, and North American accents into Mexico's pre-Columbian culinary heritage—with wonderful results. Ingredients include beans, corn, squash, tomatoes, jicama, chocolate, avocado, papaya, guava, vanilla, dozens of spices, and of course, chile peppers. The traditional Mexican wedding cake is a fruitcake soaked in rum, typically accompanied by pecan-flavored Mexican wedding cookies. For wedding entertainment, begin with a mariachi band, then step it up with salsa and merengue. And don't forget that no wedding in Mexico is complete without a piñata—usually heart-shaped!

PLANNING RESOURCES

EMBASSY AND GOVERNMENT OFFICES:
Embassy of Mexico (in the United States)
1911 Pennsylvania Avenue NW, Washington, DC 20006
www.embassyofmexico.org
202-728-1600

United States Embassy (in Mexico)
Paseo de la Reforma 305, Colonia Cuauhtemoc, 06500 Mexico, DF
www.usembassy-mexico.gov/emenu.html
52-55-5080-2000

Oficina del Registro Civil
Arcos de Belen y Doctor Andrade, 06720 Mexico, DF
52-5-578-7140

TOURISM:
Mexico Tourism Board
www.visitmexico.com
800-446-3942

PARKS, MONUMENTS, AND HISTORIC SITES:
United States-Mexico Affairs Office
2455 Missouri Suite C, Las Cruces, NM 88001
www.nps.gov/oia/around/mexico.htm
505-521-2689

VENUES

You can expect to find some of the world's most spectacular venues in Mexico. Check out the **ALLEGRO RESORT** (800-858-2258 / www.allegroresort.com) in Cozumel, a beautiful island with coral reefs made famous by Jacques Cousteau's 1961 documentary. In Cancun, pamper yourself and your guests at **AVENTURA PALACE** (800-635-1836 / www.palaceresorts.com), a state-of-the-art spa. While luxury resorts abound, Mexico also has options for small, rustic ecolodges. In Playa del Carmen, the thatched-roof beach huts of **KAILUUM** (800-538-6802 / www.kailuum.com) provide a calming romantic getaway. Mexico boasts so many wonderful destinations—Cabo San Lucas, Puerto Vallarta, Acapulco, San Miquel de Allende, and Cuernavaca, to name a few—whichever you choose is sure to be *fantástico*!

PARAÍSO DE LA BONITA RESORT & THALASSO
Carretera Cancun-Chetumal, KM 328, Bahia Petempich 77500,
Cancun QROO, Mexico
www.paraisodelabonitaresort.com
52-998-872-8300

SIZE: 14 ACRES **NUMBER OF ROOMS:** 90 SUITES (82 REGULAR, 7 MASTER, 1 PRESIDENTIAL) **WHEEL-CHAIR ACCESSIBLE:** RESTRICTED **RATES:** $$–$$$ **SPECIAL NOTES:** CHILDREN UNDER AGE 13 ARE NOT PERMITTED. SPECIAL OFFERINGS AVAILABLE FOR NONTRADITIONAL COUPLES.

REVIEW: *Condé Nast Traveler* selected Paraíso de la Bonita as one of the 50 Hot Hotels in the World and one of the World's Coolest New Places to Stay. *Travel + Leisure* magazine recognized it as one of the Top 15 Resorts to Watch in Mexico and South America. It's easy to see what all the fuss is about once you experience the resort's Mayan-style Jacuzzis, therapeutic spa services, and sunset cruises aboard La Bonita, the hotel's private 50-foot catamaran. The beautiful décor recalls the great Yucatan haciendas, with thatched roofs, thick plastered walls, hand-hewn timber beams, reflecting pools, mosaic pathways, and fountains. The large suites, luxuriously decorated with handcrafted furniture, offer exquisite views of the gardens and the Caribbean. This site is located on the Riviera Maya, the second largest reef in the world, where guests can snorkel, dive, and swim with dolphins.

CEREMONY OPTIONS: Outdoor ceremonies can take place on the beach or on a pier, which holds 60 guests. Indoor ceremonies can be held in the richly decorated lounge area, which sports open views of the beautiful property.

RECEPTION OPTIONS: Both the pier and the lounge area are available for receptions.

WEDDING SERVICES: Offers full wedding services, special wedding packages, and assistance with fulfilling legal requirements.

LAS ALAMANDAS
AP 201, San Patricio Melaque, 48980, Mexico
www.alamandas.com
866-376-7831 / 52-322-285-5500

© PHOTO BY ISABELLE BOSQUET

SIZE: 1,500 ACRES **NUMBER OF ROOMS:** 14 SUITES WITHIN 6 VILLAS **WHEELCHAIR ACCESSIBLE:** YES **RATES:** $$–$$$ **SPECIAL NOTES:** NONTRADITIONAL COUPLES WELCOME

REVIEW: Described by *Forbes* magazine as one of the world's most romantic hotels, Las Alamandas is located on acres and acres of forest, tropical gardens, estuaries, and beaches. With a reputation for providing luxury, personal attention, and privacy, this resort hosted many celebrity newlyweds, including Richard Gere and Cindy Crawford. The hotel tailors any wedding under 50 people. Elegantly appointed with all the amenities, guest rooms include Jacuzzis and incredible views.

CEREMONY OPTIONS: Wedding ceremonies for up to 50 guests can take place in an oceanside palm grove, on one of the many large grassy knolls overlooking the ocean, or in one of the flourishing gardens. Most Catholic ceremonies are held in a small church in nearby Quemaro, a five-minute drive from the hotel.

RECEPTION OPTIONS: Chef Alejandro Aguilar Morales, who specializes in regional and fusion cuisine, can prepare an elegant meal for up to 50 people in La Palala, the hotel's restaurant.

WEDDING SERVICES: Offers full wedding planning services and assistance preparing legal documentation.

ESPERANZA HOTEL AND RESORT

Carretera Transpeninsular KM 7, Punta Ballena,
Cabo San Lucas BCS 23410, México
www.esperanzaresort.com
866-311-2226 / 52-624-145-6400

SIZE: 17 ACRES **NUMBER OF ROOMS:** 50 SUITES, 6 PRIVATE VILLAS **WHEELCHAIR ACCESSIBLE:** NO **RATES:** $$$ **SPECIAL NOTES:** CHILDREN WELCOME IN RESIDENTIAL CLUB (NOT PERMITTED IN RESORT)

REVIEW: Reminiscent of a gracious Mexican villa, the Esperanza Hotel and Resort is a member of the prestigious Auberge du Soleil. It sits atop the bluffs of Punta Ballena (Whale Point), overlooking two private coves on the Sea of Cortez at the tip of the Baja Peninsula. Guests enjoy an unparalleled natural setting and nearby historic colonial towns as well as the resort's fitness center, state-of-the-art spa, and world-class oceanfront restaurant, which features *cocina del sul* (Mediterranean-influenced cooking) and over 100 selections of tequila. Rooms are decorated in a casually elegant Baja style, with original art, handcrafted furniture, fine linens, and oversized bathrooms. In the recent past, gift certificates from Esperanza have been among the goodies included in the prestigious gift baskets given to Academy Award presenters.

CEREMONY OPTIONS: Wedding ceremonies for up to 120 guests can be held poolside, by the beach, or on a grassy hilltop knoll.

RECEPTION OPTIONS: Receptions for up to 120 are held at the Signature Restaurant, overlooking the private sandy coves. It features three levels of stone terraces that flow from a circular thatched-roof dining room. Superb cuisine showcasing local resources and regional flavors is available for the reception menu.

WEDDING SERVICES: Full service. Helps facilitate marriage license.

© LAS VENTANAS AL PARAISO, A ROSEWOOD RESORT

LAS VENTANAS AL PARAÍSO

KM 19.5 Carratera Transpeninsular, San Jose del Cabo, Baja California Sur 23400, Mexico
www.lasventanas.com
52-624-144-2800

SIZE: N/A **NUMBER OF ROOMS:** 61 SUITES **WHEELCHAIR ACCESSIBLE:** NO **RATES:** $$–$$$

REVIEW: Owned by the prestigious Rosewood Hotels, this location features original Mexican art, richly appointed interiors, and panoramic views of the sparkling blue Sea of Cortez. There is also a state-of-the-art spa with treatments specially designed for the bride and her attendants. The luxury suites include marble and limestone floors and full amenities. Areas for tennis, yachts, world-class golf, fishing, horseback riding, desert excursions, and hiking are all nearby. Awards for excellence include AAA's Five-Diamond rating.

CEREMONY OPTIONS: An oceanfront patio with the Sea of Cortez as a backdrop is available for wedding ceremonies, with accommodations for up to 60 guests.

RECEPTION OPTIONS: Receptions are usually held in a private banquet room that opens up to a beautiful inlaid-pebble terrace. For intimate parties of 16 or less, La Cava, the private wine room, is a popular choice for rehearsal dinners. A traditional Mexican beach barbecue is another option for parties of less than 60.

WEDDING SERVICES: Full planning services, including help with legal documentation.

ONE&ONLY PALMILLA RESORT

KM 7.5 Carratera Transpeninsular, San Jose del Cabo,
Baja California Sur 23400, Mexico
www.palmillaresort.com
888-691-8081 / 52-624-144-7000

SIZE: 14 ACRES **NUMBER OF ROOMS:** 172 ROOMS; 18 SUITES **WHEELCHAIR ACCESSIBLE:** NO
RATES: $$–$$$

REVIEW: This welcoming resort, founded in 1956 by the son of a former interim president of Mexico, has hosted Ernest Hemingway and other prestigious guests. Located on a private peninsula overlooking the Pacific Ocean, it rests in a dramatic spot where the desert terrain meets the rugged mountains. The Old Mexican-style architectural details include red tile roofs, whitewashed walls, and gardens filed with exquisite fountains. In their leisure time, guests can enjoy a 27-hole Jack Nicklaus-designed golf course, deep-sea fishing, horseback riding, cruises, and state-of-the-art spa facilities. Rooms are located in one- to three-story casas overlooking the sea, appointed with the best amenities.

CEREMONY OPTIONS: Ceremonies for up to 50 guests can be held in a beautiful whitewashed wedding chapel located on tropical grounds; the bride can be transported by a horse-drawn carriage. A beachside location is also available for larger weddings.

RECEPTION OPTIONS: Receptions take place in one of the resort's two palapa-style restaurants, each suitable for up to 50 guests. Both restaurants offer gourmet Mediterranean cuisine and panoramic views of the Sea of Cortez.

WEDDING SERVICES: Full planning services, including help with legal documentation.

europe

Europe is a land for lovers—lovers of art, architecture, history, music, food, wine, and luxury. From the wailing of the pipes in the Scottish highlands to the dancing of the *tarantella* in an Italian villa, Europe boasts countless ways to celebrate a wedding. So, whether your ideal setting is an art museum, a vineyard, a castle, or a yacht, you're sure to find it in Europe. However, saying "I do" in some European destinations takes a lot more than merely knowing the language of love. The key to a successful wedding in Europe is *planning*. Wedding regulations in Europe are as diverse as the wedding traditions, and it is as vital to familiarize yourself with each country's legal requirements for marriage as it is to fall in love with the possible venues. I've reviewed several magnificent European destinations where the requirements are not too daunting. Keep in mind that your options may be extremely limited in some countries, such as France or Spain. If you are unable to marry in the country of your choice, you may have to plan a grand celebration of marriage abroad, then return home to sign on the dotted line at the town hall.

What is your idea of the perfect backdrop for a wedding celebration? Old-world castles? Thatched-roof cottages? Country estates? Trendy city restaurants? Victorian seaside resorts? The British Isles offer all of these—and much more. The term "the British Isles" defines a geographic area consisting of the Republic of Ireland and the United Kingdom, which is made up of England, Scotland, Wales, and Northern Ireland. The Republic of Ireland and the United Kingdom are two separate nations, each with its own government and currency. To discuss the highlights of this region, I've divided the British Isles into three sections: Ireland (Northern Ireland and the Republic of Ireland), Scotland, and England. For detailed information and Web site links regarding marriage law in the British Isles, visit www.wedding-services.demon.co.uk/marriage.htm.

IRELAND:
northern ireland and the republic of ireland

Everyone will be green with envy when you tell them you're getting married on the "Emerald Isle" of Ireland, a beautiful country where tradition runs deep. There is evidence of habitation in Ireland going back thousands of years, and today, stories and legends from the early years still abound, capturing many a visitor's imagination. In ancient times, a marriage proposal might have been, "Would you like to hang your washing next to mine?" Even if today's brides find this proposal a little less than romantic, they're sure to find plenty of romance and enchantment on the Emerald Isle.

Come to Ireland to enjoy hiking, cycling, mountain climbing, fishing, and even surfing, sailing, and scuba diving! Explore Ireland's great literary past in Dublin or visit the spiritual past of Ireland's holy wells, grottoes, ancient circles, and early Christian monasteries. When in the Republic of Ireland, all newly married couples should go to Blarney Castle, where they can kiss the legendary Blarney Stone to receive the gift of eloquence. Those couples visiting Northern Ireland should join their hands through the ancient Holestone Marriage Stone in County Antrim, a ritual that promises eternal love and happiness. Peak tourist season occurs during July and August, when swarms of visitors enjoy beautiful warm weather and long daylight hours. The crowds thin out before and after the peak season, making June and September the best months to visit.

COUNTRY OVERVIEW

CURRENCY: BRITISH POUND (NORTHERN IRELAND); EURO (REPUBLIC OF IRELAND) **TIPPING:** TIPPING IN THE REPUBLIC OF IRELAND AND IN NORTHERN IRELAND IS DISCRETIONARY. AS A GENERAL RULE, TIP TAXI DRIVERS 10% AND LEAVE HOTEL STAFF A SMALL TIP AS WELL. IF A RESTAURANT BILL OR MENU DOES NOT STATE THAT THE SERVICE CHARGE IS INCLUDED, LEAVE A 10–15% TIP. **ELECTRICITY:** 240V AC (NORTHERN IRELAND); 220V AC (REPUBLIC OF IRELAND) **INTERNATIONAL CALLING CODE:** 44 (NORTHERN IRELAND); 353 (REPUBLIC OF IRELAND)

PLANNING NOTES

SUGGESTED ASSISTANCE: Some assistance may be needed. When it comes to legal matters, it is important to distinguish between Northern Ireland and the Republic of Ireland, as the two are separate countries with different governments. Marriage law in Ireland is currently undergoing reform, so it is highly recommended that you contact the General Register Office (see page 281) to get the latest information and check the most recent changes in marriage law.

SPECIAL REQUIREMENTS: WAITING PERIOD: Three months **RESIDENCY REQUIREMENT:** 15 days

CIVIL CEREMONIES: In Northern Ireland, civil marriages can be held either at the registrar's office or at a place approved by the registrar. In the Republic of Ireland, civil ceremonies, though optional, must take place in the registrar's office. Three months prior to the planned wedding date, a preprinted notification form (available through the local general register office) must be signed and submitted to the registrar of civil marriages of the area in which you plan to marry.

RELIGIOUS CEREMONIES: Many couples opt instead for a religious ceremony, which is a legal alternative to a civil ceremony in both Northern Ireland and the Republic of Ireland, provided the officiant has been authorized by the local registrar. Almost every religious marriage ceremony is recognized in Ireland, as long as it is performed in a building certified by the government for that purpose. The exception is a Muslim marriage ceremony, which must be proceeded by a civil ceremony to make it legally binding. Contact the head of the religious organization or the place of worship nearest your intended location to check the religious requirements and to determine if the presence of the local registrar is required.

© CORINNA RAZNIKOV

DESIGN IDEAS

Known for its warmth and hospitality, Ireland has been called "the land of a thousand welcomes." Welcome your guests with baskets containing a copy of the *Book of Kells* or a book of traditional Irish blessings, Irish coffee mugs, Beleek china, and Irish linen. The Claddagh design, which features two hands holding a crowned heart, is a fitting motif for any Irish wedding. The two hands represent a couple's friendship; the crown, their loyalty and lasting fidelity; and the heart, their love for each other. For your wedding bands, you might order a pair of Claddagh rings. Celtic knotwork, another possible motif, symbolizes eternal unity. Knotwork designs are gorgeous on everything, from the invitations to the cake.

When deciding on a wedding dress and reception décor, beautiful Irish lace and linen can provide great inspiration. Orange blossoms are a popular choice for Irish brides, as they traditionally represent beauty and generosity. (Queen Victoria was said to have worn a porcelain diadem of orange blossoms on her wedding day.) You might choose to include stephanotis, the bride's good-luck blossom, in your bouquet if you are marrying in the summer, when the flower is available. You could also adopt a good-luck theme, using little pots of shamrock as gifts or centerpieces. An Irish menu could include traditional Irish soda bread, sometimes called *barmbrack*, and gooseberry crumble. No menu would be complete without some fine Irish whiskey and a few pints of Guinness Stout! Traditional Irish musicians are readily available, and many play tunes on a variety of instruments, including whistles, the uilleann pipes and the *bodhrán*, a shallow, one-sided drum.

PLANNING RESOURCES

EMBASSY AND GOVERNMENT OFFICES:
Embassy of the Republic of Ireland (in the United States)
2234 Massachusetts Avenue NW, Washington, DC 20008
www.irelandemb.org
202-462-3939 / Consulate General (New York): 212-319-2555

Embassy of the United Kingdom (in the United States)
3100 Massachusetts Avenue NW, Washington, DC 20008
www.britainusa.com
202-588-7800 / Consulate General (New York): 212-745-0200

Embassy of the United States (in the Republic of Ireland)
42 Elgin Road, Ballsbridge, Dublin 4, Ireland
http://dublin.usembassy.gov
353-1-668-8777

The General Register Office (Republic of Ireland)
Joyce House, 8-11 Lombard Street East, Dublin 2, Ireland
www.groireland.ie
353-1-635-4000

General Register Office (Northern Ireland), Marriage Section
Oxford House, 49/55 Chichester Street, Belfast, BT1 4HL, Northern Ireland, UK
www.groni.gov.uk
44-28-90-252136

TOURISM:
Fáilte Ireland (Tourist Board)
Republic of Ireland: Baggot Street Bridge, Dublin 2, Ireland
Northern Ireland: 53 Castle Street, Belfast BT1 1GH, Northern Ireland, UK
www.ireland.ie
(Republic of Ireland) 353-1-602-4000 / (Northern Ireland) 44-2890-265500

Northern Ireland Tourist Board
St. Anne's Court, 59 North St., Belfast, BT1 INB, Northern Ireland, UK
www.discovernorthernireland.com
44-2890-231221

PARKS, MONUMENTS, AND HISTORIC SITES:
Heritage Island (Republic of Ireland)
Marina House, 11/13 Clarence Street, Dun Laoghaire, County Dublin, Ireland
www.heritageisland.com
353-1-236-6890

National Trust (Northern Ireland)
Rowallane House, Saintfield, Ballynahinch, County Down, BT24 7LH,
    Northern Ireland, UK
www.thenationaltrust.org.uk
44-28-9751-0721

WEDDING RESOURCES:
HELPFUL WEB SITES:
Wed UK Wedding Service Directory: www.weduk.com
Wedding Ireland: www.wedding-ireland.com
NI Weddings: www.niweddings.co.uk

VENUES

Ireland is rich with charming venues. Arrange a quaint wedding in Donegal and stay in the traditional **DONEGAL THATCHED COTTAGES** (353-71-9177197 / www.donegalthatched cottages.com), then leave your footprints on the 12 sandy beaches of Cruit Island. Or celebrate in a traditional steel canal boat, cruising the country's inland waterways with **CANALWAYS IRELAND** (353-45-524646 / www.canalways.ie). For the ancient splendor of an Irish castle, consider **ADARE MANOR HOTEL & GOLF RESORT** (800-462-3273 / www.adaremanor.com), which was voted #1 European resort by *Condé Nast Traveler* readers in 2002. This Tudor mansion, located on 840 magnificent acres, offers golf, trails, fox hunts, and salmon fishing. The Northern Ireland Hotels Federation (44-28-9035-110 / www.nihf.co.uk) offers many venues, including the lovely **MANOR HOUSE COUNTRY HOTEL** (44-28-6862-22001 / www.manor-house-hotel.com) in the Fermanagh country-side, voted best hotel in 2002 by the Hotel Federation. Manor House's original Victorian splendor makes it a popular wedding location.

© LONGUEVILLE HOUSE

LONGUEVILLE HOUSE
Mallow, County Cork, Republic of Ireland
www.longuevillehouse.ie
800-323-5463 / 353-22-47156

SIZE: 500 ACRES **NUMBER OF ROOMS:** 20 ROOMS (NOTE: TO HAVE A WEDDING AT THIS LOCATION, ALL 20 ROOMS MUST BE RENTED BY THE WEDDING PARTY, AS THEY ONLY CATER TO WEDDINGS ON AN "EXCLUSIVE RENTAL" BASIS) **WHEELCHAIR ACCESSIBLE:** NO **RATES:** $$–$$$ **SPECIAL NOTES:** PROVIDES TRAVEL COTS, BABY LISTENING MONITORS, HIGH CHAIRS, TOYS, AND A CHILDREN'S MENU

REVIEW: The Longueville House is a 1720 Georgian mansion with sumptuous guest rooms offering views of formal gardens, pastures, and vineyards. Using fresh produce from the hotel's gardens, Longueville's award-winning chef transforms every dish into a memorable culinary experience. Both service and setting have garnered awards from every major travel guide, including *Condé Nast Traveler* and *Food & Wine*. There are several outdoor activities to enjoy around Longueville House, such as cycling, hunting, walking the formal gardens, salmon and trout fishing in the Blackwater River, and golfing on some of Europe's most famous courses. Guests can also take in a bit of theater and participate in wine-tasting parties.

CEREMONY OPTIONS: It is not possible to have a legal marriage ceremony on the Longueville grounds, though the staff can arrange an informal "blessing ceremony." You can charter a bus to transport guests to the "official" ceremony location.

RECEPTION OPTIONS: There are a variety of interconnected, uniquely appointed spaces, which can accommodate receptions of any size up to 120 guests.

WEDDING SERVICES: Provides some assistance and a list of preferred vendors.

WATERFORD CASTLE HOTEL & GOLF CLUB

The Island Ballinakill, County Waterford, Republic of Ireland

www.waterfordcastle.com

353-51-878203

SIZE: 310-ACRE ISLAND **NUMBER OF ROOMS:** 19 UNITS **WHEELCHAIR ACCESSIBLE:** THE HOTEL IS WHEELCHAIR ACCESSIBLE, BUT THE BEDROOMS THEMSELVES ARE NOT **RATES:** $$–$$$ **SPECIAL NOTES:** BABYSITTING AVAILABLE WITH ADVANCE NOTICE

REVIEW: Imagine getting married in one of Ireland's most secluded sixteenth-century castles, located on a private island and accessible by the island's private ferry! The castle is the stuff of dreams, with ancient gargoyles, fairytale turrets, towers and battlements, four-poster beds, stone fireplaces, elegant antiques, and deep claw-foot bathtubs. Once you have made this dream a reality, you and your guests can relax with skeet shooting, archery, fishing, tennis, golf on the championship course, and cuisine in the award-winning dining room.

CEREMONY AND RECEPTION OPTIONS: There are a number of local churches available for wedding ceremonies. The hotel's Munster dining room, which can accommodate groups of 35 to 60, is available for receptions.

WEDDING SERVICES: Provides some assistance. Provides list of preferred vendors.

SCOTLAND

For those who are "tartan to the core," hike up your kilts (not too far!) and head to the Highlands! Kilts, cashmere sweaters, and tweed suits abound in Scotland, as do castles, abbeys, galleries, museums, golf courses, fishing villages, and some of the most romantic destination wedding locations in the world. Keep in mind that not every wedding need be a costly affair—ask any Scot who has participated in a traditional "Penny Wedding," in which guests are expected to bring their own food and drinks to the church hall celebration. Today's brides and grooms often celebrate at one of the many local castles or country manors, complete with bagpipes, Gaelic blessings, and a lively Ceilidh band accompanying the Highland dancing and traditional sword dances.

Scotland can be divided into three major geological regions: the Southern Uplands (rolling moorlands between the English border and the central plain), the Central Lowlands (containing three valleys and estuaries of the Clyde, Forth, and Tay rivers), and the Highlands (made up of lochs, glens, mountains, and islands along the west and north). Scotland's cultural calendar of events and festivals is worth considering when planning your trip. The month-long Edinburgh International Arts Festival is one of the world's largest, and Highland games and gatherings occur throughout the country on a regular basis. July and August are the most popular months for tourists, so prices and crowds are inflated. The best time to plan a wedding is September, the sunniest month. Winter months (apart from mid-December) see hotel prices drop 20 percent, and it is a good time to see Highlanders at their heartiest!

COUNTRY OVERVIEW

CURRENCY: BRITISH POUND **TIPPING:** RESTAURANTS AND CLUBS GENERALLY ADD A 15% SERVICE CHARGE; IT IS CUSTOMARY TO TIP AN ADDITIONAL 3–5% ON TOP OF THAT. TAXI DRIVERS EXPECT 10–15% PLUS 50P PER BAG IF THEY HANDLE LUGGAGE. PORTERS GET 75P PER BAG. BARBERS AND HAIRDRESSERS GENERALLY GET 10–15%. TIPS ARE NOT EXPECTED IN PUBS. **ELECTRICITY:** 240V **INTERNATIONAL CALLING CODE:** 44

PLANNING NOTES

SUGGESTED ASSISTANCE: Anyone can do it. Marriage notice must be filled out and returned (in person or by mail) to the registrar's office.

SPECIAL REQUIREMENTS: WAITING PERIOD: You must wait a minimum of 15 days after your marriage notice has been received by the registrar's office, unless one of the couple has been previously married, in which case he or she needs to turn the form in six weeks before the wedding date. For a religious ceremony, you must go to the registrar's office seven days before the wedding to pick up the marriage schedule that has been drawn up for you. (The marriage schedule is to be completed at the ceremony, then sent back to the registrar.) **RESIDENCY REQUIREMENT:** None

CIVIL CEREMONIES: Civil ceremonies are optional. They are performed by the district registrar in the registrar's office or in locations approved by the district registrar. Detailed information is available from the General Register Office in Edinburgh and from www.gro-scotland.gov.uk/regscot/getting-married-in-scotland/index.htm.

RELIGIOUS CEREMONIES: Religious ceremonies are conducted by an officiant, who must be approved by the registrar general prior to the ceremony if he is not from one of the following religious bodies: Church of Scotland; Baptist Union of Scotland; Congregational Union of Scotland; churches of the Anglican Communion; Free Church of Scotland; Free Presbyterian Church of Scotland; Hebrew Congregation; Methodist Church in Scotland; Society of Friends; Roman Catholic Church; Salvation Army; Scottish Unitarian Association; United Free Church of Scotland. For information on Christian officiants, you can go to www.churchofscotland.org.uk, www.diocese ofedinburgh.org (Roman Catholic), and www.scotland.anglican.org. You can also find a list of Jewish congregations by visiting www.somethingjewish.co.uk. With over 50,000 Muslims in Scotland, there are several mosques throughout the country. Muslims can contact the Central Mosque of Glasgow (44-0141-429-3132), or, to find a mosque, they can check www.salaam.co.uk.

DESIGN IDEAS

Fill your guests' welcome baskets with Scottish shortbread, tea, a bottle of single-malt Scotch, and perhaps a silver teaspoon. (According to tradition, a groom who presents his bride with a silver spoon ensures that they will never go hungry.) You might use the Scottish thistle as a design theme, or you could incorporate Scottish tweed or your family tartan into your apparel and décor. Scottish brides sometimes wear a tartan sash with their gown or include tartan in their floral bouquets. Many brides also sew a miniature horseshoe in the hem of their gowns for good luck.

What an interesting menu you can create in Scotland! Delicacies include Arbroath Smokies, Selkirk bannocks, Galloway cheeses, Dundee cake and Moffat toffee. Aberdeen Angus beef, Highland venison, Loch Fyne oysters, and Clyde Valley soft fruits are all superb, too. For the toast, offer a "wee"dram of whiskey instead of champagne. No Scottish wedding is complete without a bagpipe ballad or two and a bit of Celtic music.

PLANNING RESOURCES

EMBASSY AND GOVERNMENT OFFICES:
Embassy of the United Kingdom (in the United States)
3100 Massachusetts Avenue NW, Washington, DC, 20008
www.britainusa.com
202-588-7800 / Consulate General (New York): 212-745-0200

United States Consulate General (in Scotland)
3 Regent Terrace, Edinburgh EH7 5BW, Scotland, UK
www.usembassy.org.uk/scotland
44-131-556-8315

Registrar General (in Edinburgh)
New Register House, 3 West Register Street,
    Edinburgh EH1 3YT, Scotland, UK
www.gro-scotland.gov.uk
44-131-334-0380

TOURISM:
National Tourism Board of Scotland
Fairways Business Park, Deer Park Avenue,
    Livingston EH54 8AF, Scotland, UK
www.visitscotland.com
44-845-225 5121

Highlands of Scotland Tourist Board
Peffery House, Strathpeffer IV14 9HA,
Scotland, UK
www.visithighlands.com
44-870-514-3070 / 44-146-323-4353

© EMMANUEL VAUCHER

PARKS, MONUMENTS, AND HISTORIC SITES:
National Park Headquarters
The Old Station, Balloch Road, Balloch G83 8LQ, Scotland, UK
www.lochlomond-trossachs.org
44-138-972-2600

WEDDING RESOURCES:

HELPFUL PUBLICATIONS:
The Scottish Wedding Directory: www.scottishweddingdirectory.co.uk /
    44-141-445-5545
Bride & Groom Magazine: www.brideandgroommag.com / 44-125-388-5777
The Best Scottish Weddings: www.thebestscottishweddings.co.uk /
    44-125-388-5777

HELPFUL WEB SITES:
Scotland's Online Wedding Directory: www.wedsitescotland.com
Scottish Weddings: www.scottishweddings.org
Natalie Walden's Weddings & Brides Pages: www.weddings-and-brides.co.uk
Scot Smart Scottish Directory: www.scotsmart.com

VENUES

Whether one wants to wed at a castle, a country house, or an ancient ruin, Scotland can turn the wedding dreams of any lad and lassie into reality! **BALBIRNIE HOUSE** (44-159-261-0066 / www.balbirnie.co.uk) is a Georgian country house located on a 400-acre estate in central Scotland. If couples visiting Balbirnie don't find the hotel's luxurious and romantic atmosphere relaxing enough, they can indulge in several rounds of golf on the beautiful golf course. For a more intimate wedding, **THE HOWARD** (44-131-557-3500 / www.thehoward.com) is a five-star Georgian townhouse located in the center of Scotland, available for small weddings of up to 35 guests. **MAR HALL** (44-141-812-9999 / www.marhall.com) is a newly refurbished Gothic mansion, once visited by Robert the Bruce and Mary Queen of Scots. Built on 240 acres near Glasgow and Loch Lomond, it is a member of the prestigious Small Luxury Hotels of the World.

RUFFLETS COUNTRY HOUSE

Strathkinness Low Road, St. Andrews, Fife KY16 9TX, Scotland, UK

www.rufflets.co.uk

44-133-447-2594

SIZE: 10 ACRES **NUMBER OF ROOMS:** 24 UNITS DESIGNED TO ACCOMMODATE UP TO 48 GUESTS **WHEELCHAIR ACCESSIBLE:** THE GATE HOUSE BUILDING IS HANDICAPPED-ACCESSIBLE, BUT HAS NO ELEVATOR **RATES:** $–$$$ **SPECIAL NOTES:** CHILDREN WELCOME; BABY MONITORS PROVIDED

REVIEW: A member of the prestigious Small Luxury Hotels of the World and one of the oldest established Country House Hotels in Scotland, Rufflets has been run by the same family for over 50 years. Modern rooms are available in two separate lodges, but traditionalists often request space in the main building. The house mascot, a teddy bear named Rufus, welcomes guests to their rooms. The restaurant is renowned for its use of garden-fresh ingredients in both continental and Scottish dishes. Guests can enjoy theater, tours of Edinburgh Castle, golfing, fishing, croquet, tennis, riding, water sports, and more.

CEREMONY OPTIONS: Rufflets is a licensed civil marriage venue. Ceremonies can be held indoors in the drawing room, library, or music room, or outdoors on the terrace or in the gardens. Couples planning a larger evening reception at Rufflets are required to book 14 rooms in the main building, including three turret rooms and one suite.

RECEPTION OPTIONS: The Garden Restaurant, which has stunning views and overlooks the formal rose gardens, is suitable for up to 80. Other rooms are available for more intimate receptions of 20 or less. For parties of 80 to 150, a reception tent can be added to the main builiding, complete with floors and heat.

WEDDING SERVICES: Full service. Facilitates marriage license, provides list of preferred vendors, and suggests local officiants.

LOCH TORRIDON COUNTRY HOUSE HOTEL

Torridon, By Achnasheen, Wester Ross IV22 2EY, Scotland, UK

www.lochtorridonhotel.com

44-144-579-1242

SIZE: 58 ACRES NUMBER OF ROOMS: 19 WHEELCHAIR ACCESSIBLE: FULLY ACCESSIBLE, WITH A SPECIALLY-DESIGNED EN-SUITE BEDROOM ON THE GROUND FLOOR RATES: $$$ SPECIAL NOTES: HIGH CHAIRS, COTS, BABY LISTENING DEVICES, AND BABYSITTERS AVAILABLE UPON REQUEST

REVIEW: The elegant Loch Torridon was built in 1887 as a shooting lodge for the first Earl of Lovelace. The rooms in this home of "highland excellence" offer gorgeous mountain or loch views, and many have beds large enough to accommodate the entire cast of *Braveheart*! Guests can stay entertained with activities include archery, clay pigeon shooting, mountain biking, fly-fishing, guided walks, and excursions by car, boat, or bike. Loch Torridon has received many awards, including *Hotel Review Scotland*'s Scottish Hotel of the Year 2004.

CEREMONY AND RECEPTION OPTIONS: Civil ceremonies must be held at the local registrar's office. Religious ceremonies and receptions are held in either the library or the drawing room, which both accommodate up to 40 guests. The wedding coordinator can help plan a *ceilidh* with musicians, fireworks, and dancing.

WEDDING SERVICES: Full service. Facilitates marriage license and provides list of preferred vendors. The wedding coordinator can suggest local religious officiants.

INVERLOCHY CASTLE
Torlundy, Fort William PH33 6SN, Scotland, UK
www.inverlochycastlehotel.com
888-424-0106 / 44-139-770-2177

SIZE: 50 ACRES NUMBER OF ROOMS: 17 WHEELCHAIR ACCESSIBLE: NO RATES: $$–$$$

REVIEW: Over the years, Inverlochy Castle has hosted a wide array of international politicians, celebrities, and royals. One of Inverlochy's first celebrity endorsements came from Queen Victoria, who wrote in her diary, "I have never seen a more romantic spot!" Nestled at the foot of Ben Nevis (the highest peak in the United Kingdom), the castle overlooks its own private loch. Guests enjoy medieval furnishings, walled gardens, fishing, clay pigeon shooting, falconry, snooker, hiking, biking, and even cruises on nearby Loch Ness! All 17 bedrooms—each with its own distinct design—offer splendid views of the surroundings. The hotel has received countless awards, including *Hotel Review Scotland*'s Most Luxurious Scottish Hotel.

CEREMONY AND RECEPTION OPTIONS: Wedding ceremonies and/or receptions for up to 50 guests are held in either the Great Room or the Drawing Room. These rooms are elaborately furnished with period pieces that the King of Norway presented as a gift to the owners of the castle.

WEDDING SERVICES: Full service. Inverlochy facilitates the marriage license, provides a list of preferred vendors, and helps procure an officiant to lead either a religious or civil ceremony. They can also arrange for a traditional Scottish bagpiper to lead the wedding celebration.

ENGLAND

Steeped in tradition and history, known for elegance and royalty, and synonymous with pomp and ceremony, England is *the* destination for an unforgettable wedding. It is, after all, the home of Shakespeare, one of the most famous romantics of all time.

England offers all the allure of a foreign destination without the language barrier, plus it holds countless possibilities for wedding locations. Choose from the medieval villages of the Cotswalds, the natural beauty of the Lake District, the charming Isle of Wight, the ancient spa city of Bath, the enigmatic Stonehenge monoliths, or the historic regions of Canterbury, Dover, and Hastings. At your fingertips are some of the best parks, museums, and theaters in the world. In a country known for its stunning gardens, it is no surprise that many of the stately homes and castles have a florist on staff to create magnificent bridal bouquets on request. Generally, the best time for a wedding in England is between May and August, when temperatures range from 52°F to 80°F (11°C to 27°C). The climate does not vary much across the countryside, though it does get cooler as you travel north.

COUNTRY OVERVIEW

CURRENCY: BRITISH POUND **TIPPING:** GENERALLY, RESTAURANTS DO NOT ADD A SERVICE CHARGE TO THE BILL, AND A TIP OF 12–15% IS EXPECTED FOR GOOD SERVICE. TIPS ARE NOT EXPECTED IN PUBS, THOUGH "BUYING A DRINK" FOR THE BARTENDER (WHICH HE OR SHE MAY ACCEPT IN CASH) IS COMMON. HOUSEKEEPERS MAY GET UP TO A POUND A DAY. TAXI DRIVERS ARE TIPPED 10%, DEPENDING ON THE DISTANCE. **ELECTRICITY:** 220V **INTERNATIONAL CALLING CODE:** 44

PLANNING NOTES

SUGGESTED ASSISTANCE: If a couple wants to be legally married in England, they must plan to spend a month in the country prior to the wedding in order to file the appropriate papers. (If you don't have that much time, consider having the civil ceremony at home, followed by a celebration in England.) Marriage laws are being reviewed, however, and may be changed in the future. It is always a good idea to contact the General Register Office (see page 290) to clarify civil marriage legal issues and to check on the most up-to-date information. You can also find out more about legal requirements at www.weddings.co.uk/ info/legeng.htm.

SPECIAL REQUIREMENTS: WAITING PERIOD: To marry in England, you must wait a total of 22 days, which are divided into two waiting periods. First, you must start the process by "giving notice" to the superintendent registrar of your chosen locale, who will post your intention to marry for a period of seven days. Then, you must wait an additional 15 days before you can be married. **RESIDENCY REQUIREMENT:** Seven days in all. In order to give a registrar notice of your intention to marry, you both must provide documentation that you have resided in the country for at least seven days.

CIVIL CEREMONIES: Civil ceremonies can be held at the General Register Office or another building approved for civil marriage, including licensed hotels, castles, stately homes, and manors. For a list of approved premises, call or write the Office of National Statistics (see page 290). To marry in a location other than a register office, contact the superintendent registrar of your chosen locale and discuss her attendance (which is required to officiate the ceremony) and any other necessary arrangements.

RELIGIOUS CEREMONIES: Couples of any major world religion will be able to find a religious officiant in England. For information on marriage in accordance with Anglican rites, consult the Faculty Office (44-207-222-5381 / www.facultyoffice.org.uk/ marriage.html). Jewish couples can contact the Office of the Chief Rabbi (44-208-343-8989) for resources.

DESIGN IDEAS

You can welcome your guests with Wedgwood tea cups and English Breakfast tea, scones, Cadbury chocolates, a couple of bottles of English ale, an umbrella, and a shiny new pound to spend on a souvenir of choice. Consider sending your guests illuminated gold leaf invitations designed and inscribed by **THE MEDIEVAL SCRIBE** (44-158021-1383 / www.medievalscribe.com). He can also provide you with beautiful wedding poems that could be incorporated into the ceremony, marriage certificates worth framing, and personal seals that offer an elegant, old-world touch.

If you are a superstitious bride, look for horseshoes and chimney sweeps; for English brides, wearing a decorative horseshoe around her wrist is good luck and kissing a real chimney sweep after the wedding ceremony is a good omen (considered so because a chimney sweep rescued King George III's wedding carriage when the horses bolted). To add a regal touch to your wedding, consider hiring a "toastmaster" dressed in full red regalia to serve as the master of ceremonies (44-208-550-7863 / www.toastmaster. connectfree.co.uk) or a falconer to demonstrate the ancient art of falconry (44-154348-1737 / www.britishfalconersclub.co.uk). Include with each table setting a colorful English "cracker" (traditionally used at Christmas) filled with a nice favor, such as a sterling silver trinket. The festivities begin with a bang when, at the count of three, your guests pop open their crackers. (To purchase wedding crackers, check out www.absolutely crackers.com.) After the ceremony, a group of wandering minstrals could lead the procession from the ceremony site to the reception, where English fold musicians might perfom. For a less formal celebration, serve the traditional fare of fish and chips. Or to treat your guests to a feast

© JOHN CORBETT. WWW.CORBETTPHOTOGRAPHY.NET

fit for a king, serve roasted lamb or roast beef, Yorkshire pudding, meat pies, and bangers and mash. Finish with a dessert buffet of scrumptious puddings and pies in addition to a traditional wedding cake.

PLANNING RESOURCES

EMBASSY AND GOVERNMENT OFFICES:
Embassy of the United Kingdom (in the United States)
3100 Massachusetts Avenue NW, Washington, DC 20008
www.britainusa.com
202-588-7800 / Consulate General (New York): 212-745-0200

Embassy of the United States (in England)
24 Grosvenor Square, London W1A 1AE, England, UK
www.usembassy.org.uk
44-20-7499-9000

Office of National Statistics
P.O. Box 56, Southport PR8 2GL, England, UK
www.statistics.gov.uk
44-151-471-4817

General Register Office
Trafalgar Road, Southport PR8 2HH, England, UK
www.gro.gov.uk/gro/content
44-151-471-4803

TOURISM:
Visit Britain
Thames Tower, Blacks Road, London W6 9EL, England, UK
www.visitbritain.com
44-208-846-9000

PARKS, MONUMENTS, AND HISTORIC SITES:
Association of National Park Authorities
126 Bute Street, Cardiff CF10 5LE, Wales, UK
www.anpa.gov.uk *(This site lists national parks that are registered as marriage sites; you can contact each site directly to find out how to arrange a wedding there.)*
44-292-049-9966

English Heritage
P.O. Box 569, Swindon SN2 2YP, England, UK
www.english-heritage.org.uk
44-870-333-1181

WEDDING RESOURCES:
British Association of Wedding and Event Professionals
27 Old Gloucester Road, London WC1N 3XX, England, UK

HELPFUL PUBLICATIONS:
Brides: www.bridesuk.net
You and Your Wedding: www.youandyourwedding.co.uk / 44-207-439-5000

HELPFUL WEB SITES:
Hitched: www.hitched.co.uk
Wedding Service Providers:
www.britishservices.co.uk/weddingconsultancies.htm

VENUES

England conjures up all kinds of romantic images—stately castles, rolling pastures, quaint country inns and cottages, even sophisticated clubs in London. Do you envision yours a rustic, country wedding? Look into the **COOLING CASTLE BARN** in Kent (44-163–422-2244 / www.coolingcastlebarn.com), which includes three distinctive barns all surrounded by beautiful grounds. Or, in the Northampshire countryside, consider **THE HIGHGATE HOUSE** (44-160-450-5505 / www.sundialgroup.com), a seventeeth-century coaching inn. All over

England there are dramatic castles and exquisite manor houses that are licensed for civil ceremonies. You can explore these stately options by searching the Internet for English

© CORINNA RAZNIKOV

travel, wedding, and history Web sites. Other venues include hotels, inns, schools, museums, and even pubs. You could marry at the **MUSEUM OF GARDEN HISTORY**, overlooking the River Thames (44-207-01-8865 / www.museumgardenhistory.org), or at the **ROYAL BOTANIC GARDENS** in Surrey, which has a beautiful eighteenth-century cottage available for ceremonies, in the middle of some of England's most beautiful gardens (44-203-332-5655 / www.bgkew.org.uk).

THE LANESBOROUGH HOTEL
Hyde Park Corner, London SW1X 7TA, England, UK
www.lanesborough.com
44-207-259-5599

SIZE: 5 FLOORS **NUMBER OF ROOMS:** 95 ROOMS AND SUITES **WHEELCHAIR ACCESSIBLE:** YES
RATES: $$$

REVIEW: The Lanesborough combines the best of old-world elegance with modern convenience in a central London location overlooking Hyde Park. Its rooms are exquisitely decorated with handcrafted period furnishings in a rich, Regency style. While the ambiance is more typical of a luxurious private country house than a typical city hotel, The Lanesborough provides every service and amenity (including business and technological conveniences) you could need. Every room includes the services of a butler to assist with any last-minute additions or amendments to your plans. The butler service is available for all rooms at no charge.

CEREMONY AND RECEPTION OPTIONS: The five beautiful reception rooms can accommodate every kind of celebration, be it the marriage ceremony itself, an intimate sit-down wedding breakfast, a glittering reception, or a sit-down dinner for 120 guests. Each of the rooms, uniquely decorated with its own color scheme, is available for cocktails, dancing, and more.
WEDDING SERVICES: Full service.

AMBERLEY CASTLE
Amberley, Near Arundel, West Sussex BN18 9LT, England, UK
www.amberleycastle.co.uk
44-179-883-1992

SIZE: 12 ACRES **NUMBER OF ROOMS:** 19 SUITES AND BEDROOMS (NOTE: ACCOMMODATION IS LIMITED TO THE BRIDE AND GROOM UNLESS EXCLUSIVE USE OF THE CASTLE HAS BEEN ARRANGED.) **WHEELCHAIR ACCESSIBLE:** RESTRICTED **RATES:** $$–$$$ **SPECIAL NOTES:** YOUNG GUESTS RESTRICTED TO FLOWER GIRLS, RING BEARERS, AND CHILDREN 12 AND OLDER

© EMMANUEL VAUCHER

REVIEW: Amberley Castle could be the answer to every romantic dream of a wedding in a richly historic, stunningly private, and beautiful medieval castle setting. Since 1988, the Cummings family has made this 900-year-old castle, surrounded by stone walls, into a luxurious country castle hotel. Licensed for civil marriages, the castle can be rented in its entirety. The 19 individually designed bedrooms and suites each come with their own Jacuzzi. The grounds include formal gardens, koi ponds, old stone walls, tennis courts, and a recently installed 18-hole professional putting course. Each night, the massive portcullis is lowered, giving guests total privacy, serenity, and security within the castle walls.

CEREMONY AND RECEPTION OPTIONS: For those couples having a civil ceremony, the Amberley provides a range of beautiful settings within the castle's meeting rooms. Or, for a religious service, the beautiful church of St. Michael's in Amberley village is just a short stroll away. The castle and grounds include several reception options, from an afternoon tea beside a koi pond to a formal banquet for 48 in the Baronial Great Room. For outdoor affairs, a tented reception can be held by the moat for 150 guests or by the lake for 250. The hosts will work with you to design menus that sample their exquisite cuisine and extensive wine list.

WEDDING SERVICES: Provides some assistance.

GOODWOOD HOUSE

Goodwood Chichester, West Sussex PO18 0PX, England, UK

www.goodwood.co.uk

44-124-377-5537

SIZE: 12,000 ACRES **NUMBER OF ROOMS:** 94 (AT THE MARIOTT GOODWOOD PARK HOTEL, ALSO ON THE ESTATE) **WHEELCHAIR ACCESSIBLE:** YES (LIMITED) **RATES:** $$$ SITE FEES AND CATERING FEES; $$ ACCOMMODATION FEES (AT THE MARRIOTT GOODWOOD PARK HOTEL)

REVIEW: The home of the Dukes of Richmond for over 300 years, Goodwood House is set in the heart of the 12,000-acre Goodwood Estate, surrounded on all sides by peaceful park land. So remarkable is this great Sussex house's collection of fine art and furniture (on display in every room) that there is a full-time curator on staff. The great house has a very elegant and luxurious ambiance with an art collection that could grace any museum and the service and hospitality of an exclusive country home. The Dukes of Richmond were famous for their lavish, formal entertaining, and the Goodwood House offers the same extraordinary possibilities for wedding ceremonies or receptions, or rented on an exclusive basis, for all of your wedding celebratory events. The entire estate includes horse and car racing, an aerodome, a golf course, and acres of certified organic farmland. It also includes the Marriott Goodwood Park Hotel, with accommodations for your wedding party and guests.

CEREMONY AND RECEPTION OPTIONS: Goodwood House offers eight wonderful rooms, with three that are licensed for civil marriage ceremonies. The Long Hall and Egyptian Dining Rooms can each accommodate up to 60 guests; for larger parties there is the Ballroom and the gracious Yellow Room, which can seat up to 150 guests in extraordinary style. Goodwood's talented chef will work with you to arrange menus and wines that are sure to delight.

WEDDING SERVICES: Full service. Facilitates marriage license.

The Czech Republic

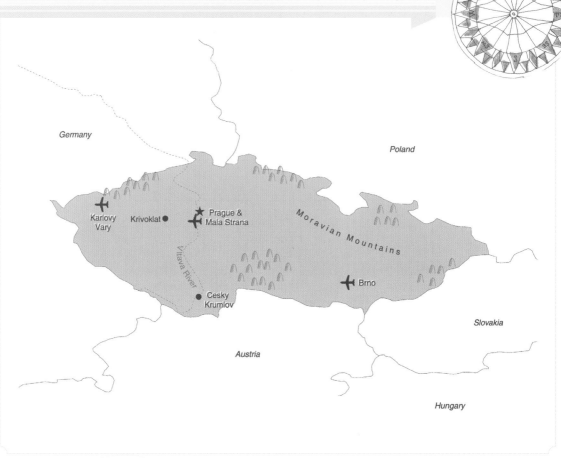

Germany

Poland

Karlovy Vary

Krivoklat ●

★ Prague & Mala Strana

Moravian Mountains

Vltava River

● Cesky Krumlov

✈ Brno

Slovakia

Austria

Hungary

The Czech Republic is a magical, historic country located in the heart of Europe. It has been a crossroads for foreign trade for hundreds of years, and its diverse architecture is a testament to the wide range of international influences. Many great composers, writers, and artists have found inspiration in the romantic Bohemian countryside and the bustling cities. Among today's visitors are couples who have discovered a wedding destination that promises both old-world charm and a cosmopolitan spirit. Many cannot resist the appeal of Prague, the Czech capital, an enchanting mixture of cathedrals, cobblestone streets, and verdant green parks. Towering over the city is picturesque Prague Castle, the largest ancient castle in the world, and St. Vitus Cathedral, located in the town of Hradcany. Many beautiful bridges in Prague span the Vltava River, the oldest and most famous being the St. Charles Bridge, the center of the community, where tourists and residents flock on warm days to socialize and shop.

As you venture out of the city, narrow, tree-lined roads take you over hill and dale into a countryside filled with green pastures, mountainside villages, turrets and towers of Gothic castles, and inviting health spas. Natural beauty abounds, with a beautifully varied terrain of cave and canyon, gentle highlands and rolling lowlands, mountain peaks, and bubbling bogs. One third of the countryside is still virgin forest, and bears and wolves still cross the Carpathians into Moravia. The best time to visit is in May, June, and September, but, with cheaper rates, April and October are also good choices.

COUNTRY OVERVIEW

CURRENCY: CZECH KORUNA (WILL EVENTUALLY BE CHANGING TO THE EURO) **TIPPING:** TIPPING HAS NOT GENERALLY BEEN A CZECH CUSTOM, BUT WITH MORE TOURISTS, IT IS BECOMING MORE COMMON. GENERALLY SPEAKING, ROUND YOUR BILL UP TO THE NEXT MULTIPLE OF 10 (IF THE BILL IS 92K, LEAVE 100K). GIVE 20K EACH TO DOORMEN; 10% TO TAXI DRIVERS. IF YOU ARE WITH A LARGE GROUP, LEAVE 10% AT A RESTAURANT. **ELECTRICITY:** 220V **INTERNATIONAL CALLING CODE:** 420

PLANNING NOTES

SUGGESTED ASSISTANCE: Some assistance may be needed. Both of you will be required to provide a Czech Foreigners Police Statement, which affirms that you are in the Czech Republic legally. All documents, including the police statement, need both translation and apostilles from the State Department before being presented at the town hall. If neither the bride nor the groom speaks Czech, a Czech translator must attend the wedding.

SPECIAL REQUIREMENTS: **WAITING PERIOD:** There is a waiting period of 14 days between the time your application is received and the date of the wedding. To be on the safe side, all paperwork should be filed at least 21 days in advance. You can send it by mail to the town hall. **RESIDENCY REQUIREMENT:** Generally speaking, there is no residency requirement. However, requirements are left to the discretion of each individual city, so they vary from place to place. You may even find that some towns do not allow nonresidents to be married there. For this reason, it is imperative to double-check with the town hall in which you intend to be married; it is also advisable to arrive a few days in advance to be certain.

CIVIL CEREMONIES: Civil ceremonies are optional. They generally take place in a public place and are usually performed by the town registrar. Special permission is required for couples wishing to wed outdoors. To find an officiant, contact the town hall or registrar's office nearest your intended location.

RELIGIOUS CEREMONIES: The predominant denomination in the Czech Republic is Roman Catholic. You will be able to find Protestant churches, but generally only in Prague or other large cities. Mosques can be found in Prague and Brno, and synagogues can be found in major cities throughout the country. Buddhism is practiced in a few of the major cities, including Prague. Hindu resources seem to be scarce in the Czech Republic.

DESIGN IDEAS

Welcome your guests with lovely linen tea towels, a small blown-glass trinket, a crystal vase, or wooden jewelry, hand-carved by Carpathian artisans. Or for a fun souvenir, surprise your guests with a lively little marionette, available from many vendors on the streets of Prague. For a special token to your beloved or your parents, give a gift made of Czech lace or Bohemian crystal, garnets, or amber.

The Czech Republic offers a wealth of items and traditions that can easily be incorporated into your wedding celebration. Traditionally, the mother or grandmother of the bride made rosemary wreaths, symbolic of remembrance, to decorate the ceremony and reception. Today, brides and their attendants often wear crowns made with rosemary, baby's breath, and miniature roses. Friends of the bride usually make the bride's wreath as a symbol of wisdom, love, and loyalty, then place it on her bed before the wedding. The same friends may also send the couple a wish for a long and healthy life together by planting a tree in the bride's yard and decorating it with ribbons and painted eggshells. They will often throw grain, nuts, coins, and figs around the yard as a symbolic offering to the gods of hearth and home.

According to tradition, the bride-to-be bakes *kolache,* small buns filled with at least three fillings, then sends them to her friends and relatives as a formal invitation to the wedding celebration. For the wedding menu, you might consider featuring *kolache* as a special treat, in addition to the traditional fare of goulash, meats, dumplings, Moravian wine, and the original Budweiser beer, as well as an impressive roasted boar with an apple in its mouth! After the wedding ceremony, guests shower the departing couple with peas rather than rice. At the reception, the groomsmen each place a dish on the table, and after each guest makes a speech, they place a monetary gift in the plate and down a glass of beer. For traditional entertainment, you could hire a traditional polka band to play upbeat folk dances, complete with dancers in costume. It is a custom for the single girls to perform a circle dance, in which they try to rip a piece of the veil from the bride, who keeps her eyes closed. To protect the bride from the girls, the men form a protective circle around her; when their circle is broken, it represents an end to the bride's innocence and virginity.

PLANNING RESOURCES

EMBASSY AND GOVERNMENT OFFICES:
Embassy of the Czech Republic (in the United States)
3900 Spring of Freedom Street NW, Washington, DC 20008
www.mzv.cz/washington
202-274-9100

Consulate General of the Czech Republic
1109 Madison Avenue, New York, NY 10028
www.mzv.cz/newyork
212-717-5643

Embassy of the United States (in the Czech Republic)
Trziste 15, 118 01 Prague 1, Czech Republic
www.usembassy.cz
Consular Services: www.usembassy.cz/consular/consular.htm
420-257-530-663

City Hall, Prague *(You must contact the city hall closest to your wedding venue)*
Matrika, Vodièkova 18, Prague 1, Czech Republic
420-221-097-111

TOURISM:
Czech Center New York/Czech Tourist Authority
1109-1111 Madison Avenue, New York, NY 10028
www.czechcenter.com
212-288-0830

Czech Tourism
Vinohradska 46, P.O. Box 32, 120 41 Prague 2,
    Vinohrady, Czech Republic
www.czechtourism.com
420-221-580-111

Prague Information Service
Betlemske namesti 2,116 98 Prague 1,
    Czech Republic
www.prague-info.cz
420-12-444

© HOTEL HOFFMEISTER

PARKS, MONUMENTS, AND HISTORIC SITES:
There is not a general overseeing body for parks, historic sites, and monuments. Parks are generally not available for weddings; castles are administered individually.

VENUES

The Czech Republic offers many venues with old-world charm and romance—castles, monasteries, manors, *vinarnas* (wine caves or cellars), and churches. Once you're in Prague, you'll quickly understand why it is called "The City of 100 Spires." The skyline is dominated by chuch spires, all seeming to compete for the most heavenly reach. If a church is what you seek, take a look at the **STRAHOV MONASTERY** (420-233-107-711 / www.strahovskyklaster.cz), which is close to Prague Castle and many luxury hotels. Instead of the city, you might opt for a venue in the Czech Republic's beautiful Hans Christian Andersen countryside, which is dotted with approximately 2,000 castles. Many of these castles have been lovingly restored since the end of Communist rule. You can find numerous options by going to www.zamky-hrady.cz or www.czechcastles.com, both Web sites dedicated to castles, manors, and monasteries in the Czech Republic. Some castles in or near Prague can be rented for special events, including the popular **ZAMEK NELAHOZEVES** (420-315-709-121) and **ZAMEK TROJA** (420-222-327-677 / www.city galleryprague.cz), which houses the City Gallery in Prague.

Outside of Prague is the Bohemian spa town of Karlovy Vary (Carlsbad). Peter the Great was reputed to rejuvenate there, as well as Emperor Franz Josef, Beethoven, Chopin, Goethe, Tolstoy, and Karl Marx. Karlovy Vary's **THE GRANDHOTEL PUPP** (420-353-109-630 / www.pupp.cz), an elegant spa hotel built in 1701, is one of the oldest and most famous hotels in central Europe. In the medieval town of Cesky Krumlov is another venue, the **CESKY KRUMLOV CASTLE** (420-380-704-711 / www.castleckrumlov.cz), first mentioned in the journal of an Austrian knight in the year 1240. With a complex of more than

40 buildings on the edge of the Vltava River, the castle—one of the largest in Europe—has been designated UNESCO World Cultural Heritage status. Located in the heart of the town, the recently renovated **HOTEL DVORAK CESKY KRUMLOV** (420-380-711-020 / http://dvorakck.genea2000.cz/en/akce.php), offers magnificent views, bright and airy rooms, top-notch service—and even morning and evening balloon rides over the castle.

HOTEL SAVOY

Keplerova 6, CZ-118 00 Prague 1, Czech Republic

www.hotel-savoy.cz

420-224-302-430

SIZE: 1 CITY BLOCK **NUMBER OF ROOMS:** 61 ROOMS, INCLUDING 6 SUITES **WHEELCHAIR ACCESSIBLE:** YES (LIMITED) **RATES:** $$-$$$

REVIEW: Frequented by presidents, heads of state, and international stars, the luxurious Hotel Savoy is located at an exclusive address in the historic Hradcany District near Prague Castle and St. Vitus Cathedral. Each room, tastefully decorated in shades of blue and yellow, includes a small sitting area and modern amenities. Both the Honeymoon and Grand Presidential Suites feature large terraces with commanding views of the nearby castle. Other famous sights, such as the National Gallery, the Strahov Monastery, the Church of St. Nicholas, and the Castle Gardens, are within easy walking distance of the hotel, and the airport is only 15 minutes away. The Savoy is a member of the Leading Small Hotels of the World and Vienna International Hotels and Resorts.

CEREMONY AND RECEPTION OPTIONS: Wedding ceremonies and receptions can be held in the hotel's library or restaurant. With its large, romantic, open-air fireplace, the library is perfect for intimate weddings of up to 36. The Restaurant Hradcany serves gourmet international and Czech specialties for as many as 120. It is known for its sliding glass cupola with windows that sink into the floor with a touch of a button, creating easy access to the outdoor patio and gardens. Also be sure to ask about the nearby Strahov Monastery, which can accommodate 120.

WEDDING SERVICES: Full service.

ARIA HOTEL

Trziste 9, 118 00, Prague 1, Czech Republic

www.ariahotel.net

888-454-2742 / 420-225-334-111

SIZE: 32,000 SQUARE FEET **NUMBER OF ROOMS:** 52 ROOMS, INCLUDING 9 LUXURY SUITES **WHEELCHAIR ACCESSIBLE:** YES; TWO HANDICAPPED-ACCESSIBLE ROOMS AVAILABLE **RATES:** $$$ **SPECIAL NOTES:** CHILDREN ARE FREE WHEN STAYING IN PARENTS' ROOM. CRIBS, HIGH CHAIRS, SPECIAL MENUS, AND BABYSITTING AVAILABLE. GAMES, BOOKS, AND DVDS ALSO AVAILABLE.

REVIEW: Each of the Aria Hotel's four guest room floors is dedicated to a different musical genre—jazz, opera, classical, and contemporary—and each guest room celebrates an individual artist or composer who has influenced the respective genre. The rooms feature original artwork, a selection of books, an in-room flat-screen computer with the artist's biography and Internet access, and plenty of other modern amenities. Guests also enjoy a state-of-the-art fitness center, a music library, and a salon with a fireplace, along with a business center, concierge services, and a rooftop terrace overlooking the capital.

CEREMONY AND RECEPTION OPTIONS: Ceremonies are not provided at the Aria but are instead held in the town hall, nearby gardens, or surrounding medieval castles. For wedding receptions, the Aria's restaurant, Coda, seats 40, and the lobby restaurant seats 80. During warm weather, the reception can be held on the rooftop terrace, which provides spectacular 360-degree views of the rooftops of Malá Strana.

WEDDING SERVICES: Provides list of vendors.

HOTEL HOFFMEISTER-LILY WELLNESS & SPA

Pod Bruskou 7, Prague 1, 118 00 Malá Strana, Czech Republic

www.hoffmeister.cz

420-251-017-111

SIZE: 9.5 ACRES **NUMBER OF ROOMS:** 30 ROOMS; 8 SUITES **WHEELCHAIR ACCESSIBLE:** YES
RATES: $$

REVIEW: This historic hotel, situated in Malá Strana at the Old Castle Steps, offers luxurious surroundings, easy access to main shopping areas in Old Towne Square, and lavishly decorated rooms featuring tile, antiques, and modern amenities. Adorning the interior are portraits of distinguished nineteenth-century personalities painted by the hotel's original owner. Guests can visit the nearby baroque gardens of Vrtbovska, receive a spa treatment in the fifteenth-century cave, or indulge in the French-influenced cuisine and gourmet delicacies created by the restaurant's award-winning chef. Hotel Hoffmeister's honeymoon packages make the venue especially enticing to newlyweds.

CEREMONY AND RECEPTION OPTIONS: Small wedding ceremonies can be held on-site, but generally the ceremonies are performed at local churches or synagogues, at the town hall (a wonderful medieval city house built in the early 1400s), or in one of the many formal gardens nearby. Ceremonies can also be held at either of the castles Nelahozeves or Troja, which feature exquisite artwork, historical costumes, and objects of cultural and historic significance. Following the ceremonies, guests usually meet for cocktails in the Hoffmeister winery before beginning the reception for up to 100 guests in the newly refurbished Restaurant ADA.

WEDDING SERVICES: Provides some assistance.

Greece

Greece attracts travelers of all kinds, from backpackers to shipping magnates. Given its incomparable beauty and romantic aura, it is no surprise that the Grecian shores lure destination couples as well. Greek song and sculpture honor Erotokritos and Aretousa, the Cretan Romeo and Juliet who, unlike Shakespeare's ill-fated lovers, lived happily ever after. The optimistically romantic spirit of this tale is prevalent all over Greece, a country of spectacular settings where you can begin your own love story! A Greek wedding is sure to be memorable, whether you marry aboard a yacht on the azure seas or high up in the mountains. To avoid the crowds, go during the early spring. May and June are the warmest months, and many hotels close from November until April.

COUNTRY OVERVIEW

CURRENCY: EURO **TIPPING:** RESTAURANT BILLS USUALLY INCLUDE A SERVICE CHARGE OF 15–20% IN ADDITION TO A COVER CHARGE FOR USE OF THE TABLE. IT IS ALSO CUSTOMARY TO LEAVE THE CHANGE FROM YOUR BILL. **ELECTRICITY:** 220V AC **INTERNATIONAL CALLING CODE:** 30

PLANNING NOTES

SUGGESTED ASSISTANCE: Some assistance may be needed. You'll need to file the standard documents, but they will need to be stamped with an apostille, translated into Greek, and then authenticated by the Greek Consulate. Call the Greek Consulate for guidance on getting an official translator. You will also need assistance in publishing your intention to marry and then applying for the license unless you are able to be there seven days in advance of the wedding to do it yourself.

SPECIAL REQUIREMENTS: WAITING PERIOD: Seven days are required to publish your intentions and apply for the license, but this can be done for you by someone in Greece. **RESIDENCY REQUIREMENT:** None.

CIVIL CEREMONIES: Civil ceremonies, which are performed by a mayor, are optional and can happen anywhere that the mayor agrees to. Greece is unusual in that it will accept a foreign marriage license as long as it does not place any restrictions on the location of the marriage. You will still be issued a Greek version of the marriage license, but the advantage is that you will not have to provide an Affidavit of Single Status along with your other documents. A marriage license can be obtained from your current place of residence prior to coming to Greece, and it will generally be accepted by Greek authorities as long as the license has a blank line on which the officiant can write in the location of the marriage. (This applies only if neither the bride nor the groom resides in Greece.) Regardless of where you get your license, you will have to publish your intention to marry in the local paper one week prior to the ceremony—unless you are planning a wedding in Santorini, which has no newspaper in which to publish an intention! Next, you'll need to bring the published announcement and all your translated documents to the *demarcheio*, or city hall, nearest your wedding location to apply for the marriage license. It is legal—and may be more convenient—to have a wedding planner publish your intentions and apply for your license so you can arrive two or three days before the wedding.

RELIGIOUS CEREMONIES: Greek Orthodox is the dominant religion, accounting for 97% of the population. However, most major world religions are found in Greece, including Judaism, Islam, Buddhism, and Hinduism as well as other Christian denominations. Check with the local spiritual leader from your faith to determine the exact requirements, as he will be required to apply for the marriage license on your behalf.

DESIGN IDEAS

When your guests arrive, greet them with something unique to the islands—perhaps tickets for a local tour, a bag of homegrown pistachios, and a bottle of vanilla. Also check out the local crafts markets for a piece of handmade jewelry or an alabaster or bronze miniature of an ancient sculpture. For Grecian wedding décor, use a blue-and-white color scheme or a traditional Greek motif, such as ancient statues, olives, Athena's Owl, or even the good-luck evil-eye icon. In addition, you could incorporate one of the many beautiful Greek wedding traditions into your ceremony. During the wedding, for example, the bride and groom wear *stephanothikes*, special crowns identifying the couple as king or queen for the day. The crowns, made of garland or of metal and semiprecious stones, are tied together by a white ribbon. On the island of Santorini, many newlywed couples follow the tradition of parading through the streets on donkeys, riding from ceremony to reception while attracting cheers from onlookers.

For the reception, whet your guests' appetites with stuffed grape leaves, marinated olives, lamb, and seafood, and wet their lips with ouzo, the aromatic drink that is said to symbolize Greek optimism and joy of life. A significant part of Greek socializing is the *meze*, a special meal intended to accompany wine and spirits, consisting of pita, hummus, baba ghanouj, tabbouleh, and other dishes. End the feast with sweet baklava—and maybe even a wedding cake shaped liked the Parthenon! For entertainment, a Greek band could lead your guests in some foot-stomping dances, including the *kalamantiano* circle dance (made famous by *Zorba the Greek*). There is usually a "money dance," during which guests dance with either the bride or the groom and pin money to their clothes. And don't be alarmed if you hear plates breaking—at many receptions, guests wish the couple luck by noisily breaking plates on the dance floor as they shout in merriment!

PLANNING RESOURCES

EMBASSY AND GOVERNMENT OFFICES:
Embassy of Greece (in the United States)
2221 Massachusetts Avenue NW, Washington, DC 20008
www.greekembassy.org
202-939-1300 / Consulate General: 202-939-1318

Embassy of the United States (in Greece)
91 Vasilissis Sophias Avenue, Athens 10160, Greece
www.usembassy.gr
30-210-721-2951

Athens City Hall
Athinas 63, Kotzia Square, Athens 10552, Greece
30-210-372-2001

Translation Department of the Greek Ministry of Foreign Affairs
10, Arionos Street, Psiri, Athens 10554, Greece
30-210-323-9514

TOURISM:
Greek National Tourism Organization
Tsoha 7 Street, Athens 11521, Greece
www.gnto.gr
30-210-870-7000

Greek National Tourist Office (in the United States)
645 Fifth Avenue, New York, NY 10022
www.greektourism.com
212-421-5777

PARKS, MONUMENTS, AND HISTORIC SITES:
Hellenic Ministry of Culture *(for special-use permits for national parks and monuments)*
20-22 Bouboulinas Street, Athens 10682, Greece
www.culture.gr
30-210-820-1100

Hellenic Society for the Protection of Nature
24 Nikis Street, Athens 10557, Greece
30-132-249-44

WEDDING RESOURCES:
HELPFUL WEB SITES:
Greek Boston: www.greekboston.com/wedding/
Athens Guide: www.athensguide.com/dorian
(This is the contact information for Dorian Kokas, a Greek American now living in Athens. He can provide resources and assistance to couples on just about any legal matter in Greece, including marriage laws among the different churches.)

VENUES

Every venue in Greece, from seaside resort to cliffside villa, offers a breathtaking setting! If you love the sea, the yachts of **POSEIDON CHARTERS** (888-372-7245 / www.poseidon charters.com) can be chartered for wedding- and honeymoon-sailings to Santorini, Crete, and Mykonos, among other destinations. For an Athens wedding, the **ST. GEORGE LYCA-BETTUS BOUTIQUE HOTEL** (30-210-729-0711 / www.sglycabettus.gr) is located in Kolonaki, the most exclusive address in Athens. This hotel offers unparalleled views of the Acropolis from its balconies and rooftop restaurant.

The most popular island for weddings is Santorini, though the islands of Mykonos and Crete are also a draw. If you are interested in Santorini, the site of the legendary sunken civilization of Atlantis, consider **THE ATLANTIS SUBMARINE** (30-228-602-8900 / www.submarine.gr), which offers underwater wedding ceremonies off the coast for up to 30 guests. **CHROMATA** (30-228-602-4850 / www.chromata-santorini.com) is a trendy hotel perched on a cliff in Imerovigli, overlooking the Caldera, the semi-submerged volcano believed to be the demise of Atlantis. Located in Oia, Santorini, **1864 THE SEA CAPTAIN'S HOUSE** (30-228-607-1983 / www.santorini-gr.com) is a luxurious neoclassical guesthouse, chosen as one of *Condé Nast Traveler* Hot and Coolest hotels. Formerly the villa of a wealthy Greek sea captain, it is furnished with items the captain purchased around the world. The cliffside accommodations of **KATIKIES** (30-228-607-1401 / www.katikies.com), which include a hotel, suites, and seven-unit villa,

© PHOTOGRAPHER WILLIAM ABRANOWICZ / PERIVOLAS TRADITIONAL HOUSES

are an architectural wonder with freeform stairways, bridges, walks, and cave houses. Katikies offers supreme service, promising one service person for every two guests on the property at all times.

On Mykonos, the **BELVEDERE HOTEL** (30-228-902-5122 / www.belvederehotel.com) is a fashionable, fully restored 1850 mansion with views of the Aegean from every balcony. Another chic hotel on the island, the **KIVOTOS CLUBHOTEL** (30-228-902-5795 / www.kivotosclubhotel.gr), has 40 rooms and suites, all individually designed by famous artists and local craftsmen, as well as five swimming pools, a private beach, and two gourmet restaurants. If you want to be married in Europe's oldest civilization, Crete is your island. **THE ELOUNDA GULF VILLAS & SUITES** (30-284-109-0300 / www.elounda villas.com), overlooking the gulf of Mirabella, has garnered many prestigious awards, including mention as one of Europe's 50 Best Villas in the *New York Times'* travel magazine. At **MINOS BEACH ART 'OTEL** (30-284-102-2345 / www.slh.com/minosbeach), you will find waterfront bungalows nestled among palm trees, olive trees, and bougainvillea.

THE TSITOURAS COLLECTION HOUSE
Firostefani, Santorini 84700, Greece
www.tsitouras.gr
30-228-602-3747

SIZE: 5,300 SQUARE FEET **NUMBER OF ROOMS:** 5 VILLAS (EACH ACCOMMODATES 2–5 PERSONS **WHEELCHAIR ACCESSIBLE:** YES (LIMITED) **RATES:** $$-$$$ **SPECIAL NOTES:** BABYSITTING AND CHILDREN'S FILM LIBRARY AVAILABLE

REVIEW: This boutique hotel includes five cliffside villas that were renovated in 1985 by Dimitris Tsitouras, a well-known Santorinian historian, writer, and collector. The main mansion is over 230 years old and will soon include a museum to house the owner's collection of Greek artifacts. Each villa has its own theme based on a different facet of Greek history. The villa houses—The House of the Sea, The House of the Wind, The House of Portraits, The House of Porcelain, and The House of Nureyev—feature exquisite antiques and *objets d'art*, including old maps and Byzantine icons. Sleeping two to five guests, each beautiful house has a white marble bathroom, wet bar, CD player, satellite television, DVD, direct-dial phone, and safety deposit box. An à-la-carte breakfast is served daily, and lunch and dinner are available on the Maria Callas Terrace.

CEREMONY AND RECEPTION OPTIONS: The Maria Callas Terrace, which seats up to 100 guests, is used for both wedding ceremonies and receptions.

WEDDING SERVICES: Full service. Facilitates marriage license and provides list of preferred vendors.

PERIVOLAS TRADITIONAL HOUSES
GR847-02, Oia, Santorini, Greece
www.perivolas.com
30-228-607-1308

SIZE: ALMOST 300 ACRES **NUMBER OF ROOMS:** 18 HOUSES **WHEELCHAIR ACCESSIBLE:** SANTORINI IN GENERAL IS NOT AN IDEAL DESTINATION FOR ANYONE IN A WHEELCHAIR **RATES:** $$$ **SPECIAL NOTES:** THIS IS NOT AN APPROPRIATE PROPERTY FOR CHILDREN

REVIEW: In 1980, the owners of Perivolas converted a group of 300-year-old cliffside caves, once part of a fishing village, into a complex of 18 exclusive romantic houses. Minimalist in style, the houses are truly unique, with arched ceilings and lots of nooks and crannies. The largest suite features an olive tree growing inside and, outside, a private pool that comes up to the glass doors of the bedroom. There are no televisions—after all, most guests choose Perivolas because they want to relax in tranquility. According to *Hideaways Magazine*, Perivolas has one of the World's Ten Best Pools, an edgeless pool that appears to drop right into the sea, where guests can be waited on hand and foot. In addition to offering spa services, Perivolas encourages its guests to explore the island's villages and archeological treasures.

CEREMONY OPTIONS: During the quiet months of April or October, couples might opt to be married by the pool. During the high season of November to March, the most private options are the terrace under the edge of the pool or a terrace of one of the houses, all accommodating up to 20. The house that is best suited for a wedding is the newest Perivolas Suite, which has its own pool and terrace. For wedding parties of more than 20, consider one of the many churches or another location off property.

RECEPTION OPTIONS: Wedding receptions can be held in the dining room. If the party desires more privacy, the chef can cater a meal on one of the private terraces. For larger groups, a wedding planner can also recommend restaurants in town.

WEDDING SERVICES: Provides list of preferred vendors.

VEDEMA RESORT
Megalohori, Santorini 84700, Greece

www.vedema.gr

30-210-899-3790

SIZE: 12,000 SQUARE METERS **NUMBER OF ROOMS:** 45 HOUSES AND VILLAS **WHEELCHAIR ACCESSIBLE:** NO **RATES:** $$–$$$ **SPECIAL NOTES:** CHILDREN WELCOME; BABYSITTING AVAILABLE

REVIEW: Surrounded by a medieval village, Vedema Resort is a world unto itself, with buildings designed around a fifteenth-century winery. In 2001, this member of The Luxury Collection of Starwood Hotels & Resorts was voted one of the world's best hotels by the British newspaper *The Independent*. Vinsanto, the old vaulted dining room, is the most exclusive restaurant on the island, and the Canava wine bar offers daily wine tastings. All the villas, pastel-hued townhouses domed with distinctive cupolas, have marble bathrooms, island-style furnishings, and terraces. The ten pool suites are models of fresh minimalism, inspired by the "barefoot chic" philosophy. Guests enjoy impeccable service, private beaches, a spa, a swimming pool, Jacuzzis, private bicycles, a fitness and business center, and private verandas.

CEREMONY AND RECEPTION OPTIONS: The pool restaurant accommodates up to 250 people. The Vinsanto restaurant, which accommodates up to 80, is located in a 400-year-old, medieval-themed winery and offers the finest Mediterranean cuisine. The Canava wine bar, located in the catacombs in the center of the property, offers more privacy for parties up to 80.

WEDDING SERVICES: Full service. An officiant can be provided to perform the wedding; special circumstances will be dealt with upon request.

Italy

Viva *Italia*—a bastion of romance and a top pick for destination weddings. Popular spots include the Tuscan countryside, the Amalfi and Sorrento coasts, the Italian Alps, Rome, Venice, and Florence. Dubbed the world's "living art gallery," Italy boasts more culture than you can shake a paintbrush at! For a colorful backdrop to any wedding celebration, consider the many cultural events in Italy, including Venice's Carnivale, Sicily's Holy Week festivities, and Abruzzo's Festival of Snakes. Peak tourist season begins shortly before Easter and runs through October. Spring and autumn are the best times to visit, though winter means shorter lines at tourist attractions. Many shops and restaurants in Rome close during August, when most Italians are on holiday.

COUNTRY OVERVIEW

CURRENCY: EURO **TIPPING:** MOST RESTAURANTS ADD A 15% SERVICE CHARGE TO THE BILL, BUT IT IS CUSTOMARY TO GIVE THE WAITER AN ADDITIONAL 5–10% IF THE FOOD AND SERVICE HAVE WARRANTED IT (ALWAYS TIP IN CASH). IN BARS AND CAFÉS, TIP WITH A FEW COINS. TIP CAB DRIVERS 5–10% AND CONCIERGES 15%. TIP TOUR GUIDES AT LEAST ONE EURO PER PERSON PER HALF-DAY—MORE IF THEY ARE VERY GOOD. SMALL TIPS TO WEDDING SERVICE PROVIDERS ARE APPROPRIATE AND ALWAYS APPRECIATED. **ELECTRICITY:** 220V **INTERNATIONAL CALLING CODE:** 39

PLANNING NOTES

SUGGESTED ASSISTANCE: Assistance is a must, as requirements are quite complex. Though the American Embassy Web site (www.usembassy.it/cons/acs/marriage.htm) provides details on marriage license requirements, it is wise to contact the local civil registry office nearest your intended location to confirm other specific requirements.

SPECIAL REQUIREMENTS: WAITING PERIOD: None. However, if you are an Italian or American citizen residing in Italy, the posting of the banns must occur on two consecutive Sundays prior to the ceremony. **RESIDENCY REQUIREMENT:** None

CIVIL CEREMONIES: Civil ceremonies are required if you wish to have a legally binding wedding in Italy, unless you are Catholic and find a priest to take care of the legal matters for you. (Most couples proceed to the church after the civil ceremony for a blessing ceremony.) Your civil ceremony can be done prior to going to Italy or can be held at any city hall or civil registry office throughout Italy. Civil ceremonies can be beautiful affairs because they are often held in lovely historic buildings, complete with flowers and music. In Florence, civil weddings can take place in the Sala Rossa, or "Red Room," in the famous Palazzo Vecchio. In Sorrento, civil ceremonies take place in a beautiful monastery, and in Positano they are held on a terrace overlooking the sea (weather permitting). If neither party speaks Italian, you are required to hire a translator for the service. Always make arrangements months in advance.

RELIGIOUS CEREMONIES: Most non-Catholic marriage officiants insist that couples first legally marry in a civil ceremony before going through a religious ceremony. They do this to ensure the legality of the marriage, as anything other than a Catholic wedding has no legal standing in Italy. For matrimony in a Catholic church, the priest can simply give a religious blessing (when the couple arrives already legally bound) or he can perform both a Catholic and civil ceremony simultaneously. Such full wedding services, however, are rarely extended to visitors. Protestant couples seeking a religious ceremony often choose one of Italy's many Anglican churches. There are officiants available from several faiths throughout Italy; photographs and information describing Italy's synagogues can be found at www.kosherdelight.com/italy synagogues.htm. Muslims can find three Islamic masjids in Rome alone. Hindus looking for ashrams in Italy can find a list on www.hindunet.org.

DESIGN IDEAS

The tradition of giving wedding favors dates back to the Middle Ages, when the couple's families exchanged gifts. Since then, Italians have developed an elaborate tradition of giving keepsakes, called *bomboniere*. The gifts might be anything from terra-cotta figurines to crystal vases. One item, however, remains constant—*confetti*, the five sugar-coated Jordan almonds given to guests, representing fertility, happiness, health, longevity, and wealth. To welcome your guests, you could give them *confetti* and *bomboniere* in a pretty ceramic bowl, along with a bottle of Chianti or Asti Spumanti, packages of pasta, and perhaps a bottle of limoncello.

When decorating, consider using fragrant bunches of lavender, rosemary, and thyme, which grow in profusion in Italy. Orchids, gladioli, and irises are also plentiful, as are roses, which are most commonly used for Italian weddings. Lemons, grapes, olives, and eggplants could all be incorporated into the décor for a Tuscan theme. Get ready for culinary euphoria because Italian wedding banquets are bountiful and mouthwatering! Menu choices depend on your locale; you might have anything from fondues in the north to *componata* in the south. Most meals include an antipasta (appetizer), a pasta, and then the main course, consisting of your choice of meat (often roasted pig or lamb) or seafood. When choosing your reception music, be sure to request the *tarantella*, a lively traditional Italian wedding dance.

PLANNING RESOURCES

EMBASSY AND GOVERNMENT OFFICES:
Embassy of Italy (in the United States)
3000 Whitehaven Street NW, Washington, DC 20008
www.italyemb.org
202-612-4400 / Consulate General: 202-612-4402

Embassy of the United States (in Italy)
Via Vittorio Veneto 119/A, 00187 Rome, Italy
www.usembassy.it
for information on weddings: www.usembassy.it/cons/acs/marriage.htm
39-066-729-4633

© GREG JANSEN

Consulate General of the United States
Florence: Lungarno Vespucci 38, 50123, Florence, Italy
39-055-266-951
Milan: Via Principe Amadeo 2/10, 20121, Milan, Italy
39-02-290-351
Naples: Piazza della Repubblica, 80122 Naples, Italy
39-081-5838-111

To find out about legal requirements, contact the local city hall or civil registry nearest your destination location.
Rome: Anagrafe, Marriage Office
Via Petroselli, 50, Rome, Italy
39-066-710-3066

To find out about English-language marriages at the Vatican, contact:
The Church of Santa Susanna
Via Venti Settembre, 15, 00187, Rome, Italy
www.santasusanna.org
39-064-201-4554

TOURISM:
Italian Government Tourism Board
630 Fifth Avenue, Suite 1565, New York, NY 10111
www.italiantourism.com
212-245-5618

Italian State Tourist Board
Central Office, Via Marghera 2/6, 00185, Rome, Italy
www.enit.it
39-06-49711

PARKS, MONUMENTS, AND HISTORIC SITES:
Italian Federation of Parks and Natural Reserves
Via Cristoforo Colombo 149, 00147, Rome, Italy
www.parks.it
39-06-5160-4940

VENUES

Villas, spas, *palazzi*, basilicas, monasteries, hotels, restaurants—there are so many wonderful venues in Italy! Rest assured, you cannot go wrong, no matter which you choose. In Rome consider the **EXCELSIOR LIDO HOTEL** (39--041-526-0201 / www.starwood hotels.com), a magnificent palace, which having just undergone a multimillion-dollar renovation, boasts an opulent façade and Belle Epoch splendor. **THE HOTEL CASTELLO DELLA CASTELLUCCIA** (39-063-020-7041 / www.hotelcastelluciarome.com) is a medieval castle in the countryside of Sardinia, north of Rome.

If your interest is Venice, there is the **HOTEL GRITTI PALACE** (39-041-794-611 / www.hotelgrittivenice.com), which is situated right on the Grand Canal. It is one of the most celebrated hotels in the world, having been frequented by ambassadors, royal families, and Hollywood stars. Ernest Hemingway called it "the best hotel in a city of great hotels." Not too far away from Venice, you'll find the **HOTEL VILLA MICHELANGELO** (39-044-455-0300 / www.hotelvillamichelangelo.com), a popular venue among Italian couples. Only minutes from the city of Vincenza, Hotel Villa Michelangelo is a country house retreat converted from an eighteenth-century monastery overlooking the Berici Hills.

Tuscany is a popular region for weddings. For a comprehensive list of Tuscan venues, go to www.rent-a-villa-in-tuscany.com. You may also want to check out **VILLA CONTRONI** (www.villacontroni.com/villa.htm) in Lucca, where you can rent an entire villa for yourself and 12 guests, complete with a gardener, chef, housekeeper, stocked wine cellar, antique camellia gardens—and even a chapel for small weddings. If you love the Renaissance, look into Florence's **VILLA LA VEDETTA** (39-055-681631 / www.villalavedetta hotel.com), a hotel on *Condé Nast Traveler*'s 2004 Hot List!, where you can spend your wedding night on a terrace overlooking the famous Piazza Michelangelo in Florence.

What about a seaside wedding? The **GRAND HOTEL EXCELSIOR VITTORIA** (39-081-807-1044 / www.excelsiorvittoria.com) is located on the cliffs of Sorrento on five acres of citrus and olive trees, overlooking Mount Vesuvius and the Bay of Naples. A little less expensive is the **BELLEVUE SYRENE** (39-081-878-1024 / www.bellevue.it), equally as lovely with gorgeous views of the sea. On the Amalfi Coast in the charming city of Positano, there is a tiny cliffside chapel called the Chapel of San Pietro, an ideal setting for an intimate wedding. Nearby in the town of Ravello, you will find the **PALAZZO SASSO** (39-089-818-181 / www.palazzosasso.com), a five-star, twelfth-century villa perched high on a seaside cliff.

If you cannot decide on one single region in Italy, you can always plan to honeymoon in one or more areas after your wedding. Relax in one of the many thermal spas, such as the **GROTTO GIUSTI THERME HOTEL** (39-057-290-771 / www.grottagiustispa.com) in Tuscany, a natural thermal cavern with amazing rock formations and a subterranean lake that bathes guests luxuriously. Or visit the **TERME DI SATURNIA SPA RESORT** (39-056-460-0800 / www.termedisaturnia.it), another state-of-the-art Tuscan spa that caters to honeymooners. For a captivating honeymoon option, why not go to the island of Capri, where you can stay at either the **GRAND HOTEL QUISISANA** (39-081-837-0788 / www.quisi.com) or the **CAPRI PALACE HOTEL & SPA** (39-081-978-0111 / www.capripalace.it).

MONSIGNOR DELLA CASA COUNTRY RESORT
Via di Mucciano 16, 50032 Borgo San Lorenzo, Florence, Italy
www.monsignore.com
39-055-840-821

SIZE: 200 PRIVATE FENCED ACRES **NUMBER OF ROOMS:** 2 DOUBLE ROOMS, 19 SUITES, 5 VILLAS **WHEELCHAIR ACCESSIBLE:** 1 ROOM **RATES:** $$–$$$

REVIEW: This historic Tuscan estate was the birthplace of Monsignor della Casa, the Vatican Secretary of State that wrote *Galateo*, a highly regarded sixteenth-century treatise on etiquette. It is situated in Florence, in an area once frequented by the Medici family as well as artists Giotto, Cimabue, and Fra Angelico. A living fresco of fields and gardens, the tranquil resort is a member of the Great Hotels of the World. Each apartment has its own private entrance and garden, with rustic Tuscan furnishings, terracotta floors, fireplaces, and wrought iron canopied beds. Two of the villas have their own private pools. Guests enjoy a fully equipped wellness center and fitness room, whirlpools, swimming pools, biking, horseback riding, golf, and evening barbecues.

CEREMONY AND RECEPTION OPTIONS: Wedding and receptions can be held for up to 60 guests. In the Wine Bar Restaurant, guests can taste the greatest wines of Tuscany and enjoy cuisine that fuses creativity and ancient tradition.

WEDDING SERVICES: Full service.

VILLA D'ESTE
Via Regina, 40 Como 22012, Cernobbio, Italy
www.villadeste.it
39-031-3481

SIZE: 25 ACRES **NUMBER OF ROOMS:** 160 ROOMS, INCLUDING 79 DOUBLES/TWINS, 6 SINGLES, 55 JUNIOR SUITES, AND 17 SUITES **WHEELCHAIR ACCESSIBLE:** 2 DOUBLE ROOMS **RATES:** $$–$$$
SPECIAL NOTES: BABYSITTING AND OUTDOOR CHILDREN'S POOL AVAILABLE

REVIEW: Villa d'Este was converted into a grand hotel in 1873, after it had served for several centuries as a residence for European aristocrats. Located on pristine Lake Como, this luxurious wedding destination has been accorded top awards by *Condé Nast Traveler*, *Gourmet*, and *Travel + Leisure* . The elegantly appointed rooms feature period pieces, "Como" silk coverlets, linen sheets, oil paintings, modern amenities, and a marble bath with a Jacuzzi. The main restaurant, overlooking the lake, specializes in Italian and international cuisine. Another restaurant serves Japanese specialties. The Swiss border and Lugano are less than 30 minutes away, as is the Casino of Campione. Daily sightseeing and boat trips are part of the excitement, as Villa d'Este is close to Milan and the Italian Riviera.

CEREMONY OPTIONS: Wedding ceremonies can be held in the Mosaic Gardens, which holds up to 200 people. The Mantero Terrace is also available for 90 or fewer guests.

RECEPTION OPTIONS: The Napoleon Room is ideal for small receptions of up to 50 people, while the Impero Room can host up to 200 guests. Each banquet room is elegantly furnished, and the staff can plan a lavish event, complete with cocktails, canapes, a four-course feast, wedding cake, and a spumante cup for the final toast!

WEDDING SERVICES: Full service, though unable to assist in finding officiants.

HOTEL DANIELI VENICE

Riva Deglia Schiavori, Castello 4196, Venice, Italy

www.hoteldanielivenice.com

39-041-522-6480

SIZE: 1 CITY BLOCK **NUMBER OF ROOMS:** 222 ROOMS; 11 SUITES **WHEELCHAIR ACCESSIBLE:** 1 ROOM; LIMITED FACILITIES **RATES:** $$–$$$ **SPECIAL NOTES:** CHILDREN WELCOME; BABYSITTING AVAILABLE UPON REQUEST

REVIEW: The Danieli is the most famous palazzo hotel in all of Venice. Picture being transported on the red velvet seats of a golden wedding gondola to your turreted palace on the Grand Canal. And imagine having your wedding photos taken in the nearby Piazza San Marco, one of the most romantic squares in the world. Originally built in the late fourteenth century as Doge Dandalo's grand showcase and private residence, the Danieli was converted in the nineteenth century as a "hotel for kings." Through the years, it has been visited by literati and glitterati alike, including Johann Wolfgang von Goethe, Charles Dickens, Steven Spielberg, and Elizabeth Taylor. The guest rooms, accessible from the lavish lobby by a cascading marble staircase, have silk coverlets, antique beds, and rich Oriental carpeting covering parquet floors—and even heated towel bars! The smaller but more romantic Gothic-style rooms are the most popular, located in the original building, the Palazzo Dandolo.

CEREMONY AND RECEPTION OPTIONS: Cocktails begin in the lavishly opulent lounge, which has a huge chandelier, marble columns, and a massive stone fireplace. Receptions for as many as 120 can be held in one of the four elegant banquet salons or on the rooftop terrace restaurant, where guests enjoy the most spectacular 180-degree view of Venice, San Giorgio Maggiore, and St. Mark's Basin.

WEDDING SERVICES: Full service.

africa

Africa, a continent rich in natural beauty, gems, wildlife, culture, and history, is characterized by astounding diversity. But, from Algeria to South Africa, most Africans place symbolic importance upon a wedding. In an African wedding, not only are two lives involved but often two different communities. Because she is the link between her and her husband's ancestors and future generations, the African bride is deeply revered. For a wedding in Africa, start planning early—determine which shots and vaccinations you will need, and check on travel warnings posted on embassy Web sites. Then get creative! Will your wedding be shaped by a song from the Serengeti, the revelry of a *zaffa* parade, or another colorful tradition? Turn the page and explore the possibilities for a wedding in Egypt, South Africa, and Tanzania. I encourage you to explore other options, too. Morocco, the Canary Islands, the Seychelles, Madagascar, Botswana, Kenya, and Zimbabwe are all magnificent destinations. If you want to learn more about the countries of Africa, visit www.africaguide.com.

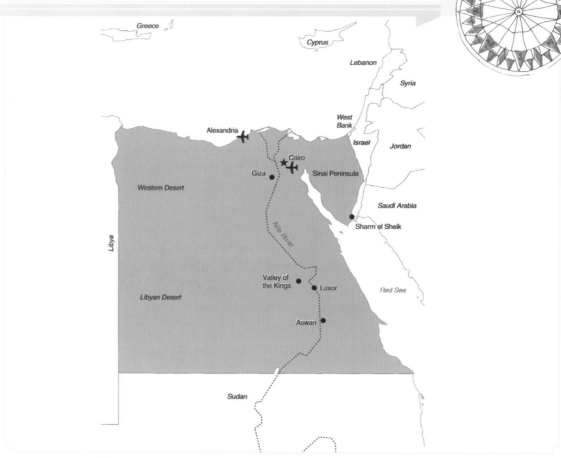

Egypt makes all of one's senses—including one's sense of history—come alive! This country is perhaps the most fitting destination for a wedding, as it was the first to codify marriage laws, making the union both a civic and a religious institution. Egypt offers a host of fabled spots that combine the ancient with the exotic. Couples can cruise the mystical Nile aboard a *felucca* (an Egyptian sailboat), stand in the shadows of the Great Pyramids of Giza, join a quiet camel caravan for a desert trek, go diving in the Red Sea, or experience King Tut's tomb at the Egyptian Antiquities Museum. Autumn and winter are the best time to visit, as mild weather prevails. Be prepared for April sandstorms, summer heat, and rain and cold from December to February.

COUNTRY OVERVIEW

CURRENCY: EGYPTIAN POUND **TIPPING:** TIPPING IS VERY IMPORTANT IN EGYPT. 15% IS EXPECTED, BUT HAVE SMALL AMOUNTS AVAILABLE FOR DOORMEN AND ANYONE ELSE WHO OFFERS YOU ASSISTANCE IN ANY WAY. IT IS CONSIDERED OFFENSIVE TO OFFER TIPS TO PROFESSIONALS, BUSINESSMEN, OR OTHERS WHO WOULD CONSIDER THEMSELVES YOUR EQUALS. **ELECTRICITY:** 220V **INTERNATIONAL CALLING CODE:** 20

PLANNING NOTES

SUGGESTED ASSISTANCE: Some assistance may be needed. Application forms must be completed at the marriage court, and these forms can only be obtained at the Department of Justice's Office of Marriage either the day before or the day of the wedding. Applicants should have original versions and photocopies of all their documents, as well as notarized Arabic translations for all authenticated documents. To use the Egyptian marriage certificate in your country of origin, it should be translated into English by the Translation Office in the Egyptian Ministry of Justice, then authenticated by the Egyptian Ministry of Foreign Affairs.

SPECIAL REQUIREMENTS: WAITING PERIOD: None, unless the bride-to-be is in *idda*, the waiting period following a divorce or the death of her husband; a divorcée must wait approximately three months after the divorce to remarry, and a widow must wait four months and ten days after her husband's death to remarry. **RESIDENCY REQUIREMENT:** None

CIVIL CEREMONIES: Civil ceremonies are required and must be performed by a court-appointed officiant at the local marriage court (religious marriages may be performed later). When applying for the marriage license, two male witnesses with proper identification must also be present. Marriage is illegal if the bride is Muslim and groom is of a different faith; Muslim men, however, can marry non-Muslims. Forms are available through the United States Embassy in Cairo. While at the embassy, you must pick up a form that states whether you are Muslim, Jewish, or Christian; the form will then need to be certified by the Egyptian Ministry of Foreign Affairs. All documents must be translated into Arabic.

RELIGIOUS CEREMONIES: Egypt is predominantly Muslim, but there is a sizable Orthodox Coptic Christian minority. Egyptian priests (for Christian couples) will only perform ceremonies in a church setting, such as the Orthodox Coptic Christian Church in Cairo (20-2-350-7781). For other Christian denominations contact your denominational headquarters at home or visit http://ww3.interoz.com/hotels/toursearch8.ihtml. For information on Hindu weddings in Egypt, contact the Consular Wing of the Indian Embassy in Cairo (20-2-392-5162). The Six-Day War in 1967 resulted in the expulsion of most Jews from Egypt. Today, Cairo has Egypt's only functioning synagogue, Shaarey HaShamayim (20-2-749-025), maintained by the Israeli diplomatic staff.

DESIGN IDEAS

Looking for the perfect way to set the tone for your Egyptian wedding? There's nothing more appropriate—and more beautiful—than invitations printed on a scroll of papyrus paper. Welcome your guests to Egypt with spices, rich Egyptian coffee, and hand-blown perfume bottles—all stashed in an alabaster bowl or a wooden box decorated with mother-of-pearl inlay. (You can find many of these items on www.bazaarontheweb.com and www.egypt7000.com.) Because Egypt is rich in gold, copper, and gems such as peridot, emeralds, and turquoise, it is easy to create a dazzling wedding celebration. On this note, you might also present each of your guests with a gold cartouche, an ancient pendant worn by Egyptian pharaohs or kings as a symbol of long life and good fortune. When considering your wedding décor, feel free to embrace the exotic. Dress up your wedding site with rich tones of gold and ruby, fine Egyptian cotton linens covered with elegantly embroidered *mashrabiya* (www.mashrabiya.com), copper or brass chargers, ceramic dishes, hand-blown lanterns, and water-filled glass bowls with floating blue water lilies. For a Bedouin theme, furnish the space with sumptuous Persian carpets, silk drapery, and plenty of pillows for guests to lounge upon. You could also incorporate columns, urns, Egyptian statuary, and even miniature pyramids.

Egyptian weddings are traditionally huge celebrations, usually preceded by a noisy parade of festooned cars. When the bride and groom arrive, they are received by a *zaffa*, a joyful parade of belly dancers, flaming swords, and drummers. Once they finally make it to the reception hall, the couple sits in the *kosha*, where they reign as king and queen of the festivities. The toast to the couple's health is given, and then the bride and groom switch their wedding bands from right to left index fingers, signaling the beginning of the party! For your celebration, tantalize your guests' tastebuds with the best of Egyptian fare, including the famous *kebabs*, grilled to perfection, as well as *shish tawook* (grilled chicken). In ancient Egypt, wines were produced from grapes, dates, palm, pomegranates, and other fruits. Because modern Egypt is primarily Muslim, alcoholic beverages are generally discouraged. However, most hotels will provide whatever you wish, and it may be fun to include something unusual such as pomegranate wine on the menu. Ancient hieroglyphics indicate that music has always been an important part of Egyptian celebrations, religious or secular. To hear a selection of contemporary Egyptian music, go to www.egyptiancastle.com and click on the "music" section.

PLANNING RESOURCES

EMBASSY AND GOVERNMENT OFFICES:
Embassy of the Arab Republic of Egypt (in the United States)
3521 International Court NW, Washington, DC 20008
www.egyptembassy.us
205-895-5400 / Consular Section: 205-966-6342 /
Consulate General (New York): 212-759-7120

Embassy of the United States (in Egypt)
8 Kamal El Din Salah Street, Garden City, Cairo, Egypt
Consular Section: 5 Latin America Street, Garden City, Cairo, Egypt
http://cairo.usembassy.gov
202-797-3300

Civil Marriage Registration Office, Office of Marriage of Foreigners
Ministry of Justice Annex, Fourth Floor, Lazoughly Square, Abdin, Cairo, Egypt
202-792-2263 / 202-792-2267

Translation Office, Ministry of Justice
Ministry of Justice Building, Thirteenth Floor, Lazoughly Square, Abdin, Cairo, Egypt
20-10-103-3754

Authentication Offices, Ministry of Foreign Affairs
Maspero, Cornish El Nile, Cairo, Egypt
202-574-6861

TOURISM:
Egyptian Tourist Authority
630 Fifth Avenue, Suite 2305, New York, NY 10111
www.egypttourism.org
212-332-2570

Sharm el Sheikh Tourism
67 El Makrizy Street, 11341 Heliopolis, Cairo, Egypt
www.sharmelsheikh.com
202-257-8514

PARKS, MONUMENTS, AND HISTORIC SITES:
Egyptian Environmental Affairs Agency
30 Misr Helwan El-Zyrae Road, Maadi, Cairo, Egypt
www.eeaa.gov.eg
202-525-6452

Supreme Council of Antiquities
14 Fakhry Abdel Nour Street, Abbassyria, Cairo, Egypt
202-685-9253

WEDDING RESOURCES:
HELPFUL WEB SITES:
The Egyptian Wedding: www.touregypt.net/featurestories/weddings.htm

VENUES

If couples come to Egypt having had a civil ceremony elsewhere, re-enactment ceremonies can be held anywhere, even at the Pyramids or at some of the temples. Be aware, however, that fees for these locations are very high. If you're looking for inspiration, contact **TRAVEL IN STYLE** (888-466-8242 / www.travelinstyle.com), a California-based company that caters to couples seeking unique wedding experiences in Egypt (and elsewhere). They can help organize a wedding cruise for you and your guests—a unique opportunity to see Egypt from the banks of the Nile—with everything from belly dancers to an Antony and Cleopatra costume party. Travel in Style can also plan weddings in the Luxor Temple, with waiters and staff dressed as pharaohs and high priests! Egypt has many lavish hotels and resorts, among them **THE FOUR SEASONS HOTEL CAIRO AT THE FIRST RESIDENCE** (202-573-1212 / www.fourseasons.com/cairofr). Located right by Cairo's Zoological and Botanical Gardens, this five-star hotel sits on the west bank of the Nile, affording guests wonderful views of the Great Pyramids. Divers will no doubt be lured to the famous diving destination of Sharm El-Sheikh, where **RED SEA DIVING SAFARI** (202-337-9942 / www.redsea-divingsafari.com) manages three ecolodges. Their oceanside Shagra Village lodge even gives die-hard divers the opportunity to marry underwater, with the assistance of the owner, a lawyer who helps with the legal documentation and witnesses the occasion. Sharm El-Sheikh is for golfers, too, with the **JOLIE VILLE MOEVEN-PICK GOLF AND RESORT** (20-69-360-3200 / www.moevenpick-hotels.com/ hotels/hksshyy). Managed by a Swiss company, this resort offers the area's only 18-hole PGA golf course. It also features 300 guest rooms, six oceanside villas with private pools, a large water-theme park, snorkeling, a dive center, and a fully equipped fitness center. You might also head to Aswan, where you'll find the historic **OLD CATARACT HOTEL** (20-97-231-6000 / www

.sofitel.com), the favorite hotel of the British elite during Egypt's British colonial period. This luxurious five-star gem is perched atop a granite ledge overlooking the Nile and Elephantine Island. Winston Churchill stayed here in celebration of the opening of the Aswan Dam, and Agatha Christie found inspiration here for *Death on the Nile*.

ABERCROMBIE & KENT LUXURY NILE CRUISES

1520 Kensington Road, Suite 212, Oak Brook, IL 60523

www.abercrombiekent.com

800-554-7016

SIZE: N/A **NUMBER OF ROOMS**: THE 36-PASSENGER *SUN BOAT III* HAS 15 SUPERIOR DOUBLES, 2 PRESIDENTIAL, AND 2 ROYAL SUITES; THE 80-PASSENGER *SUN BOAT IV* HAS 36 SUPERIOR DOUBLES, 2 PRESIDENTIAL, AND 2 ROYAL SUITES **WHEELCHAIR ACCESSIBLE:** LIMITED. ITINERARIES REQUIRE SOME MOBILITY TO ENJOY THE SHORE EXCURSIONS. ON SOME PROGRAMS, MODIFICATIONS CAN BE MADE TO ACCOMMODATE MANY DISABILITIES. SUN BOAT III HAS 8 WHEELCHAIR-ACCESSIBLE CABINS AND SUN BOAT IV HAS 10 WHEELCHAIR-ACCESSIBLE CABINS **RATES**: $$$

REVIEW: Abercrombie & Kent's cruise ships stand apart from the many other ships that tour the Nile. That's because they are, according to the magazine *Opinionated Traveler*, "Cadillacs of the waterways, offering cleanliness, comfort, and excellent food and service." Abercrombie & Kent was founded as a safari company in Kenya in 1962, but now offers travel and tour operations in more than 100 countries. These Nile cruises are some of the few that also offer visits to King Tut's tomb and the mummy room at Cairo's Egyptian Museum. For a small group of up to 36 guests, a 14-day "Pharoahs and Pyramids" cruise aboard the *Sun Boat III* allows visits to also explore Luxor, the Temple of Karnak, the Valley of the Kings, and Aswan. For a larger party, the wedding could begin at the Four Seasons Hotel in Cairo, then follow with a 12-day journey that includes a five-day Nile cruise on the larger *Sun Boat IV*. A shorter itinerary upon the same yacht is available with the "Highlights of Egypt" cruise. A personal Egyptologist accompanies you on each of these three options. The luxurious cabins on both boats face outside, with two large picture windows, full en-suite bathrooms, air conditioning, a mini-bar, and full amenities.

CEREMONY AND RECEPTION OPTIONS: The Abercrombie & Kent Cruise Lines offers small wedding parties that begin at the Four Seasons in Cairo. The wedding takes place on two beautiful *feluccas* (traditional Nile sailing boats). A meal can be served on board by costumed staff, and arrangements can be made for the couple to be showered with flowers by flower girls and serenaded by a local wind instrument band. If you are interested, they can also arrange for a maazoun to perform a Muslim service. After enjoying your A & K Nile cruise, your final night(s) is spent in Sharm El Sheikh's Four Seasons, considered one of the best resorts in the Middle East.

WEDDING SERVICES: Full service.

MENA HOUSE OBEROI

Pyramids' Road, Giza, Cairo, Egypt

www.oberoimenahouse.com

202-383-3222

SIZE: 40 ACRES **NUMBER OF ROOMS:** 486 **WHEELCHAIR ACCESSIBLE:** CURRENTLY IN THE PROCESS OF COMPLETING SEVERAL WHEELCHAIR-ACCESSIBLE ROOMS **RATES:** $$–$$$ **SPECIAL NOTES:** BABYSITTING, CHILDREN'S MENUS, AND CHILDREN'S OUTDOOR PLAY STATIONS ARE AVAILABLE

REVIEW: Mena House Oberoi was built in 1869 as a palace. Today it is one of the most famous hotels in Egypt, recognized for its excellence by *Condé Nast Traveler*, *Travel + Leisure*, and others. The hotel's exquisite interior is traditional in style, complete with carved paneling, murals, gilding, mother-of-pearl inlay, handcrafted mosaics,

© EMBRATUR

and original art and antiques, and its exterior is replete with minarets, domes, and towers. Surrounded by 40 acres of gardens, Mena House stands amidst palms, jasmine, and bougainvillea. A more romantic destination would be difficult to find! All 13 suites, 21 palace rooms, and 140 garden rooms offer views of the Pyramids. Guests have access to an 18-hole golf course, tennis courts, a fitness center, swimming pools, and horseback and camel riding.

CEREMONY AND RECEPTION OPTIONS: For a wedding with a unique touch, you could plan your celebration around one of the hotel's theme evenings. Consider "Bedouin Night," which features a camel trek to a desert encampment under the Pyramids, dinner and dancing included. Receptions for up to 520 guests can take place in one of the hotel's five banquet rooms.

WEDDING SERVICES: Full service.

South Africa, which recently celebrated its tenth anniversary as a democracy, invites visitors to share its spirit of harmony and optimism. The greatest challenge in planning a wedding in South Africa may be choosing which venue most appeals to your sense of romance and adventure. Couples can choose from big-game safaris, rustic mountain huts, overnight caves, UNESCO World Heritage Sites, national parks, ecotourism retreats, beautiful beaches on the capes, and villas in the wine district near Cape Town. Temperatures are generally pleasant, but the best time to visit depends on what you plan to do. Whale watching is popular mid-June to December, game watching runs from August to October, and diving and surfing is marvelous from April to September.

COUNTRY OVERVIEW

CURRENCY: RAND **TIPPING:** TIPPING IS CUSTOMARY. TIP TAXI DRIVERS 10% AND RESTAURANT STAFF 10–15%. **ELECTRICITY:** 220/230V **INTERNATIONAL CALLING CODE:** 27

PLANNING NOTES

SUGGESTED ASSISTANCE: Some assistance may be needed. While it is quite easy to be married in South Africa, it is recommended that you hire your officiant as soon as possible so that she can assist you through the process.

SPECIAL REQUIREMENTS: WAITING PERIOD: None; be aware, however, that it takes six months to process the wedding certificate once the wedding has been performed. RESIDENCY REQUIREMENT: None.

CIVIL CEREMONIES: Civil ceremonies are not required but are accepted as legal if performed by an authorized marriage officer. They can take place anywhere.

RELIGIOUS CEREMONIES: Christianity is the major religion in South Africa, but mosques and synagogues are easily found in most major cities. Buddhism is growing in South Africa, where the the Nan Hua Temple in KwaZulu-Natal—the largest Buddhist temple in the southern hemisphere—was completed in 2003.

DESIGN IDEAS

To welcome your guests, fill baskets with wooden carvings, beaded dolls, African masks, and traditional specialties, such as *biltong* (a type of jerky) and *droewors* (dried sausage). As one of the world's leading producers of diamonds, gold, and platinum, South Africa is an ideal place to find wedding jewelry. And, for decorations, think flowers. South Africa is home to over ten percent of the world's flowering species! For your ceremony, you might take inspiration from a beautiful South African wedding tradition, in which the parents of the bride and groom take a flame from their own fireplaces, then gather in the home of their children to begin a new fire. Treat your guests to South African steak (rump, sirloin, or prime rib) or fish, such as kingklip, hake, or kebeljou. And don't forget to serve South Africa's famous local wines from Nederburg, Tassenberg, Meerlust, and Douglas Green. For wedding music, consider *isicathamiya,* the traditional music of South Africa made famous by Paul Simon's *Graceland* album. This music originated in the South African work mines, where "tip-toe guys" sung and quietly danced to the music (so as not to awaken security guards) until the wee hours on Sunday mornings.

PLANNING RESOURCES

EMBASSY AND GOVERNMENT OFFICES:
Embassy of the Republic of South Africa (in the United States)
3051 Massachusetts Avenue NW, Washington, DC 20008
www.saembassy.org
202-232-4400 / Consulate General: (New York) 212-213-4880

Embassy of the United States (in South Africa)
P.O. Box 9536, Pretoria 0001, 877 Pretorius Street, Pretoria, South Africa
http://pretoria.usembassy.gov
27-12-431-4000 / Consulate General: (Johannesburg) 27-11-644-8160 / (Cape Town) 27-21-421-4280

South African Department of Home Affairs
Private Bag X114, Pretoria 0001, South Africa
www.home-affairs.gov.za
for marriage-related information: www.southafrica-newyork.net/homeaffairs/index.htm
27-12-810-8911

TOURISM:
South Africa Tourism
Bojanala House, 90 Protea Road, Chislehurston, Johannesburg 2146, South Africa
Mailing Address: Private Bag X10012, Sandton 2146, South Africa
www.southafrica.net
(United States) 800-593-1318 / (South Africa) 27-11-895-3000

PARKS, MONUMENTS, AND HISTORIC SITES:
South African National Parks
P. O. Box 787, Pretoria 0001, South Africa
www.sanparks.org
27-12-428-9111

VENUES

Intrigued by the idea of waking each morning to the bellowing of elephants? Then consider **GORAH ELEPHANT CAMP** (27-44-532-7818 / www.gorah.com). Situated in the Addo Elephant Camp, the Gorah House is a nineteenth-century colonial lodge restored into a luxurious hotel. To wed in beautiful Kruger National Park, contact **THE SABI SABI LODGES** (27-11-483-3939 / www.sabisabi.com), who have three venues: Selati Camp, whose thatch-roofed bungalows convey colonial elegance, the Bush Lodge, whose aesthetic is more contemporary, and the Earth Lodge, whose design reflects the environment. For your wedding, Sabi Sabi can organize traditional Shangaan dancing, bush barbecues, and assistance with officiants and wedding licenses. In Cape Town, check out the elegant **MOUNT NELSON HOTEL** (27-21-483- 1000 / www.mountnelsonhotel.orient-express.com). Built in 1924, the hotel, known as the "Nellie," is nestled below the Table Mountain on nine lush acres of gardens. Guests enjoy high tea, local beaches, wineries, and the scenic fishing village of Hout Bay. **THE BIRKENHEAD HOUSE** (27-15-793-0150 / www.birkenhead house.com), 75 miles from Cape Town, is a modern cliffside beachhouse that made *Condé Nast Traveler's* Hot List the minute it opened in 2003. Every room affords spectacular ocean vistas, which sometimes include views of breaching whales. Adventurous couples can arrange scuba diving, sea-kayaking, deep-sea fishing, and for the fearless, shark diving in steel cages. Those with calmer passions can tour local wineries, Birkenhead Brewery, and the Grootbas Private Nature Preserve.

EKLAND SAFARIS
P.O. Box 3187, Louis Trichardt 0920, South Africa
www.eklandsafaris.com
27-15-517-7062

SIZE: 37,065 ACRES **NUMBER OF ROOMS:** 14 ROOMS (8 DOUBLES, 6 SUITES) **WHEELCHAIR ACCESSIBLE:** NO **RATES:** $$$ **SPECIAL NOTES:** CHILDREN UNDER 3 STAY FREE WITH PARENTS (50% OFF FOR CHILDREN AGES 3–12)

REVIEW: This venue, located near Kruger National Park, makes it possible to experience pure luxury in the heart of the untamed African bushveld. Ekland, a member of the Small Luxury Hotels of the World, provides unparalleled service and accommodations. The lodges' primitive exteriors shelter magnificent living quarters, immersing guests in the magic of Africa. The suites, which all have two bedrooms, come with a full bath, living room, small kitchenette and mini-bar, fireplace, veranda, and full amenities. Guests can experience big game drives in ATVs, guided treks on foot, and treetop walks in the nearby forest canopies.

CEREMONY AND RECEPTION OPTIONS: Ceremonies can take place on the grounds or in the main lodge, which can accommodate up to 100 guests. For larger wedding parties, tents can be set up outdoors. There is only a site fee if you use an off-site caterer.

WEDDING SERVICES: Provides some assistance.

© EKLAND SAFARIS

THE SAXON

36 Saxon Road, Sandhurst, Johannesburg, South Africa

www.thesaxon.com

27-11-292-6000

SIZE: 6 ACRES NUMBER OF ROOMS: 26 SUITES WHEELCHAIR ACCESSIBLE: YES (1 SUITE) RATES: $$$ SPECIAL NOTES: CHILDREN WELCOME; BABYSITTING SERVICES AVAILABLE

REVIEW: In 2001, 2002, and 2003, The Saxon Hotel was named Best Boutique Hotel by World Travel Awards. This bastion of African eloquence and sophistication is located in Johannesburg, the "City of Gold." Water is a main design element at The Saxon, reflected in the huge central swimming pool, koi ponds, heated lap pools with underwater music, saunas, and steam rooms. African art accents all the suites, which feature lattice-covered bay windows, large-screen televisions with surround-sound systems, and state-of-the-art Internet and business facilities. Four luxurious presidential suites have private elevators, a reception area, lounge, two bedrooms, a dining room, bar, and butler's kitchen. When hunger strikes, guests can indulge at the Saxon's dining room, which showcases an impressive wine list and the skills of world-class chefs. In their leisure time, guests can also enjoy Johannesburg's cultural offerings and visit nearby national parks and lion preserves.

CEREMONY AND RECEPTION OPTIONS: Couples may be married poolside near the hotel's huge reflecting pool. Indoor weddings for 50 guests are also possible in the elegantly appointed boardrooms. For dinner receptions, the Saxon offers highly flexible menu options, making provisions for any special dietary requirements.

WEDDING SERVICES: Full service. Local officiants can be procured for ceremonies.

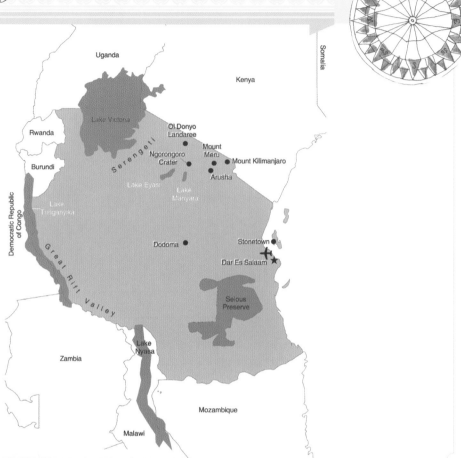

Couples who travel to Tanzania and its island state, Zanzibar, will discover friendly people, marvelous wildlife, and fascinating cultures. Tanzania is home to the Massai tribe and the Hadzabe Bushmen, and its Serengeti is the stomping grounds for some three million large mammals, including giraffe and zebra. Tanzania's Lake Tanganyika is the world's second-largest freshwater lake, Gombe Streams National Park shelters thousands of chimpanzees, Ngorongoro Crater serves as a Garden of Eden for East African wildlife, and Mount Kilimanjaro claims the highest peak in Africa. The country has two rainy seasons—the "long rains" (late March to June) and the "short rains" (November to January), and the best times to visit are December to March and June to October.

COUNTRY OVERVIEW

CURRENCY: TANZANIAN SHILLING **TIPPING:** TANZANIANS ARE TIP-HAPPY! RESTAURANTS ADD 10% TO YOUR BILL, BUT YOU SHOULD GIVE THEM AN ADDITIONAL 5%. A 15% TIP IS APPROPRIATE FOR ANY SERVICE PROVIDER. **ELECTRICITY:** 220V **INTERNATIONAL CALLING CODE:** 255

PLANNING NOTES

SUGGESTED ASSISTANCE: Assistance is a must. To avoid the complexities of the legal process, you may want to be legally married at home. Marriage laws are varied to accommodate the diverse needs of the population. Rules differ for various religions and regions; there are differing rules for Christian, Muslim, Hindu, and traditional African marriages, and though it is a state of Tanzania, Zanzibar has its own marriage laws. Should you decide to be legally married in Tanzania, begin the process at least three months in advance, as the laws are often unclear. It is also recommended to have a knowledgeable person act on your behalf through the process.

SPECIAL REQUIREMENTS: WAITING PERIOD: In both Zanzibar and mainland Tanzania, all required documentation must be submitted 21 days in advance. In Zanzibar, the couple must appear before the ceremony in order to verify all the documentation. In Tanzania, the 21-day waiting period can be waived by making a special application in person at the Registrar of Births and Deaths in Dar es Salaam. You can get the most up-to-date information by contacting the Consulate at the American Embassy in Tanzania. **RESIDENCY REQUIREMENT:** Two days

CIVIL CEREMONIES: On mainland Tanzania, civil ceremonies are optional. Special permission must be obtained to hold a marriage ceremony at a private place or residence. In Zanzibar, civil ceremonies are required and are held in town, followed by a symbolic or religious ceremony on location, if desired. For a civil ceremony on the mainland, couples usually apply for the license at the local District Registrar of Marriages; however, in some towns and in Zanzibar, they must apply at the Regional Commissioner's Office.

RELIGIOUS CEREMONIES: In a religious ceremony on the mainland, the religious officiant issues the marriage certificate. Therefore, if you are hoping to have a legal wedding in Tanzania, it may be easier to plan a religious ceremony. Choose an officiant early, and first be sure he can lead you through the process. There is no shortage of churches, mosques, and even Hindu temples in Tanzania. There is a Buddhist temple (255-22-215-0422 / www.geocities.com/pannasekara) in Dar es Salaam. Zanzibar and the smaller islands are predominantly Muslim, though Christian officiants are easily found. The country's Jewish community is very small, so Jewish couples hoping to marry in Tanzania should bring their own rabbi. Because Muslim fundamentalism has been on the rise since the 1990s, it is important to check the United States State Department's travel advisories before planning a wedding in Tanzania.

DESIGN IDEAS

In earlier times, a bride-to-be from Tanzania's Ngoni tribe would be presented with items for starting a new life with her husband. Capture the spirit of this tradition with symbolic welcome gifts for your guests—perhaps a handmade *lidengu* (basket), *mkele* (ceramic bowl), and *kipepeo* (fan). Other gift ideas include beeswax and honey (a major Tanzanian export), wood carvings, beaded Maasai jewelry, and colorful batiks. And, for a gift to yourselves, consider having your wedding bands made with tanzanite, a gem found only in Tanzania. Decorate your venue with Maasai beading, safari designs, or African violets, which are native to Tanzania. If you are lucky, your site will feature some of the country's loveliest trees, such as the flowering jacaranda, the leafy acacia, or the giant baobab. For your menu, consider local cuisine, typically flavored with curry and cardamom. *Nyama choma* (barbecued meat) is popular, as are traditional Swahili seafood dishes. Native music and dance are an integral part of Tanzanian culture. At nearly every wedding in Tanzania, you'll hear Patrick Balisidya's beloved song, *Harusi*. The lyrics of this song instruct newlyweds to be humble and generous, respect their parents, and teach their children manners. Traditional dance styles vary among the country's 120 tribes; the Makonde shake their hips, the Maasai leap high into the air, and the Sukuma twist and turn with live snakes.

PLANNING RESOURCES

EMBASSY AND GOVERNMENT OFFICES:
Embassy of Tanzania (in the United States)
2139 R Street NW, Washington, DC 20008
www.tanzaniaembassy-us.org
202-939-6125

Consulate of Tanzania (in the United States)
205 East Forty-second Street, Suite 1300, New York, NY 10017
212-972-9160

Embassy of the United States (in Tanzania)
P.O. Box 9123, 686 Old Bagamoyo Road, Msasani, Dar es Salaam, Tanzania
http://usembassy.state.gov/tanzania/
255-22-266-8001

Registrar of Marriages (in Dar es Salaam)
255-22-286-3045

Regional Commissioner's Office
Arusha: 255-27-250-2078
Zanzibar: 255-24-230-246/7

TOURISM:
The United Republic of Tanzania
www.tanzania.go.tz

Zanzibar Tourism
www.zanzibar-web.com

PARKS, MONUMENTS, AND HISTORIC SITES:
Tanzania National Parks
P.O. Box 3134, Arusha, Tanzania
255-27-250-8040

VENUES

Created to reflect the wild environs, Tanzania's luxury camps, safari lodges, beach resorts, colonial hotels, and eco-adventure venues have preserved the country's natural beauty. Couples seeking a safari experience will be interested in **THE MIGRATION CAMP SERENGETI** (www.serengetimigrationcamp.com) in the northern Serengeti, where visitors can count on close encounters with the "Big Five" (elephant, rhino, lion, leopard, and buffalo). There is a honeymoon tent, and the owners love to surprise newlyweds with a special bush dinner following a hard day of trekking. Consider an early-morning flight over the Serengeti in a hot air balloon with SERENGETI BALLOON SAFARIS (255-27-250-8578 / www.balloon safaris.com), followed by a traditional full breakfast in the bush à la *Out of Africa*, with china, linen, silver, and champagne!

CONSERVATION CORPORATION AFRICA (888-882-3742 / www.ccafrica.com) owns two of Tanzania's best luxury bush camp lodges. The 30 stone and thatched suites of NGORON-GORO CRATER LODGE (888-882-3742 / www.ngorongorocrater.com) sit on the rim of the crater, allowing guests a spectacular view. The staff is happy to facilitate romantic bush, safari, and African wedding banquets, using local choirs, drummers, and dancers. LAKE MANYARA TREE LODGE (888-882-3742 / www.lakemanyara.com), the only lodge in Lake Manyara National Park, offers ten stilted treehouse suites in the middle of a mahogany forest overlooking the Great Rift Valley. Another good resource for quality venues is SER-ENA HOTELS (www.serenahotels.com), who own a variety of unique hotels in mainland Tanzania and Zanzibar. THE SERENA MOUNTAIN VILLAGE (255-27-250-4158) in Arusha is set in the flower gardens of a coffee plantation farmhouse. Its makuti- thatched *rondavel* are appointed with Makonde art and wide-timbered decks overlooking Lake Duluti. NGORONGORO SERENA SAFARI LODGE (255-27-253-7050), built on the rim of the Ngoron-goro crater, offers traditional Maasai wedding ceremonies on the floor of the crater. The thatched *rondavel* and winding paths of the SERENGETI SERENA SAFARI LODGE (255-28-262-2612) stand among groves of indigenous trees, sparkling streams, and papyrus-fringed ponds. They, too, offer elegant, traditional safari wedding banquets in the bush. THE ZANZIBAR SERENA INN (255-24-223-3587) is housed in two historic, seafront build-ings overlooking the Indian Ocean. Reflecting an aesthetic typical of Zanzibar, the restored interiors fuse Arabian and East African influences.

SELOUS SAFARI COMPANY
P.O. Box 1193, Dar es Salaam, Tanzania

www.selous.com

255-22-213-4802

SIZE: OVER 22,000 SQUARE MILES NUMBER OF ROOMS: THE RAS KUTANI HAS 13 LARGE COTTAGES (EXECUTIVE COTTAGE HAS 2 BEDROOMS); THE SELOUS SAFARI CAMP HAS 12 RAISED TENTS. WHEEL-CHAIR ACCESSIBLE: NO RATES: $$

REVIEW: The Selous Safari Company, established in 1989, runs two properties, the Ras Kutani and the Selous Safari Camp. Together these properties are the perfect option for couples wanting to experience both the coast and the bush. Many couples marry at Ras Kutani and then honeymoon at the Selous Safari Camp. Located on the Indian Ocean, the Ras Kutani Beach Lodge is surrounded by lush tropical undergrowth, palm trees, and bougainvillea. The lodge's thatched cottages are appointed with Swahili furnishings, and each has its own deck overlooking either the lagoon or the ocean. Guest activities include boogie boarding, deep-sea fishing, snorkeling, kayak-ing, and guided treks to observe monkeys, baboons, and civet cats. The Selous Safari Camp, located on the Selous Preserve, once hosted His Royal Highness Prince Charles and Princes William and Harry. The 12 tents, each on its own raised plat-form, has a bedroom furnished with two single beds (convertible to a king), rush carpets, solar-powered lights, an en-suite bathroom, and an outdoor shower with privacy screen. The camp also has a *dungo* (open-air dining room) built on stilts overlooking the river. In addition to relaxing in the pool, dining on gourmet cuisine, and savoring excellent wines, guests will enjoy the thrill of seeing animals wandering freely through the camp—the hippos are so close, you can hear them eating at night!

CEREMONY AND RECEPTION OPTIONS: Commitment ceremonies and receptions can be held at Ras Kutani, on the beach adjacent to a freshwater lagoon—often with whales breaching in the background! Dinner receptions can be provided, but for a wedding party of 24 or more, the entire beach lodge would need to be rented. The cuisine is generally European with African influences.

WEDDING SERVICES: Provides some assistance.

THE PALMS

P.O. Box 1298, Zanzibar, Tanzania

www.palms-zanzibar.com

254-20-272-9394

SIZE: 5 ACRES **NUMBER OF ROOMS:** 6 LARGE PRIVATE VILLAS **WHEELCHAIR ACCESSIBLE:** YES RATES: $$–$$$ **SPECIAL NOTES:** MINIMUM AGE REQUIREMENT FOR GUESTS IS 16 YEARS OLD

REVIEW: This boutique hotel, situated on the southeastern coast of the island, includes six private palm-thatched villas with a bedroom, living room, en-suite bathroom, full amenities, *banda* (large furnished terrace) with a private Jacuzzi, and a traditional Zanzibari bed for lounging. Recently lauded in *Italian Architectural Digest*, The Palms' décor is a brilliant fusion of Zanzibari sophistication and colonial elegance. There is a wonderful pool and pool bar, evening bar, dining room, private beachfront *banda*, massage boutique, and Internet lounge. Guests can also take full advantage of the fitness center, the exclusive Frangipani Spa, water sports, and tennis courts at the nearby Breezes Beach Club (The Palms' parent resort) at no additional expense.

CEREMONY AND RECEPTION OPTIONS: The Palms can be rented in its entirety, making it a perfect venue for small weddings. There are two featured wedding packages, both of which require a minimum stay of three nights. The "Palms Escape" package focuses on the bride and groom, and includes procurement of an officiant, assistance with legal documentation, complimentary henna tattooing, massages, dolphin excursions, and discovery dives. The "Ultimate Dream Wedding" package includes exclusive private rental of the entire resort for your family and friends, and includes everything from the cocktail party the night before to the beach barbecue the following day. In both cases, the wedding ceremony is held under a beachside palm and bougainvillea canopy on the white sandy beach. This location is only available for those staying at The Palms, which can accommodate up to 17 guests.

WEDDING SERVICES: Full service.

BREEZES BEACH CLUB & SPA

P.O. Box 1361, Zanzibar, Tanzania

www.breezes-zanzibar.com

255-74-741-5049

SIZE: 20 ACRES **NUMBER OF ROOMS:** 20 SUITES, 40 DELUXE ROOMS, 10 STANDARD ROOMS **WHEEL-CHAIR ACCESSIBLE:** LIMITED **RATES:** $$–$$$ **SPECIAL NOTES:** CHILDREN WELCOME; SAFE GARDENS, A CHILDREN'S POOL AND MANY CHILDREN'S ACTIVITIES ARE AVAILABLE

REVIEW: The Breezes, a family-owned, beachside luxury resort, offers a European atmosphere. Each of the resort's ten "houses" have four deluxe rooms on the ground floor and two suites on the first floor; secluded bungalows house the standard rooms. All the rooms have recently been renovated, and the en-suite bathrooms are small but adequate. Guests enjoy windsurfing, pedal boats, snorkeling, and diving, with "Learn to Dive" courses available. There is also a crafts bazaar, a pool bar, a spa, a fully equipped fitness center, four restaurants, and live entertainment nightly.

CEREMONY AND RECEPTION OPTIONS: Three different wedding options are available, with special services available for each. A beachside "Renewal of Vows" (minimum three-night stay) includes a cocktail party followed by a gala wedding dinner in a private settings. The "Romantic Getaway" (minimum three-night stay) provides assistance with legal documentation, procuring an officiant, arranging the civil ceremony at the Registrar's Office, organizing the beachside nuptials and reception, and more! The "Classic" (minimum four-night stay) includes special entertainment the night before the wedding, a beachside barbecue the next day, and traditional henna painting for the couple before the service. The Breezes can also provide special wedding "extras," including welcome gifts for the guests, snorkeling safaris, discovery dives, and live entertainment. The Breezes can accommodate wedding parties of 30 to 40.

WEDDING SERVICES: Full service.

© EMBRATUR

asia

Some couples see destination weddings as the opportunity to diverge from the conventional ceremony/reception routine. If this describes you and your beloved, consider Asia, a continent that boasts beauty and variety. For many Westerners, Asian-themed weddings are becoming very popular. Why not go a step further and have an unforgettably unique wedding *in* Asia? Some Asian weddings embrace simplicity, with a design aesthetic based on elegant minimalism. Others are high-spirited royal affairs, with dramatic ceremonies and electrifying celebrations. In many traditional Chinese weddings, the bride wears an exotic red and black *cheongsam;* in Japan, the bride dresses in a white kimono; and in India, the bride adorns her body with jewels and her skin with red henna designs. This section discusses your options in Indonesia, Thailand, and India, but these three countries represent only a smattering of what Asia has to offer. To investigate other popular destinations in Asia, such as Singapore, Taiwan, Hong Kong, Tokyo, and Malaysia, contact the Pacific Asia Travel Association (www.pata.org).

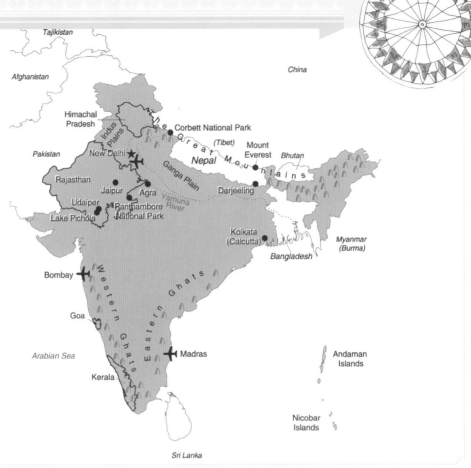

A land of ancient tradition and exotic beauty, India conjures up images of snake charmers, silk saris, and sumptuous palaces. What could be more romantic than India's most famous palace, the Taj Mahal, an enduring testimony to the love of Emperor Shahjahan for his wife, Mumtaz Mahal? While in India, couples can visit one of the 25 national preserves protecting the Royal Bengal tiger, India's national animal. They can also explore the Himalaya mountains, relax on palm-fringed beaches, rejuvenate at an Ayurvedic spa, share a cup of chai in a marketplace, and ride a tinsel-covered Tata truck over bumpy byways. The best time to visit India depends on your particular destination, but, in general, October to March provides the most pleasant conditions.

COUNTRY OVERVIEW

CURRENCY: RUPEE **TIPPING:** LEAVE 10% IF A SERVICE CHARGE HAS NOT ALREADY BEEN ADDED TO THE BILL **ELECTRICITY:** 220V **INTERNATIONAL CALLING CODE:** 91

PLANNING NOTES

SUGGESTED ASSISTANCE: India's marriage laws are very complicated and depend on religion. For this reason, the civil marriage should be done in your home country.

SPECIAL REQUIREMENTS: WAITING PERIOD: 30 days **RESIDENCY REQUIREMENT:** 30 days

CIVIL CEREMONIES: Due to the complexity of the marriage laws, I do not recommend a foreign couple attempt to be legally married in India. That said, civil marriages can be held anywhere and are only required if the couple is of different faiths. If the bride and groom share the same religion, they are not obliged to have a civil ceremony, as their religious leader can register the marriage.

RELIGIOUS CEREMONIES: Hindus, Buddhists, Muslims, and Christians coexist in India. Indians are predominantly Hindu; for a list of India's Hindu temples, visit www.mandir net.org/temples_list. Mosques are listed on www.indiantravelportal.com/mosques; synagogues on www.kosherdelight.com/india.htm; and Buddhists temples on www.buddhanet.net/asia_dir/abc_i.htm. To locate resources for other faiths in India, including Christianity, couples should contact their local denominational headquarters.

DESIGN IDEAS

India is a treasure trove for unique welcome gifts, such as leather or embroidered *mojaris* or *juttees* (sandals), traditional *phad* paintings, *katpulis* (string marionettes), and clothing made from block-printed cottons. Marriage is the most important social ritual for any family in India, so weddings are gala events held over several days. Brides bedeck themselves with body jewelry and wear richly colored saris of gold-embroidered silk. Muslim brides traditionally have intricate designs painted on their hands and feet with henna; today, Indian women of all faiths have this done the night before their wedding. In traditional Hindu weddings, families gather at the bride's home for singing, dancing, and eating. The groom, carrying a sword, arrives on horseback, and the bride is carried on a platform to meet her groom beneath a floral canopy, where the ceremony takes place. The couple exchange floral garlands and vows, then circle a symbolic flame seven times. (For more details on wedding traditions in India, visit www.go4marriage.com.) Indian weddings feasts are as delicious as they are varied; you might enjoy a fish fry at a Bengali wedding, *biryani* (a mixture of meat, rice, nuts, and spices) at a Muslim celebration, and *meethi daal* (soup) at a Gujarati reception.

PLANNING RESOURCES

EMBASSY AND GOVERNMENT OFFICES:
Embassy of India (in the United States)
2107 Massachusetts Avenue NW, Washington, DC 20008
www.indianembassy.org
202-939-7000

Consulate General of India (in the United States)
3 East Sixty-fourth Street, New York, NY 10021
www.indiacgny.org *(applications available on Web site)*
212-774-0600

Embassy of the United States (in India)
Shantipath, Chanakyapuri, New Delhi 110021, India
http://newdelhi.usembassy.gov/
for information on marriage laws: http://usembassy.state.gov/posts/in1/wwwhacsirr.html
91-112-419-8000

TOURISM:
Government of India Tourist Office
1270 Avenue of the Americas, Suite 1808, New York, NY 10020
www.tourindia.com
800-464-6342 / 212-586-4901

PARKS, MONUMENTS, AND HISTORIC SITES:
National Parks in India
www.indianwildlifeportal.com/national-parks/

VENUES

To explore a vast range of hotel venues across India, look into **OBEROI HOTELS** (www
.oberoihotels.com) and **TAJ HOTELS** (www.tajhotels.com). The Himalayas will put you on
top of the world, especially if your venue of choice is **WILDFLOWER HALL** (91-177-264-
8585 / www.oberoihotels.com). This romantic hotel, recognized on *Condé Nast Traveler*'s
2002 Hot List, is perched atop a knoll overlooking snow-capped mountains, meadows, and
cedar forests. The luxurious ecolodge of **INFINITY RESORTS** (91-115-160-8508 /
www.tigercorbettindia.com) rests in the foothills of the Himalayas, close to Corbett
National Park, famous for its protected population of Bengal tigers, leopards, deer, and
birdlife. On the west coast of India, you'll find the popular beach destination of Goa. **THE
LEELA** (800-426-3135 / 91-832-287-1234 / www.theleela.com) is one of Goa's most inviting beachside resorts. A wedding at this resort includes Goan serenaders, folk music,
and fireworks. **TOUR INDIA** offers some unique wedding venues in the southern Kerala
region, such as **THE GREEN MAGIC TREEHOUSE AND NATURE RESORT** (91-471-233-0437
/ www.tourindiakerala.com). There you can spend your wedding night in a banyan tree,
towering 86 feet above the forest floor. Tour India can also organize a memorable excur-
sion through lagoons, locks, and lakes on a *kettuvallum*, an original rice boat made of
bamboo and woven coconut fiber. These amazing boats have single, double, and triple
rooms with sundecks, balconies, full baths, and equipped kitchens.

AMAN-I-KHÁS
Ranthambhore, Rajasthan, India
www.amanresorts.com
800-477-9180

SIZE: 8 ACRES **NUMBER OF ROOMS:** 10 TENTS (NOTE: ENTIRE SITE MUST BE RENTED FOR WED-
DINGS) **WHEELCHAIR ACCESSIBLE:** NO **RATES:** $$$

REVIEW: Aman-i-Khás is situated in the Aravalli Hills near ancient temple ruins just out-
side Ranthambhore National Park, where animals roam freely. Once the hunting
grounds of the Maharajah of Jaipur, it is today a wildlife sanctuary for leopards and
endangered tigers. Don't let the prospect of tent accommodations scare you—they
are nothing short of astounding. Every October, tents are set up on a concrete foun-

dation, each with air conditioning, a living area, bedroom, dressing area, and a bathroom compete with a shower and a soaking tub. Days are filled with spotting wildlife, soaking in the newly added pool, enjoying Ayurvedic oil massages, or reading in the library tent. In the evenings, there are fine Indian meals and roaring campfires.

CEREMONY AND RECEPTION OPTIONS: Aman-i-Khás can arrange spiritual or religious ceremonies (blessings) and receptions for up to 20 guests. Weddings take place by the central campfire area, under the stars. The couple can arrive by camel to an opulent setting, complete with Indian rugs, candles, flowers, and live traditional music.

WEDDING SERVICES: Provides some assistance.

TAJ LAKE PALACE
P.O. Box No. 5, Pichola Lake,
Udaipur 313 001, India
www.tajhotels.com
91-294-252-8800

SIZE: OCCUPIES AN ENTIRE ISLAND IN THE MIDDLE OF PICHOLA LAKE **NUMBER OF ROOMS:** 66 ROOMS; 19 SUITES **RATES:** $$–$$$

© PHOTO BY ISABELLE BOSQUET

REVIEW: Imagine boarding your own personal water taxi, to be whisked across Lake Pichola to a 250-year-old marble castle that seemingly floats on water. Welcome to nirvana—also known as Taj Lake Palace. Epitomizing luxury and romance, Taj Lake Palace is a member of the Small Leading Hotels of the World. The suites have ornate glass windows, bohemian crystal lights, and original paintings, and the recently renovated guest rooms feature murals, marble baths, and Rahasthani furniture. From the rooms and suites, guests enjoy a vista of the lake, fountain pavilions, hilltop fortresses, temples, and medieval gardens. There are plenty of activities to keep guests busy, including camel and horseback rides, heritage treks, *shikara* boat rides on the lake, drives in vintage Cadillacs, and cultural performances.

CEREMONY AND RECEPTION OPTIONS: You can begin your wedding at the Taj Lake Palace with an elephant procession, followed by a gourmet reception featuring Udaipur specialties, then finish with fireworks over the lake. There are banquet facilities for up to 55 guests on the palace terraces, with breathtaking views of both the castle and the lake. Small wedding parties of ten guests can be held in the Neel Kamal restaurant, where some of the recipes have been passed down from the kitchens of the original Maharana! Cocktails and dinner can also be held in the Lily Pond Courtyard or on the royal barge, a 50-year-old Ganguar boat.

WEDDING SERVICES: Full service. Taj Lake Palace will help locate an officiant and provide a translator for the event.

Indonesia

Indonesia is the world's largest archipelago, comprised of more than 17,000 islands. No two places in this country are alike, and with more than 300 ethnic groups and 500 dialects, "diverse" does not even begin to describe it. Bali, Java, Tengarra, and Sumatra are just some of the breathtaking destinations, offering surfing, scuba diving, and safari touring as well as traditional dancing, singing, and puppet performances. As the epicenter of the 2004 tsunami, northern and western Indonesia suffered extensive damage, while Bali and other areas survived unscathed. Tsunami damage notwithstanding, Indonesia is a superb wedding destination of natural beauty, kind people, fascinating wedding traditions, and a tropical climate with little temperature variation.

COUNTRY OVERVIEW

CURRENCY: INDONESIAN RUPIAH **TIPPING:** TIP GOOD SERVICE PROVIDERS 5–10%. GIVE AIRPORT PORTERS RP.2000–3000 PER BAG AND HELPFUL TAXI DRIVERS RP.1000. **ELECTRICITY:** 220/250V IN LARGE CITIES (110V IS STILL USED IN SOME AREAS) **INTERNATIONAL CALLING CODE:** 62

PLANNING NOTES

SUGGESTED ASSISTANCE: Assistance is a must. It is possible to be legally married in Indonesia, but the country's laws, particularly those regarding religion, are complex. Unless you've hired professional assistance, I recommend having the religious ceremony there and taking care of the legal marriage at home. Even with help, you will need to have your documents in order at least eight weeks before the wedding.

SPECIAL REQUIREMENTS: WAITING PERIOD: There is a waiting period of ten days if you want to register with the Civil Registry Office. Verify this when you are planning, as this area seems to be a bit gray for tourists. **RESIDENCY REQUIREMENT:** None

CIVIL CEREMONIES: There is no such thing as a nonreligious civil marriage in Indonesia. Both civil and religious ceremonies are required unless the couple is Muslim. After the religious ceremony, the couple must register the marriage at the Kantor Catatan Sipil (Civil Registry Office). There is a Civil Registry Office in each district (*kabupaten*) in Indonesia, and foreign citizens must file with the Civil Registry Office in the regency where they are staying. If the couple is Muslim and is married by the Kantor Urusan Agama (Office of Religious Affairs), they are not obligated to register at the Civil Registry Office. To find out more details, go to www.baliguide.com/baliwedding.html.

RELIGIOUS CEREMONIES: Anyone may be married in Indonesia as long as they are members of a religion recognized by the Indonesian Government (Islam, Hinduism, Buddhism, or Christian Catholic/Protestant). This is not good news for Jewish couples or those of other beliefs, including agnostics or atheists. Additionally, couples must share the same religion in order for their wedding to be legal. Most Indonesians are Muslim, though Hinduism dominates the population of Bali. If the couple is Christian, Buddhist, or Hindu, they must hold the ceremony in a church or temple first, then register with the Kantor Catatan Sipil (Civil Registry). If one or both persons wish to convert to Islam and be married according to Islamic law, the marriage must be reported and registered with the Kantor Urusan Agama (Religious Affairs Office).

DESIGN IDEAS

Welcome guests to your Indonesian wedding with a wicker basket filled with local goods, including wood carvings, jewelry, pottery, masks, statues, or batiked textiles. To create a festive environment, decorate your wedding venue with woven garlands, floating floral arrangements, and candles wrapped in banana bark, and set your tables with bamboo plates and silk or batiked linens. Indonesian weddings are characterized by pageantry and great reverence for the bride and groom. The couple, dressed in dramatic costume attire, is treated like royalty. Indonesian cuisine is delicious, and it reflects the country's diverse culture. While every region has its own specialties, you can expect wonderful seafood, vegetables, poultry, and beef. There are plenty of spicy, hot dishes prepared with coconut milk and peanut sauces, and some of the world's best coffee and beer (as long as it is not an Islamic celebration). *Wayang kulit*, the art of storytelling with shadow puppets, is a common form of entertainment at wedding celebrations. You might also consider the mysterious, melodic sounds of a traditional Gamelan orchestra. These orchestras, which are unique to Indonesia, can have as many as 20 musicians.

PLANNING RESOURCES

EMBASSY AND GOVERNMENT OFFICES:
Embassy of the Republic of Indonesia (in the United States)
2020 Massachusetts Avenue NW, Washington, DC 20036
www.embassyofindonesia.org
202-775-5200

Embassy of the United States (in the Republic of Indonesia)
Jl. Merdeka Selatan 4-5, Jakarta 10110, Indonesia
http://jakarta.usembassy.gov/embassy.html
62-213-435-9000
for the Notice of Intention to Marry: United States Consular Agency
    (Surabaya) 62-31-568-2287 / (Bali) 62-361-233-605

TOURISM:
Tourism Indonesia
3457 Wilshire Boulevard, Suite 104, Los Angeles,
    CA 90010
www.tourismindonesia.com

VENUES

Among Indonesia's many options, Bali and Java are perhaps the most popular, with wedding venues that attract couples seeking both romance and adventure. There are five exquisite **TUGU HOTELS** (62-361-731-701 / www.tugu hotels.com) locations on Bali and Java, including Bali's Hotel Tugu, a Relais & Châteaux property with open-air balconies, sunken limestone baths, private plunge pools, and personal spa treatments. There, newlyweds can choose to spend their wedding night in a "floating" villa on a private lotus pond. **THE FOUR SEASONS** (800-819-5053) has a beautiful hotel in Jakarta, Java (www.four seasons.com/jakarta), which features several ballrooms, and two equally lovely resorts in Bali (www.fourseasons .com/bali), which boast traditional pavilions with private, outdoor baths. With its impressive marble-accented four-story atrium lobby and palatial staircase, **THE GRAND HYATT** (62-21-390-1234 / http://jakarta.grand.hyatt.com) in Jakarta is another appealing site for weddings. You can even plan a safari wedding on the east side of Java at **ROSAS ECOLODGE AND BALURAN NATIONAL PARK** (62-338-453-005 / www.rosasecolodgecom), located in a gorgeous region barely touched by tourism. There are plentry of unique options on the other islands, too. One worth mentioning is **THE BANYAN TREE** (62-770-693-100 / www.banyantree.com/ bintan/index.htm) on the lesser known but no less mystical island of Bintan. This picturesque resort, situated above a secluded bay dotted with ancient mangroves, offers full-service weddings.

THE OBEROI BALI

P.O. Box 3351, Denpasar 80033, Bali, Indonesia

www.oberoihotels.com

62-361-730-361

SIZE: 40 ACRES **NUMBER OF ROOMS:** 75 LANAIS AND VILLAS **WHEELCHAIR ACCESSIBLE:** YES, BUT LIMITED **RATES:** $$-$$$ **SPECIAL NOTES:** CRIBS AND BABYSITTING SERVICES AVAILABLE

REVIEW: The Oberoi Bali, one of the most exclusive resorts in Bali, topped the *Condé Nast Traveler* 2004 Gold List. The Oberoi chain is noted for impeccable service, and the Oberoi Bali is no exception. The resort is designed to look like a Balinese village, with 15 villas and 60 thatched lanais surrounded by tropical gardens and beaches. High coral walls enclose each villa and lanai, giving guests a sense of privacy. Accented with Balinese artifacts, the rooms have glass-walled bathrooms with sunken tubs that look out onto the gardens. The luxury villas have terraces, garden courtyards, and pavilions for private dining. Guests can take full advantage of the Oberoi's two restaurants, gym and health club, and extensive spa services.

CEREMONY OPTIONS: The Oberoi Bali can accommodate wedding ceremonies in the oceanfront lobby garden or on the lawn near the Frangipani Café.

RECEPTION OPTIONS: Receptions for up to 30 guests can be held in the Bale Banjar meeting room or poolside at a private villa. For added ambience, Obor Obor torches can be lit and the pool can be covered with tropical flowers and floating candles.

WEDDING SERVICES: For a fee, the Oberoi can procure an officiant and assist with the legal marriage certificate, provided you submit the documentation six weeks in advance.

AMANDARI

Kedewatan, Ubud, Bali, Indonesia

www.amanresorts.com

62-361-975-333

SIZE: 5 ACRES **NUMBER OF ROOMS:** 30 SUITES **WHEELCHAIR ACCESSIBLE:** YES **RATES:** $$$

REVIEW: Amandari, one of five Amanresorts in Indonesia, is located in central Bali on a slope overlooking the Ayung River Gorge. Amandari (meaning "peaceful island") is close to the city of Ubud, home to the colorful Pasar Seni market, and several villages that specialize in jewelry, woodcarving, and pottery. And, because the resort is integrated with the local village, villagers walk through the grounds on their way to the fields. River-stone walkways guide guests past gardens and shrines to their private, thatched-roofed suites, each with its own walled garden. Suites feature Javanese marble floors, carved teak furniture, and luxurious beds. One separate villa—perfect for a small party of guests—has five separate pavilions (one with a glass-walled living room), three bedrooms, a landscaped deck, and a double-tiered pool.

CEREMONY AND RECEPTION OPTIONS: Small weddings of up to ten people can be held beside a lotus pond, in a private dining room or villa, or in one of the special outdoor bales located by the pool. Ceremonies for up to 30 guests can be accommodated in a garden alcove, followed by a candlelit dinner by the pool, in a private villa or in the lush fields overlooking the valley and rice terraces. Another option is a fully inclusive event with ceremony, reception, and dinner, all staged at a nearby temple.

WEDDING SERVICE: Full service, including facilitation of marriage license.

Thailand

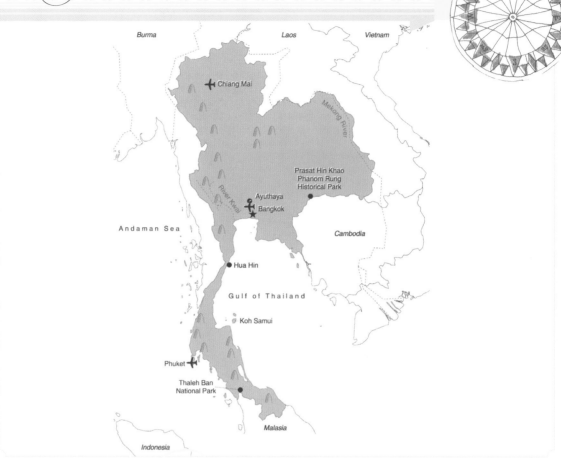

Why not "Thai" the knot in Thailand? The warm, gracious people of Thailand invite visitors to enjoy their ecotourism lodges, spa resorts, meditation centers, and national preserves—making the country truly "The Land of Smiles." From the canals of Bangkok to the colorful bazaars of Chiang Mai, there's always an exciting experience around the corner, like elephant safaris, kayak excursions, visits to *wats* (old temples) and sapphire mines, and more. The climate is tropical with three seasons—the summer (March to May), the wet season (June to September), and the cool season (October to February). The climate varies from region to region, so it may be best to determine where you'll be visiting first, then decide on which time of year to go.

COUNTRY OVERVIEW

CURRENCY: THAI BAHT **TIPPING:** TAXI DRIVERS DO NOT EXPECT A TIP BUT DO APPRECIATE 5 OR 10 BAHT. GIVE PORTERS 10–20 BAHT, AND TIP ANY SERVICE PROVIDER WHO IS ESPECIALLY HELPFUL 5–10%. **ELECTRICITY:** 220V AC **INTERNATIONAL CALLING CODE:** 66

PLANNING NOTES

SUGGESTED ASSISTANCE: Assistance is a must. To register for marriage, papers must be notarized and translated at your embassy, then certified at the Information Department. A lawyer or wedding coordinator is highly recommended to help you through this process. A lawyer can also help with the laws regarding prenuptial agreements.

SPECIAL REQUIREMENTS: WAITING PERIOD: There is no official waiting period. However, you should expect the paper processing to take at least three days before you can be married. **RESIDENCY REQUIREMENT:** None

CIVIL CEREMONIES: Civil ceremonies are required, and must be performed at the *Amphur* or *Khet* (Civil Registry Office).

RELIGIOUS CEREMONIES: Religious ceremonies, which follow the civil ceremony, can be held anywhere the officiant allows. Buddhism is the dominant religion in Thailand. Muslims form the country's largest religious minority, but Hindus, Sikhs, and Christians also have a presence. To find Jewish resources, visit www.jewishthailand.com.

DESIGN IDEAS

While you are waiting for your legal documents to be processed, hit the local bazaars (or visit www.chiangmaicraft.com) to find welcome gifts with local flavor, such as celadon pottery, silks, gemstones, and handmade wicker baskets to hold everything. Create a festive atmosphere with painted bamboo fans, paper parasols, lacquer vases, lotus-shaped floating lanterns, intricate garlands, origami, or flowers (some 15,000 species grow in Thailand, where floral arranging is considered an art).

At traditional Buddhist weddings in Thailand, couples go to the local *wat* (temple) to make an offering to the monks, who in turn bestow their blessings. During the ceremony, the monk pours holy water over the couple's hands and into a pot of flowers, then the guests are invited to do the same. At the reception, food is served on *kantokes*, a platter of several different items, as the guests sit on mats. You can't go wrong with traditional Thai dishes, which are seasoned with sauces made of curry, coconut, and peanut. Also consider serving seasonal fruits and gold-colored sweets, symbolizing sweetness and wealth for the couple. Entertainment could include sword and fire dancers and *kom loi*, large paper fire balloons that are released into the sky to "float away" bad luck.

PLANNING RESOURCES

EMBASSIES AND GOVERNMENT OFFICES:
Royal Thai Embassy (in the United States)
1024 Wisconsin Avenue NW, Washington, DC 20007
www.thaiembdc.org
202-944-3600

Embassy of the United States (in Thailand)
95 Wireless Road, Bangkok 10330, Thailand
http://bangkok.usembassy.gov/
66-2-205-4005 / Consulate: 66-2-205-4000

Khet Pathumwan Registration Office *(one of three in Bangkok)*
216/1 Chula 7, Kwang-Mai, Bangkok 10330, Thailand
66-2-214-3004

Information Department, Legalization Division, Ministry of Foreign Affairs
123 Changwattana Road, Thungsonghong, Laksi, Bangkok 10210, Thailand
66-2-575-1057

TOURISM:
Tourism Authority of Thailand
304 Park Avenue, Eighth Floor, New York, NY 10010
www.tourismthailand.org
212-219-7447

© THE ORIENTAL, BANGKOK

PARKS, MONUMENTS, AND HISTORIC SITES:
Royal Forest Department
61 Phaholyathin Ladyao Jatujak, Bangkok
 10900, Thailand
www.forest.go.th
66-2-561-4292 / National Parks: 66-2-579-4842

VENUES

The results of the tsunami that hit Thailand, particularly the Phuket Bay area, in December of 2004 were still being assessed as this book went to publication. The venues discussed here sustained little or no damage, and I encourage you to explore these and other possibilities in Thailand, as this beautiful country needs tourists' support more than ever.

 With mountains, waterfalls, and rivers, Thailand's rural north appeals to adventurous couples. Experience it from a hot air balloon with **ORIENTAL BALLOON FLIGHTS** (31-74-2761100 [Netherlands] / www.orientalballoon flights.com) or from an ultralight with **CHIANG MAI SKY ADVENTURE** (66-5-386-8460 / www.skyadventures.info). If you want a traditional Thai ceremony, contact the **FOUR SEASONS RESORT CHIANG MAI** (66-53-298-181 / www.fourseasons.com/chiang mai). The hotel hosts weddings for up to 100, complete with traditional dancers, Siam guitarists, and a morning blessing ceremony by local monks. With two months advance notice, they can also arrange your legal documentation. In the central region, you'll find the **RIVER KWAI FLOATEL** (66-2-542-6361 / www.riverkwaifloatel.com), a hotel on water. The "floatel" accommodates wedding parties of up to 200, offering guests the cruise of a lifetime that includes candlelit dinners, waterfalls, jungles, caves, and temples. The southern region, famed for its beaches and islands, has the rugged west Andaman coast and the calmer east gulf coast. **ROCKY RESORT** (66-7-741-8367 / www.rocky resort.com) is on the island of Koh Samui, Thailand's third largest island, where beach weddings are a specialty.

THE ORIENTAL, BANGKOK

48 Oriental Avenue, Bangkok 10500, Thailand

www.mandarinoriental.com

66-2-659-9000

SIZE: 3 CITY BLOCKS **NUMBER OF ROOMS:** 358 ROOMS; 35 SUITES **WHEELCHAIR ACCESSIBLE:** NO **RATES:** $$$ **SPECIAL NOTES:** CHILDREN ARE WELCOME; DAYCARE IS AVAILABLE

REVIEW: Located on the shores of Chao Phya River (River of the Kings) in the heart of Bangkok, The Oriental offers decadent weddings that blend European elegance and Asian beauty. Two modern additions offer spectacular views, but many visitors prefer the older, more romantic section, now called the "Author's Wing." (Noel Coward, Joseph Conrad, and Graham Greene were but a few of its literary visitors.) The rooms reflect a taste for grandeur, with teak furnishings, Thai silk, and parquet floors. The Oriental features a spa, a pool, cooking programs, and nine dining choices, ranging from Le Normandie's French cuisine to the China House's fine Cantonese dishes.

CEREMONY AND RECEPTION OPTIONS: From October to February, ceremonies are held in the gardens overlooking the river. The most elegant events take place in the magnificent Royal Ballroom. Seating 450, this ornate ballroom is decorated with hand-woven Thai silk panels and crystal chandeliers. The Author's Lounge and Regency Room, both located in the Old Wing, are equally elegant but smaller, seating 160.

WEDDING SERVICES: Full service. The Oriental will assist you with legal documentation and locating an officiant.

AMANPURI

Pansea Beach, Phuket 83000, Thailand

www.amanresorts.com

66-7-632-4333

SIZE: 14 ACRES **NUMBER OF ROOMS:** 40 PAVILIONS AND 30 VILLA HOMES WITH 2–6 BEDROOMS **WHEELCHAIR ACCESSIBLE:** NO **RATES:** $$$

REVIEW: Amanpuri, meaning "place of peace," is aptly named. Guests stay in pavilions and villa homes, whose peaked roofs ascend into the tropical foliage. There is an open-air lobby, a library with over 1,000 books, a freshwater pool, two restaurants, a beach terrace offering torch-lit barbecues, and Aman Spa, featuring treatments to nurture body and soul. Amanpuri also has the largest fleet of cruising vessels in Asia, from 20 to 110 feet in length! Guests can charter dinghies for beach picnics, or yachts for day, cocktail, dinner, sunset, or overnight cruises.

CEREMONY OPTIONS: Amanpuri can help arrange traditional Thai Buddhist, Catholic, or nondenominational ceremonies for up to 50 guests at the private villa homes. They are most often held by the pool, with the Andaman Sea in the background. The bride and groom also have the option of hiring the Amanpuri tailor, who can custom make your wedding attire with Thai flair, provided you arrive a few days early.

RECEPTION OPTIONS: Following the ceremony, guests are treated to canapés, cocktails, and traditional Thai music. Dinner can be set up around the private villa pool or in the air-conditioned living salas, with candles and tiki torches softly illuminating the space. A small stage, laid over part of the swimming pool, is perfect for toasts.

WEDDING SERVICES: Full service.

oceania

——— ✦ ———

For couples seeking an atmosphere of paradise with opportunities for adventure, Oceania is tempting indeed. Oceania, which includes Australia, New Zealand, the Fiji Islands, Papua New Guinea, and the islands of Polynesia, Melanesia, and Micronesia, claims wedding venues beyond compare. How do you choose which island is right for your celebration? Let your passions be your guide. No matter what your adventure of choice, from scuba diving to bungee jumping, you'll find a destination in Oceania to fulfill your dreams. Those interested in experiencing the islands' indigenous cultures can celebrate with a Maori *powhiri* in New Zealand or a *lovo* feast in Fiji. This section showcases wedding possibilities in Australia, New Zealand, and the Fiji Islands, but there's lots more to explore. Tahiti, Bora Bora, Samoa, and the Cook Islands are just a few of the other utopian options that promise the ultimate in excitement *and* relaxation.

The old adage calls for "something old, something new, something borrowed, something blue." Choose Australia as your destination, and you've got all your bases covered! For something old, visit Australia's aboriginal people—living evidence of the planet's oldest continuous culture. For something new, relax at one of the country's modern island resort spas. For something borrowed, adopt the Aussies' laid-back attitude. And for something blue, see the deep indigo of the Great Barrier Reef. Australia boasts culture, cuisine, and plenty of natural beauty, with snowcapped mountains, a rugged outback, and over 7,000 beaches. December through February is beach season, June through August is ski season, and the shoulder seasons are mild and comfortable.

COUNTRY OVERVIEW

CURRENCY: AUSTRALIAN DOLLAR **TIPPING:** LEAVING A TIP OF 10–15% IS BECOMING MORE COMMON IN AUSTRALIA, PARTICULARLY IN CITY RESTAURANTS. HOWEVER, SINCE THIS IS A FAIRLY NEW PRACTICE, YOU WILL NOT OFFEND IF YOU DO NOT TIP. TAXI DRIVERS ARE ALWAYS GRATEFUL IF YOU LEAVE THE CHANGE. **ELECTRICITY:** 230V **INTERNATIONAL CALLING CODE:** 61

PLANNING NOTES

SUGGESTED ASSISTANCE: Some assistance may be needed.

SPECIAL REQUIREMENTS: WAITING PERIOD: None **RESIDENCY REQUIREMENT:** None

CIVIL CEREMONIES: You can have a civil or a religious ceremony anywhere in Australia. To do so, you must complete a Notice of Intended Marriage Form, which can be downloaded from the Consular section of the Australian Embassy Web site (www.austemb.org/consular.html). Your officiant may be able to provide the form as well. The form must be signed before a local notary public in the United States and sent to your officiant within six months—and no later than one month and one day—prior to your wedding date. Both civil and religious officiants will help with all further legal documentation. Civil officiants are appointed by the federal attorney general's office (www.ag.gov.au). To find listings for both religious or civil officiants, visit www.i-do.com.au, then click on "Civil Marriage Celebrants and Chaplains."

RELIGIOUS CEREMONIES: Christianity is the most prominent religion in Australia, but there are also Buddhist, Hindu, Jewish, and Muslim communities. Unique to Australia are the Australian Aboriginal Traditional Religions. Note that a clergy person will only marry in a house of worship; if you wish to have your ceremony anywhere other than a house of worship, you will need to choose a civil officiant. For a listing of officially recognized religions and officiants in Australia, go to www.ag.gov.au, click on "Family Law," then on "Relationships," and look for the section on marriage.

DESIGN IDEAS

Let your guests buy their own boomerangs—welcome them instead with a basket filled with Australia's other specialties! A bottle of Southern Australia virgin olive oil, along with farmhouse cheeses and fruits, would complement a bottle of wine from one of the country's 1,000-plus wineries. And if you include a jar of Vegemite (the quintessential Australian breakfast food with the slogan, "It puts a rose in every cheek"), the bride won't be the only one blushing! You might also add a fine merino wool sweater, an Akubra hat, or a selection of the finest in botanical cosmetics. Indeed, Australia's clean air, water, and remarkable plant biodiversity have allowed companies such as Jurlique, Aesop, and Natio to create some of the world's best cosmetics—a sure crowd-pleaser for the ladies.

An aboriginal theme would make any wedding a uniquely Australian celebration. For décor, explore the possibilities of aboriginal art (www.aboriginalart.com.au), using anything from bark paintings and dot paintings to sculpture and jewelry. And for entertainment, consider hiring aboriginal musicians and dancers. You might request a few tunes on the didgeridoo, a long wooden flute believed to be the oldest musical instrument on Earth. Any Australian menu, be it inexpensive country fare or four-star modern fusion, is based on the freshest of basic ingredients: dairy, meats, seafood, and produce. Favorite dishes include green and king prawns, blue-eye fish, Tasmanian crayfish (lobster), and lamb roast.

© DAVID BECKSTEAD

PLANNING RESOURCES

EMBASSY AND GOVERNMENT OFFICES:
Embassy of Australia (in the United States)
1601 Massachusetts Avenue NW, Washington, DC 20036-2273
www.austemb.org
202-797-3000

Consulate General of Australia (in the United States)
150 East Forty-second Street, Thirth-fourth Floor, New York, NY 10017
www.australianyc.org/consulate/welcome.php
212-351-6500

Embassy of the United States (in Australia)
Moonah Place, Yarralumla ACT 2600, Australia
www.travel.state.gov
61-2-6214-5600

Federal Attorney General's Office
Robert Garran Offices, National Circuit, Barton, ACT, 2600, Australia
www.ag.gov.au
61-2-6250-6666

TOURISM:
Australian Tourism Commission
G.P.O. Box 2721, Level Four, 80 William Street, Woolloomooloo,
    NSW, 2011, Australia
www.australia.com
61-2-9360-1111

VENUES

Nuptials exchanged in the land "Down Under" can't be topped! For luxury, the **FOUR SEASONS HOTEL** (800-545-4000 / www.fourseasons.com/sydney) in downtown Sydney prides itself on pampering newlyweds, with a staff that tends to the smallest of details. **THE OBSERVATORY HOTEL** (61-2-9256-2222 / www.observatoryhotel.com.au), located near the city center and historic "Rocks" area, has been named one the world's most luxurious hotels by the Zagat Survey. **THE LILIANFELS BLUE MOUNTAINS** (61-2-4780-1200 / www.lilianfels.com.au), a picturesque romantic hideaway, is a five-star European-style country house perched high on a ledge overlooking the World Heritage Blue Mountains. And, recently renovated, **THE WINDSOR** (61-3-9633-6000 / www.oberoiwindsor.com) is a sophisticated grand Victorian hotel from 1883, known for hosting such celebrities as Lauren Bacall and Omar Sharif.

For those with a smaller budget, the **KEWARRA BEACH RESORT** (61-7-4057-6666 / www.kewarrabeachresort.com.au) is a modestly priced resort, cradled on 75 acres of tropical gardens, rock pools, and lagoons, overlooking the Great Barrier Reef. Located outside of Cairns, the resort is decorated with aboriginal art, paintings, and sculptures. **THE LIZARD ISLAND LODGE** (800-225-9849 / www.lizardisland.com) is an exclusive resort on a rugged 2,500-acre national park island. It offers scuba lessons, snorkeling, glass-bottomed boat trips, and beach weddings with receptions in the open-air restaurant. The lodge is part of **VOYAGES** (800-225-9849 / www.voyages.com), an Australian travel company that offers eight other resorts in some of the country's most spectacular locations.

Adventurers should check out the **EMMA GORGE RESORT** (61-8-9169-1777), a spic-and-span safari camp on the one-million-acre El Questro cattle station. Guests stay in tents with wooden floors and electric lights, eat at a rustic gourmet restaurant, and join in hikes, guided horseback rides, bird-watching tours, river cruises, and more. **PJ'S UNDER-GROUND B&B** (61-8-8091-6626 / www.babs.com.au/pj), located in the opal-mining town of White Cliff, features three underground rooms, accessed by a maze of spacious tunnels in the rock. Couples can marry at the bed and breakfast itself or in town, where there is a small, old stone church for just such an occasion. **THE PRAIRIE HOTEL** (61-8-8648-4606 / www.prairiehotel.com.au) is a remarkable tin-roofed, stone-walled outback pub in the Flinders Ranges. It offers you the opportunity to sample an outback feast, complete with emu egg frittata, kangaroo stir fry, camel sausage, mango chutney, and a "feral" mixed grill—only in Australia, mate!

TOWER LODGE

Halls Road, Pokolbin, New South Wales 2320, Australia

www.towerestate.com

61-2-4998-7022

SIZE: 70 ACRES **NUMBER OF ROOMS:** 12 SUITES **WHEELCHAIR ACCESSIBLE:** YES **RATES:** $$$
SPECIAL NOTES: THE LODGE DOES NOT CATER TO CHILDREN UNDER 16

REVIEW: Tucked away in Australia's Hunter Valley wine region, Tower Lodge forms part of a chic compound known as Tower Estate. The Estate also includes the Tower Winery, Robert's Restaurant, and Blaxland's Café-Restaurant. Eclectically decorated with artifacts from around the world, the distinctive lodge features furniture from a French château, Chinese tapestries, stained-glass windows, and even a 300-year-old Sri Lankan bed. The lodge's central area has a dining room, bar and lounge room, a library, and a fountain courtyard. Guests enjoy rooms with deep-soaking spa baths and separate showers as well as an impressive recreational facility, where they can take advantage of an 18-hole golf course, a 1.6km walking track, heated pool, sauna, gym, and massage treatment room.

CEREMONY OPTIONS: Tower Lodge is available on a sole occupancy basis for small, exquisite weddings. With sole occupancy, the wedding party has all of the lodge's ambience exclusively at its fingertips for the ceremony, the reception, and guest accommodations.There are many beautiful locations for a wedding ceremony on the estate, and an officiant can be arranged.

RECEPTION OPTIONS: When the couple reserves the lodge on a sole-occupancy basis, they can have anything from a cocktail reception in the courtyard to a five-course degustation menu in the dining room. When guest numbers exceed 24, a reception can be held at Robert's Restaurant or Blaxland's, each of which caters to 100 or more guests.

WEDDING SERVICES: Provides some assistance.

ANGSANA RESORT & SPA

1 Veivers Road, Palm Cove, Cairns, Queensland 4879, Australia

www.angsana.com

61-7-4055-3000

SIZE: 8 ACRES **NUMBER OF ROOMS:** 67 SUITES **WHEELCHAIR ACCESSIBLE:** YES **RATES:** $$–$$$
SPECIAL NOTES: BABYSITTING SERVICES AND CHILDREN'S VIDEOS AVAILABLE

REVIEW: Located on the shore of the Coral Sea in Australia's North Queensland area, Angsana is a haven for couples who seek ultimate relaxation. With its paradise-like atmosphere, the resort has won many awards over the years. Guests can unwind with wonderful massages and treatments, administered in special rooftop spa pavilions overlooking the sea and in air-conditioned spa suites. Shaded by palms and eucalyptus trees, the resort features an open-air design. Each suite has a view of either the ocean or one of the three saltwater ponds. In addition to water sports and swimming pools, Angsana offers fine beachside dining. For discerning guests who wish to take home the Angsana experience, there is a gift shop/gallery that sells specially blended essential oils, spa amenities, artwork, and furnishings.

CEREMONY AND RECEPTION OPTIONS: The Angsara offers a variety of ceremony and reception options, depending on the size of your party. The new multifunction venue, Chapel on the Beach, is used to perform nondenominational ceremonies during the day. It seats 40 for the ceremony and has standing room for 30 more guests. The chapel converts to Reflections restaurant, which caters evening receptions for 20 to 50 guests. Cocktail receptions for 80 to 100 guests are held on the grass area in front of the beach pool. In the case of inclement weather, guests can move into the Ulysses Lounge, which accommodates up to 40 for cocktails, or the Lobby Lounge, which seats 60 people. The beautiful Far Horizons restaurant can also cater functions of up to 50, offering a variety of delicious fixed menus. If you wish to have a smaller, more intimate dinner in the restaurant, an à la carte menu is also available. With a minimum of 80 guests, couples can secure exclusive use of Far Horizons. Angsara also offers a "marquee" wedding package. The party of 60 to 100 enjoys the ceremony in the beautiful chapel, followed by relaxing pre-dinner drinks on the beachfront. Once darkness falls, guests move to the marquee dinner venue, where a romantic dinner is served on a grassy area behind the Lobby Lounge.

WEDDING SERVICES: Full service. Officiants can be arranged.

THORNGROVE MANOR HOTEL

2 Glenside Lane, Stirling, Adelaide 5152,
South Australia
www.slh.com/australia/adelaide/
hotel_oveaus.html
61-8-8339-6748

SIZE: .75 ACRE **NUMBER OF ROOMS:** 5 SUITES **WHEELCHAIR ACCESSIBLE:** LIMITED (2 SUITES) **RATES:** $$$ **SPECIAL NOTES:** ROOMS FOR COUPLES WITH YOUNG CHILDREN LOCATED ON GROUND FLOOR; CHILDREN'S MENUS, TOYS AND BOOKS AVAILABLE.

REVIEW: The Thorngrove Manor, inspired by European architecture, is a vision of imagination with a genuine Australian twist. Often described as one of the world's most outstanding properties, the Manor has been decorated with several international awards. Its baroque turrets are as theatrical and romantic as the elegant interiors, which are richly decorated in gold leaf and antiques. On the hotel grounds, guests can explore the colorful European-style gardens. Or, for a little more peace and quiet, they can take the walking lane down to the sheep meadow and relax by the century-old holly and hawthorn bushes.

CEREMONY OPTIONS: The Thorngrove Manor only accommodates wedding guests residing at the Manor at the time of the wedding. Weddings can be held inside the manor or in the garden, or at one of the historic churches nearby. The staff will arrange for officiants and help facilitate legal procedures for the marriage license.

RECEPTION OPTIONS: Intimate receptions for small wedding parties (up to eight guests) range from elaborate wedding breakfasts held on the terrace to romantic evening receptions held in the formal dining room under the 24-carat gold-plated chandelier.

WEDDING SERVICES: Full service

The Fiji Islands

"*Bula*" (greetings) from Fiji, an ideal destination where the scenery is stunning, the native wedding customs are beautiful, and the marriage laws are relaxed. Of the country's 300 islands, only 100 are inhabited. Whether you're exploring Viti Levu, the Mamauca Islands, or the Yasawa Islands, you—like many adventurers, backpackers, snorkelers, and ecotourists—are sure to fall in love with Fiji. Below the crystal waters of the Fijian reefs, there's an exciting world of tropical fish, dolphins, manta rays, and underwater caves, and on land, there's a paradise of beaches, mountains, and tropical rainforests. Visit the islands March through November, as December to April can be rainy. Average year-round temperatures range from 77°F to 85°F (25°C to 29°C).

COUNTRY OVERVIEW

CURRENCY: FIJIAN DOLLAR **TIPPING:** TIPPING IS NOT REQUIRED ANYWHERE IN FIJI. HOWEVER, IF YOU WANT TO SHOW YOUR GRATITUDE TO SOMEONE, YOU CAN GIVE THEM A KILO OF KAVA (SEE DESIGN IDEAS) TO SHARE WITH THEIR FRIENDS—AND THEY ALWAYS APPRECIATE A SMILE AND A *"VINAKA"* ("THANK YOU") **ELECTRICITY:** 240V **INTERNATIONAL CALLING CODE:** 679

PLANNING NOTES

SUGGESTED ASSISTANCE: Little or no assistance needed.

SPECIAL REQUIREMENTS: **WAITING PERIOD:** None **RESIDENCY REQUIREMENT:** None; however, you need one working day to obtain the license. **SPECIAL NOTES:** The couple must apply for the marriage license in person at the Registry Office, bringing with them original copies of the necessary documents. The process takes about 15 minutes. The marriage license, which is ready by the next working day, is valid for 21 days. Once married, it will take 15 working days to obtain the marriage certificate; however, the certificate can be sent to you.

CIVIL CEREMONIES: You may have either a religious or a civil ceremony. If you opt for a civil ceremony and you want to have it at the Registrar General or the district office, make an appointment a day or two in advance. To be married at any other location, or to have the ceremony performed by a spiritual leader, you need special permits.

RELIGIOUS CEREMONIES: There is no official state religion in the Fiji Islands. Christianity (Methodist, Protestant, Catholic) is predominant, but a large minority of Fijans practice Hinduism and Islam. Nadi is home to Sri Siva Subramaniya, the largest Hindu temple in the southern hemisphere. Jewish couples can contact the Fiji Jewish Association (679-387-980); most Jewish residents live in Suva and attend services at the Israeli Embassy (679-303-420). For more about religion in Fiji, visit www.fiji-island.com/tourist-information/religion.html.

DESIGN IDEAS

The original inhabitants of Fiji are called *Lapita* people, after a distinctive type of pottery they produced 3,000 years ago. Today, you can buy similar pottery as well as fine weaving and woodcarvings in Fiji's colorful markets. These handmade items would make wonderful welcome gifts for your guests, as would a beach-themed basket, filled with suntan lotion, a snorkel, a beach towel, and a Pandanus hat.

In Fiji, the bride and groom wear flowers on their heads and around their necks, and garments made from *tapa* or *masi* cloth, which is hand-painted and made from finely-pounded mulberry bark. If wearing bark is not your bridal style, consider wearing a traditional *sulu*, a loose-fitting sarong (available on www.sarongs-online.com). In Fiji, traditional weddings often take place on the beach, beginning at sunset with the blowing of a conch shell. After the bride is ceremoniously chauffeured in on a *billy, billy* (raft), the ceremony commences with a rhythmic *meke* dance and chant. If you want your wedding to be uniquely Fijian, include a *kava* (or *yaqona*) ceremony, which is celebrated during all momentous occasions. Kava, a nonalcoholic yet tranquilizing drink made from a local pepper plant mixed with water, is served in a *bilo* (a half-coconut shell). The groom, and then the bride, are offered the drink, clap once, accept the bilo, and say *"bula"* (meaning "cheers," or literally, "life"). In the past, the groom then presented his new father-in-law with *tabua*, a large whale tooth that is today a valuable artifact. *Lovo*, the Fijian feast that follows, consists of seafood baked beneath sand lined with hot volcanic stones. Evening entertainment could be provided by Luli drums, a string band, or an a cappella village choir.

PLANNING RESOURCES

EMBASSY AND GOVERNMENT OFFICES:
Embassy of the Republic of Fiji Islands (in the United States)
2233 Wisconsin Avenue NW, Suite 240, Washington, DC 20007
www.fijiembassy.org
202-337-8320

Embassy of the United States (in the Fiji Islands)
31 Loftus Street, P.O. Box 218, Suva, Fiji
www.amembassy-fiji.gov
679-331-4466

Office of the Registrar-General
Registrar of Births, Deaths, and Marriages, Cohil Complex, Toorak Road,
    P.O. Box 2236, Government Buildings, Suvavou House, Victoria Parade, Fiji
679-331-5280

TOURISM:
Fiji Visitors Bureau
G.P.O. Box 92, Thomson Street, Suva, Fiji
www.bulafiji.com
800-932-3454 / 679-330-2433

PARKS, MONUMENTS, AND HISTORIC SITES:
The National Trust of Fiji *(administers six national parks in the Fiji Islands)*
P.O. Box 2089, 3 Maafu Street, Suva, Fiji
www.culture.gov.fj/statorg.htm
679-330-1807

VENUES

Fiji offers venue options for every taste and budget. You can have a simple ceremony (for $11!) at the civil registry office, or you can spend thousands at any of the country's many luxurious resorts. For a one-of-a-kind experience, you can book an entire island at the **TOBERUA ISLAND RESORT** (679-347-2777 / www.toberua.com), a very private venue that was one of Fiji's first boutique resorts. Weddings for no more than 30 are held on the beach, by the pool, in the gardens, or in a special wedding *bure*. (*Bures* are Fijian-style thatched bungalows popular in most resorts.) A traditional-tree planting ceremony follows each wedding, and a small carved sign bearing the couple's name is placed beneath the tree. **THE PEARL SOUTH PACIFIC** (679-345-0022 / www.raessouthpacific.com.fj) is a wonderful beachside resort that specializes in weddings—especially for the ecoadventurer who loves surfing, diving, golfing, and exploring culture. You can continue your ecoadventure in the same area with whitewater rafting and sea kayaking trips offered by **RIVERS FIJI** (800-446-2411 / www.riversfiji.com). Ecotourists are also lured to the island of Taveuni, home to Ravilevu Nature Preserve on the east coast and the Taveuni Forest Preserve in the center. **MARAVU PLANTATION RESORT** (888-345-4669 / www.maravu.com) is a five-star Taveuni Island resort that offers its guests a unique slice of native life, with Fijian storytelling, traditional Kava ceremonies, workshops on natural medicines, and Fijian cooking classes. (It also happens to be where the movie *Castaway* was filmed.) If you are a diver or snorkeling aficionado, consider Treasure Island, one of the Mamanuca

Islands, accessible by seaplane, catamaran, speedboat or helicopter. At **TREASURE ISLAND RESORT** (679-666-6999 / www.fiji-treasure.com), couples can be married on the beach or in the lovely, open-air chapel in traditional Fijian style.

Some couples choose to marry in Fiji, then skip over to French Polynesia for a honeymoon in Tahiti or Bora Bora. (Weddings in Tahiti are not legally recognized in the United States.) For the ultimate in romance, check into **HOTEL KIA ORA RANGIROA** (689-93-1117 / www.hotelkiaora.com), where you can sleep in one of several bungalows on stilts over the blue water—connected to each other by floating pontoon catwalks. Guests can enjoy all kinds of water sports, shark feeding, dolphin watches, and shopping at the market in Papeete. **THE BORA BORA LAGOON RESORT & SPA** (800-860-4095 / www.borabora lagoon.com) sits on its own small *motu* (island), Motu Toopua, in the middle of Bora Bora's spectacular crystal blue lagoon. The resort made *Condé Nast Traveler*'s The Worlds Best Place to Stay Gold List in both 2003 and 2004. Having recently undergone a four-million-dollar renovation, it boasts Polynesian-style bungalows with hardwood floors and beamed ceilings. The over-water bungalows have sun decks with glass-top coffee tables that open so you can feed the tropical fish below! Among other things, guests enjoy beach barbecues with traditional entertainment, a large freshwater swimming pool, a relaxing spa, canoeing and other sports, and private sunset or dinner cruises.

TURTLE ISLAND
Yasawa Islands, Fiji
www.turtlefiji.com
800-255-4347

SIZE: 500 ACRES **NUMBER OF ROOMS:** 14 BURES **WHEELCHAIR ACCESSIBLE:** THE ISLAND IS NOT HANDICAPPED ACCESSIBLE, NOR ARE ANY OF THE BURES. **RATES:** $$$ **SPECIAL NOTES:** SINCE TURTLE ISLAND FOCUSES ON ROMANCE, THEY ONLY ALLOW CHILDREN DURING 2 "FAMILY TIMES,"

© BORA BORA LAGOON RESORT & SPA

REVIEW: Turtle Island is not just a resort—it is an experience. Because the resort accommodates only 28 people, you and your guests can take over the entire 500-acre paradise. One of the sole truly all-inclusive resorts in Fiji, Turtle Island is a paragon of ecotourism, an unparalleled romantic hideaway and a second home to many celebrities. Among other honors, the resort has been named one of the top ten hotels in the entire Pacific Region by *Travel + Leisure*. The 14 bures are two-room, thatched cottages, with 21-foot vaulted ceilings, wood and terra-cotta floors, and a veranda overlooking the Blue Lagoon—yes, *that* Blue Lagoon (Turtle Island was the location for both *Blue Lagoon* movies). Each bure is assigned a manager (affectionately known as a "bure mama"), a personal concierge who tends to the guests' needs and wants. Guests are also given two-way radios to be used anywhere on the resort for requesting drinks or service of any kind. Staff will even wade into the lagoon to deliver your order! There's kayaking, sailing, and snorkeling adventures, private beach picnics, mountaintop dinners under the stars, and much more. With hydroponic gardens and a vast wine cellar, the Turtle's chef, Jacques Reymond, promises gourmet meals. Guests can also participate in the Turtle Conservation Program. In an effort to save sea turtles, Turtle Island buys captured turtles from fishermen and auctions them to the highest bidders, whose winning bid earns them the opportunity to paint a message on the turtle's shell—rendering its shell worthless to poachers. Now that is a special way to commemorate your wedding!

WEDDING AND RECEPTION OPTIONS: Turtle Island offers all the best of a traditional Fijian wedding. The ceremony can take place on the beach, followed by a large feast held indoors or out. Intimate beach weddings for two are common. On their wedding night, couples can even sleep under the stars in a primitive bure on a private beach.

WEDDING SERVICES: Full service.

VATULELE ISLAND RESORT
Vatulele Island, Fiji

www.vatulele.com

679-672-0300

SIZE: 12 SQUARE MILES **NUMBER OF ROOMS:** 19 BURES **WHEELCHAIR ACCESSIBLE:** NO **RATES:** $$$ **SPECIAL NOTES:** CHILDREN OVER 12 YEARS WELCOME (CHILDREN UNDER 12 ALLOWED ONLY DURING CERTAIN WEEKS; CONTACT RESORT FOR DETAILS)

REVIEW: Vatulele Island Resort was created as a haven for jet-setters and celebrities seeking repose in coral sands, a crystal-clear lagoon, and jungle setting. Guests stay in colorful, private bures or villas, each with its own stretch of beach, a living room, and a split-level sleeping area. Newlyweds often choose The Point or The Grande Bure, the more deluxe and private villas. Vatulele has won numerous awards, including a 2004 "Secluded Honeymoon" award by *Modern Bride*. For fun, guests visit island villages, explore inland caves, take jungle excursions, and enjoy the five-star scuba facility. In the evening, couples can dine with others under the stars on the terrace or at the water's edge—or have a romantic dinner for two on the beach.

CEREMONY AND RECEPTION OPTIONS: Because Vatulele only hosts three weddings a month, you can be certain each one is special. The resort arranges traditional Fijian wedding ceremonies and receptions for up to 40 guests. Ceremonies can be held on the beach, complete with floral arbors and arches. Note that there is only one minister and one choir for ceremonies. Open-air receptions are held on the terrace or on the beach.

WEDDING SERVICES: Full service. The staff will help procure a wedding officiant and facilitate the marriage license.

JEAN-MICHEL COUSTEAU FIJI ISLANDS RESORT

Private Mail Bag, Savusavu, Fiji

www.fijiresort.com

800-246-3454 / 679-885-0188

SIZE: 17 ACRES **NUMBER OF ROOMS:** 25 BURES **WHEELCHAIR ACCESSIBLE:** YES **RATES:** $$–$$$
SPECIAL NOTES: THE FIRST TWO CHILDREN AGE 12 AND UNDER IN ANY BURE STAY FREE. ANY ADDITIONAL CHILDREN ARE $75 PER NIGHT. ON SOME DATES, CHILDREN ARE RESTRICTED.

REVIEW: This five-star island resort, built on a former coconut plantation, features traditional thatched bures by the teal blue waters of Savusavu Bay. Each bure has a king-size bed, comfortable rattan furniture, louvered windows, oversized bathrooms, and a private deck with garden or ocean views. The more secluded Point Reef Bures are popular among newlyweds, as is the Honeymoon Point Reef Bure. The newest and most sought-after bure is the first of the Point Reef Villas—a large, beachfront villa with exquisite landscaping, a private pool, whirlpool tubs, and outdoor showers. Offering a full-time, on-staff marine biologist to educate guests, Jean-Michel Cousteau is

© BORA BORA LAGOON RESORT & SPA

the perfect resort for those who want to explore Fiji's underwater world. World-class diving, gourmet dining, a relaxing spa, and eco-friendly activities have made this a favorite wedding destination. The resort was awarded *Travel + Leisure*'s #1 Resort in Fiji in 2001 and *Condé Nast Johansens* Award for Excellence in 2005.

CEREMONY AND RECEPTION OPTIONS: The resort itself accommodates 60 to 70 guests; however, they can arrange for a traditional Fijian wedding for as many as 100 guests. If the wedding party takes over the entire property, the reception can be held in the open-air dining room. Romantic wedding dinners for two can be served on the beachfront pier or under one of the private dining bures on the beach.

WEDDING SERVICES: Full service.

Located in the South Pacific about 1,000 miles southeast of Australia, New Zealand consists of two main islands (the North and South Islands) and many smaller islands. New Zealand showcases the full glory of Mother Nature, with a landscape of mountain ranges, volcanic regions, glaciers, lakes, grassy plains, farmland, rainforests, and coasts. Adventuresome couples will be in their glory, as a destination wedding here is not to be observed but experienced. And if there is anything more enticing than the country's natural beauty, it is the casual warmth and good humor of New Zealanders, affectionately known as "Kiwis." The north of New Zealand is subtropical, and the south temperate, so be prepared for beautiful weather and mild to warm temperatures.

COUNTRY OVERVIEW

CURRENCY: NEW ZEALAND DOLLAR **TIPPING:** TIPPING IS UNUSUAL; HOWEVER, FOR EXCEPTIONAL SERVICE, LEAVE 5–10%. **ELECTRICITY:** 240V **INTERNATIONAL CALLING CODE:** 64

PLANNING NOTES

SUGGESTED ASSISTANCE: Little or no assistance needed.

SPECIAL REQUIREMENTS: **WAITING PERIOD:** Three days (You must apply for the license three days before the ceremony). **RESIDENCY REQUIREMENT:** None

CIVIL CEREMONIES: Civil marriages are not required, but you must be married by a registered marriage celebrant. A list of civil marriage celebrants can be found in the New Zealand yellow pages or online at www.celebrant.co.nz.

RELIGIOUS CEREMONIES: New Zealand's population enjoys religious diversity. Indigenous faith traditions are practiced side-by-side with Christianity (mostly Anglican, Catholic, and Presbyterian), Buddhism, Hinduism, Islam, and Judaism. For Jewish synagogues in New Zealand, check http://vital.org.nz/nzjews.html. For Buddhist temples, go to www.bodhinyanarama.net.nz and click on "Directory." To locate a Hindu temple, contact the Radha Krishna Temple (64-9-379-4463).

DESIGN IDEAS

New Zealand is well known for its sheepskin, leather, pottery, glass, and jewelry. If these options are too costly for welcome gifts, consider giving your guests a bottle of New Zealand's famous wine, or small items made of paua shell, such as coasters or pendants. You can find many gift ideas on www.maoritreasures.com. You might draw some inspiration from the indigenous Maori culture, whose wedding ceremonies begin with the welcome call, *Te Karanga*. After they are greeted with a song and dance known as *Te Powhiri*, the couple exchanges vows, sings the traditional Maori love song, *Pokarekare ana*, receives a blessing from the priest, then seals their love and friendship by touching noses. A traditional Maori feast follows, featuring ingredients such as pork, mutton, chicken, cabbage, and pumpkin, that have been baked in an underground hole lined with hot volcanic rock. More traditional New Zealand cuisine fuses Maori, Asian, Polynesian, and European influence. Choices range from country fare to nouvelle cuisine, with highlights including seafood, lamb, and venison. (To learn more about New Zealand cuisine and wines, visit www.cuisine.co.nz.) For dessert, consider serving pavlova (or *pav*, as Kiwis call it)—a meringue shell topped with fresh whipped cream and fruit. Complete the celebration with local entertainment, perhaps some Maori folk music and dance.

PLANNING RESOURCES

EMBASSY AND GOVERNMENT OFFICES:

Embassy of New Zealand (in the United States)
37 Observatory Circle NW, Washington, DC 20008
www.nzemb.org
202-328-4800

Embassy of the United States (in New Zealand)
P.O. Box 1190, Wellington, New Zealand
http://usembassy.org.nz
64-4-462-6000

General Registry Office: Births, Deaths, and Marriages
P.O. Box 10-526, Wellington, 47 Boulcott Street, Wellington, New Zealand
www.bdm.govt.nz
64-4-474-8150

TOURISM:
New Zealand Tourism
222 East Forty-first Street, Suite 2510, New York, NY 10017
www.newzealand.com/travel
866-639-9325 / 212-661-7088

PARKS, MONUMENTS, AND HISTORIC SITES:
Department of Conservation
www.doc.govt.nz
*(Check with the Visitor Center closest to your destination venue to seek
permission for a wedding ceremony.)*

WEDDING RESOURCES:
New Zealand Weddings and Wedding Services: www.nzweddingplanner.co.nz
NZ Wedding: www.nz-wedding.co.nz

© DAVID ELLIOT

VENUES

If you want to explore the very best of New Zealand's dramatic venues, be sure to check into the national parks (www.doc.govt.nz). **FIORDLAND NATIONAL PARK** (64-3-249-7924), a United Nations Heritage site, offers picturesque fiords, waterfalls, and wildlife; for accommodations there, contact **TE ANAU** (www.fiordland.org.nz). If you'd like to fly above the mountains by helicopter or land on a glacier in a ski plane, check out your options at **AORAKI MOUNT COOK NATIONAL PARK** (64-3-4351186). Near Mt. Cook, there is **THE CHURCH OF THE GOOD SHEPHERD** (64-3-685-8383), a magical church built on the shores of Lake Tekapo, and the **GODLEY RESORT HOTEL** (64-3-377-5700 / www.tekapo.co.nz), a lovely reception site. If you'd like to marry on a warm New Zealand beach, head north to **ABEL TASMAN NATIONAL PARK** (64-3-525-8026) or to the popular **HAWKE'S BAY REGION** (www.hawkes baynz.com) on the North Island. The North Island is home to Auckland, "The City of Sails," where you'll find **FLO-RENCE COURT MANOR** (64-9-623-9333 / www.florence court .co.nz), an opulent Edwardian mansion that offers the most elegant of weddings. Auckland also boasts **SORRENTO IN THE PARK** (64-9-625-1122 / www.sorrento .co.nz), an estate-like venue overlooking Manukau Harbour. The most unique wedding venue has to be **WHITE ISLAND VOLCANO** (64-25-273-4090 / www.wi.co.nz), an active volcano on a private island off the north coast of the North Island, accessible only by helicopter or boat. The island's spectacular scenery makes it an irresistible destination for many adventure-seeking couples.

EICHARDT'S PRIVATE HOTEL

Marine Parade, P.O. Box 1340, Queenstown, New Zealand

www.eichardtshotel.co.nz

64-3-441-0450

SIZE: 1 ACRE **NUMBER OF ROOMS:** 5 SUITES **WHEELCHAIR ACCESSIBLE:** LIMITED **RATES:** $$$

REVIEW: Eichardt's is an iconic landmark in the center of Queenstown, a former mining town that enjoys the reputation of "adventure sport capital of the world." Completely renovated by a leading New Zealand designer, Eichardt's proudly mixes its own historic charm with state-of-the-art amenities. Nestled in the "Remarkables" mountain range by Wakatipu Lake, the hotel boasts five sophisticated suites, each with a king-size bed, fireplace, dressing room, double bathroom, and lake or mountain views. Guests can choose how to relax—luxurious health and beauty treatments, jet boat rides from the hotel's pier, movies at the nearby theater, and more. Eichardt's, a member of the Small Luxury Hotels of the World, has been featured in many major travel guides and publications, such as *Vogue* and *Condé Nast Traveler*.

CEREMONY AND RECEPTION OPTIONS: Eichardt's hosts exclusive weddings and intimate receptions for up to ten guests, provided the entire hotel is reserved for the event. Wedding ceremonies are held in the hotel's Parlour Room, comfortably decorated with overstuffed leather wingback chairs, exquisite antiques, and *objets d'art*.

WEDDING SERVICES: Full service.

WHAREKAUHAU COUNTRY ESTATE

Western Lake Road, Palliser Bay, RD3 Featherston, Wairarapa, New Zealand

www.wharekauhau.co.nz

64-6-307-7581

SIZE: 5,000 ACRES **NUMBER OF ROOMS:** 12 SUITES **WHEELCHAIR ACCESSIBLE:** LIMITED **RATES:** $$$ **SPECIAL NOTES:** THE ESTATE HAS A "ONE FAMILY PER NIGHT" POLICY

REVIEW: Wharekauhau, a Small Luxury Hotel of the World and Andrew Harpers Grand Award winner, is a luxurious Edwardian-style estate, situated on a working sheep station by Palliser Bay, with views of coastline and cloud-capped mountains. The estate welcomes up to 36 guests, providing accommodations in the three-bedroom Wharepapa Cottage, the 4,600 square foot Château Wellington, and individual cottage suites, each outfitted with a four-post king-size bed, fireplace, and private veranda. Guests convene and dine in the Edwardian Lodge, which has a grand hall with an elegant stairway, fireplaces, and mullioned windows. For leisure activities, Wharekauhau offers an indoor pool, a fitness center, spa treatments, croquet, horseback riding, clay target shooting, scenic helicopter flights, and delicious cuisine. Guests can also take day excursions to the nearby Martinborough Vineyards and Cape Palliser Seal Rookery.

CEREMONY AND RECEPTION OPTIONS: Wharekauhau hosts ceremonies and receptions for up to 36 people, either in the main lodge or at any number of outdoor settings on the property. The bride and her bridesmaids often get ready in the Château Wellington, while the groom and groomsmen use the Wharepapa Cottage.

WEDDING SERVICES: Full service. The estate can help couples find assistance for legal documentation and can also help locate an officiant or a master of ceremony.

THE REST OF THE WORLD—
and Beyond

"Too often we are so occupied with the destination, we forget the journey."

ANONYMOUS

In the Orient, it is said that once you have completed 95 percent of your journey, you are only halfway there. Your journey as a couple began the day you met, and your destination wedding marks the day you formally declare that love and commitment to one another in front of your family and friends. We have explored a myriad of options for the couple who wants their wedding to reflect who they are and what kind of adventure they hope to share in life together. In this book we have journeyed to the four corners of the world, but I have only begun to show you the possibilities! As couples engage in more and more amazing destination weddings, and tell their stories to the world, the possibilities open even further: to the North and South Poles, to cyberspace, and even to outer space! In this final chapter, I challenge you to "think beyond," to consider unexplored paths yet to be discovered!.

The number of venues I have reviewed and discussed were limited only by the number of pages in this book; there are countless more options for wedding venues throughout the world that could have been included. This conclusion will offer a few more wedding ideas that, I hope, will encourage you to plan a wedding that is uniquely your own. Should you feel inspired to adopt some of these ideas, simply use the methods laid out in Part I to put your dreams into action. Save this book as a resource for the future—for planning a romantic vacation, your silver wedding anniversary, or a trip to renew your vows in the years ahead. Don't forget to visit the *Destination Bride* Web site (www.destinationbride.com) to learn about even more venues, detailed legal requirements, tried-and-true service providers in each destination (including photographers, caterers, and musicians), and many details and information we could not fit in the book. And please share your experiences with us and our readers by sending or e-mailing your destination wedding stories!

WEDDINGS ON ICE

In 2000, the first married couple to make it to the South Pole renewed their wedding vows there! After a record-breaking 730-mile trek, adventurers Fiona and Mike Thorne from Nottingham, England, made history with their special ceremony. Afterwards, Fiona's mum commented, "I knew Fiona would follow Mike to the end of the world, which she now has." Four years after Fiona and Mike renewed their vows, Katrina Sandling and Robert Follows were married on the summit of Vinson Massif, the highest point in Antarctica, with Guy Cotter, from Adventure Associates (61-2-9389-7466 / www.adventureassociates.com), acting as the officiant. Does this kind of once-in-a-lifetime experience appeal to you? If so, check the Antarctic Connection Web site (www.antarcticconnection.com) for a list of other possible Antarctic adventures.

There's also the North Pole—an option for ambitious couples who want to feel "on top of the world." If this interests you, contact Quark Expeditions (800-356-5699 / www.quarkexpeditions.com) to book a July cruise out of Oslo or Helsinki aboard the Russian nuclear icebreaker, *Yamal*. The price may be a little steep, but it boasts many features that you probably won't find at any other wedding celebration, including an on-deck "ice barbecue," complete with a heated swim-ming pool! Adventure Associates (see contact information above) also offer North Pole options. If you and your fiancé like the idea of traveling to the North Pole, but you still need a little something extra to get your adrenaline pumping, contact Curtis Lieber of Global Expeditions (800-770-5961 / www.north-pole-expeditions.com). He can organize North Pole skydiving and ski trips, South Pole excursions, icebreaker cruises, and more. Imagine being able to say that you exchanged vows on the frozen surface of 14,000-foot deep arctic water!

© DAVID BECKSTEAD

What could be more romantic than double-zipping your arctic sleeping bags on the first night of your honeymoon, then rising at dawn for a dog sled ride through the snowy terrain? Or climbing down a ladder through the ice for a quick under-ice dip before breakfast? If these ideas are not met with a chilly reception, consider the following options: Ice Hotel Quebec-Canada Inc. (877-505-0423 / www.icehotel-canada.com) and its sister company, Ice Hotel in Sweden (www.icehotel.com) are two of the only hotels in the world made entirely of snow and ice. The Ice Hotel has 32 rooms and theme suites, a theater, a chapel, an art gallery, two exhibit rooms, the Absolut Ice Bar, the N'ice Club, and special wedding packages that include rental of fur coats. Hotel & Igloo Village Kakslauttanen (358-16-667-100 / www.kakslauttanen.fi) in Lapland, Finland offers luxurious log cabins for rent and 20 snow igloos. The Village also has an ice gallery, bar, ice chapel, and the world's largest snow restaurant for 150 persons. With five glass igloos, guests have the opportunity to sleep under the Lapp sky while comfortably admiring the northern lights. Weddings can be held in a romantic wooden chapel, in a beautiful snow chapel, or outdoors under the midnight sun. In addition to civil marriages, Kakslauttanen can arrange Lutheran, Catholic, and Jewish blessings in English or Finnish.

UNDERGROUND WEDDINGS

If you are looking for an extraordinary experience—or if you and your beloved share a passion for spelunking—think caves! Before Mammoth Cave in Kentucky became a National Park, weddings were regularly held at the cave's "Bridal Altar," a natural formation of three stalactites, symbolizing the bride, the groom, and the clergyman.

© DAVID BECKSTEAD

According to a legend told by early guides of Mammoth Cave, there was a young girl who promised her dying mother that she would marry no man on the face of the Earth. But the young girl fell in love and, in order to keep her promise, she chose to wed beneath the earth in Mammoth Cave. You may be surprised to find out that underground wedding ceremonies can be arranged all over the globe. Bridal Cave Thunder Mountain Park (573-346-2676 / www.bridalcave.com/weddings.htm) in Missouri provides a private dressing area for the bride and groom, just outside their underground chapel. New York is home to Howe Caverns (518-296-8900 / www.howecaverns.com), and in the Aussie outback, there's PJ's Underground B&B (61-8-8091-6626 / www.babs.com.au/pj), which is discussed on page 349. Now *that* is a wedding that your guests will never forget!

SAILING THE SEVEN SEAS

Every kind of boat is available for weddings and honeymoons—floating hotels in Thailand, canal boats in the British Isles, shikaras in India, gondolas in Venice, and many more. When navigating nautical nuptials, be prepared to hear "no" from a few cruise lines, such as Crystal Cruises and the Cunard Line, as not every cruise ship welcomes weddings. (For a list of cruise lines that offer wedding and/or honeymoon packages, see the Appendix, page 375.) Weddings at sea can take extra planning, but they may save you thousands in the process. Why? Your wedding will most likely be smaller, and the honeymoon is included! In most cases, the actual legal ceremony happens in port, not at sea, so you must follow the port's requirements for weddings. Once in port, you typically leave the ship, present your previously prepared paperwork before a judge, then go back to the ship for your ceremony. Through Bermuda law, captains aboard the new Golden Princess and the Grand Princess of Princess Cruises can perform ceremonies both at sea and on land. (This is true of some other destinations as well.) In order for a ship captain to perform a marriage at sea, he must be a judge, a justice of the peace, a minister, or an officially recognized officiant, such as a notary public. If you want to renew your vows at sea, you need to show proof of a valid marriage.

CYBERSPACE WEDDINGS

It is a little known fact that, in some states, couples can be married "by proxy," meaning that the couple is not physically together at the time of the marriage. In the United States, proxy marriages are only allowed in four states—Texas, Montana, California, and Colorado —and only under special circumstances. California, for example, only allows proxy marriages for members of the armed services deployed during times of international conflict. To be married over the Internet, you would have to follow laws regarding weddings by proxy. Some couples have a ceremonial Internet wedding, followed by a legal marriage at the town hall. For more information about proxy marriage laws, search "about proxy marriages" online or ask at your town hall.

Most cruise lines offer complete wedding packages and/or honeymoon packages that include everything you'll need.

If you are a water enthusiast, you might be intrigued by having a guest list that includes dolphins, mantas, eels, and sharks! In some places, it is possible to be married underwater—though you might not actually be able to *say* "I do"! In scuba diving weddings, vows are exchanged using a combination of hand signals, underwater slates, and wax pencils. Check with the laws of the nation in which you choose to marry, as legal procedures vary. For example, in order for an underwater marriage to be legal in Australia, the underwater wedding party (bride, groom, witnesses, and officiant) must be able to hear the spoken words and vows. To accommodate this, the weddings are conducted using a special underwater mask that incorporates a communication device. According to the *Guinness Book of World Records*, the largest underwater wedding was held on September 13, 2003, off the island of St. Croix, with over 103 guests in scuba gear! Hotel Caravelle (800-524-2030 / www.hotelcaravelle.com) offers wet wedding packages in St. Croix. For an aquatic officiant in Hawaii, call Reverend Eve Hogan

(800-833-6483 / www.mauiunderwater.com), who is licensed to perform nondenominational weddings above, below, and beside the sea. Off the coast of southern Thailand, couples celebrate Valentine's Day with a mass underwater wedding. The inaugural ceremony, held in Trang in 1994, was attended by brides and grooms from 28 different countries. Participating couples get to experience several customs of a Thai wedding, such as the "khan maak" procession and a traditional blessing ceremony. This event was cancelled in 2005 due to the tsunami, but it should continue again in the future.

WEDDINGS IN THE CLOUDS

For jet-setting couples, the perfect wedding may involve chartering a jet, picking up guests from the east and west coast, saying "I do!" in the heavens (complete with decorations, live music, and a gourmet meal), then landing in Europe, Africa, or Asia for an extended celebration. Since 1994, Air Royale International (800-776-9253 / www.airroyale.com) has offered couples just such a charter service, with more than 5,500 aircraft available, from Learjets and Gulfstreams to Boeing 747s.

Helicopter weddings allow couples to reach awesome, secluded locations that are otherwise not accessible. Because helicopters cannot fit many passengers—remember, the officiant and the photographer take up two seats!—this kind of wedding may be best for elopements or small weddings, unless you are able to rent and land more than one helicopter. Check out Heli USA (www.heliusa.com) for helicopter weddings in Las Vegas, the Grand Canyon, and Hawaii. To experience Niagara Falls from above, contact Skyway Helicopters in Niagara-on-the-Lake, Ontario, Canada (800-491-3117 / www.skywayhelicopters.com). Skyway Helicopters, which calls itself "your chapel in the sky," can perform an official ceremony in-flight, with red roses for the bride, a rose boutonniere for the groom, and a special reception upon landing. The ceremony is officially recognized worldwide.

For those with "lofty" wedding aspirations, why not plan a sunrise or sunset ceremony in a hot air balloon! You, your wedding officiant, and a

OUTERSPACE WEDDINGS

Even extraterrestrial destinations are possible! In 2003, the first outerspace wedding took place between cosmonaut Yuri Malenchenko and Ekaterina Dmitriev. The marriage was by proxy; while Yuri was in the space station, his orbital home, the bride walked down the aisle in NASA's Johnson Space Center, escorted by Yuri's best friend, who stood in proxy for the groom. Dmitriev told reporters, "An orbital wedding reflects mankind's desire and need to go one step further..." And, for interested "civilians," outerspace weddings may soon be a reality. The Virgin Group, a company owned by Richard Branson, launched the first private spacecraft called *Space Ship One*. Now, the Virgin Group is taking reservations ($205,000 each) for the next suborbital space trip, scheduled for as early as 2007 or 2008. Hundreds of "astourists" have already signed up, including William Shatner and Sigourney Weaver. Weddings in space are sure to follow!

few guests can celebrate your nuptials while quietly drifting over field and forest. Hot air balloon weddings are becoming increasingly popular throughout the world, and the Web site www.launch.net reviews over 50 possibilities across the globe, including options in Belgium, Switzerland, South Africa, and New Zealand. Head in the Clouds (44-1635-43719 / www.headinthecloudsballoonflights.co.uk) offers balloon weddings in the United Kingdom.

© PHOTO BY ISABELLE BOSQUET

If these options are just too tame for you and your beloved, you can always get your adrenaline going with a skydiving or a bungee-jumping wedding! Have you ever considered "tying the knot and taking the plunge" (literally!) with bungee cords attached to your ankles? If you are interested in an "extreme" wedding adventure, contact Wedding Dreams (888-293-3659 / www.weddingdreams.com), who can arrange for a mid-air ceremony, conducted by a minister as you and yours bungee jump or skydive. Thrill-seeking bungee-jumpers can find other locations for extreme weddings, bungee-style, by visiting www.bungeezone.com/links or www.bungee-experience.com. Remember, the sky's the limit!

WEDDINGS ON THE MOVE

Are your wheels always in motion? Then maybe a "wedding on the move" is for you! If you are seeking a venue with a touch of old-fashioned romance, consider a train wedding. In addition to the train options already mentioned in Part II, there are plenty of possibilities to be explored. In Boulder City, Nevada, you can book your own private train on the now-defunct Boulder City Railroad with the Nevada State Railroad Museum (775-687-6953 / www.nsrm-friends.org). The wedding party celebrates as they ride the railway bed used by the Union Pacific Railroad during the construction of the Hoover Dam in the 1930s. A restored 1939 parlor car (now with working air conditioning) is available for the bridal party, and the lounge car is perfect for a small reception. For a train wedding in the Canadian Rockies, contact Rocky Mountaineer Vacations (877-460-3200 / www.rockymountaineer.com) in Vancouver, British Columbia. Passing through Vancouver, Whistler, Victoria, Calgary, Banff, and Jasper, the train takes guests through the unparalleled scenery of majestic snowy peaks, glittering glacial lakes, roaring waterfalls, and towering trees.

Do you love your motorcycle as much as your mate? If so, consider kick-starting your marriage by saying "I do" biker-style! At the Harley-Davidson First Factory dealership (877-740-3770 / www.orlandoharley.com) in Orlando, Florida, couples can go "hog"-wild with a truly unforgettable wedding for up to 500 guests. Options include Harley accessories and rings, motorcycle-themed invitations, his and her Harley

© PHOTO BY ISABELLE BOSQUET

rentals, wedding leather attire, and a bridal bouquet of orange "Harley" roses in motorcycle grip holders. To celebrate, you and your guests can enjoy temporary tattoos, professional rides on Harley motorcycles, gourmet barbecue catering, and entertainment by biker bands.

For couples who are children at heart, there are countless opportunities for fun weddings on the move—especially in theme parks. Just think how exhilarating it would be to celebrate your nuptials on the twists and turns of a roller coaster! In Buena Park, California, wedding ceremonies can be performed at Knott's Berry Farm (714-220-5200 / www.knotts.com) in the Church of Reflections, the park's nondenominational church overlooking Reflection Lake. After your wedding, experience GhostRider (a thrilling wooden roller coaster), Supreme Scream (30 stories up, 3 seconds down), and Xcelerator (sending riders 0 to 80

mph in 2.3 seconds!). One of the most popular destinations for fantasy weddings is Disneyland (www.disneylandweddings.com), where you can even ride Cinderella's glass coach to your wedding at Sleeping Beauty's castle! For more information on other amusement park possibilities in the United States, check the Appendix (page 375).

WACKY WEDDINGS

If you feel compelled to make your wedding as outlandish as possible, try searching the Internet for "Wacky Weddings." You might be surprised by some of the ideas you find. For example, Andrea C. Poe of *Modern Bride* has compiled a list of "20 Wacky Wedding Locations" (www.modernbride.com/sites/?wr_20wackmbm0701.html). This list is worth perusing, if not for inspiration, at least for a chuckle or two. You can exchange vows peering from atop a skyscraper, hanging ten off a surf board, or sitting high up in a ferris wheel car (tightly squeezed between the officiant and your honey). And for couples with special inter- ests, options abound. There are Trekkie weddings for Star Trek fans (complete with Vulcan ears and phaser guns), Renaissance-festival weddings for medieval history buffs, Graceland weddings for Elvis fanatics, and more. If these more unusual ceremonies and celebrations are right up your alley, you'll want to explore the Internet to research the wealth of possibilities.

ENJOY THE JOURNEY!

No matter what destination you choose and no matter what kind of adventure you plan, I hope you enjoy the journey there—and I wish you and your future spouse a long and intriguing journey through life together.

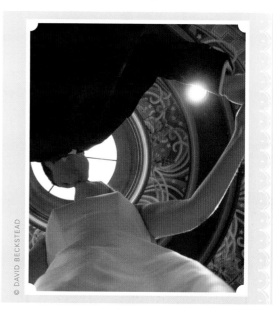

© DAVID BECKSTEAD

Appendix

This appendix is an invaluable resource for couples researching destination wedding possibilities. Included in the list is contact information for many wedding service providers. Keep in mind that I have not worked with every company on this list, so I cannot guarantee the quality of every provider. For this reason, it is important to always ask for references and samples of the providers' work. For links to the service providers with whom I have worked, visit the *Destination Bride* Web site (www.destinationbride.com), an online resource for planning a wedding anywhere in the world.

GOING ABROAD

EMBASSY & CONSULATE INFORMATION:

FOREIGN EMBASSIES IN THE UNITED STATES
www.state.gov/misc/10125.htm

FOREIGN EMBASSIES OF WASHINGTON, DC
www.embassy.org/embassies

UNITED STATES EMBASSIES AND CONSULATES
http://usembassy.state.gov

AMERICAN EMBASSY DIRECTORY
www.americanembassy.com

LEGAL DOCUMENTATION FOR TRAVELING ABROAD:

AMERICAN PASSPORT EXPRESS
www.americanpassport.com
for online passport and visa services

NATIONAL BIRTH CERTIFICATE
www.nationalbirthcertificate.com
for information on birth certificates, divorce decrees, marriage licenses, and death certificates

TRAVEL WARNINGS & ENTRY REQUIREMENTS:

UNITED STATES BUREAU OF CONSULAR AFFAIRS
www.travel.state.gov

TRAVEL & TOURISM

LUXURY HOTELS:

AMAN RESORTS
www.amanresorts.com

EPOQUE HOTELS
www.epoquehotels.com

FAIRMONT HOTELS AND RESORTS
www.fairmonthotels.com

FOUR SEASONS HOTELS
www.fourseasonshotels.com

GREAT HOTELS OF THE WORLD
www.ghotw.com

HIP HOTELS
www.hiphotels.net

HISTORIC HOTELS OF AMERICA
www.historichotels.org

ISLAND OUTPOST
www.islandoutpost.com

THE LEADING HOTELS OF THE WORLD
www.lhw.com

LE MERIDIEN
www.lemeridien.com

MANDARIN ORIENTAL HOTEL GROUP
www.mandarin-oriental.com

OBEROI HOTELS AND RESORTS
www.oberoihotels.com

ONE & ONLY RESORTS
www.oneandonlyresorts.com

PREFERRED HOTELS AND RESORTS WORLDWIDE
www.preferredhotels.com

RELAIS & CHÂTEAUX
www.relaischateaux.com

RITZ-CARLTON HOTELS
www.ritzcarlton.com

ROSEWOOD HOTELS AND RESORTS
www.rosewoodhotels.com

SMALL LUXURY HOTELS OF THE WORLD
www.slh.com

TAJ HOTELS, RESORTS AND PALACES
www.tajhotels.com

WYNDHAM HOTELS AND RESORTS
www.wyndham.com

ONLINE TRAVEL RESERVATIONS:

EXPEDIA
www.expedia.com

HOTELS.COM
www.hotels.com

ORBITZ
www.orbitz.com

TRAVELOCITY
www.travelocity.com

TOURISM BUREAUS WORLDWIDE:

INTERNATIONAL ASSOCIATION OF CONVENTION
& VISITORS BUREAUS (IACVB)
www.iacvb.org

INTERNATIONAL CHAMBER OF COMMERCE &
CITY-STATE-PROVINCE DIRECTORY
www.chamber-of-commerce.com

TOURISM OFFICES WORLDWIDE DIRECTORY
www.towd.com

TRANSPORTATION:

AMERICAN AUTOMOBILE ASSOCIATION
www.aaa.com

AIRPORT CAR RENTALS AND AIRPORT SHUTTLES
www.airportrentals.us

TRAVEL AGENTS:

AMERICAN SOCIETY OF TRAVEL AGENTS
www.astanet.com

TRAVEL INSURANCE:

INSURE MY TRIP
www.insuremytrip.com

TRAVEL GUARD INTERNATIONAL
www.travelguard.com

TRAVEL PUBLICATIONS:

CONDÉ NAST TRAVELER
www.cntraveler.com

ISLANDS
www.islands.com

NATIONAL GEOGRAPHIC TRAVELER
www.nationalgeographic.com/traveler/

TRAVEL + LEISURE
www.travelandleisure.com

VILLAS & PRIVATE ESTATES:

LACURE, THE EXPERIENCE COMPANY
www.lacure.com

VILLAS AND APARTMENTS ABROAD
www.vaanyc.com

CULTURAL INFORMATION

CURRENCY:

AMERICAN EXPRESS
www.americanexpress.com
for purchasing traveler's checks

INTERNATIONAL CURRENCY EXPRESS, INC.
www.foreignmoney.com
for purchasing foreign currency

ONANDA.COM
www.onanda.com
for foreign currency conversion

WESTERN UNION
www.westernunion.com
for wiring money

XE.COM
www.xe.com
for foreign currency conversion

ELECTRICITY:

VOLTAGE VALET
www.voltagevalet.com
*directory for using electrical appliances
and adapters abroad*

FOOD & CUISINE:

GLOBAL GOURMET
www.globalgourmet.com/destinations/

METRIC CONVERSION:

ONLINE CONVERSION
www.onlineconversion.com
*for converting measurements, temperature,
and much more*

MUSIC:

WORLD MUSIC CENTRAL
www.worldmusiccentral.org

TIME ZONES:

TIME AND DATE
www.timeanddate.com
for current world times

TIPPING:

TRAVEL CHANNEL
http://travel.discovery.com/tips/international/
tipping.html

TRANSLATIONS & MULTILINGUAL DICTIONARIES:

FOREIGN WORD
www.foreignword.com

WEATHER:

ACCUWEATHER WORLD WEATHER
www.accuweather.com

WORLD CLIMATE
www.worldclimate.com

RELIGIOUS INFORMATION

FAITH COMMUNITIES & HOUSES OF WORSHIP:

BELIEFNET
www.beliefnet.com
for information on world religions

CATHOLIC ONLINE
www.catholic.org
for Catholic resources

DHARMANET INTERNATIONAL
www.dharmanet.org
for information on Buddhism

DIRECTORY OF HINDU RESOURCES ONLINE
www.hindu.org
for Hindu resources

ISLAM ONLINE
www.islamonline.net
for Islamic resources

ISLAMIC FINDER
www.islamicfinder.org
for Islamic resources

KOSHER DELIGHT: JEWISH ONLINE MAGAZINE
www.kosherdelight.com
for Jewish resources

NET MINISTRIES
www.netministries.org
for Christian resources

GAY & LESBIAN

INTERNATIONAL LESBIAN AND GAY ASSOCIATION
www.ilga.info

PURPLE UNIONS: GAY AND LESBIAN WEDDING DIRECTORY
www.purpleunions.com

RAINBOW WEDDING DIRECTORY
www.rainbowweddingnetwork.com

LOCATION RESOURCES

See also "Luxury Hotels" and "Villas and Private Estates" under TRAVEL AND TOURISM, pages 370–371.

AMERICAN BED AND BREAKFAST ASSOCIATION
www.abba.com

CASTLES OF BRITAIN
www.castles-of-britain.com

CASTLES OF THE WORLD
www.castles.org

CASTLES OF TUSCANY
www.castellitoscani.com

CASTLES ON THE WEB
www.castlesontheweb.com

CELTIC CASTLES
www.celticcastles.com

LIGHTHOUSE DEPOT ONLINE
www.lhdepot.com

NATIONAL PARKS WORLDWIDE
www.world-national-parks.net

NATIONAL TRUST FOR HISTORIC PRESERVATION
www.nationaltrust.org

U.S. INNS: BED AND BREAKFAST RESOURCES
www.usinns.com

UNITED STATES NATIONAL PARKS SERVICES
www.nps.gov

WORLD HERITAGE SITES
http://whc.unesco.org/

GENERAL WEDDING INFORMATION

GENERAL WEDDING RESOURCES:
ABOUT WEDDINGS
www.weddings.about.com

THE KNOT, INC.
www.theknot.com

MY EVENT
www.myevent.com
for creating your own customized wedding Web site

WEDDING CHANNEL
www.weddingchannel.com

DESTINATION WEDDINGS:
DESTINATION BRIDE
www.destinationbride.com

MARRIAGE LAWS & LICENSES:
MARRIAGE LAWS
www.usmarriagelaws.com

SOURCES OF VITAL STATISTICS RECORDS IN FOREIGN COUNTRIES
http://policy.ssa.gov/poms.nsf/lnx/0200307990
listing of international civil registry offices

WORLDWIDE WEDDING TRADITIONS AND THEMES:
WEDDING DETAILS
www.weddingdetails.com

ASK GINKA
www.askginka.com

WEDDING SERVICE PROVIDERS

GENERAL SERVICE PROVIDER INFORMATION:
BETTER BUSINESS BUREAU
www.bbb.org

DESTINATION BRIDE
www.destinationbride.com

WEDDING SITES AND SERVICES
www.weddingsitesandservices.com

ATTIRE:

ASSOCIATION OF WEDDING GOWN SPECIALISTS
www.weddinggownspecialists.com

INTERNATIONAL FORMAL WEAR ASSOCIATION
www.formalwear.org

ENTERTAINMENT:

AMERICAN DISC JOCKEY ASSOCIATION (ADJA)
www.adja.org

FLORISTS:

FLOWERS AND PLANTS ASSOCIATION
www.flowers.org.uk

BLOOM CENTRAL
www.bloomcentral.com
international directory of florists and flower shops

FOOD, CATERING, AND RENTAL:

AMERICAN RENTAL ASSOCIATION (ARA)
www.ararental.org

INTERNATIONAL CATERERS ASSOCIATION (ICA)
www.icacater.org

NATIONAL ASSOCIATION OF CATERING
EXECUTIVES (NACE)
www.nace.net

HONEYMOON REGISTRY:

THE BIG DAY
www.thebigday.com

THE HONEYMOON
www.thehoneymoon.com

TRAVEL BRIDE
www.travelbride.com

HONEY LUNA
www.honeyluna.com

JEWELRY:

INTERNATIONAL COLORED GEMSTONE
ASSOCIATION (ICGA)
www.gemstone.org

JEWELERS OF AMERICA (JA)
www.jewelers.org

WORLD DIAMOND COUNCIL (WDC)
www.worlddiamondcouncil.com

PHOTOGRAPHERS AND VIDEOGRAPHERS:

WEDDING BUREAU
www.weddingbureau.com

WEDDING PHOTOJOURNALISTS ASSOCIATION
(WPJA)
www.wpja.org

WEDDING AND EVENT VIDEOGRAPHERS
ASSOCIATION INTERNATIONAL (WEVA)
www.weva.com

WEDDING CONSULTANTS AND PLANNERS:

ASSOCIATION OF BRIDAL CONSULTANTS (ABC)
www.bridalassn.com

ASSOCIATION FOR WEDDING PROFESSIONALS
INTERNATIONAL (AFWPI)
www.afwpi.com

INTERNATIONAL SPECIAL EVENTS SOCIETY (ISES)
www.ises.com

WEDDING INSURANCE:

R.V. NUCCIO & ASSOCIATES INC.
www.rvnuccio.com

WEDSAFE
www.wedsafe.com

WEDDING OFFICIANTS:

Don't forget to check embassy and tourism Web sites for
your destination in addition to the following Web sites.

INTERNET DIRECTORY OF PROFESSIONAL
WEDDING MINISTERS
www.weddingministers.com

NATIONAL ASSOCIATION OF WEDDING MINISTERS
www.aweddingministers.com

NATIONAL ASSOCIATION OF WEDDING
OFFICIANTS
www.nawoonline.com

WEDDING OFFICIANTS
www.weddingofficiants.com

WEDDING PUBLICATIONS:

BRIDAL GUIDE
www.bridalguide.com

BRIDES
www.brides.com

DESTINATION WEDDINGS & HONEYMOONS
www.islands.com/weddings/magazine

GRACE ORMONDE WEDDING STYLE
www.weddingstylemagazine.com

ELEGANT BRIDE
www.elegantbride.com

MARTHA STEWART WEDDINGS
www.marthastewart.com

MODERN BRIDE
www.modernbride.com

PERFECT WEDDING GUIDE
www.pwg.com

CRUISE LINES

CARNIVAL CRUISE LINES
www.carnivalcruise.com

CELEBRITY CRUISES/ROYAL CARIBBEAN
INTERNATIONAL
www.royalcaribbean.com

DISNEY CRUISE LINE
www.disneycruise.com

HOLLAND AMERICA
www.hollandamerica.com

NORWEGIAN CRUISE LINE
www.ncl.com

OCEANIA CRUISES
www.oceaniacruises.com

ORIENT LINES
www.orientlines.com

PRINCESS CRUISES
www.princess.com

RADISSON SEVEN SEAS CRUISES
www.rssc.com

SEABOURN CRUISE LINE
www.seabourn.com

WINDJAMMER BAREFOOT CRUISES
www.windjammer.com

WINDSTAR CRUISES
www.windstarcruises.com

THEME PARKS OFFERING WEDDINGS

BUSCH GARDENS (TAMPA, FL;
WILLIAMSBURG, VA)
www.buschgardens.com

CHAPEL OF LOVE, THE MALL OF AMERICA
(MINNEAPOLIS, MN)
www.chapeloflove.com

DOLLYWOOD (PIGEON FORGE, TN)
www.dollywood.com

DUTCH WONDERLAND (E. LANCASTER, PA)
www.dutchwonderland.com

HERSHEY'S CHOCOLATE WORLD (HERSHEY, PA)
www.hersheys.com

SEA WORLD (ORLANDO, FL; SAN DIEGO, CA;
SAN ANTONIO, TX)
www.seaworld.com

SIX FLAGS (SEVERAL LOCATIONS)
www.sixflags.com

Index

D-F

The best in wedding inspiration
is from **NORTH LIGHT BOOKS**!

Intimate Weddings

Christina Friedrichsen

In *Intimate Weddings*, you'll find stories and wisdom from real-life couples who planned their own small weddings. You'll get advice on involving family and friends in the big day, from decorating to the actual ceremony, and inspring suggestions for personalizing a wedding with themes and traditions that have special meaning. You'll also find creative ideas for venues and unique cost-saving tips for getting married on a budget. Perfect for anyone planning a wedding wtih 75 or fewer guests, this book walks the bride-to-be through every step she needs to make her big day a success.

ISBN 1-55870-592-5, paperback, 192 pages, #70642

Wedding Papercrafts

Editors of North Light Books

In projects using the latest techniques in papercrafting, rubber stamping and collage, *Wedding Papercrafts* shows you how to create your own invitations, decorations and favors. All of the projects show you how to personalize your wedding with unique handmade touches. The book includes 50 gorgeous projects made easy with patterns and step-by-step instruction.

ISBN 1-55870-653-4, paperback, 128 pages, #70603

Creative Wedding Showers

Laurie Dewberry

Whether you'd like to throw a traditional hen party or a nontraditional couples shower, the ten shower themes in *Creative Wedding Showers* will give you plenty of ideas and inspiration. From recipes for the perfect party snacks and meals to games and favors, this book has everything you need to throw a wonderful shower that suits the bride-to-be. You'll find step-by-step instructions for making invitations, decorations and even party favors that will show you how to give an unforgettable shower.

ISBN 1-55870-710-7, paperback, 96 pages, #70662

New Inspirations in Wedding Florals

Terry Rye

You can create beautiful wedding florals that look professionally crafted with the guidance of Terry Rye. Whether you're an experienced flower arranger or a beginner, this book provides expert tips and techniques to make your wedding even more lovely. Included are 30 unique, step-by-step projects with variations such as bridal and bridesmaid bouquets, arrangements for the ceremony, table centerpieces, cake toppers and more!

ISBN 1-55870-634-8, paperback, 128 pages, #70582

These books and other fine North Light titles
are available from your local art & craft retailer,
bookstore or online supplier.